of Congress Cataloging-in-Publication Data
Craig.
lying UML and patterns : an introduction to object-oriented analysis and design and
Unified Process / Craig Larman.— 2nd ed.
o. cm.
ncludes index.
SBN 0-13-092569-1 (alk. paper)
. Object-oriented methods (Computer science) 2. UML (Computer science) 3. System
lysis. 4. System design. I. Title.

76.9.O35 L37 2001
.1'17--dc21   2001036446

production supervision: *Patti Guerrieri*
ons editor: *Paul Petralia*
g manager: *Debby vanDijk*
turing manager: *Alexis R. Heydt*
assistant: *Justin Somma*
sign director: *Jerry Votta*
signer: *Nina Scuderi*

© 2002 by Craig Larman
Published by Prentice Hall PTR
Prentice-Hall, Inc.
Upper Saddle River, NJ 07458

Hall books are widely used by corporations and government agencies
ng, marketing, and resale.

isher offers discounts on this book when ordered in bulk quantities.
information, contact: Corporate Sales Department, Phone: 800-382-3419;
-236-7141; E-mail: corpsales@prenhall.com; or write: Prentice Hall PTR,
les Dept., One Lake Street, Upper Saddle River, NJ 07458.

ucts or services mentioned in this book are the trademarks or service marks of their respective companies or
tions.

knowledgements:
aul Erdos: From "The Man Who Only Loved Numbers" by Paul Hoffman.
.G. Wells: Used by permission of A.P. Watt Ltd. On behalf of the Executors of the Estate of H.G. Wells.

-13-092569-1

Education LTD.
Education Australia PTY, Limited
Education Singapore, Pte. Ltd.
Education North Asia Ltd.
Education Canada, Ltd.
Educación de Mexico, S.A. de C.V.
Education — Japan
Education Malaysia, Pte. Ltd.

General Responsibility Assignment Software Patterns (GRASP)

Pattern	Description
Information Expert	A general principle of object design and responsibility assignment? Assign a responsibility to the information expert—the class that has the information necessary to fulfill the responsibility.
Creator	Who creates? (Note that Factory is a common alternate solution.) Assign class B the responsibility to create an instance of class A if one of these is true: 1. B contains A 4. B records A 2. B aggregates A 5. B closely uses A 3. B has the initializing data for A
Controller	Who handles a system event? Assign the responsibility for handling a system event message to a class representing one of these choices: 1. Represents the overall system, device, or a subsystem (facade controller). 2. Represents a use case scenario within which the system event occurs (use-case or session controller)
Low Coupling (evaluative)	How to support low dependency and increased reuse? Assign responsibilities so that (unnecessary) coupling remains low.
High Cohesion (evaluative)	How to keep complexity manageable? Assign responsibilities so that cohesion remains high.
Polymorphism	Who is responsible when behavior varies by type? When related alternatives or behaviors vary by type (class), assign responsibility for the behavior—using polymorphic operations—to the types for which the behavior varies.
Pure Fabrication	Who is responsible when you are desperate, and do not want to violate high cohesion and low coupling? Assign a highly cohesive set of responsibilities to an artificial or convenience "behavior" class that does not represent a problem domain concept—something made up, in order to support high cohesion, low coupling, and reuse.
Indirection	How to assign responsibilities to avoid direct coupling? Assign the responsibility to an intermediate object to mediate between other components or services, so that they are not directly coupled.
Protected Variations	How to assign responsibilities to objects, subsystems, and systems so that the variations or instability in these elements do not have an undesirable impact on other elements? Identify points of predicted variation or instability; assign responsibilities to create a stable "interface" around them.

APPLYING
AND PA

AN
OBJECT-ORIENTED ANA
AND THI

Prentice Hall PTR
Upper Saddle River, NJ 07458
www.phptr.com

For Julie

Without your support, this would not have been possible.

For Haley and Hannah

Thanks for putting up with a distracted Daddy, again!

CONTENTS AT A GLANCE

TABLE OF CONTENTS

FOREWORD

Programming is fun, but developing quality software is hard. In between the nice ideas, the requirements or the "vision," and a working software product, there is much more than programming. Analysis and design, defining how to solve the problem, what to program, capturing this design in ways that are easy to communicate, to review, to implement, and to evolve is what lies at the core of this book. This is what you will learn.

The Unified Modeling Language (UML) has become the universally-accepted language for software design blueprints. UML is the visual language used to convey design ideas throughout this book, which emphasizes how developers really apply frequently used UML elements, rather than obscure features of the language.

The importance of patterns in crafting complex systems has long been recognized in other disciplines. Software design patterns are what allow us to describe design fragments, and reuse design ideas, helping developers leverage the expertise of others. Patterns give a name and form to abstract heuristics, rules and best practices of object-oriented techniques. No reasonable engineer wants to start from a blank slate, and this book offers a palette of readily usable design patterns.

But software design looks a bit dry and mysterious when not presented in the context of a software engineering process. And on this topic, I am delighted that for his second edition, Craig Larman has chosen to embrace and introduce the Unified Process, showing how it can be applied in a relatively simple and low-ceremony way. By presenting the case study in an iterative, risk-driven, architecture-centric process, Craig's advice has realistic context; he exposes the dynamics of what really happens in software development, and shows the external forces at play. The design activities are connected to other tasks, and they no longer appear as a purely cerebral activity of systematic transformations or creative intuition. And Craig and I are convinced of the benefits of iterative development, which you will see abundantly illustrated throughout.

So for me, this book has the right mix of ingredients. You will learn a systematic method to do Object-Oriented Analysis and Design (OOA/D) from a great teacher, a brilliant methodologist, and an "OO guru" who has taught it to thousands around the world. Craig describes the method in the context of the Unified Process. He gradually presents more sophisticated design patterns—this will make the book very handy when you are faced with real-world design challenges. And he uses the most widely accepted notation.

I'm honored to have had the opportunity to work directly with the author of this major book. I enjoyed reading the first edition, and was delighted when he asked me to review the draft of his second edition. We met several times and exchanged many e-mails. I have learned much from Craig, even about our own process work on the Unified Process and how to improve it and position it in various organizational contexts. I am certain that you will learn a lot, too, in reading this book, even if you are already familiar with OOA/D. And, like me, you will find yourself going back to it, to refresh your memory, or to gain further insights from Craig's explanations and experience.

In an iterative process, the result of the second iteration improves on the first. Similarly, the writing matures, I suppose; even if you have the first edition, you'll enjoy and benefit from the second one.

Happy reading!

Philippe Kruchten
Rational Fellow
Rational Software Canada
Vancouver, BC

PREFACE

Thank you for reading this book! This is a practical introduction to object-oriented analysis and design (OOA/D), and to related aspects of iterative development. I am grateful that the first edition was received as a popular introduction to OOA/D throughout the world, translated into many languages. Therefore, this second edition builds upon and refines—rather than replaces—the content in the first. I want to sincerely thank all the readers of the first edition.

Here is how the book will benefit you.

Design robust and maintainable object systems.

First, the use of object technology has proliferated in the development of software, and mastery of OOA/D is critical for you to create robust and maintainable object systems.

Follow a roadmap through requirements, analysis, design, and coding.

Second, if you are new to OOA/D, you are understandably challenged about how to proceed through this complex subject; this book presents a well-defined roadmap—the Unified Process—so that you can move in a step-by-step process from requirements to code.

Use the UML to illustrate analysis and design models.

Third, the Unified Modeling Language (UML) has emerged as the standard notation for modeling; so it is useful for you to be conversant in it. This book teaches the skills of OOA/D using the UML notation.

Improve designs by applying the "gang-of-four" and GRASP design patterns.

Fourth, design patterns communicate the "best practice" idioms and solutions that object-oriented design experts apply in order to create systems. In this book you will learn to apply design patterns, including the popular "gang-of-four" patterns, and the GRASP patterns which communicate fundamental principles of responsibility assignment in object design. Learning and applying patterns will accelerate your mastery of analysis and design.

Learn efficiently by following a refined presentation.

Fifth, the structure and emphasis in this book is based on years of experience in training and mentoring thousands of people in the art of OOA/D. It reflects that experience by providing a refined, proven, and efficient approach to learning the subject so your investment in reading and learning is optimized.

Learn from a realistic exercise.

Sixth, it exhaustively examines a single case study—to realistically illustrate the entire OOA/D process, and goes deeply into thorny details of the problem; it is a realistic exercise.

Translate to code.

Seventh, it shows how to map object design artifacts to code in Java.

Design a layered architecture.

Eighth, it explains how to design a layered architecture and relate the graphical user interface layer to domain and technical services layers.

Design a framework. **Finally**, it shows you how to design an object-oriented framework and applies this to the creation of a framework for persistent storage in a database.

Objectives

The overarching objective is this:

> Help students and developers create object designs through the application of a set of explainable principles and heuristics.

By studying and applying the information and techniques presented here, you will become more adept at understanding a problem in terms of its processes and concepts, and designing a solid solution using objects.

Intended Audience

This book is an *introduction* to OOA/D, related requirements analysis, and to iterative development with the Unified Process as a sample process; it is not meant as an advanced text. It is for the following audience:

- Developers and students with experience in an object-oriented programming language, but who are new—or relatively new—to object-oriented analysis and design.

- Students in computer science or software engineering courses studying object technology.

- Those with some familiarity in OOA/D who want to learn the UML notation, apply patterns, or who want to sharpen and deepen their analysis and design skills.

Prerequisites

Some prerequisite knowledge is assumed—and necessary—to benefit from this book:

- Knowledge and experience in an object-oriented programming language such as Java, C#, C++, or Smalltalk.

- Knowledge of fundamental object technology concepts, such as class, instance, interface, polymorphism, encapsulation, interfaces, and inheritance.

Fundamental object technology concepts are not defined.

Java Examples

In general, the book presents code examples in Java or discusses Java implementations, due to its widespread familiarity. However, the ideas presented are applicable to most—if not all—object-oriented programming languages.

Book Organization

The overall strategy in the organization of this book is that analysis and design topics are introduced in an order similar to that of a software development project running across an "inception" phase (a Unified Process term) followed by three iterations (see Figure P.1).

1. The inception phase chapters introduce the basics of requirements analysis.

2. Iteration 1 introduces fundamental OOA/D and how to assign responsibilities to objects.

3. Iteration 2 focuses on object design, especially on introducing some high-use "design patterns."

4. Iteration 3 introduces a variety of subjects, such as architectural analysis and framework design.

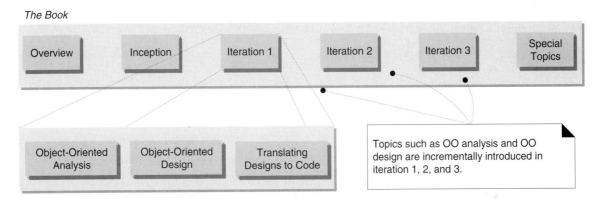

Figure P.1. The organization of the book follows that of a development project.

Web-Related Resources

- Please see www.craiglarman.com for articles related to object technology, patterns, and process.

- Some instructor resources can be found at www.phptr.com/larman.

Enhancements to the First Edition

While retaining the same core as the first edition, the second is refined in many ways, including:

- Use cases are updated to follow the very popular approach of [Cockburn01].

- The well-known Unified Process (UP) is used as the example iterative process within which to introduce OOA/D. Thus, all artifacts are named according to UP terms, such as Domain Model.

- New requirements in the case study, leading to a third iteration.

- Updated treatment of design patterns.

- Introduction to architectural analysis.

- Introduction of Protected Variations as a GRASP pattern.

- A 50/50 balance between sequence and collaboration diagrams.

- The latest UML notation updates.

- Discussion of some practical aspects of drawing using whiteboards or UML CASE tools.

Acknowledgments

First, a very special thanks to my friends and colleagues at Valtech, world-class object developers and iterative development experts, who in some way contributed to, supported, or reviewed the book, including Chris Tarr, Michel Ezran, Tim Snyder, Curtis Hite, Celso Gonzalez, Pascal Roques, Ken DeLong, Brett Schuchert, Ashley Johnson, Chris Jones, Thomas Liou, Darryl Gebert, Frank Rodorigo, Jean-Yves Hardy, and many more than I can name.

To Philippe Kruchten for writing the foreword, reviewing, and helping in so many ways.

To Martin Fowler and Alistair Cockburn for many insightful discussions on process and design, quotes, and reviews.

To John Vlissides and Cris Kobryn for the kind quotes.

To Chelsea Systems and John Gray for help with some requirements inspired by their Java technology ChelseaStore POS system.

To Pete Coad and Dave Astels at TogetherSoft for their support.

Many thanks to the other reviewers, including Steve Adolph, Bruce Anderson, Len Bass, Gary K. Evans, Al Goerner, Luke Hohmann, Eric Lefebvre, David Nunn, and Robert J. White.

Thanks to Paul Becker at Prentice-Hall for believing the first edition would be a worthwhile project, and to Paul Petralia and Patti Guerrieri for shepherding the second.

Finally, a special thanks to Graham Glass for opening a door.

About the Author

Craig Larman serves as Director of Process for Valtech, an international consulting company with divisions in Europe, Asia, and North America, specializing in e-business systems development, object technologies, and iterative development with the Unified Process.

Since the mid 1980s, Craig has helped thousands of developers to apply object-oriented programming, analysis, and design, and assisted organizations adopt iterative development practices.

After a failed career as a wandering street musician, he built systems in APL, PL/I, and CICS in the 1970s. Starting in the early 1980s—after a full recovery—he became interested in artificial intelligence (having little of his own), natural language processing, and knowledge representation, and built knowledge systems with Lisp machines, Lisp, Prolog, and Smalltalk. He plays bad lead guitar in his part-time band, the *Changing Requirements* (it used to be called the *Requirements*, but some band members changed...).

He holds a B.Sc. and M.Sc. in computer science from Simon Fraser University in Vancouver, Canada.

Contact

Craig can be reached at clarman@ieee.org and www.craiglarman.com. He welcomes questions from readers and educators, and speaking, mentoring, and consulting enquiries.

Typographical Conventions

This is a **new term** in a sentence. This is a *Class* or *method* name in a sentence. This is an author reference [Bob67]. A language independent scope resolution operator "--" is used to indicate a class and its associated method as follows: *ClassName--methodName*.

Production Notes

The manuscript of this book was created with Adobe FrameMaker. All drawings were done with Microsoft Visio. The body font is New Century Schoolbook. The final print images were generated as PDF files using Adobe Acrobat Distiller, from PostScript generated by an AGFA driver.

PART 1 INTRODUCTION

OBJECT-ORIENTED ANALYSIS AND DESIGN

The shift of focus (to patterns) will have a profound and enduring effect on the way we write programs.

—Ward Cunningham and Ralph Johnson

Objectives

- Compare and contrast analysis and design.
- Define object-oriented analysis and design (OOA/D).
- Illustrate a brief example.

1.1 Applying UML and Patterns in OOA/D

What does it mean to have a good object design? This book is a tool to help developers and students learn core skills in object-oriented analysis and design (OOA/D). These skills are essential for the creation of well-designed, robust, and maintainable software using object technologies and languages such as Java, C++, Smalltalk, and C#.

The proverb "owning a hammer doesn't make one an architect" is especially true with respect to object technology. Knowing an object-oriented language (such as Java) is a necessary but insufficient first step to create object systems. Knowing how to "think in objects" is also critical.

This is an introduction

This is an introduction to OOA/D while applying the Unified Modeling Language (UML), patterns, and the Unified Process. It is not meant as an advanced text; it emphasizes mastery of the fundamentals, such as how to assign responsibilities to objects, frequently used UML notation, and common design patterns. At the same time, primarily in later chapters, the material progresses to a few intermediate-level topics, such as framework design.

Applying UML

The book is not just about the UML. The **UML** is a standard diagramming notation. As useful as it is to learn notation, there are more critical object-oriented things to learn; specifically, how to think in objects—how to design object-oriented systems. The UML is not OOA/D or a method, it is simply notation. It is not so helpful to learn syntactically correct UML diagramming and perhaps a UML CASE tool, but then not be able to create an excellent design, or evaluate and improve an existing one. This is the harder and more valuable skill. Consequently, this book is an introduction to object design.

Yet, one needs a language for OOA/D and "software blueprints," both as a tool of thought and as a form of communication with others. Therefore, this book explores how to *apply* the UML in the service of doing OOA/D, and covers frequently used UML notation. But the emphasis is on helping people learn the art and science of building object systems, rather than notation.

Applying patterns and assigning responsibilities

How should **responsibilities** be allocated to classes of objects? How should objects interact? What classes should do what? These are critical questions in the design of a system. Certain tried-and-true solutions to design problems can be (and have been) expressed as best-practice principles, heuristics, or **patterns**—named problem-solution formulas that codify exemplary design principles. This book, by teaching how to apply patterns, supports quicker learning and skillful use of these fundamental object design idioms.

One case study

This introduction to OOA/D is illustrated in a **single case study** that is followed throughout the book, going deep enough into the analysis and design so that some of the gory details of what must be considered and solved in a realistic problem are considered, and solved.

Use cases and requirements analysis

OOA/D (and all software design) is strongly related to the prerequisite activity of **requirements analysis**, which includes writing **use cases**. Therefore, the case study begins with an introduction to these topics, even though they are not specifically object-oriented.

An example iterative process— the Unified Process

Given many possible activities from requirements through to implementation, how should a developer or team proceed? Requirements analysis and OOA/D needs to be presented in the context of some development process. In this case, the well-known **Unified Process** is used as the *sample* **iterative development process** within which these topics are introduced. However, the analysis and design topics that are covered are common to many approaches, and learning them in the context of the Unified Process does not invalidate their applicability to other methods.

> In conclusion, this book helps a student or developer:
>
> ■ Apply principles and patterns to create better object designs.
>
> ■ Follow a set of common activities in analysis and design, based on the Unified Process as an example.
>
> ■ Create frequently used diagrams in the UML notation.
>
> It illustrates this in the context of a single case study.

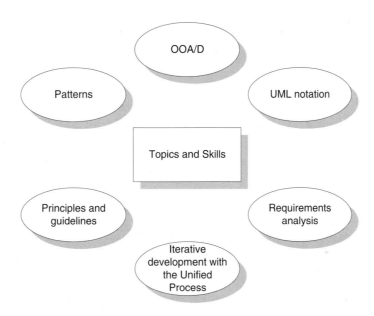

Figure 1.1 Topics and skills covered

Many Other Skills Are Important

Building software involves myriad skills and steps beyond requirements analysis, OOA/D, and object-oriented programming. For example, usability engineering and user interface design are critical to success; so is database design.

However, this introduction emphasizes OOA/D, and does not attempt to cover all topics in software development. It is one piece of a larger picture.

1.2   Assigning Responsibilities

There are many possible activities and artifacts in introductory OOA/D, and a wealth of principles and guidelines. Suppose we must choose a single practical skill from all the topics discussed here—a "desert island" skill. What would it be?

> A critical, fundamental ability in OOA/D is to skillfully assign responsibilities to software components.

Why? Because it is one activity that must be performed—either while drawing a UML diagram or programming—and it strongly influences the robustness, maintainability, and reusability of software components.

Of course, there are other necessary skills in OOA/D, but responsibility assignment is emphasized in this introduction because it tends to be a challenging skill to master, and yet vitally important. On a real project, a developer might not have the opportunity to perform any other analysis or design activities—the "rush to code" development process. Yet even in this situation, assigning responsibilities is inevitable.

Consequently, the design steps in this book emphasize principles of responsibility assignment.

> Nine fundamental principles in object design and responsibility assignment are presented and applied. They are organized in a learning aid called the GRASP patterns.

1.3   What Is Analysis and Design?

Analysis emphasizes an *investigation* of the problem and requirements, rather than a solution. For example, if a new computerized library information system is desired, how will it be used?

"Analysis" is a broad term, best qualified, as in *requirements analysis* (an investigation of the requirements) or *object analysis* (an investigation of the domain objects).

Design emphasizes a *conceptual solution* that fulfills the requirements, rather than its implementation. For example, a description of a database schema and software objects. Ultimately, designs can be implemented.

As with analysis, the term is best qualified, as in *object design* or *database design*.

Analysis and design have been summarized in the phase *do the right thing (analysis), and do the thing right (design)*.

1.4   What Is Object-Oriented Analysis and Design?

During **object-oriented analysis**, there is an emphasis on finding and describing the objects—or concepts—in the problem domain. For example, in the case of the library information system, some of the concepts include *Book, Library,* and *Patron.*

During **object-oriented design**, there is an emphasis on defining software objects and how they collaborate to fulfill the requirements. For example, in the library system, a *Book* software object may have a *title* attribute and a *getChapter* method (see Figure 1.2).

Finally, during implementation or object-oriented programming, design objects are implemented, such as a *Book* class in Java.

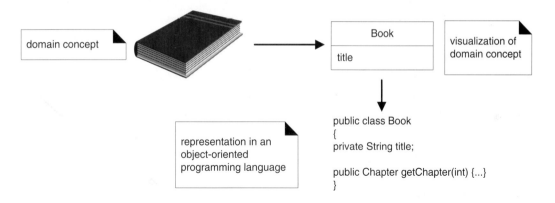

Figure 1.2 Object-orientation emphasizes representation of objects.

1.5   An Example

Before diving into the details of requirements analysis and OOA/D, this section presents a birds-eye view of a few key steps and diagrams, using a simple example—a "dice game" in which a player rolls two die. If the total is seven, they win; otherwise, they lose.

Define Use Cases

Requirements analysis may include a description of related domain processes; these can be written as **use cases**.

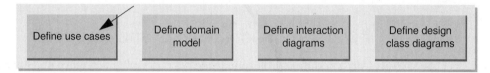

Use cases are not an object-oriented artifact—they are simply written stories. However, they are a popular tool in requirements analysis and are an important part of the Unified Process. For example, here is a brief version of the *Play a Dice Game* use case:

> **Play a Dice Game**: A player picks up and rolls the dice. If the dice face value total seven, they win; otherwise, they lose.

Define a Domain Model

Object-oriented analysis is concerned with creating a description of the domain from the perspective of classification by objects. A decomposition of the domain involves an identification of the concepts, attributes, and associations that are considered noteworthy. The result can be expressed in a **domain model**, which is illustrated in a set of diagrams that show domain concepts or objects.

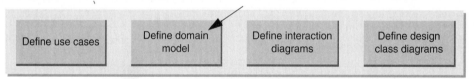

For example, a partial domain model is shown in Figure 1.3.

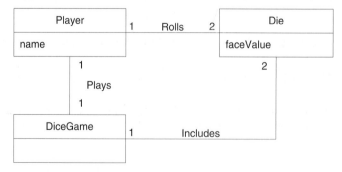

Figure 1.3 Partial domain model of the dice game.

This model illustrates the noteworthy concepts *Player, Die,* and *DiceGame,* with their associations and attributes.

Note that a domain model is not a description of software objects; it is a visualization of concepts in the real-world domain.

Define Interaction Diagrams

Object-oriented design is concerned with defining software objects and their collaborations. A common notation to illustrate these collaborations is the **interaction diagram**. It shows the flow of messages between software objects, and thus the invocation of methods.

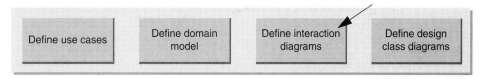

For example, assume that a software implementation of the dice game is desired. The interaction diagram in Figure 1.4 illustrates the essential step of playing, by sending messages to instances of the *DiceGame* and *Die* classes.

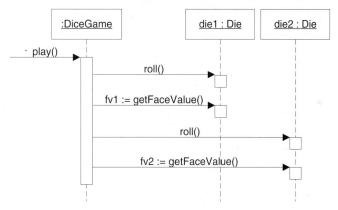

Figure 1.4 Interaction diagram illustrating messages between software objects.

Notice that although in the real world a *player* rolls the dice, in the software design the *DiceGame* object "rolls" the dice (that is, sends messages to *Die* objects). Software object designs and programs do take some inspiration from real-world domains, but they are *not* direct models or simulations of the real world.

Define Design Class Diagrams

In addition to a *dynamic* view of collaborating objects shown in interaction diagrams, it is useful to create a *static* view of the class definitions with a **design class diagram**. This illustrates the attributes and methods of the classes.

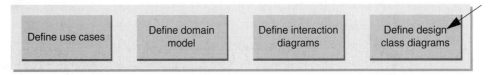

For example, in the dice game, an inspection of the interaction diagram leads to the partial design class diagram shown in Figure 1.5. Since a *play* message is sent to a *DiceGame* object, the *DiceGame* class requires a *play* method, while class *Die* requires a *roll* and *getFaceValue* method.

In contrast to the domain model, this diagram does not illustrate real-world concepts; rather, it shows software classes.

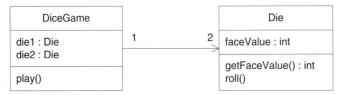

Figure 1.5 Partial design class diagram.

Summary

The dice game is a simple problem, presented to focus on a few steps and artifacts in analysis and design. To keep the introduction simple, not all the illustrated UML notation was explained. Future chapters explore analysis and design and these artifacts in closer detail.

1.6   The UML

To quote:

> The Unified Modeling Language (UML) is a language for specifying, visualizing, constructing, and documenting the artifacts of software systems, as well as for business modeling and other non-software systems [OMG01].

The UML has emerged as the de facto and de jure standard diagramming notation for object-oriented modeling. It started as an effort by Grady Booch and Jim Rumbaugh in 1994 to combine the diagramming notations from their two popular methods—the Booch and OMT (Object Modeling Technique) methods. They were later joined by Ivar Jacobson, the creator of the Objectory method, and as a group came to be known as the *three amigos*. Many others contributed to the UML, perhaps most notably Cris Kobryn, a leader in its ongoing refinement.

The UML was adopted in 1997 as a standard by the OMG (Object Management Group, an industry standards body), and has continued to be refined in new OMG UML versions.

This book does not cover every minute aspect of the UML, which is a large body of notation (some say, too large[1]). It focuses on diagrams which are frequently used, the most commonly used features within those diagrams, and core notation that is unlikely to change in future versions of the UML.

Why Won't We See Much UML for a Few Chapters?

This is not just a UML notation book, but one that explores the larger picture of applying the UML, patterns, and an iterative process in the context of software development. The UML is primarily applied during OOA/D, which is normally preceded by requirements analysis. Therefore, the initial chapters present an introduction to the important topics of use cases and requirements analysis, which are then followed by chapters on OOA/D and more UML details.

1.7 Further Readings

A very readable and popular summary of essential UML notation is *UML Distilled*, by Martin Fowler.

A succinct and popular introduction to the Unified Process (and its refinement in the Rational Unified Process) is *The Rational Unified Process—An Introduction* by Philippe Kruchten.

For a detailed discussion of UML (version 1.3) notation, *The Unified Modeling Language Reference Manual* and *The Unified Modeling Language User Guide,* by Booch, Jacobson, and Rumbaugh are worthwhile. Note that these texts were not meant for learning how to do object modeling or OOA/D—they are UML diagram notation references.

For a description of the current version of the UML, the on-line *OMG Unified Modeling Language Specification* at www.omg.org is necessary. UML revision work and soon-to-be released versions can be found at www.celigent.com/uml.

There are many books on software patterns, but the seminal classic is *Design Patterns*, by Gamma, Helm, Johnson, and Vlissides. It is truly required reading

---

1. The UML 2.0 effort includes exploration of the goal of simplifying and reducing the notation. This book presents high-use UML likely to survive future simplification.

for those studying object design. However, it is not an introductory text and is best read after developing comfort with the fundamentals of object design and programming.

Iterative Development and the Unified Process

People are more important than any process.

*Good people with a good process will
outperform good people with no process every time.*

—Grady Booch

Objectives

- Provide motivation for the content and order of subsequent chapters.
- Define an iterative and adaptive process.
- Define fundamental concepts in the Unified Process.

Introduction

Iterative development is a skillful approach to software development, and lies at the heart of how OOA/D is presented in this book. The Unified Process is an example iterative process for projects using OOA/D, and it shapes the book's presentation. Consequently, it is useful to read this chapter so that these core concepts and their influence on the book's structure are clear.

This chapter summarizes a few key ideas; please see Chapter 37 for further discussion of the UP and iterative process practices.

Informally, a **software development process** describes an approach to building, deploying, and possibly maintaining software. The **Unified Process** [JBR99] has emerged as a popular software development process for building object-oriented systems. In particular, the **Rational Unified Process** or **RUP**

[Kruchten00], a detailed refinement of the Unified Process, has been widely adopted.

The Unified Process (UP) combines commonly accepted best practices, such as an iterative lifecycle and risk-driven development, into a cohesive and well-documented description. Consequently, it is used in this book as the example process within which to introduce OOA/D.

This book starts with an introduction to the UP for two reasons:

1. The UP is an *iterative* process. Iterative development is a valuable practice that influences how this book introduces OOA/D, and how it is best practiced.

2. UP practices provide an example structure to talk about how to do—and how to learn—OOA/D.

> This text presents an introduction to the UP, not complete coverage. It emphasizes common ideas and artifacts related to an introduction to OOA/D and requirements analysis.

What If I Don't Care About the UP?

The UP is used as an example process within which to explore requirements analysis and OOA/D, since it is necessary to introduce the subject in the context of some process, and the UP (or the RUP refinement) is relatively widely used. Also, the UP presents common activities and best practices. Nevertheless, the central ideas of this book—such as use cases and design patterns—are independent of any particular process, and apply to many.

2.1 The Most Important UP Idea: Iterative Development

The UP promotes several best practices, but one stands above the others: **iterative development**. In this approach, development is organized into a series of short, fixed-length (for example, four week) mini-projects called **iterations**; the outcome of each is a tested, integrated, and executable system. Each iteration includes its own requirements analysis, design, implementation, and testing activities.

The iterative lifecycle is based on the successive enlargement and refinement of a system through multiple iterations, with cyclic feedback and adaptation as core drivers to converge upon a suitable system. The system grows incrementally over time, iteration by iteration, and thus this approach is also known as **iterative and incremental development** (see Figure 2.1).

Early iterative process ideas were known as spiral development and evolutionary development [Boehm88, Gilb88].

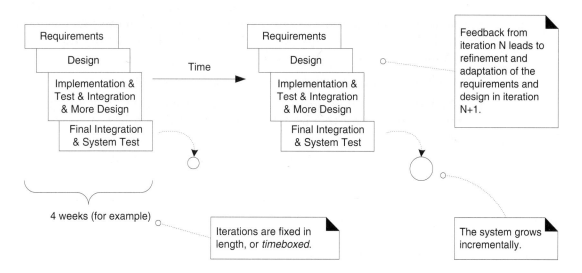

Figure 2.1 Iterative and incremental development.

Example

As an example (not a recipe), in a two-week iteration half-way through a project, perhaps Monday is spent primarily on distributing and clarifying the tasks and requirements of the iteration, while one person reverse-engineers the last iteration's code into UML diagrams (via a CASE tool), and prints and displays noteworthy diagrams. Tuesday is spent at whiteboards doing pair design work drawing rough UML diagrams captured on digital cameras, and writing some pseudocode and design notes. The remaining eight days are spent on implementation, testing (unit, acceptance, usability, ...), further design, integration, daily builds, system testing, and stabilization of the partial system. Other activities include demonstrations and evaluations with stakeholders, and planning for the next iteration.

Notice in this example that there is neither a rush to code, nor a long drawn-out design step that attempts to perfect all details of the design before programming. A "little" forethought regarding the design with visual modeling using rough and fast UML drawings is done; perhaps a half or full day by developers doing design work in pairs.

The result of each iteration is an executable but incomplete system; it is not ready to deliver into production. The system may not be eligible for production deployment until after many iterations; for example, 10 or 15 iterations.

The output of an iteration is *not* an experimental or throw-away prototype, and iterative development is not prototyping. Rather, the output is a production-grade subset of the final system.

Although, in general, each iteration tackles new requirements and incrementally extends the system, an iteration may occasionally revisit existing software and improve it; for example, one iteration may focus on improving the performance of a subsystem, rather than extending it with new features.

Embracing Change: Feedback and Adaptation

The subtitle of one book that discusses iterative development is *Embrace Change* [Beck00]. This phrase is evocative of a key attitude of iterative development: Rather than fighting the inevitable change that occurs in software development by trying (usually unsuccessfully) to fully and correctly specify, freeze, and "sign off" on a frozen requirement set and design before implementation, iterative development is based on an attitude of embracing change and adaptation as unavoidable and indeed essential drivers.

This is not to say that iterative development and the UP encourages an uncontrolled and reactive "feature creep"-driven process. Subsequent chapters explore how the UP balances the need—on the one hand—to agree upon and stabilize a set of requirements, with—on the other hand—the reality of changing requirements, as stakeholders clarify their vision or the marketplace changes.

Each iteration involves choosing a small subset of the requirements, and quickly designing, implementing, and testing. In early iterations the choice of requirements and design may not be exactly what is ultimately desired. But the act of swiftly taking a small step, before all requirements are finalized, or the entire design is speculatively defined, leads to rapid feedback—feedback from the users, developers, and tests (such as load and usability tests).

This early feedback is worth its weight in gold; rather than *speculating* on the correct requirements or design, the feedback from realistic building and testing something provides crucial practical insight and an opportunity to modify or adapt understanding of the requirements or design. End-users have a chance to quickly see a partial system and say, "Yes, that's what I asked for, but now that I try it, what I really want is something slightly different."[1] This "yes...but" process is not a sign of failure; rather, early and frequent structured cycles of "yes...buts" are a skillful way to make progress and discover what is of real value to the stakeholders. Yet, as mentioned, this is not an endorsement of chaotic and reactive development in which developers continually change direction—a middle way is possible.

In addition to requirements clarification, activities such as load testing will prove if the partial design and implementation are on the right path, or if in the

---

1. Or more likely, "You didn't understand what I wanted!"

next iteration, a change in the core architecture is required. Better to resolve and *prove* the risky and critical design decisions early rather than late—and iterative development provides the mechanism for this.

Consequently, work proceeds through a series of structured build-feedback-adapt cycles. Not surprisingly, in early iterations the deviation from the "true path" of the system (in terms of its final requirements and design) will be larger than in later iterations. Over time, the system converges towards this path, as illustrated in Figure 2.2.

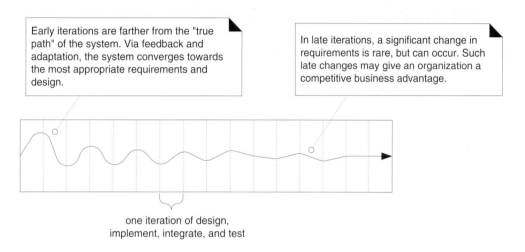

Figure 2.2 Iterative feedback and adaptation leads towards the desired system. The requirements and design instability lowers over time.

Benefits of Iterative Development

Benefits of iterative development include:

- early rather than late mitigation of high risks (technical, requirements, objectives, usability, and so forth)

- early visible progress

- early feedback, user engagement, and adaptation, leading to a refined system that more closely meets the real needs of the stakeholders

- managed complexity; the team is not overwhelmed by "analysis paralysis" or very long and complex steps

- the learning within an iteration can be methodically used to improve the development process itself, iteration by iteration

Iteration Length and Timeboxing

The UP (and experienced iterative developers) recommends an iteration length between two and six weeks. Small steps, rapid feedback, and adaptation are central ideas in iterative development; long iterations subvert the core motivation for iterative development and increase project risk. Much less than two weeks, and it is difficult to complete sufficient work to get meaningful throughput and feedback; much more than six or eight weeks, and the complexity becomes rather overwhelming, and feedback is delayed. A very long iteration misses the point of iterative development. Short is good.

A key idea is that iterations are **timeboxed**, or fixed in length. For example, if the next iteration is chosen to be four weeks long, then the partial system should be integrated, tested, and stabilized by the scheduled date—date slippage is discouraged. If it seems that it will be difficult to meet the deadline, the recommended response is to remove tasks or requirements from the iteration, and include them in a future iteration, rather than slip the completion date. Chapter 37 summarizes reasons for timeboxing.

Massive teams (for example, several hundred developers) may require longer than six-week iterations to compensate for the overhead of coordination and communication; but no more than three to six months is recommended. For example, the successful replacement in the 1990s of the Canadian air traffic control system was developed with an iterative lifecycle and other UP practices. It involved 150 programmers and was organized into six-month iterations.[2] But note that even in the case of an overall six-month project iteration, a subsystem team of 10 or 20 developers can break down their work into a series of six one-month iterations.

A six-month iteration is the exception for massive teams, not the rule. To reiterate, the UP recommends that normally an iteration should be between two and six weeks in duration.

2.2   Additional UP Best Practices and Concepts

The central idea to appreciate and practice in the UP is short timeboxed iterative, adaptive development.

Another implicit, but core, UP idea is the use of object technologies, including OOA/D and object-oriented programming.

---

2. Philippe Kruchten, who also led the development of the RUP, served as chief architect for the project.

Some additional best practices and key concepts in the UP include:

- tackle high-risk and high-value issues in early iterations
- continuously engage users for evaluation, feedback, and requirements
- build a cohesive, core architecture in early iterations
- continuously verify quality; test early, often, and realistically
- apply use cases
- model software visually (with the UML)
- carefully manage requirements
- practice change request and configuration management

See Chapter 37 for a more detailed description of these practices.

2.3 The UP Phases and Schedule-Oriented Terms

A UP project organizes the work and iterations across four major phases:

1. **Inception**— approximate vision, business case, scope, vague estimates.

2. **Elaboration**—refined vision, iterative implementation of the core architecture, resolution of high risks, identification of most requirements and scope, more realistic estimates.

3. **Construction**—iterative implementation of the remaining lower risk and easier elements, and preparation for deployment.

4. **Transition**—beta tests, deployment.

These phases are more fully defined in subsequent chapters.

This is *not* the old "waterfall" or sequential lifecycle of first defining all the requirements, and then doing all or most of the design.

Inception is not a requirements phase; rather, it is a kind of feasibility phase, where just enough investigation is done to support a decision to continue or stop.

Similarly, elaboration is not the requirements or design phase; rather, it is a phase where the core architecture is iteratively implemented, and high risk issues are mitigated.

Figure 2.3 illustrates common schedule-oriented terms in the UP. Notice that one development cycle (which ends in the release of a system into production) is composed of many iterations.

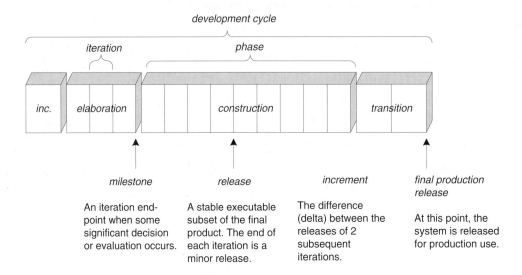

Figure 2.3 Schedule-oriented terms in the UP.

2.4   The UP Disciplines (was Workflows)

The UP describes work activities, such as writing a use case, within **disciplines** (originally called **workflows**).[3] Informally, a discipline is a set of activities (and related artifacts) in one subject area, such as the activities within requirements analysis. In the UP, an **artifact** is the general term for any work product: code, Web graphics, database schema, text documents, diagrams, models, and so on.

There are several disciplines in the UP; this book focuses on some artifacts in the following three:

- **Business Modeling**—When developing a single application, this includes domain object modeling. When engaged in large-scale business analysis or business process reengineering, this includes dynamic modeling of the business processes across the entire enterprise.

- **Requirements**—Requirements analysis for an application, such as writing use cases and identifying non-functional requirements.

- **Design**—All aspects of design, including the overall architecture, objects, databases, networking, and the like.

---

3. In 2001, the old UP term "workflow" was replaced by the new term "discipline" in order to harmonize with an international standardization effort called the OMG SPEM; because of its prior meaning in the UP, many continue to use the term workflow to mean discipline, although this is not strictly correct. The term "workflow" took on a new but slightly different meaning within the UP: On a particular project, it is a particular sequence of activities (perhaps *across* disciplines)—a flow of work.

A longer list of UP disciplines is shown in Figure 2.4.

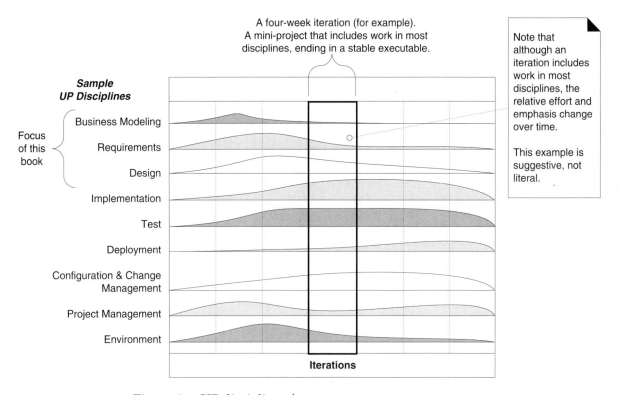

Figure 2.4 UP disciplines.[4]

In the UP, **Implementation** means programming and building the system, not deployment. The **Environment** discipline refers to establishing the tools and customizing the process for the project—that is, setting up the tool and process environment.

Disciplines and Phases

As illustrated in Figure 2.4, during one iteration work goes on in most or all disciplines. However, the relative effort across these disciplines changes over time. Early iterations naturally tend to apply greater relative emphasis to requirements and design, and later ones less so, as the requirements and core design stabilize through a process of feedback and adaptation.

Relating this to the UP phases (inception, elaboration, ...), Figure 2.5 illustrates the changing relative effort with respect to the phases; please note these are suggestive, not literal. In elaboration, for example, the iterations tend to have a

---

4. Diagram adapted from the RUP product.

relatively high level of requirements and design work, although definitely some implementation as well. During construction, the emphasis is heavier on implementation and lighter on requirements analysis.

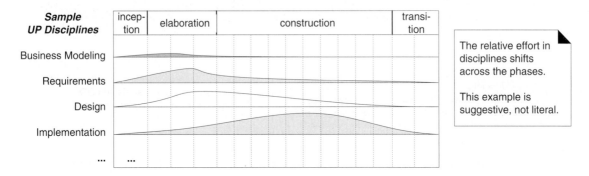

Figure 2.5 Disciplines and phases.

Book Structure and UP Phases and Disciplines

With respect to the phases and disciplines, what is the focus of the case study? Answer:

> The case study emphasizes the inception and elaboration phase. It focuses on some artifacts in the Business Modeling, Requirements, and Design disciplines, as this is where requirements analysis, OOA/D, patterns, and the UML are primarily applied.

The earlier chapters introduce activities in inception; later chapters explore several iterations in elaboration. The following list and Figure 2.6 describe the organization with respect to the UP phases.

1. The inception phase chapters introduce the basics of requirements analysis.

2. Iteration 1 introduces fundamental OOA/D and how to assign responsibilities to objects.

3. Iteration 2 focuses on object design, especially on introducing some high-use "design patterns."

4. Iteration 3 introduces a variety of subjects, such as architectural analysis and framework design.

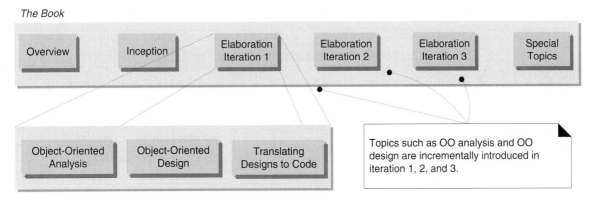

Figure 2.6 Book organization is related to the UP phases and iterations.

2.5 Process Customization and the Development Case

Optional Artifacts

Some UP practices and principles are invariant, such as iterative and risk-driven development, and continuous verification of quality.

However, a key insight into the UP is that all activities and artifacts (models, diagrams, documents, ...) are *optional*—well, maybe not the code! The set of possible artifacts described in the UP should be viewed like a set of medicines in a pharmacy. Just as one does not indiscriminately take many medicines, but matches the choice to the ailment, likewise on a UP project, a team should select a small subset of artifacts that address its particular problems and needs. In general, focus on a *small* set of artifacts that demonstrate high practical value.

The Development Case

The choice of UP artifacts for a project may be written up in a short document called the **Development Case** (an artifact in the Environment discipline). For example, Table 2.1 could be the Development Case describing the artifacts for the "NextGen Project" case study explored in this book.

Subsequent chapters describe the creation of some of these artifacts, including the Domain Model, Use-Case Model, and Design Model.

The example artifacts presented in this case study are by no means sufficient for, or suitable for, all projects. For example, a machine control system may benefit from doing many state diagrams. A Web-based e-commerce system may require a focus on user interface prototypes. A "green-field" new development project has very different design artifact needs than a systems integration project.

Discipline	Artifact	Incep.	Elab.	Const.	Trans.
	Iteration→	I1	E1..En	C1..Cn	T1..T2
Business Modeling	Domain Model		s		
Requirements	Use-Case Model	s	r		
	Vision	s	r		
	Supplementary Specification	s	r		
	Glossary	s	r		
Design	Design Model		s	r	
	SW Architecture Document		s		
	Data Model		s	r	
Implementation	Implementation Model		s	r	r
Project Management	SW Development Plan	s	r	r	r
Testing	Test Model		s	r	
Environment	Development Case	s	r		

Table 2.1 Sample Development Case of UP artifacts. s - start; r - refine

2.6   The Agile UP

Methodologists speak of processes as heavy vs. light, and predictive vs. adaptive. A **heavy process** is a pejorative term meant to suggest one with the following qualities [Fowler00]:

- many artifacts created in a bureaucratic atmosphere
- rigidity and control
- elaborate, long-term, detailed planning
- predictive rather than adaptive

A **predictive process** is one that attempts to plan and predict the activities and resource (people) allocations in detail over a relatively long time span, such as the majority of a project. Predictive processes usually have a "waterfall" or sequential lifecycle—first, defining all the requirements; second, defining a detailed design; and third, implementing. In contrast, an **adaptive process** is one that accepts change as an inevitable driver and encourages flexible adaptation; they usually have an iterative lifecycle. An **agile process** implies a light and adaptive process, nimble in response to changing needs.

The UP was not meant by its authors to be either heavy or predictive, although its large optional set of activities and artifacts have understandably led to that impression in some. Rather, it was meant to be adopted and applied in the spirit of an agile process—**agile UP**. Some examples of how this applies:

- Prefer a small set of UP activities and artifacts. Some projects will benefit from more than others, but, in general, keep it simple.

- Since the UP is iterative, requirements and designs are not completed before implementation. They adaptively emerge through a series of iterations, based on feedback.

- There isn't a *detailed* plan for the entire project. There is a high level plan (called the **Phase Plan**) that estimates the project end date and other major milestones, but it does not detail the fine-grained steps to those milestones. A detailed plan (called the **Iteration Plan**) only plans with greater detail one iteration in advance. Detailed planning is done adaptively from iteration to iteration. Please see Chapter 36 for some comments on planning iterative projects, and the justification for this approach.

The case study emphasizes a relatively small number of artifacts, and iterative development, in the spirit of an agile UP.

2.7   The Sequential "Waterfall" Lifecycle

In contrast to the iterative lifecycle of the UP, an old alternative was the sequential, linear, or "waterfall" lifecycle [Royce70]. In common usage, it defined steps similar to the following:

1. Clarify, record, and commit to a set of complete and frozen requirements.

2. Design a system based on these requirements.

3. Implement, based on the design.

A two year study reported in the *MIT Sloan Management Review* of successful software projects identified four common factors for success; iterative development, rather than a waterfall process, was first on the list [MacCormack01].[5]

A brief description of its problems, and how they are mitigated by iterative development, is presented in Chapter 37.

---

5. The others were: 2) at least daily incorporation of new code into a complete system build, and rapid feedback on design changes (via testing); 3) a team experienced in shipping multiple products; and 4) an early focus on building and proving a cohesive architecture. Three of these four factors are explicit practices in the UP.

2.8   You Know You Didn't Understand the UP When...

Here are some signs that indicate when you have not understood what it means to adopt the UP and iterative development in the agile spirit intended by the UP.

■ You think that inception = requirements, elaboration = design, and construction = implementation (that is, superimposing a waterfall lifecycle on to the UP).

■ You think that the purpose of elaboration is to fully and carefully define models, which are translated into code during construction.

■ You try to define most of the requirements before starting design or implementation.

■ You try to define most of the design before starting implementation; you try to fully define and commit to an architecture before iterative programming and testing.

■ A "long time" is spent doing requirements or design work before programming starts.

■ You believe that a suitable iteration length is four months long, rather than four weeks long (excluding projects with hundreds of developers).

■ You think UML diagramming and design activities are a time to fully and accurately define designs and models in great detail, and of programming as a simple mechanical translation of these into code.

■ You think that adopting the UP means to do many of the possible activities and create many documents, and thinks of or experiences the UP as a formal, fussy process with many steps to be followed.

■ You try to plan a project in detail from start to finish; you try to speculatively predict all the iterations, and what should happen in each one.

■ You want believable plans and estimates for projects before the elaboration phase is finished.

2.9   Further Readings

A very readable introduction to the UP and its refinement in the RUP is *The Rational Unified Process—An Introduction* by Philippe Kruchten, the lead architect of the RUP.

A description of the original UP can be found in *The Unified Software Development Process* by Jacobson, Booch, and Rumbaugh. It is worth study, but Kruchten's introduction is recommended first, as it is smaller and more succinct, and the RUP updates and refines the original UP.

Rational Software sells the online Web-based RUP documentation product, which provides comprehensive reading on RUP artifacts and activities, and templates for most artifacts. See Chapter 37 for a brief discussion. An organization can run a UP project just using mentors and books as learning resources, but some find the RUP product a useful learning and process aid.

UP activities are also loosely described in a series of books edited by Ambler and Constantine (for example, *The Unified Process: Elaboration Phase* [Ambler00]). These books contain reprints of articles published over the years in *Software Development* magazine, categorized into their respective phase and activity in terms of a UP taxonomy. Note that the articles were not originally written for the UP, although they definitely contain useful advice. Also note one slight error in the series: They describe the UP elaboration phase as a phase in which throw-away prototypes are created, thus reducing the need for attention to care in the programming or design. This is not accurate; production-quality (albeit partial) designs and code are created during elaboration. Ambler recognizes the inaccuracy and may correct it in a subsequent edition.[6]

For other agile methods, the **Extreme Programming** (XP) series of books [Beck00, BF00, JAH00] are recommended, such as *Extreme Programming Explained*. Some XP practices are mentioned in later chapters. Most XP practices (such as test-first programming and iterative development) are compatible—or identical—with UP practices, and I encourage their adoption on a UP project. Note that the XP did not (nor did it claim to) invent short timeboxed iterative and adaptive development, which has been a practice in the UP and other iterative methods for years. Two noteworthy differences—this is not a complete list—between the UP and XP are: 1) The UP recommends incrementally writing use cases and a non-functional requirements document (XP does not); and, 2) The UP recommends more visual design diagramming (such as a half-day or day) near the start of an iteration, before major programming. The XP leaders recommend very little, such as 30 minutes.

Highsmith provides justification for the value of adaptive development in *Adaptive Software Development* [Highsmith00].

---

6. Ambler, private communication.

CASE STUDY: THE NEXTGEN POS SYSTEM

Few things are harder to put up with than a good example.

—*Mark Twain*

Introduction

This chapter briefly describes the case study. If you understand the problem domain, it may be skipped. Indeed, this problem was chosen because it is familiar, but rich with interesting design and architectural problems, and thus allows one to concentrate on how to do analysis and design, rather than explain the problem and domain.

3.1   The NextGen POS System

The case study is the NextGen point-of-sale (POS) system. In this apparently straightforward problem domain, we shall see that there are very interesting requirement and design problems to solve. In addition, it is a realistic problem; organizations really do write POS systems using object technologies.

A POS system is a computerized application used (in part) to record sales and handle payments; it is typically used in a retail store. It includes hardware components such as a computer and bar code scanner, and software to run the system. It interfaces to various service applications, such as a third-party tax calculator and inventory control. These systems must be relatively fault-tolerant; that is, even if remote services are temporarily unavailable (such as the inventory system), they must still be capable

of capturing sales and handling at least cash payments (so that the business is not crippled).

A POS system increasingly must support multiple and varied client-side terminals and interfaces. These include a thin-client Web browser terminal, a regular personal computer with something like a Java Swing graphical user interface, touch screen input, wireless PDAs, and so forth.

Furthermore, we are creating a commercial POS system that we will sell to different clients with disparate needs in terms of business rule processing. Each client will desire a unique set of logic to execute at certain predictable points in scenarios of using the system, such as when a new sale is initiated or when a new line item is added. Therefore, we will need a mechanism to provide this flexibility and customization.

Using an iterative development strategy, we are going to proceed through requirements, object-oriented analysis, design, and implementation.

3.2   Architectural Layers and Case Study Emphasis

A typical object-oriented information system is designed in terms of several architectural layers or subsystems (see Figure 3.1). The following is not a complete list, but provides an example:

- **User Interface**—graphical interface; windows.

- **Application Logic and Domain Objects**—software objects representing domain concepts (for example, a software class named *Sale*) that fulfill application requirements.

- **Technical Services**—general purpose objects and subsystems that provide supporting technical services, such as interfacing with a database or error logging. These services are usually application-independent and reusable across several systems.

> OOA/D is generally most relevant for modeling the application logic and technical service layers.

The NextGen case study primarily emphasizes the problem domain objects, allocating responsibilities to them to fulfill the requirements of the application. Object-oriented design is also applied to create a technical service subsystem for interfacing with a database.

In this design approach, the UI layer has very little responsibility; it is said to be *thin*. Windows do *not* contain code that performs application logic or processing. Rather, task requests are forwarded on to other layers.

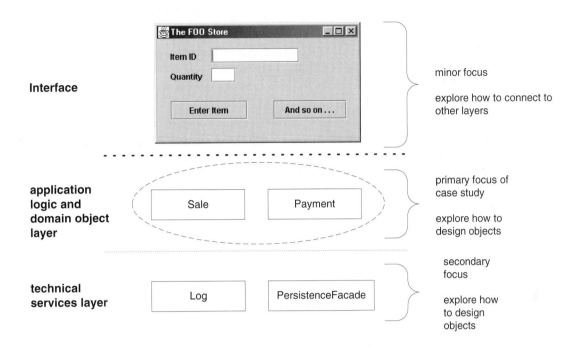

Figure 3.1 Sample layers and objects in an object-oriented system, and the case study focus.

3.3   The Book's Strategy: Iterative Learning and Development

This book is organized to follow an iterative development strategy. OOA/D is applied to the NextGen POS system in multiple iterations; the first iteration is for some core functions. Later iterations expand the functionality of the system (see Figure 3.2). In conjunction with iterative development, the *presentation* of analysis and design topics, UML notation, and patterns are introduced iteratively and incrementally. In the first iteration, a core set of analysis and design topics and notation is presented. The second iteration expands into new ideas, UML notation, and patterns. And likewise in the third iteration.

Figure 3.2 Learning path follows iterations.

PART 2 INCEPTION

4

INCEPTION

Le mieux est l'ennemi du bien (The best is the enemy of the good).

—*Voltaire*

Objectives

- Define the inception step.
- Motivate the following chapters in this section.

Introduction

This chapter defines the inception phase of a project. If process ideas are not your priority, or you prefer to first focus on learning the main practical activity in this phase—use case modeling—then this chapter can be skipped.

Most projects require a short initial step in which the following kinds of questions are explored:

- What is the vision and business case for this project?
- Feasible?
- Buy and/or build?
- Rough estimate of cost: Is it $10K-100K or in the millions?
- Should we proceed or stop?

Defining the vision and obtaining an order-of-magnitude (unreliable) estimate necessitates doing some requirements exploration. However, the purpose of the inception step is not to define all the requirements, or generate a believable estimate or project plan. At the risk of over-simplification, the idea is to do just enough investigation to form a rational, justifiable opinion of the overall purpose and feasibility of the potential new system, and decide if it is worthwhile to invest in deeper exploration (the purpose of the elaboration phase).

35

Thus, the inception phase should be relatively short for most projects, such as one or a few weeks long. Indeed, on many projects, if it is more than a week long, then the point of inception has been missed: It is to decide if the project is worth a serious investigation (during elaboration), not to do that investigation.

Inception in one sentence:

Envision the product scope, vision, and business case.

The main problem solved in one sentence:

Do the stakeholders have basic agreement on the vision of the project, and is it worth investing in serious investigation?

4.1   Inception: An Analogy

In the oil business, when a new field is being considered, some of the steps include:

1. Decide if there is enough evidence or a business case to even justify exploratory drilling.

2. If so, do measurements and exploratory drilling.

3. Provide scope and estimate information.

4. Further steps...

The inception phase is like step one in this analogy. In step one people do not predict how much oil there is, or the cost or effort to extract it. It is premature—there is insufficient information. Although it would be nice to be able to answer "how much" and "when" questions without the cost and effort of the exploration, in the oil business it is understood to not be realistic.

In UP terms, the realistic exploration step is the elaboration phase. The preceding inception phase is akin to a feasibility study to decide if it is even worth investing in exploratory drilling. Only after exploration (elaboration) do we have the data and insight to make somewhat believable estimates and plans. Therefore, in iterative development and the UP, plans and estimates are not to be considered reliable in the inception phase. They merely provide an order-of-magnitude sense of the level of effort, to aid the decision to continue or not.

4.2   Inception May Be Very Brief

The intent of inception is to establish some initial common vision for the objectives of the project, determine if it is feasible, and decide if it is worth some serious investigation in elaboration. If it has been decided beforehand that the project will definitely be done, and it is clearly feasible (perhaps because the team has done projects like this before), then the inception phase will be especially brief. It may include the first requirements workshop, planning for the first iteration, and then quickly moving forward to elaboration.

4.3   What Artifacts May Start in Inception?

Table 4.1 lists common inception (or early elaboration) artifacts and indicates the issues they address. Subsequent chapters will examine some of these in greater detail, especially the Use-Case Model. A key insight regarding iterative development is to appreciate that these are only partially completed in this phase, will be refined in later iterations, and should not even be created unless it is deemed likely they will add real practical value. And since it is inception, the investigation and artifact content should be light.

For example, the Use-Case Model (to be described in following chapters) may list the *names* of most of the expected use cases and actors, but perhaps only describe 10% of the use cases in detail—done in the service of developing a rough high-level vision of the system scope, purpose, and risks.

Note that some programming work may occur in inception in order to create "proof of concept" prototypes, to clarify a few requirements via (typically) UI-oriented prototypes, and to do programming experiments for key "show stopper" technical questions.

Artifact[†]	Comment
Vision and Business Case	Describes the high-level goals and constraints, the business case, and provides an executive summary.
Use-Case Model	Describes the functional requirements, and related non-functional requirements.
Supplementary Specification	Describes other requirements.
Glossary	Key domain terminology.
Risk List & Risk Management Plan	Describes the business, technical, resource, schedule risks, and ideas for their mitigation or response.
Prototypes and proof-of-concepts	To clarify the vision, and validate technical ideas.
Iteration Plan	Describes what to do in the first elaboration iteration.

Artifact[†]	Comment
Phase Plan & Software Development Plan	Low-precision guess for elaboration phase duration and effort. Tools, people, education, and other resources.
Development Case	A description of the customized UP steps and artifacts for this project. In the UP, one always customizes it for the project.

Table 4.1 Sample inception artifacts.

†-These artifacts are only partially completed in this phase. They will be iteratively refined in subsequent iterations. Name capitalization implies it is an officially named UP artifact.

Isn't That a Lot of Documentation?

Recall that artifacts should be considered optional. Choose to create only those that really add value for the project, and drop them if their worth is not proved.

The point of an artifact is not the document or diagram itself, but the thinking, analysis, and proactive readiness (and then its recording, to avoid re-invention or having to repeat things verbally). As General Eisenhower said, "In preparing for battle I have always found that plans are useless, but planning indispensable" [Nixon90, BF00].

Record artifacts digitally and online—available on the project's website—rather than on paper.

Note also that UP artifacts from previous projects can be reused on later ones. It is common for there to be many similarities in risk, project management, testing, and environment artifacts across projects. All UP projects will (or should) organize artifacts the same way, with the same names (Risk List, Development Case, and so on). This simplifies finding reusable artifacts from prior projects on new UP engagements.

4.4   You Know You Didn't Understand Inception When...

- It is more than "a few" weeks long for most projects.
- There is an attempt to define most of the requirements.
- Estimates or plans are expected to be reliable.
- You define the architecture; rather, this should be done iteratively in elaboration.

- You believe that the proper sequence of work should be: 1) define the requirements; 2) design the architecture; 3) implement.

- There is no Business Case or Vision artifact.

- The names of most of the use cases and actors were not identified.

- All the use cases were written in detail.

- None of the use cases were written in detail; rather, 10-20% should be written in detail to obtain some realistic insight into the scope of the problem.

UNDERSTANDING REQUIREMENTS

Ours is a world where people don't know what they want and are willing to go through hell to get it.

—*Don Marquis*

Objectives

- Define the FURPS+ model.
- Relate types of requirements to UP artifacts.

Introduction

Not all requirements are created equal. This chapter introduces the FURPS+ requirements categories.

Requirements are capabilities and conditions to which the system—and more broadly, the project—must conform [JBR99]. A prime challenge of requirements work is to find, communicate, and remember (that usually means record) what is really needed, in a form that clearly speaks to the client and development team members.

The UP promotes a set of best practices, one of which is *manage requirements*. This does not refer to the waterfall attitude of attempting to fully define and stabilize the requirements in the first phase of a project, but rather—in the context of inevitably changing and unclear stakeholder's wishes—"a systematic approach to finding, documenting, organizing, and tracking the changing requirements of a system" [RUP]; in short, doing it skillfully and not being sloppy. Note the word *changing*; the UP embraces change in requirements as a fundamental driver on projects. *Finding* is another important term; that is, skillful elicitation via techniques such as use case writing and requirements workshops.

As indicated in Figure 5.1, one study of factors on challenged projects revealed that 37% of factors related to problems with requirements, making requirements issues the largest single contributor to problems [Standish94]. Consequently, masterful requirements management is important. The waterfall response to this data would be to try harder to polish, stabilize, and freeze the requirements before any design or implementation, but history shows this to be a losing battle. The iterative response is to use a process that embraces change and feedback as core drivers in discovering requirements.

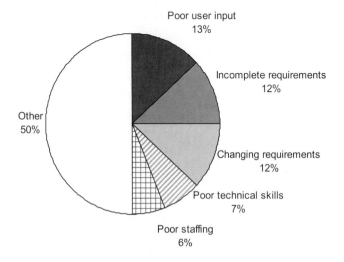

Figure 5.1 Factors on challenged software projects.

5.1 Types of Requirements

In the UP, requirements are categorized according to the FURPS+ model [Grady92], a useful mnemonic with the following meaning:[1]

- **Functional**—features, capabilities, security.

- **Usability**—human factors, help, documentation.

- **Reliability**—frequency of failure, recoverability, predictability.

---

1. There are several systems of requirements categorization and quality attributes published in books and by standards organizations, such as ISO 9126 (which is similar to the FURPS+ list), and several from the Software Engineering Institute (SEI); any can be used on a UP project.

- **Performance**—response times, throughput, accuracy, availability, resource usage.

- **Supportability**—adaptability, maintainability, internationalization, configurability.

The "+" in FURPS+ indicates ancillary and sub-factors, such as:

- **Implementation**—resource limitations, languages and tools, hardware, ...

- **Interface**—constraints imposed by interfacing with external systems.

- **Operations**—system management in its operational setting.

- **Packaging**

- **Legal**—licensing and so forth.

It is helpful to use FURPS+ categories (or some categorization scheme) as a checklist for requirements coverage, to reduce the risk of not considering some important facet of the system.

Some of these requirements are collectively called the **quality attributes**, **quality requirements**, or the "-ilities" of a system. These include usability, reliability, performance, and supportability. In common usage, requirements are categorized as **functional** (behavioral) or **non-functional** (everything else); some dislike this broad generalization [BCK98], but it is very widely used.

Functional requirements are explored and recorded in the Use-Case Model, the subject of the next chapter, and in the system features list of the Vision artifact. Other requirements can be recorded in the use cases they relate to, or in the Supplementary Specifications artifact. The Vision artifact summarizes high-level requirements that are elaborated in these other documents. The Glossary records and clarifies terms used in the requirements. The Glossary in the UP also encompasses the concept of the **data dictionary**, which records requirements related to data, such as validation rules, acceptable values, and so forth. Prototypes are a mechanism to clarify what is wanted or possible.

As we shall see when exploring architectural analysis, the quality requirements have a strong influence on the architecture of a system. For example, a high-performance, high-reliability requirement will influence the choice of software and hardware components, and their configuration. The need for easy adaptability due to frequent changes in the functional requirements would likewise fundamentally shape the design of the software.

5.2 Further Readings

References related to requirements with use cases are covered in a subsequent chapter. Use-case-oriented requirements texts, such as *Writing Effective Use Cases* [Cockburn01] are the recommended starting point in requirements study, rather than more general (and usually, traditional) requirements texts.

There is a broad effort to discuss requirements—and a wide variety of software engineering topics—under the umbrella of the Software Engineering Body of Knowledge (**SWEBOK**), available at www.swebok.org.

The SEI (www.sei.cmu.edu) has several proposals related to quality requirements. The ISO 9126, IEEE Std 830, and IEEE Std 1061 are standards related to requirements and quality attributes, and available on the Web at various sites.

Some cautions regarding general requirements books, even those that purport to cover use cases, iterative development, or indeed even requirements in the UP:

1. Most are written with a waterfall bias of significant or "thorough" up-front requirements definition before moving on to design and implementation. This is not meant to invalidate their broader value or often deep and useful method-independent requirements insights, but to clarify that they do not represent an accurate view of iterative development. This is because the authors may have a primary background in waterfall projects, working to refine, carefully and thoroughly define, and finalize the requirements before continuing to design. Those books that also mention iterative development may do so superficially, perhaps with "iterative" material added to appeal to modern trends. Thus, requirements books and articles should be read with alertness; one could be lulled into the idea of trying to carefully define all the requirements in the initial phase, which is not consistent with an iterative process.

2. Many general requirements books that also purport to include use cases do so superficially, or misunderstand what use-case driven requirements really means. This may be because the authors' primary background is in traditional requirements methods, and there has been an attempt to recently append use cases to their prior method, without appreciating that a central idea of use cases as envisioned by Ivar Jacobson and the UP is to make use cases the heart-and-center overarching requirements approach—replacing other requirements documents as the central element; use cases suffuse and drive the requirements work, rather than being some minor or medium-level adjunct technique appended to traditional requirements documents or approaches.

In summary, general requirements books offer useful advice on techniques and issues of requirements gathering, written by skilled practitioners, but often present the advice in a waterfall process context, and without great insight into the deeper implications of use cases. Any variant of process advice implying "try to define most of the requirements, and then move forward to design and implementation" is not consistent with iterative development and the UP.

USE-CASE MODEL: WRITING REQUIREMENTS IN CONTEXT

The indispensable first step to getting the things you want out of life: decide what you want.

—*Ben Stein*

Objectives

- Identify and write use cases.
- Relate use cases to user goals and elementary business processes.
- Use the brief, casual, and fully dressed formats, in an essential style.
- Relate use case work to iterative development.

Introduction

This chapter is worth studying during a first read of the book because use cases are a widely used mechanism to discover and record requirements (especially functional); they influence many aspects of a project, including OOA/D. It is worth both knowing about and creating use cases.

Writing use cases—stories of using a system—is an excellent technique to understand and describe requirements. This chapter explores key use case concepts and presents sample use cases for the NextGen application.

The UP defines the **Use-Case Model** within the Requirements discipline. Essentially, this is the set of all use cases; it is a model of the system's functionality and environment.

6.1   Goals and Stories

Customers and end users have goals (also known as *needs* in the UP) and want computer systems to help meet them, ranging from recording sales to estimating the flow of oil from future wells. There are several ways to capture these goals and system requirements; the better ones are simple and familiar because this makes it easier—especially for customers and end users—to contribute to their definition or evaluation. That lowers the risk of missing the mark.

Use cases are a mechanism to help keep it simple and understandable for all stakeholders. Informally, they are stories of using a system to meet goals. Here is an example *brief format* use case:

> **Process Sale**: A customer arrives at a checkout with items to purchase. The cashier uses the POS system to record each purchased item. The system presents a running total and line-item details. The customer enters payment information, which the system validates and records. The system updates inventory. The customer receives a receipt from the system and then leaves with the items.

Use cases often need to be more elaborate than this, but the essence is discovering and recording functional requirements by writing stories of using a system to help fulfill various stakeholder goals; that is, *cases of use*.[1] It isn't supposed to be a difficult idea, although it may indeed be difficult to discover or decide what is needed, and write it coherently at a useful level of detail.

Much has been written about use cases, and while worthwhile, there is always the risk among creative, thoughtful people to obscure a simple idea with layers of sophistication. It is usually possible to spot a novice use-case modeler (or a serious Type A analyst) by an over-concern with secondary issues such as use case diagrams, use case relationships, use case packages, optional attributes, and so forth, rather than writing the stories. That said, a strength of the use case mechanism is the capacity to scale both up and down in terms of sophistication and formality, depending on need.

6.2   Background

The idea of use cases to describe functional requirements was introduced in 1986 by Ivar Jacobson [Jacobson92], a main contributor to the UML and UP. Jacobson's use case idea was seminal and widely appreciated; simplicity and

---

1. The original term in Swedish literally translates as "usage case."

utility being its chief virtues. Although many have made contributions to the subject, arguably the most influential, comprehensive, and coherent next step in defining what use cases are (or should be) and how to write them came from Alistair Cockburn, summarized in the very popular text *Writing Effective Use Cases* [Cockburn01], based on his earlier work and writings stemming from 1992 onwards. This introduction is therefore based upon and consistent with the latter work.

6.3   Use Cases and Adding Value

First, some informal definitions: an **actor** is something with behavior, such as a person (identified by role), computer system, or organization; for example, a cashier.

A **scenario** is a specific sequence of actions and interactions between actors and the system under discussion; it is also called a **use case instance**. It is one particular story of using a system, or one path through the use case; for example, the scenario of successfully purchasing items with cash, or the scenario of failing to purchase items because of a credit card transaction denial.

Informally then, a **use case** is a collection of related success and failure scenarios that describe actors using a system to support a goal. For example, here is a *casual format* use case that includes some alternate scenarios:

> **Handle Returns**
>
> *Main Success Scenario*: A customer arrives at a checkout with items to return. The cashier uses the POS system to record each returned item ...
>
> *Alternate Scenarios*:
>
> If they paid by credit, and the reimbursement transaction to their credit account is rejected, inform the customer and pay them with cash.
>
> If the item identifier is not found in the system, notify the Cashier and suggest manual entry of the identifier code (perhaps it is corrupted).
>
> If the system detects failure to communicate with the external accounting system, ...

An alternate, but similar definition of a use case is provided by the RUP:

> A set of use-case instances, where each instance is a sequence of actions a system performs that yields an observable result of value to a particular actor [RUP].

The phrasing *"an observable result of value"* is subtle but important, because it stresses the attitude that the system behavior should emphasize providing value to the user.

> A key attitude in use case work is to focus on the question "How can using the system provide observable value to the user, or fulfill their goals?", rather than merely thinking of system requirements in terms of a "laundry list" of features or functions.

Perhaps it seems obvious to stress providing observable user value, but the software industry is littered with failed projects that did not deliver what people really needed. The feature and function list approach to capturing requirements can contribute to that negative outcome because it does not encourage the stakeholders to consider the requirements in a larger context of using the system in a scenario to achieve some observable result of value, or some goal. In contrast, use cases place features and functions in a goal-oriented context. Hence the chapter title.[2]

This is a key idea that Jacobson was trying to convey in the use case concept: Do requirements work with a focus on how a system can add value and fulfill goals.

6.4   Use Cases and Functional Requirements

Use cases are requirements; primarily they are functional requirements that indicate what the system will do. In terms of the FURPS+ requirements types, they emphasize the "F" (functional or behavioral), but can also be used for other types, especially when those other types strongly relate to a use case. In the UP—and most modern methods—use cases are the central mechanism that is recommended for their discovery and definition. Use cases define a promise or contract of how a system will behave.

To be clear: Use cases *are* requirements (although not all requirements). Some think of requirements only as "the system shall do..." function or feature lists. Not so, and a key idea of use cases is to (usually) reduce the importance or use of detailed older-style feature lists and rather, write use cases for the functional requirements. More on this point in a later section.

Use cases are text documents, not diagrams, and use-case modeling is primarily an act of writing text, not drawing. However, the UML defines a use case diagram to illustrate the names of use cases and actors, and their relationships.

---

2. Originally from the aptly titled *Uses Cases: Requirements in Context* [GK00] (chapter title adapted with permission of the authors).

6.5   Use Case Types and Formats

Black-Box Use Cases and System Responsibilities

Black-box use cases are the most common and recommended kind; they do not describe the internal workings of the system, its components, or design. Rather, the system is described as having *responsibilities*, which is a common unifying metaphorical theme in object-oriented thinking—software elements have responsibilities and collaborate with other elements that have responsibilities.

By defining system responsibilities with black-box use cases, it is possible to specify *what* the system must do (the functional requirements) without deciding *how* it will do it (the design). Indeed, the definition of "analysis" versus "design" is sometimes summarized as "what" versus "how." This is an important theme in good software development: During requirements analysis avoid making "how" decisions, and specify the external behavior for the system, as a black box. Later, during design, create a solution that meets the specification.

Black-box style	Not
The system records the sale.	The system writes the sale to a data-base. ...or (even worse): The system generates a SQL INSERT statement for the sale...

Formality Types

Use cases are written in different formats, depending on need. In addition to the black-box versus white-box *visibility* type, use cases are written in varying degrees of *formality*:

- **brief**—terse one-paragraph summary, usually of the main success scenario. The prior *Process Sale* example was brief.

- **casual**—informal paragraph format. Multiple paragraphs that cover various scenarios. The prior *Handle Returns* example was casual.

- **fully dressed**—the most elaborate. All steps and variations are written in detail, and there are supporting sections, such as preconditions and success guarantees.

The following example is a fully dressed case for our NextGen case study.

6.6   Fully Dressed Example: Process Sale

Fully dressed use cases show more detail and are structured; they are useful in order to obtain a deep understanding of the goals, tasks, and requirements. In the NextGen POS case study, they would be created during one of the early requirements workshops in a collaboration of the system analyst, subject matter experts, and developers.

The usecases.org Format

Various format templates are available for fully dressed use cases. However, perhaps the most widely used and shared format is the template available at www.usecases.org. The following example illustrates this style.

Please note that this is the book's primary case study example of a detailed use case; it shows many common elements and issues.

Use Case UC1: Process Sale

Primary Actor: Cashier

Stakeholders and Interests:
- Cashier: Wants accurate, fast entry, and no payment errors, as cash drawer shortages are deducted from his/her salary.
- Salesperson: Wants sales commissions updated.
- Customer: Wants purchase and fast service with minimal effort. Wants proof of purchase to support returns.
- Company: Wants to accurately record transactions and satisfy customer interests. Wants to ensure that Payment Authorization Service payment receivables are recorded. Wants some fault tolerance to allow sales capture even if server components (e.g., remote credit validation) are unavailable. Wants automatic and fast update of accounting and inventory.
- Government Tax Agencies: Want to collect tax from every sale. May be multiple agencies, such as national, state, and county.
- Payment Authorization Service: Wants to receive digital authorization requests in the correct format and protocol. Wants to accurately account for their payables to the store.

Preconditions: Cashier is identified and authenticated.

Success Guarantee (Postconditions): Sale is saved. Tax is correctly calculated. Accounting and Inventory are updated. Commissions recorded. Receipt is generated. Payment authorization approvals are recorded.

Main Success Scenario (or Basic Flow):
1. Customer arrives at POS checkout with goods and/or services to purchase.
2. Cashier starts a new sale.
3. Cashier enters item identifier.
4. System records sale line item and presents item description, price, and running total. Price calculated from a set of price rules.

Cashier repeats steps 3-4 until indicates done.

5. System presents total with taxes calculated.
6. Cashier tells Customer the total, and asks for payment.
7. Customer pays and System handles payment.
8. System logs completed sale and sends sale and payment information to the external Accounting system (for accounting and commissions) and Inventory system (to update inventory).
9. System presents receipt.
10. Customer leaves with receipt and goods (if any).

Extensions (or Alternative Flows):

*a. At any time, System fails:

    To support recovery and correct accounting, ensure all transaction sensitive state and events can be recovered from any step of the scenario.

    1. Cashier restarts System, logs in, and requests recovery of prior state.
    2. System reconstructs prior state.
        2a. System detects anomalies preventing recovery:
            1. System signals error to the Cashier, records the error, and enters a clean state.
            2. Cashier starts a new sale.

3a. Invalid identifier:
    1. System signals error and rejects entry.

3b. There are multiple of same item category and tracking unique item identity not important (e.g., 5 packages of veggie-burgers):
    1. Cashier can enter item category identifier and the quantity.

3-6a: Customer asks Cashier to remove an item from the purchase:
    1. Cashier enters item identifier for removal from sale.
    2. System displays updated running total.

3-6b. Customer tells Cashier to cancel sale:
    1. Cashier cancels sale on System.

3-6c. Cashier suspends the sale:
    1. System records sale so that it is available for retrieval on any POS terminal.

4a. The system generated item price is not wanted (e.g., Customer complained about something and is offered a lower price):
    1. Cashier enters override price.
    2. System presents new price.

5a. System detects failure to communicate with external tax calculation system service:
    1. System restarts the service on the POS node, and continues.
        1a. System detects that the service does not restart.
            1. System signals error.
            2. Cashier may manually calculate and enter the tax, or cancel the sale.

5b. Customer says they are eligible for a discount (e.g., employee, preferred customer):
    1. Cashier signals discount request.
    2. Cashier enters Customer identification.
    3. System presents discount total, based on discount rules.

5c. Customer says they have credit in their account, to apply to the sale:
    1. Cashier signals credit request.
    2. Cashier enters Customer identification.
    3. Systems applies credit up to price=0, and reduces remaining credit.

6a. Customer says they intended to pay by cash but don't have enough cash:
    1a. Customer uses an alternate payment method.
    1b. Customer tells Cashier to cancel sale. Cashier cancels sale on System.

7a. Paying by cash:
    1. Cashier enters the cash amount tendered.
    2. System presents the balance due, and releases the cash drawer.
    3. Cashier deposits cash tendered and returns balance in cash to Customer.
    4. System records the cash payment.

7b. Paying by credit:
    1. Customer enters their credit account information.
    2. System sends payment authorization request to an external Payment Authorization Service System, and requests payment approval.
        2a. System detects failure to collaborate with external system:
            1. System signals error to Cashier.
            2. Cashier asks Customer for alternate payment.
    3. System receives payment approval and signals approval to Cashier.
        3a. System receives payment denial:
            1. System signals denial to Cashier.
            2. Cashier asks Customer for alternate payment.
    4. System records the credit payment, which includes the payment approval.
    5. System presents credit payment signature input mechanism.
    6. Cashier asks Customer for a credit payment signature. Customer enters signature.

7c. Paying by check...

7d. Paying by debit...

7e. Customer presents coupons:
    1. Before handling payment, Cashier records each coupon and System reduces price as appropriate. System records the used coupons for accounting reasons.
        1a. Coupon entered is not for any purchased item:
            1. System signals error to Cashier.

9a. There are product rebates:
    1. System presents the rebate forms and rebate receipts for each item with a rebate.

9b. Customer requests gift receipt (no prices visible):
    1. Cashier requests gift receipt and System presents it.

Special Requirements:
– Touch screen UI on a large flat panel monitor. Text must be visible from 1 meter.
– Credit authorization response within 30 seconds 90% of the time.
– Somehow, we want robust recovery when access to remote services such the inventory system is failing.
– Language internationalization on the text displayed.
– Pluggable business rules to be insertable at steps 3 and 7.
– . . .

Technology and Data Variations List:
3a. Item identifier entered by bar code laser scanner (if bar code is present) or keyboard.
3b. Item identifier may be any UPC, EAN, JAN, or SKU coding scheme.
7a. Credit account information entered by card reader or keyboard.
7b. Credit payment signature captured on paper receipt. But within two years, we predict many customers will want digital signature capture.

Frequency of Occurrence: Could be nearly continuous.

Open Issues:
– What are the tax law variations?
– Explore the remote service recovery issue.
– What customization is needed for different businesses?
– Must a cashier take their cash drawer when they log out?
– Can the customer directly use the card reader, or does the cashier have to do it?

This use case is illustrative rather than exhaustive (although it is based on a real POS system's requirements). Nevertheless, there is enough detail and complexity here to offer a realistic sense that a fully-dressed use case can record many requirement details. This example will serve well as a model for many use case problems.

The Two-Column Variation

Some prefer the two-column or conversational format, which emphasizes the fact that there is an interaction going on between the actors and the system. It was first proposed by Rebecca Wirfs-Brock in [Wirfs-Brock93], and is also promoted by Constantine and Lockwood to aid usability analysis and engineering [CL99]. Here is the same content using the two-column format:

Use Case UC1: Process Sale

Primary Actor: ...
... as before ...

Main Success Scenario:

Actor Action (or Intention)	System Responsibility
1. Customer arrives at a POS checkout with goods and/or services to purchase.	
2. Cashier starts a new sale.	
3. Cashier enters item identifier.	4. Records each sale line item and presents item description and running total.
Cashier repeats steps 3-4 until indicates done.	5. System presents total with taxes calculated.
6. Cashier tells Customer the total, and asks for payment.	
7. Customer pays.	8. Handles payment.

> 9. Logs the completed sale and sends information to the external accounting (for all accounting and commissions) and inventory systems (to update inventory). System presents receipt.
>
> ...   ...

The Best Format?

There isn't one best format; some prefer the one-column style, some the two-column. Sections may be added and removed; heading names may change. None of this is particularly important; the key thing is to write the details of the main success scenario and its extensions, in some form. [Cockburn1] summarizes many usable formats.

Personal Practice

This is my practice, not a recommendation. For some years, I used the two-column format because of its clear visual separation in the conversation. However, I have reverted to a one-column style as it is more compact and easier to format, and the slight value of the visually separated conversation does not for me outweigh these benefits. I find it still simple to visually identify the different parties in the conversation (Customer, System, ...) if each party and the System responses are usually allocated to their own steps.

6.7   Explaining the Sections

Preface Elements

Many optional preface elements are possible. Only place elements at the start which are important to read before the main success scenario. Move extraneous "header" material to the end of the use case.

Primary Actor: The principal actor that calls upon system services to fulfill a goal.

Important: Stakeholders and Interests List

This list is more important and practical than may appear at first glance. It suggests and bounds what the system must do. To quote:

> The [system] operates a contract between stakeholders, with the use cases detailing the behavioral parts of that contract...The use case, as the contract for behavior, captures *all and only* the behaviors related to satisfying the stakeholders' interests [Cockburn01].

This answers the question: What should be in the use case? The answer is: That which satisfies all the stakeholders' interests. In addition, by starting with the stakeholders and their interests before writing the remainder of the use case, we have a method to remind us what the more detailed responsibilities of the system should be. For example, would I have identified a responsibility for salesperson commission handling if I had not first listed the salesperson stakeholder and their interests? Hopefully eventually, but perhaps I would have missed it during the first analysis session. The stakeholder interest viewpoint provides a thorough and methodical procedure for discovering and recording all the required behaviors.

> **Stakeholders and Interests:**
> – Cashier: Wants accurate, fast entry and no payment errors, as cash drawer shortages are deducted from his/her salary.
> – Salesperson: Wants sales commissions updated.
> – ...

Preconditions and Success Guarantees (Postconditions)

Preconditions state what *must always* be true before beginning a scenario in the use case. Preconditions are *not* tested within the use case; rather, they are conditions that are assumed to be true. Typically, a precondition implies a scenario of another use case that has successfully completed, such as logging in, or the more general "cashier is identified and authenticated." Note that there are conditions that must be true, but are not of practical value to write, such as "the system has power." Preconditions communicate noteworthy assumptions that the use case writer thinks readers should be alerted to.

Success guarantees (or **postconditions**) state what must be true on successful completion of the use case—either the main success scenario or some alternate path. The guarantee should meet the needs of all stakeholders.

> **Preconditions**: Cashier is identified and authenticated.
> **Success Guarantee (Postconditions)**: Sale is saved. Tax is correctly calculated. Accounting and Inventory are updated. Commissions recorded. Receipt is generated.

Main Success Scenario and Steps (or Basic Flow)

This has also been called the "happy path" scenario, or the more prosaic "Basic Flow." It describes the typical success path that satisfies the interests of the stakeholders. Note that it often does *not* include any conditions or branching. Although not wrong or illegal, it is arguably more comprehensible and extendible to be very consistent and defer all conditional handling to the Extensions section.

Suggestion

Defer all conditional and branching statements to the Extensions section.

The scenario records the steps, of which there are three kinds:

1. An interaction between actors.[3]

2. A validation (usually by the system).

3. A state change by the system (for example, recording or modifying something).

Step one of a use case does not always fall into this classification, but indicates the trigger event that starts the scenario.

It is a common idiom to always capitalize the actors' names for ease of identification. Observe also the idiom that is used to indicate repetition.

Main Success Scenario:
1. Customer arrives at a POS checkout with items to purchase.
2. Cashier starts a new sale.
3. Cashier enters item identifier.
4. ...
Cashier repeats steps 3-4 until indicates done.
5. ...

Extensions (or Alternate Flows)

Extensions are very important. They indicate all the other scenarios or branches, both success and failure. Observe in the fully dressed example that the Extensions section was considerably longer and more complex than the Main Success Scenario section; this is common and to be expected. They are also known as "Alternative Flows."

In thorough use case writing, the combination of the happy path and extension scenarios should satisfy "nearly" all the interests of the stakeholders. This point is qualified, because some interests may best be captured as non-functional

---

3. Note that the system under discussion itself should be considered an actor when it plays an actor role collaborating with other systems.

requirements expressed in the Supplementary Specification rather than the use cases.

Extension scenarios are branches from the main success scenario, and so can be notated with respect to it. For example, at Step 3 of the main success scenario there may be an invalid item identifier, either because it was incorrectly entered or unknown to the system. An extension is labeled "3a"; it first identifies the condition and then the response. Alternate extensions at Step 3 are labeled "3b" and so forth.

Extensions:
3a. Invalid identifier:
    1. System signals error and rejects entry.
3b. There are multiple of same item category and tracking unique item identity not
    important (e.g., 5 packages of veggie-burgers):
    1. Cashier can enter item category identifier and the quantity.

An extension has two parts: the condition and the handling.

Guideline: Write the condition as something that can be *detected* by the system or an actor. To contrast:

> 5a. System detects failure to communicate with external tax calculation system service:

> 5a. External tax calculation system not working:

The former style is preferred because this is something the system can detect; the latter is an inference.

Extension handling can be summarized in one step, or include a sequence, as in this example, which also illustrates notation to indicate that a condition can arise within a range of steps:

3-6a: Customer asks Cashier to remove an item from the purchase:
    1. Cashier enters the item identifier for removal from the sale.
    2. System displays updated running total.

At the end of extension handling, by default the scenario merges back with the main success scenario, unless the extension indicates otherwise (such as by halting the system).

Sometimes, a particular extension point is quite complex, as in the "paying by credit" extension. This can be a motivation to express the extension as a separate use case.

This extension example also demonstrates the notation to express failures within extensions.

7b. Paying by credit:
    1. Customer enters their credit account information.
    2. System requests payment validation from external Payment Authorization Ser-
       vice System.

      2a. System detects failure to collaborate with external system:
         1. System signals error to Cashier.
         2. Cashier asks Customer for alternate payment.
    3. ...

If it is desirable to describe an extension condition as possible during any (or at least most) steps, the labels *a, *b, ..., can be used.

*a. At any time, System crashes:
    In order to support recovery and correct accounting, ensure all transaction sensitive
      state and events can be recovered at any step in the scenario.
    1. Cashier restarts the System, logs in, and requests recovery of prior state.
    2. System reconstructs prior state.

Special Requirements

If a non-functional requirement, quality attribute, or constraint relates specifically to a use case, record it with the use case. These include qualities such as performance, reliability, and usability, and design constraints (often in I/O devices) that have been mandated or considered likely.

Special Requirements:
– Touch screen UI on a large flat panel monitor. Text must be visible from 1 meter.
– Credit authorization response within 30 seconds 90% of the time.
– Language internationalization on the text displayed.
– Pluggable business rules to be insertable at steps 2 and 6.

Recording these with the use case is classic UP advice, and a reasonable location when first writing the use case. However, many practitioners find it useful to ultimately consolidate all non-functional requirements in the Supplementary Specification, for content management, comprehension, and readability, because these requirements usually have to be considered as a whole during architectural analysis.

Technology and Data Variations List

Often there are technical variations in *how* something must be done, but not what, and it is noteworthy to record this in the use case. A common example is a technical constraint imposed by a stakeholder regarding input or output technologies. For example, a stakeholder might say, "The POS system must support credit account input using a card reader and the keyboard." Note that these are examples of early design decisions or constraints; in general, it is skillful to avoid premature design decisions, but sometimes they are obvious or unavoidable, especially concerning input/output technologies.

It is also necessary to understand variations in data schemes, such as using UPCs or EANs for item identifiers, encoded in bar code symbology.

This list is the place to record such variations. It is also useful to record variations in the data that may be captured at a particular step.

Technology and Data Variations List:
3a. Item identifier entered by laser scanner or keyboard.
3b. Item identifier may be any UPC, EAN, JAN, or SKU coding scheme.
7a. Credit account information entered by card reader or keyboard.
7b. Credit payment signature captured on paper receipt. But within two years, we predict many customers will want digital signature capture.

Suggestion

This section should *not* contain multiple steps to express varying behavior for different cases. If that is necessary, say it in the Extensions section.

6.8   Goals and Scope of a Use Case

How should use cases be discovered? It is common to be unsure if something is a valid (or more practically, a useful) use case. Tasks can be grouped at many levels of granularity, from one or a few small steps, up to enterprise-level activities.

At what level and scope should use cases be expressed?

The following sections examine the simple ideas of elementary business processes and goals as a framework for identifying the use cases for an application.

Use Cases for Elementary Business Processes

Which of these is a valid use case?

- Negotiate a Supplier Contract

- Handle Returns

- Log In

An argument can be made that all of these are use cases *at different levels*, depending on the system boundary, actors, and goals. Evaluation of these candidates is presented after an introduction to elementary business processes.

Rather than asking in general, "What is a valid use case?", a more relevant question for the POS case study is: What is a useful level to express use cases for application requirements analysis?

Guideline: The EBP Use Case

For requirements analysis for a computer application, focus on use cases at the level of **elementary business processes** (EBPs).

EBP is a term from the business process engineering field,[4] defined as:

> A task performed by one person in one place at one time, in response to a business event, which adds measurable business value and leaves the data in a consistent state. e.g., Approve Credit or Price Order [original source lost].

This can be taken too literally: Does a use case fail as an EBP if two people are required, or if a person has to walk around? Probably not, but the feel of the definition is about right. It's not a single small step like "delete a line item" or "print the document." Rather, the main success scenario is probably five or ten steps. It doesn't take days and multiple sessions, like "negotiate a supplier contract;" it is a task done during a single session. It is probably between a few minutes and an hour in length. As with the UP's definition, it emphasizes adding observable or measurable business value, and it comes to a resolution in which the system and data are in a stable and consistent state.

A common use case mistake is defining many use cases at too low a level; that is, as a single step, subfunction, or subtask within an EBP.

Reasonable Violations of the EBP Guideline

Although the "base" use cases for an application should satisfy the EBP guideline, it is frequently useful to create separate "sub" use cases representing subtasks or steps within a base use case. Use cases can exist that fail the EBP test; many potentially exist at a lower level. The guideline is only used to find the dominant level of use cases in requirements analysis for an application; that is, the level to focus on for naming and writing them.

---

4. EBP is similar to the term **user task** in usability engineering, although the meaning is less strict in that domain.

For example, a subtask or extension such as "paying by credit" may be repeated in several base use cases. It is desirable to separate this into its own use case (that does not satisfy the EBP guideline) and link it to several base use cases, to avoid duplication of the text.

Chapter 25 explores the issue of use case relationships.

Use Cases and Goals

Actors have goals (or needs) and use applications to help satisfy them. Consequently, an EBP-level use case is called a **user goal**-level user case, to emphasize that it serves (or should serve) to fulfill a goal of a user of the system, or the primary actor.

And it leads to a recommended procedure:

1. Find the user goals.

2. Define a use case for each.

This is slight shift in emphasis for the use-case modeler. Rather than asking "What are the use cases?", one starts by asking: "What are your goals?" In fact, the name of a use case for a user goal should reflect its name, to emphasize this viewpoint—Goal: capture or process a sale; use case: *Process Sale*.

Note that because of this symmetry, the EBP guideline can be equally applied to decide if a goal or a use case is at a suitable level.

Thus, here is a key idea regarding investigating user goals vs. investigating use cases:

Imagine we are together in a requirements workshop. We could ask either:

- "What do you do?" (roughly a use case-oriented question) or,

- "What are your goals?"

Answers to the first question are more likely to reflect current solutions and procedures, and the complications associated with them.

Answers to the second question, especially combined with an investigation to move higher up the goal hierarchy ("what is the goal of that goal?") open up the vision for new and improved solutions, focus on adding business value, and get to the heart of what the stakeholders want from the system under discussion.

Example: Applying the EBP Guideline

As the system analyst responsible for the NextGen system requirements discovery, you are investigating user goals. The conversation goes like this: During a requirements workshop:

> **System analyst**: "What are some of your goals in the context of using a POS system?"
> **Cashier**: "One, to quickly log in. Also, to capture sales."
> **System analyst**: "What do you think is the higher level goal motivating logging in?"
> **Cashier**: "I'm trying to identify myself to the system, so it can validate that I'm allowed to use the system for sales capture and other tasks."
> **System analyst**: "Higher than that?"
> **Cashier**: "To prevent theft, data corruption, and display of private company information."

Note the analyst's strategy of searching up the goal hierarchy to find higher level user goals that still satisfy the EBP guideline, to get at the real intent behind the action, and also to understand the context of the goals.

"Prevent theft, ..." is higher than a user goal; it may be called an enterprise goal, and is not an EBP. Therefore, although it can inspire new ways of thinking about the problem and solutions (such as eliminating POS systems and cashiers completely), we will set it aside for now.

Lowering the goal level to "identify myself and be validated" appears closer to the user goal level. But is it at the EBP level? It does not add observable or measurable business value. If the CEO asked, "What did you do today?" and you said "I logged in 20 times!", she would not be impressed. Consequently, this is a secondary goal, always in the service of doing something useful, and is not an EBP or user goal. By contrast, "capture a sale" does fit the criteria of being an EBP or user goal.

As another example, in some stores there is a process called "cashing in", in which a cashier inserts their own cash drawer tray into the terminal, logs in, and tells the system how much cash is in drawer. *Cashing In* is an EBP-level (or user goal level) use case; the log in step, rather than being a EBP-level use case, is a subfunction goal in support of the goal of cashing in.

Subfunction Goals and Use Cases

Although "identify myself and be validated" (or "log in") has been eliminated as a user goal, it is a goal at a lower level, called a **subfunction goal**—subgoals that support a user goal. Use cases should only occasionally be written for these subfunction goals, although it is a common problem that use case experts observe when asked to evaluate and improve (usually simplify) a set of use cases.

It is not illegal to write use cases for subfunction goals, but it is not always help-ful, as it adds complexity to a use-case model; there can be hundreds of subfunc-tion goals—or subfunction use cases—for a system.

Important point: The number and granularity of use cases influences the time and difficulty to understand, maintain, and manage the requirements.

The most common, valid motivation to express a subfunction goal as a use case is when the subfunction is repeated in or is a precondition for multiple user goal-level use cases. This in fact is probably true of "identify myself and be vali-dated," which is a precondition of most, if not all, other user goal-level use cases.

Consequently, it may be written as the use case *Authenticate User*.

Goals and Use Cases Can Be Composite

Goals are usually composite, from the level of an enterprise ("be profitable"), to many supporting intermediate goals while using applications ("sales are cap-tured"), to supporting subfunction goals within applications ("input is valid").

Similarly, use cases can be written at different levels to satisfy these goals, and can be composed of lower level use cases.

> These varying goal and use case levels are a common source of confusion in identifying the appropriate level of use cases for an application. The EBP guideline provides guidance to filter out excessive low-level use cases.

6.9   Finding Primary Actors, Goals, and Use Cases

Use cases are defined to satisfy the user goals of the primary actors. Hence, the basic procedure is:

1. Choose the system boundary. Is it just a software application, the hardware and application as a unit, that plus a person using it, or an entire organiza-tion?

2. Identify the primary actors—those that have user goals fulfilled through using services of the system.

3. For each, identify their user goals. Raise them to the highest user goal level that satisfies the EBP guideline.

4. Define use cases that satisfy user goals; name them according to their goal. Usually, user goal-level use cases will be one-to-one with user goals, but there is at least one exception, as will be examined.

Step 1: Choosing the System Boundary

For this case study, the POS system itself is the system under design; everything outside of it is outside the system boundary, including the cashier, payment authorization service, and so on.

If it is not clear, defining the boundary of the system under design can be clarified by defining what is outside—the external primary and supporting actors. Once the external actors are identified, the boundary becomes clearer. For example, is the complete responsibility for payment authorization within the system boundary? No, there is an external payment authorization service actor.

Steps 2 and 3: Finding Primary Actors and Goals

It is artificial to strictly linearize the identification of primary actors before user goals; in a requirements workshop, people brainstorm and generate a mixture of both. Sometimes, goals reveal the actors, or vice versa.

Guideline: Emphasize brainstorming the primary actors first, as this sets up the framework for further investigation.

Reminder Questions to Find Actors and Goals

In addition to obvious primary actors and user goals, the following questions help identify others that may be missed:

Who starts and stops the system?	Who does system administration?
Who does user and security management?	Is "time" an actor because the system does something in response to a time event?
Is there a monitoring process that restarts the system if it fails?	Who evaluates system activity or performance?
How are software updates handled? Push or pull update?	Who evaluates logs? Are they remotely retrieved?

Primary and Supporting Actors

Recall that primary actors have user goals fulfilled through using services of the system. They call upon the system to help them. This is in contrast to *supporting actors*, which provide services to the system under design. For now, the focus is on finding the primary actors, not the supporting ones.

Recall also that primary actors can be—among other things—other computer systems, such as "watchdog" software processes.

> *Suggestion*
>
> Be suspicious if no primary actors are external computer systems.

The Actor-Goal List

Record the primary actors and their user goals in an actor-goal list. In terms of UP artifacts it should be a section in the Vision artifact (which is described in the next chapter).

For example:

Actor	Goal	Actor	Goal
Cashier	process sales process rentals handle returns cash in cash out . . .	System Administrator	add users modify users delete users manage security manage system tables . . .
Manager	start up shut down . . .	Sales Activity System	analyze sales and performance data
. . .	. . .	. . .	. . .

The Sales Activity System is a remote application that will frequently request sales data from each POS node in the network.

Project Planning Dimension

In practice, this list has additional columns for priority, effort, and risk; this is briefly covered in Chapter 36.

The Messy Reality

This list looks neat, but the reality of its creation is anything but. Lots of brainstorming and thrashing about in a requirements workshop goes on. Consider the earlier example that illustrated applying the EBP rule to the "log in" goal. During the workshop while creating this list the cashier may offer "log in" as one of the user goals. The system analyst digs deeper and raises the level of the goal beyond the low-level mechanism of logging in (the cashier was probably thinking of using a dialog box on a GUI) up to the level of "identify and authenticate user." Yet, the analyst then realizes it does not pass the EBP guideline, and discards it as a user goal. Of course, the reality is even somewhat different than this because an experienced analyst has a set of heuristics from past experience or study, one of which is "user authentication is seldom an EBP," and so is likely to have filtered this out quickly.

Primary Actor and User Goals Depend on System Boundary

Why is the cashier, and not the customer, the primary actor in the use case *Process Sale*? Why doesn't the customer appear in the actor-goal list?

The answer depends on the system boundary of the system under design, as illustrated in Figure 6.1. If viewing the enterprise or checkout service as an aggregate system, the customer *is* a primary actor, with the goal of getting goods or services and leaving. However, from the viewpoint of just the POS system (which is the choice of system boundary for this case study), it services the goal of the cashier (and the store) to process the customer's sale.

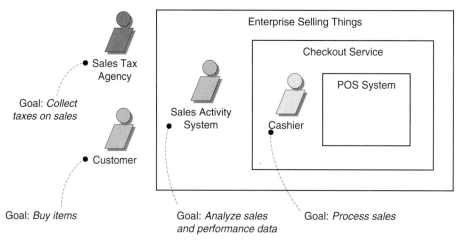

Figure 6.1 Primary actors and goals at different system boundaries.

Actors and Goals via Event Analysis

Another approach to aid in finding actors, goals, and use cases is to identify external events. What are they, where from, and why? Often, a group of events belong to the same EBP-level goal or use case. For example:

External Event	From Actor	Goal
enter sale line item	Cashier	process a sale
enter payment	Cashier or Customer	process a sale
. . .		

Step 4: Define Use Cases

In general, define one EBP-level use case for each user goal. Name the use case similar to the user goal—for example, Goal: process a sale; Use Case: *Process Sale.*

> Also, name use cases starting with a verb.

A common exception to one use case per goal is to collapse CRUD (create, retrieve, update, delete) separate goals into one CRUD use case, idiomatically called *Manage <X>*. For example, the goals "edit user," "delete user," and so forth are all satisfied by the *Manage Users* use case.

"Define use cases" has several levels of effort, ranging from a few minutes to simply record names, up to weeks to write fully dressed versions. The later UP process section of this chapter puts this work—when and how much—in the context of iterative development and the UP.

6.10   Congratulations: Use Cases Have Been Written, and Are Imperfect

The Need for Communication and Participation

The NextGen POS team is writing use cases in multiple requirements workshops over a series of short development iterations, incrementally adding to the set, and refining and adapting based on feedback. Subject matter experts, cashiers, and programmers actively participate in the writing process. There are no intermediaries between the cashiers, other users, and the developers; rather, there is direct communication.

Good, but not good enough. Written requirement specifications give the illusion of correctness; they are not. The use cases and other requirements still will not be correct—guaranteed. They will lack critical information and contain wrong statements. The solution is not the "waterfall" process attitude of trying harder to record requirements perfect and complete at the start, although of course we do the best we can in the time available. But it will never be enough.

A different approach is required. A large part of this is iterative development, but something else is needed: *ongoing personal communication*. Continual—daily—close participation and communication between the developers and someone who understands the domain and can make requirement decisions. Someone the programmers can walk up to in a matter of seconds and get clarification, whenever a question arises. For example, the XP practices [Beck00] contain an excellent recommendation: *User full-time on the project, in the project room*.

6.11   Write Use Cases in an Essential UI-Free Style

New and Improved! The Case for Fingerprinting

Investigating and asking about goals rather than tasks and procedures encourages a focus on the essence of the requirements—the intent behind them. For example, during a requirements workshop, the cashier may say one of his goals is to "log in." The cashier was probably thinking of a GUI, dialog box, user ID, and password. This is a mechanism to achieve a goal, rather than the goal itself. By investigating up the goal hierarchy ("What is the goal of that goal?"), the system analyst arrives at a mechanism-independent goal: "identify myself and get authenticated," or an even higher goal: "prevent theft ...".

This discovery process can open up the vision to new and improved solutions. For example, keyboards and mice with biometric readers, usually for a fingerprint, are now common and inexpensive. If the goal is "identification and authentication" why not make it easy and fast, using a biometric reader on the keyboard? But properly answering that question involves some usability analysis work as well, such as knowing the typical users' profiles. Are their fingers covered in grease? Do they have fingers?

Essential Style Writing

This idea has been summarized in various use case guidelines as "keep the user interface out; focus on intent" [Cockburn01]. Its motivation and notation has been most fully explored by Larry Constantine in the context of creating better user interfaces (UIs) and doing usability engineering [Constantine94, CL99]. Constantine calls the writing style **essential** when it avoids UI details and focuses on the real user intent.[5]

---

5. The term comes from "essential models" in *Essential Systems Analysis* [MP84].

In an essential writing style, the narrative is expressed at the level of the user's *intentions* and system's *responsibilities* rather than their concrete actions. They remain free of technology and mechanism details, especially those related to the UI.

> Write use cases in an essential style; keep the user interface out and focus on actor intent.

All the previous example use cases in this chapter, such as *Process Sale*, were written aiming towards an essential style.

Note that the dictionary defines *goal* as a synonym for intention [MW89], illustrating the connection between the *essential* style idea of Constantine and the goal-oriented viewpoint previously stressed in this chapter. Indeed, many actor *intention* steps in an essential use case can also be characterized as subfunction *goals*.

Contrasting Examples

Essential Style

Assume that the *Manage Users* use case requires identification and authentication. The Constantine-inspired essential style uses the two-column format. However, it can be written in one column.

. . .	
Actor Intention	**System Responsibility**
1. Administrator identifies self.	2. Authenticates identity.
3. . . .	

In the one-column format this is shown as:

. . .
1. Administrator identifies self.
2. System authenticates identity.
3. . . .

The design solution to these intentions and responsibilities is wide open: biometric readers, graphical user interfaces (GUIs), and so forth.

Concrete Style—Avoid During Early Requirements Work

In contrast, there is a **concrete use case** style. In this style, user interface decisions are embedded in the use case text. The text may even show window screen shots, discuss window navigation, GUI widget manipulation and so forth. For example:

```
. . .
1. Adminstrator enters ID and password in dialog box (see Picture 3).
2. System authenticates Adminstrator.
3. System displays the "edit users" window (see Picture 4).
4. . . .
```

These concrete use cases may be useful as an aid to concrete or detailed GUI design work during a later step, but they are not suitable during the early requirements analysis work. During early requirements work, "keep the user interface out—focus on intent."

6.12 Actors

An actor is anything with behavior, including the system under discussion (SuD) itself when it calls upon the services of other systems.[6] Primary and supporting actors will appear in the action steps of the use case text. Actors are not only roles played by people, but organizations, software, and machines. There are three kinds of external actors in relation to the SuD:

■ **Primary actor**—has user goals fulfilled through using services of the SuD. For example, the cashier.

  ❍ Why identify? To find user goals, which drive the use cases.

■ **Supporting actor**—provides a service (for example, information) to the SuD. The automated payment authorization service is an example. Often a computer system, but could be an organization or person.

  ❍ Why identify? To clarify external interfaces and protocols.

■ **Offstage actor**—has an interest in the behavior of the use case, but is not primary or supporting; for example, a government tax agency.

  ❍ Why identify? To ensure that *all* necessary interests are identified and satisfied. Offstage actor interests are sometimes subtle or easy to miss unless these actors are explicitly named.

---

6. This was a refinement and improvement to alternate definitions of actors, including those in early versions of the UML and UP [Cockburn97]. Older definitions inconsistently excluded the SuD as an actor, even when it called upon services of other systems. All entities may play multiple *roles*, including the SuD.

6.13   Use Case Diagrams

The UML provides use case diagram notation to illustrate the names of use cases and actors, and the relationships between them (see Figure 6.2).

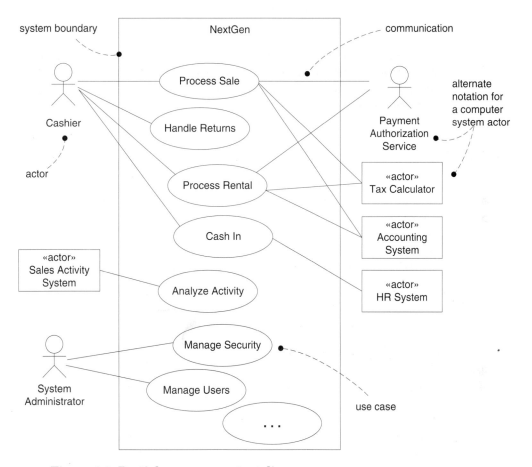

Figure 6.2 Partial use case context diagram.

Use case diagrams and use case relationships are secondary in use case work. Use cases are text documents. Doing use case work means to write text.

A common sign of a novice (or academic) use-case modeler is a preoccupation with use case diagrams and use case relationships, rather than writing text. World-class use case experts such as Anderson, Fowler, Cockburn, among others, downplay use case diagrams and use case relationships, and instead focus on writing. With that as a caveat, a simple use case diagram provides a succinct visual context diagram for the system, illustrating the external actors and how they use the system.

Suggestion

Draw a simple use case diagram in conjunction with an actor-goal list.

A use case diagram is an excellent picture of the system context; it makes a good **context diagram**, that is, showing the boundary of a system, what lies outside of it, and how it gets used. It serves as a communication tool that summarizes the behavior of a system and its actors. A sample *partial* use case context diagram for the NextGen system is shown in Figure 6.2.

Diagramming Suggestions

Figure 6.3 offers some diagram advice. Notice the actor box with the symbol «actor». This symbol is called a UML **stereotype**; it is a mechanism to categorize an element in some way. A stereotype name is surrounded by guillemets symbols—special *single*-character brackets (not "<<" and ">>") most widely known by their use in French typography to indicate a quote.

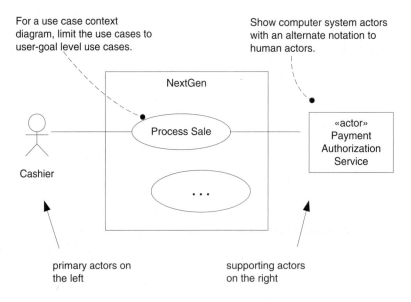

Figure 6.3 Notation suggestions.

To clarify, some prefer to highlight external computer system actors with an alternate notation, as illustrated in Figure 6.4.

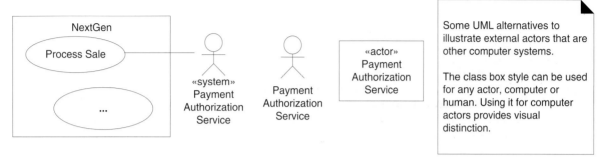

Figure 6.4 Alternate actor notation.

A Caution on Over-Diagramming

To reiterate, the important use case work is to write text, not diagram or focus on use case relationships. If an organization is spending many hours (or worse, days) working on a use case diagram and discussing use case relationships, rather than focussing on writing text, relative effort has been misplaced.

6.14   Requirements in Context and Low-Level Feature Lists *See 6.12 onwards*

As implied by the title of the book *Uses Cases: Requirements in Context* [GK00], a key motivation of the use case idea is the consideration and organization of requirements in the context of the goals and scenarios of using a system. That's a good thing—it improves cohesion and comprehension. However, use cases are not the only necessary requirements artifact. Some non-functional requirements, domain rules and context, and other hard-to-place elements are better captured in the Supplementary Specification, which is described in the next chapter.

One idea behind use cases is to replace detailed, low-level feature lists (which were common in traditional requirements methods) with use cases (with some exceptions). These lists tended to look as follows, usually grouped into functional areas:

ID	Feature
FEAT1.9	The system shall accept entry of item identifiers.

ID	Feature
. . .	. . .
FEAT2.4	The system shall log credit payments to the accounts receivable system.

Such detailed lists of low-level features are somewhat usable. However, the complete list is not a half-page; more likely it is dozens or a hundred pages. This leads to some drawbacks, which use cases help address. These include:

- Long, detailed function lists do not relate the requirements in a cohesive context; the different functions and features increasingly appear like a disjointed "laundry list" of items. In contrast, use cases place the requirements in the context of the stories and goals of using the system.

- If both use case and detailed feature lists are used, there is duplication. More work, more volume to write and read, more consistency and synchronization problems.

Suggestion

Strive to replace detailed, low-level feature lists with use cases.

High-Level System Feature Lists Are Acceptable

It is common and useful to summarize system functionality with a terse, high-level feature list called system features in a Vision document. In contrast to 100 pages of low-level, detailed features, a system features list tends to include only a few dozen items. The list provides a very succinct summary of system functionality, independent of the use case view. For example:

Summary of System Features

- sales capture
- payment authorization (credit, debit, check)
- system administration for users, security, code and constants tables, and so on
- automatic offline sales processing when external components fail
- real-time transactions, based on industry standards, with third-party systems, including inventory, accounting, human resources, tax calculators, and payment authorization services
- definition and execution of customized "pluggable" business rules at fixed, common points in the processing scenarios
- . . .

This is explored in the next chapter.

When Are Detailed Feature Lists Appropriate?

Sometimes use cases do not really fit; some applications call out for a feature-driven viewpoint. For example, application servers, database products, and other middleware or back-end systems need to be primarily considered and evolved in terms of *features* ("We need XML support in the next release"). Use cases are not a natural fit for these applications or the way they need to evolve in terms of market forces.

6.15   Use Cases Are Not Object-Oriented

There is nothing object-oriented about use cases; one is not doing object-oriented analysis if writing use cases. This is not a defect, but a point of clarification. Indeed, use cases are a broadly applicable requirements analysis tool that can be applied to non-object-oriented projects, which increases their usefulness as a requirements method. However, as will be explored, use cases are a pivotal input into classic OOA/D activities.

6.16   Use Cases Within the UP

Use cases are vital and central to the UP, which encourages **use-case driven development**. This implies:

- Requirements are primarily recorded in use cases (the Use-Case Model); other requirements techniques (such as functions lists) are secondary, if used at all.

- Use cases are an important part of iterative planning. The work of an iteration is—in part—defined by choosing some use case scenarios, or entire use cases. And use cases are a key input to estimation.

- **Use-case realizations** drive the design. That is, the team designs collaborating objects and subsystems in order to perform or realize the use cases.

- Use cases often influence the organization of user manuals.

The UP distinguishes between system and business use cases. **System use cases** are what have been examined in this chapter, such as *Process Sale*. They are created in the Requirements discipline, and are part of the Use-Case Model.

Business use cases are less commonly written. If done, they are created in the Business Modeling discipline as part of a large-scale business process reengineering effort, or to help understand the context of a new system in the business. They describe a sequence of actions of a business as a whole to fulfill a goal of a **business actor** (an actor in the business environment, such as a customer or supplier). For example, in a restaurant, one business use case is *Serve a Meal*.

Use Cases and Requirements Specification Across the Iterations

This section reiterates a key idea in the UP and iterative development: The timing and level of effort of requirements specification across the iterations. Table 6.1 presents a sample (not a recipe) which communicates the UP strategy of how requirements are developed.

Note that a technical team starts building the production core of the system when only perhaps 10% of the requirements are detailed, and in fact, there is a deliberate delay in continuing with concerted requirements work until near the end of the first elaboration iteration.

This is the key difference in iterative development to a waterfall process: Production-quality development of the core of a system starts quickly, long before all the requirements are known.

Discipline	Artifact	Comments and Level of Requirements Effort				
		Incep 1 week	Elab 1 4 weeks	Elab 2 4 weeks	Elab 3 3 weeks	Elab 4 3 weeks
Requirements	Use-Case Model	2-day requirements workshop. Most use cases identified by name, and summarized in a short paragraph. Only 10% written in detail.	Near the end of this iteration, host a 2-day requirements workshop. Obtain insight and feedback from the implementation work, then complete 30% of the use cases in detail.	Near the end of this iteration, host a 2-day requirements workshop. Obtain insight and feedback from the implementation work, then complete 50% of the use cases in detail.	Repeat, complete 70% of all use cases in detail.	Repeat with the goal of 80-90% of the use cases clarified and written in detail. Only a small portion of these have been built in elaboration; the remainder are done in construction.
Design	Design Model	none	Design for a small set of high-risk architecturally significant requirements.	repeat	repeat	Repeat. The high risk and architecturally significant aspects should now be stabilized.
Implementation	Implementation Model (code, etc.)	none	Implement these.	Repeat. 5% of the final system is built.	Repeat. 10% of the final system is built.	Repeat. 15% of the final system is built.
Project Management	SW Development Plan	Very vague estimate of total effort.	Estimate starts to take shape.	a little better...	a little better...	Overall project duration, major milestones, effort, and cost estimates can now be rationally committed to.

Table 6.1 Sample requirements effort across the early iterations; this is not a recipe.

Observe that near the end of the first iteration of elaboration, there is a second requirements workshop, during which perhaps 30% of the use cases are written in detail. This staggered requirements analysis benefits from the feedback of having built a little of the core software. The feedback includes user evaluation, testing, and improved "knowing what we don't know." That is, the act of building software rapidly surfaces assumptions and questions that need clarification.

Timing of UP Artifact Creation

Table 6.2 illustrates some UP artifacts, and an example of their start and refinement schedule. The Use-Case Model is started in inception, with perhaps only 10% of the use cases written in any detail. The majority are incrementally written over the iterations of the elaboration phase, so that by the end of elaboration, a large body of detailed use cases and other requirements (in the Supplementary Specification) are written, providing a realistic basis for estimation through to the end of the project.

Discipline	Artifact	Incep.	Elab.	Const.	Trans.
	Iteration→	I1	E1..En	C1..Cn	T1..T2
Business Modeling	Domain Model		s		
Requirements	*Use-Case Model*	s	r		
	Vision	s	r		
	Supplementary Specification	s	r		
	Glossary	s	r		
Design	Design Model		s	r	
	SW Architecture Document		s		
	Data Model		s	r	
Implementation	Implementation Model		s	r	r
Project Management	SW Development Plan	s	r	r	r
Testing	Test Model		s	r	
Environment	Development Case	s	r		

Table 6.2 Sample UP artifacts and timing. s - start; r - refine

Use Cases Within Inception

The following discussion expands on the information in Table 6.1.

Not all use cases are written in their fully dressed format during the inception phase. Rather, suppose there is a two-day requirements workshop during the early NextGen investigation. The earlier part of the day is spent identifying goals and stakeholders, and speculating what is in and out of scope of the project. An actor-goal-use case table is written and displayed with the computer projector. A use case context diagram is started. After a few hours, perhaps 20 user goals (and thus, user goal level use cases) are identified, including *Process*

Sale, Handle Returns, and so on. Most of the interesting, complex, or risky use cases are written in brief format; each averaging around two minutes to write. The team starts to form a high-level picture of the system's functionality.

After this, 10% to 20% of the use cases that represent core complex functions, or which are especially risky in some dimension, are rewritten in a fully dressed format; the team investigates a little deeper to better comprehend the magnitude, complexities, and hidden demons of the project, through a small sample of interesting use cases. Perhaps this means two use cases: *Process Sale* and *Handle Returns.*

A requirements management tool that integrates with a word processor is used for the writing, and the work is displayed via a projector while the team collaborates on the analysis and writing. The *Stakeholders and Interests* lists are written for these use cases, to discover more subtle (and perhaps costly) functional and key non-functional requirements—or system qualities—such as for reliability or throughput.

The analysis goal is not to exhaustively complete the use cases, but spend a few hours to obtain some insight.

The project sponsor needs to decide if the project is worth significant investigation (that is, the elaboration phase). The inception work is not meant to do that investigation, but to obtain low-fidelity (and admittedly error-prone) insights regarding scope, risk, effort, technical feasibility, and business case, in order to decide to move forward, where to start if they do, or if to stop.

Perhaps the NextGen project inception step lasts five days. The combination of the two day requirements workshop and its brief use case analysis, and other investigation during the week, lead to the decision to continue on to an elaboration step for the system.

Use Cases Within Elaboration

The following discussion expands on the information in Table 6.1.

This is a phase of multiple timeboxed iterations (for example, four iterations) in which risky, high-value, or architecturally significant parts of the system are incrementally built, and the "majority" of requirements identified and clarified. The feedback from the concrete steps of programming influences and informs the team's understanding of the requirements, which are iteratively and adaptively refined. Perhaps there is a two-day requirements workshop in each iteration—four workshops. However, not all use cases are investigated in each workshop. They are prioritized; early workshops focus on a subset of the most important use cases.

Each subsequent short workshop is a time to adapt and refine the vision of the core requirements, which will be unstable in early iterations, and stabilizing in later ones. Thus, there is an iterative interplay between requirements discovery, and building parts of the software.

During each requirements workshop, the user goals and use case list are refined. More of the use cases are written, and rewritten, in their fully dressed format. By the end of elaboration, "80-90%" of the use cases are written in detail. For the POS system with 20 user goal level use cases, 15 or more of the most complex and risky should be investigated, written, and rewritten in a fully dressed format.

Note that elaboration involves programming parts of the system. At the end of this step, the NextGen team should not only have a better definition of the use cases, but some quality executable software.

Use Cases Within Construction

The construction step is composed of timeboxed iterations (for example, 20 iterations of two weeks each) that focus on completing the system, once the risky and core unstable issues have settled down in elaboration. There will still be some minor use case writing and perhaps requirements workshops, but much less so than in elaboration. By this step, the majority of core functional and non-functional requirements should have iteratively and adaptively stabilized. That does not mean to imply requirements are frozen or investigation finished, but the degree of change is much lower.

6.17 Case Study: Use Cases in the NextGen Inception Phase

As described in the previous section, not all use cases are written in their fully dressed form during inception. The Use-Case Model at this phase of the case study could be detailed as follows:

Fully Dressed	Casual	Brief
Process Sale Handle Returns	Process Rental Analyze Sales Activity Manage Security ...	Cash In Cash Out Manage Users Start Up Shut Down Manage System Tables ...

6.18 Further Readings

The most popular use-case guide, translated into several languages, is *Writing Effective Use Cases* [Cockburn01].[7] This has emerged with good reason as the most widely read and followed use-case book and is therefore recommended as a primary reference. This introductory chapter is consequently based on and consistent with its content. Suggestion: Do not be put off the book by the author's use of icons for different use case levels, or the early emphasis on levels and use case taxonomy. The icons are optional and minor. And although the discussion of levels and goals may at first seem a diversion to those new to use cases, those who have worked with them for some time appreciate that the level and scope of use cases are key practical issues, because their misunderstanding is a common source of complication in use-case modeling.

"Structuring Use Cases with Goals" [Cockburn97] is the most widely cited paper on use cases, available online at *www.usecases.org*.

Use Cases: Requirements in Context [GK00] is another useful text. It emphasizes the important viewpoint—as the title states—that use cases are not just another requirements artifact, but that they are the central vehicle that drives requirements work and information.

Another worthwhile read is *Applying Use Cases: A Practical Guide* [SW98], written by an experienced use case teacher and practitioner that understand and communicate how to apply use cases in an iterative lifecycle.

---

7. Note that Cockburn rhymes with *slow burn*.

6.19   UP Artifacts and Process Context

As illustrated in Figure 6.5, use cases influence many UP artifacts.

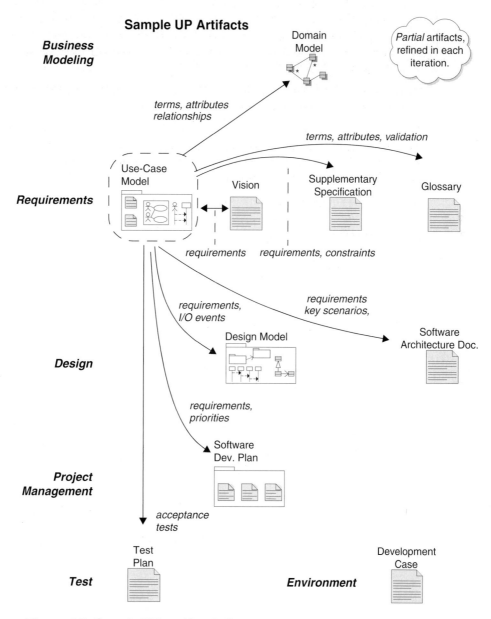

Figure 6.5 Sample UP artifact influence.

In the UP, use case work is a requirements discipline activity which could be initiated during a requirements workshop. Figure 6.6 offers suggestions on the time and space for doing this work.

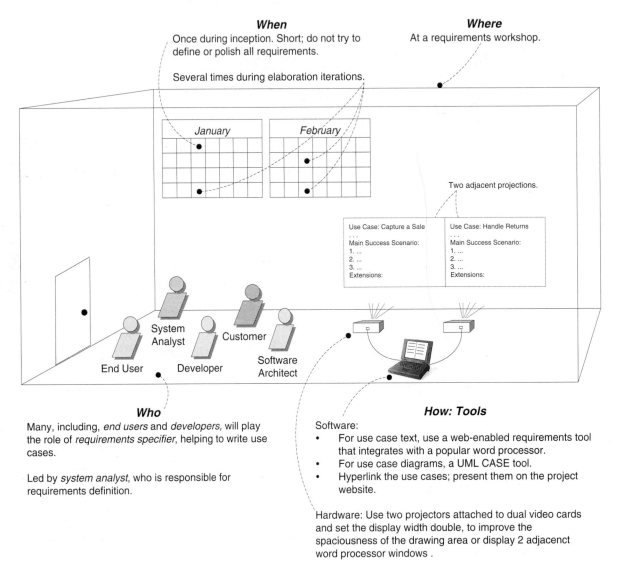

Figure 6.6 Process and setting context.

IDENTIFYING OTHER REQUIREMENTS

When ideas fail, words come in very handy.

—*Johann Wolfgang von Goethe*

Objectives

- Write a Supplementary Specification, Glossary, and Vision.
- Compare and contrast system features with use cases.
- Relate the Vision to other artifacts, and to iterative development.
- Define quality attributes.

Introduction

It is not sufficient to write use cases. There are other kinds of requirements that need to be identified, such as documentation, packaging, supportability, licensing, and so forth. These are captured in the **Supplementary Specification**.

The **Glossary** captures terms and definitions; it can also play the role of a data dictionary.

The **Vision** summarizes the "vision" of the project. It serves to tersely communicate the big ideas regarding why the project was proposed, what the problems are, who the stakeholders are, what they need, and what the proposed solution looks like.

To quote:

> The Vision defines the stakeholders' view of the product to be
> developed, specified in terms of the stakeholders' key needs and

features. Containing an outline of the envisioned core requirements, it provides the contractual basis for the more detailed technical requirements [RUP].

7.1   NextGen POS Examples

The purpose of the following examples is not to present an exhaustive Vision, Glossary, or Supplementary Specification, as some of the sections—although useful for a project—are not relevant to the learning objectives.[1] The book's goal is core skills in object design, use case requirements analysis, and object-oriented analysis, not POS problems or Vision statements. Therefore, only some sections are briefly touched upon in order to make connections between prior and future work, highlight noteworthy issues, provide a feel for the contents, and move forward quickly.

7.2   NextGen Example: (Partial) Supplementary Specification

Supplementary Specification

Revision History

Version	Date	Description	Author
Inception draft	Jan 10, 2031	First draft. To be refined primarily during elaboration.	Craig Larman

Introduction

This document is the repository of all NextGen POS requirements not captured in the use cases.

Functionality

(Functionality common across many use cases)

Logging and Error Handling

Log all errors to persistent storage.

Pluggable Business Rules

At various scenario points of several use cases (to be defined) support the ability to customize the functionality of the system with a set of arbitrary rules that execute at that point or event.

Security

All usage requires user authentication.

---

1. Scope creep is not only a problem in requirements, but in *writing* about requirements.

Usability

Human Factors

The customer will be able to see a large-monitor display of the POS.Therefore:

- Text should be easily visible from 1 meter.

- Avoid colors associated with common forms of color blindness.

Speed, ease, and error-free processing are paramount in sales processing, as the buyer wishes to leave quickly, or they perceive the purchasing experience (and seller) as less positive.

The cashier is often looking at the customer or items, not the computer display. Therefore, signals and warnings should be conveyed with sound rather than only via graphics.

Reliability

Recoverability

If there is failure to use external services (payment authorizer, accounting system, ...) try to solve with a local solution (e.g., store and forward) in order to still complete a sale. Much more analysis is needed here...

Performance

As mentioned under human factors, buyers want to complete sales processing *very* quickly. One potential bottleneck is external payment authorization. Our goal is to achieve authorization in less than1 minute, 90% of the time.

Supportability

Adaptability

Different customers of the NextGen POS have unique business rule and processing needs while processing a sale. Therefore, at several defined points in the scenario (for example, when a new sale is initiated, when a new line item is added) pluggable business rule will be enabled.

Configurability

Different customers desire varying network configurations for their POS systems, such as thick versus thin clients, two-tier versus N-tier physical layers, and so forth. In addition, they desire the ability to modify these configurations, to reflect their changing business and performance needs. Therefore, the system will be somewhat configurable to reflect these needs. Much more analysis is needed in this area to discover the areas and degree of flexibility, and the effort to achieve it.

Implementation Constraints

NextGen leadership insists on a Java technologies solution, predicting this will improve long-term porting and supportability, in addition to ease of development.

Purchased Components

- Tax calculator. Must support pluggable calculators for different countries.

Free Open Source Components

In general, we recommend maximizing the use of free Java technology open source components on this project.

Although it is premature to definitively design and choose components, we suggest the following as likely candidates:

■ JLog logging framework

■ ...

Interfaces

Noteworthy Hardware and Interfaces

■ Touch screen monitor (this is perceived by operating systems as a regular monitor, and the touch gestures as mouse events)

■ Barcode laser scanner (these normally attach to a special keyboard, and the scanned input is perceived in software as keystrokes)

■ Receipt printer

■ Credit/debit card reader

■ Signature reader (but not in release 1)

Software Interfaces

For most external collaborating systems (tax calculator, accounting, inventory, ...) we need to be able to plug in varying systems and thus varying interfaces.

Domain (Business) Rules

ID	Rule	Changeability	Source
RULE1	Signature required for credit payments.	Buyer "signature" will continue to be required, but within 2 years most of our customers want signature capture on a digital capture device, and within 5 years we expect there to be demand for support of the new unique digital code "signature" now supported by USA law.	The policy of virtually all credit authorization companies.
RULE2	Tax rules. Sales require added taxes. See government statutes for current details.	High. Tax laws change annually, at all government levels.	law
RULE3	Credit payment reversals may only be paid as a credit to the buyer's credit account, not as cash.	Low	credit authorization company policy
RULE4	Purchaser discount rules. Examples: Employee—20% off. Preferred Customer—10% off. Senior—15% off.	High. Each retailer uses different rules.	Retailer policy.

ID	Rule	Changeability	Source
RULE5	Sale (transaction-level) discount rules. Applies to pre-tax total. Examples: 10% off if total greater than $100 USD. 5% off each Monday. 10% off all sales between 10am and 3pm today. Tofu 50% off from 9am-10am today.	High. Each retailer uses different rules, and they may change daily or hourly.	Retailer policy.
RULE6	Product (line item level) discount rules. Examples: 10% off tractors this week. Buy 2 veggieburgers, get 1 free.	High. Each retailer uses different rules, and they may change daily or hourly.	Retailer policy.

Legal Issues

We recommend some open source components if their licensing restrictions can be resolved to allow resale of products that include open source software.

All tax rules must, by law, be applied during sales. Note that these can change frequently.

Information in Domains of Interest

Pricing

In addition to the pricing rules described in the domain rules section, note that products have an *original price*, and optionally a *permanent markdown price*. A product's price (before further discounts) is the permanent markdown price, if present. Organizations maintain the original price even if there is a permanent markdown price, for accounting and tax reasons.

Credit and Debit Payment Handling

When an electronic credit or debit payment is approved by a payment authorization service, they are responsible for paying the seller, not the buyer. Consequently, for each payment, the seller needs to record monies owing in their accounts receivable, from the authorization service. Usually on a nightly basis, the authorization service will perform an electronic funds transfer to the seller's account for the daily total owing, less a (small) per transaction fee that the service charges.

Sales Tax

Sales tax calculations can be very complex, and regularly change in response to legislation at all levels of government. Therefore, delegating tax calculations to third-party calculator software (of which there are several available) is advisable. Tax may be owing to city, region, state, and national bodies. Some items may be tax exempt without qualification, or exempt depending on the buyer or target recipient (for example, a farmer or a child).

Item Identifiers: UPCs, EANs, SKUs, Bar Codes, and Bar Code Readers

The NextGen POS needs to support various item identifier schemes. UPCs (Universal Product Codes), EANs (European Article Numbering) and SKUs (Stock Keeping Units) are three common identifier systems for products that are sold. Japanese Article Numbers (JANs) are a kind of EAN version.

SKUs are completely arbitrary identifiers defined by the retailer.

However, UPCs and EANs have a standards and regulatory component. See www.adams1.com/pub/russadam/upccode.html for a good overview. Also see www.uc-council.org and www.ean-int.org.

7.3   Commentary: Supplementary Specification

The **Supplementary Specification** captures other requirements, information, and constraints not easily captured in the use cases or Glossary, including system-wide "URPS+" quality attributes or requirements. Note that requirements specific to a use case can (and probably should) be first written with the use case, in a *Special Requirements* section, but some prefer to also consolidate all of them in the Supplementary Specification.. Elements of the Supplementary Specification could include:

- FURPS+ requirements—functionality, usability, reliability, performance, and supportability

- reports

- hardware and software constraints (operating and networking systems, ...)

- development constraints (for example, process or development tools)

- other design and implementation constraints

- internationalization concerns (units, languages, ...)

- documentation (user, installation, administration) and help

- licensing and other legal concerns

- packaging

- standards (technical, safety, quality)

- physical environment concerns (for example, heat or vibration)

- operational concerns (for example, how do errors get handled, or how often to do backups?)

- domain or business rules

- information in domains of interest (for example, what is the entire cycle of credit payment handling?)

Constraints are not behaviors, but some other kind of restriction on the design or project. They are also requirements, but are commonly called "constraints" to emphasize their *restrictive* influence. For example:

> *Must use Oracle (we have a licensing arrangement with them).*

> *Must run on Linux (it will lower cost).*

Suggestion

Early design decisions and constraints ("premature elaboration") are almost always a bad idea, so it is worth being suspicious and challenging of these, especially during the inception phase when very little has been carefully analyzed. Some constraints are imposed for unavoidable reasons, such as a legal restriction or an existing external system interface that must be invoked.

Quality Attributes

Some requirements are called **quality attributes** [BCK98] (or "-ilities") of a system. These include usability, reliability, and so forth. Note that these refer to the qualities of the system, not that these attributes are necessarily of high quality (the word is overloaded in English). For example, the quality of supportability might deliberately be chosen to be low if the product is not intended to serve a long-term purpose.

They are of two types:

1. Observable at execution (functionality, usability, reliability, performance, ...)

2. Not observable at execution (supportability, testability, ...)

Functionality is specified in the use cases, as are other quality attributes related to specific use cases (for example, the performance qualities in the *Process Sale* use case).

Other system-wide FURPS+ quality attributes are described in the Supplementary Specification.

Although functionality is a valid quality attribute, in common usage, the term "quality attribute" is most often meant to imply "qualities of the system other than functionality." Herein, the term is likewise used. This is not exactly the same as non-functional requirements, which is a broader term including *everything* but functionality (for example, packaging and licensing).

When we put on our "architect hat," the system-wide quality attributes (and thus the Supplementary Specification where one records them) are especially interesting because—as will be introduced in Chapter 32—architectural analysis and design are largely concerned with the identification and resolution of the quality attributes in the context of the functional requirements. For example, suppose one of the quality attributes is that the NextGen system must be quite fault-tolerant when remote services fail. From an architectural viewpoint, that will have an overarching influence on large-scale design decisions.

Quality attributes have interdependencies and involve trade-offs. As a simple example in the POS, "very reliable (fault-tolerant)" and "easy to test" are in some opposition, because there are many subtle ways a distributed system can fail.

Domain (Business) Rules

Domain rules [Ross97, GK00] dictate how a domain or business may operate. They are not requirements of any one application, although an application's requirements are often influenced by domain rules. Company policies, physical laws, and government laws are common domain rules.

They are commonly called **business rules**, which is the most common type, but that term is limited, as some software applications are for non-business problems, such as weather simulation or military logistics. A weather simulation has "domain rules" that influence the application requirements, related to physical laws and relationships.

It is often useful to identify and record those domain rules that influence the requirements, usually realized in the use cases, because they can clarify incomplete or ambiguous use case content. For example, in the NextGen POS, if someone asks if the *Process Sale* use case should be written with an alternative to allow credit payments without signature capture, there is a business rule (RULE1) that clarifies whether this will not be allowed by any credit authorization company.

Caution

Rules are not application requirements. Do not record system features as rules. They describe the constraints and behaviors of how the domain works, not the application.

Information in Domains of Interest

It is often valuable for a subject matter expert to write (or provide URLs to) some explanation of domains related to the new software system (sales and accounting, the geophysics of underground oil/water/gas flows, ...), to provide context and deeper insight for the development team. It may contain pointers to important literature or experts, formulas, laws, or other references. For example, the arcana of UPC and EAN coding schemes, and bar code symbology, must be understood to some degree by the NextGen team.

7.4   NextGen Example: (Partial) Vision

Vision

Revision History

Version	Date	Description	Author
inception draft	Jan 10, 2031	First draft. To be refined primarily during elaboration.	Craig Larman

Introduction

The analysis in this example is illustrative, but fictitious.

We envision a next generation fault-tolerant point-of-sale (POS) application, NextGen POS, with the flexibility to support varying customer business rules, multiple terminal and user interface mechanisms, and integration with multiple third-party supporting systems.

Positioning

Business Opportunity

Existing POS products are not adaptable to the customer's business, in terms of varying business rules and varying network designs (for example, thin client or not; 2, 3, or 4 tier architectures). In addition, they do not scale well as terminals and business increase. And, none can work in either on-line or off-line mode, dynamically adapting depending on failures. None easily integrate with many third-party systems. None allow for new terminal technologies such as mobile PDAs. There is marketplace dissatisfaction with this inflexible state of affairs, and demand for a POS that rectifies this.

Problem Statement

Traditional POS systems are inflexible, fault intolerant, and difficult to integrate with third-party systems. This leads to problems in timely sales processing, instituting improved processes that don't match the software, and accurate and timely accounting and inventory data to support measurement and planning, among other concerns. This affects cashiers, store managers, system administrators, and corporate management.

Product Position Statement

—*Terse summary of who the system is for, its outstanding features, and what differentiates it from the competition.*

Alternatives and Competition...

Understand who the players are, and their problems.

Stakeholder Descriptions

Market Demographics...

Stakeholder (Non-User) Summary...

User Summary...

Key High-Level Goals and Problems of the Stakeholders

Consolidate input from the Actor and Goals List, and the Stakeholder Interests section of the use cases.

A one day requirements workshop with subject matter experts and other stakeholders, and surveys at several retail outlets led to identification of the following key goals and problems:

High-Level Goal	Priority	Problems and Concerns	Current Solutions
Fast, robust, integrated sales processing	high	Reduced speed as load increases. Loss of sales processing capability if components fail. Lack of up-to-date and accurate information from accounting and other systems due to non-integration with existing accounting, inventory, and HR systems. Leads to difficulties in measuring and planning. Inability to customize business rules to unique business requirements. Difficulty in adding new terminal or user interface types (for example, mobile PDAs).	Existing POS products provide basic sales processing, but do not address these problems.
. . .	. . .	. . .	. . .

User-Level Goals

The users (and external systems) need a system to fulfill these goals:

This may be the Actor-Goal List created during use-case modeling, or a more terse summary.

- *Cashier*: process sales, handle returns, cash in, cash out
- *System administrator*: manage users, manage security, manage system tables
- *Manager*: start up, shut down
- *Sales activity system*: analyze sales data
- . . .

User Environment...

Product Overview

Product Perspective

The NextGen POS will usually reside in stores; if mobile terminals are used, they will be in close proximity to the store network, either inside or close outside. It will provide services to users, and collaborate with other systems, as indicated in Figure Vision-1.

Summarized from the use case diagram.

Context diagrams come in different formats with varying detail, but all show the major external actors related to a system.

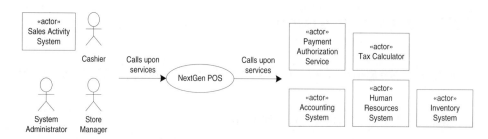

Figure Vision-1. NextGen POS system context diagram

Summary of Benefits

Similar to the Actor-Goal list, this table relates goals, benefits, and solutions, but at a higher level not solely related to use cases.

It summarizes the value and differentiating qualities of the product.

Supporting Feature	Stakeholder Benefit
Functionally, the system will provide all the common services a sales organization requires, including sales capture, payment authorization, return handling, and so forth.	Automated, fast point-of-sale services.
Automatic detection of failures, switching to local offline processing for unavailable services.	Continued sales processing when external components fail.
Pluggable business rules at various scenario points during sales processing.	Flexible business logic configuration.
Real-time transactions with third-party systems, using industry standard protocols.	Timely, accurate sales, accounting, and inventory information, to support measuring and planning.
. . .	. . .

Assumptions and Dependencies...

Cost and Pricing...

Licensing and Installation...

As discussed below, system features are a terse format to summarize functionality.

Summary of System Features

- sales capture
- payment authorization (credit, debit, check)
- system administration for users, security, code and constants tables, and so forth.
- automatic offline sales processing when external components fail
- real-time transactions, based on industry standards, with third-party systems, including inventory, accounting, human resources, tax calculators, and payment authorization services
- definition and execution of customized "pluggable" business rules at fixed, common points in the processing scenarios
- . . .

Other Requirements and Constraints

Including design constraints, usability, reliability, performance, supportability, design constraints, documentation, packaging, and so forth: See the Supplementary Specification and use cases.

7.5   Commentary: Vision

Are We Solving the Same Problem? The Right Problem?

The Problem Statement

During early requirements work in the inception phase, collaborate to define a terse problem statement; it will reduce the likelihood that stakeholders are trying to solve slightly different problems, and is usually quickly created. Occasionally, the effort reveals fundamental differences of opinion in what the parties are trying to achieve.

Rather than plain prose, a table format offered in the RUP templates for problem statements is:

The problem of	...
affects	...
the impact of which is	...
a successful solution would be	...

The Key High-Level Goals and Problems of the Stakeholders

This table summarizes the goals and problems at a higher level than task level use cases, and reveals important nonfunctional and quality goals that may belong to one use case or span many, such as:

- *We need fault-tolerant sales processing.*

- *We need the ability to customize the business rules.*

What Are the Root Problems and Goals?

It is common for stakeholders to express their goals in terms of envisioned solutions, such as: "We need a full-time programmer to customize the business rules as we change them." The solutions are sometimes perceptive, because they understand their problem domain and options well. But sometimes stakeholder jump to solutions that are not the most appropriate or do not address the root underlying major problems.

Thus, the system analyst needs to investigate the problem and goal chain—as discussed in the previous chapter on use cases and goals—in order to learn the underlying problems, and their relative importance and impact, in order to prioritize and solve the most egregious concerns with a skillful solution.

Group Idea Facilitation Methods

Although outside the scope of this discussion, it is especially during activities such as high-level problem definition and goal identification that creative, investigative group work occurs. Here are some useful group facilitation techniques to discover root problems and goals, and support idea generation and prioritization: mind mapping, fishbone diagrams, pareto diagrams, brainstorming, multi-voting, dot voting, nominal group process, brainwriting, and affinity grouping. Check them out on the web. I prefer to apply several of these during the same workshop, to discover common problems and requirements from different angles.

System Features—Functional Requirements

Use cases are not necessarily the only way one needs to express functional requirements for the following reasons:

- They are detailed. Stakeholders often want a short summary that identifies the most noteworthy functions.

- What about simply listing the use case names (*Process Sale, Handle Returns, ...*) to summarize the functionality? First, the list may still be too long. Also, the names can hide interesting functionality stakeholders really want to know about; that is, the level of granularity can obscure noteworthy functions. For example, suppose that the description of automated payment authorization functionality is embedded in the *Process Sale* use case. A reader of a list of use case names cannot tell if the system will do payment authorization. Furthermore, one may wish to group a set of use cases into one feature (for brevity), such as *System administration for users, security, code and constants tables, and so forth*.

- Some noteworthy functionality is naturally expressed as short statements that do not conveniently map to use case names or Elementary Business Process-level goals. It may span or be orthogonal to the use cases. For example, during the first NextGen requirements workshop, someone might say "The system should be able to do transactions with existing third-party accounting, inventory, and tax calculation systems." This statement of functionality does not represent one particular use case, but is a comfortable and succinct way to express, record, and communicate features.

  - As a stronger variation of the last point, some applications call out primarily for a description of functionality as features; use cases are not a natural fit. This is common, for example, with middleware products such as application servers—use cases are not really motivated. Suppose the team is considering their next release. During a requirements discussion, people (such as marketing) will say, "The next version needs EJB 2.0 entity bean support." The requirements are primarily conceived in terms of a list of features, not use cases.

Therefore, an alternative, a complementary way to express system functions is with **features**, or more specifically in this context, **system features**, which are high-level, terse statements summarizing system functions. More formally, in the UP, a **system feature** is "an externally observable service provided by the system which directly fulfills a stakeholder need" [Kruchten00].

Features are things a system can *do*. They should pass this linguistic test:

The system shall do <feature X>.

For example:

> *The system shall do payment authorization.*

Recall that the Vision may be used as a formal or informal contract between development and business. System features are a mechanism to summarize in this contract what the system will *do*. This is complementary to the use cases, as the features are terse.

Features are to be contrasted with various kinds of non-functional requirements and constraints, such as: *"The system must run on Linux, must have 24/7 availability, and must have a touch-screen interface."* Note that these fail the linguistic test.

At times, the admonition "an externally observable service..." is difficult to decide upon. For example, should the following be a system feature:

> *The system shall do transactions with third-party accounting, inventory, human resource, and tax calculation systems.*

It is a kind of behavior, and probably noteworthy to the stakeholders, but the collaboration itself may not be externally visible, depending on your time frame, and how close and where you look. Include it—fine-grained classification questions are seldom worth the worry.

Finally, note that most system features will find detailed expression in use case text.

Notation and Organization

First and foremost, short high-level descriptions are important. One should be able to read the system features list quickly.

It is not necessary to include the canonical "The system shall do..." or a variant phrase, although it is common.

Here is a features example at a high level, for a large multi-system project of which the POS is just one element:

The major features include:

- *POS services*

- *Inventory management*

- *Web-based shopping*

- *. . .*

It is common to organize a two-level hierarchy of system features. But in the Vision document more than two levels leads to excessive detail; the point of system features in the Vision is to summarize the functionality, not decompose it into a long list of fine-grained elements. A reasonable example in terms of detail:

The major features include:

- *POS services:*
  - *sales capture*
  - *payment authorization*
  - *. . .*
- *Inventory management:*
  - *automatic reordering*
  - *. . .*

Sometimes, these second level features are essentially equivalent to use case names (or user-level goals), but that is not required; features are an alternative way to summarize functionality. Nevertheless, most system features will find detailed expression in the use cases.

How many system features should the Vision contain?

Suggestion

A Vision with less than 50 features is desirable. If more, consider grouping and abstracting the features.

Other Requirements in the Vision

In the Vision, system features briefly summarize functional requirements expressed in detail in the use cases. Likewise, the Vision *can* summarize other requirements (for example, reliability and usability) that are detailed in the *Special Requirements* sections of use cases, and in the Supplementary Specification (SS). However, there is some risk of unhelpful duplication. For example, the RUP product provides templates for the Vision and SS that contain identical or similar sections for other requirements such as usability, reliability, performance, and so forth. Such duplication is inevitably awkward to maintain. Furthermore, the level of detail for similar sections (for example, performance) in the Vision and the SS needs to be quite similar to be meaningful; that is, "essential" and "detailed" other requirement descriptions tend to be much the same,

---

Suggestion

For other requirements, avoid their duplication or near-duplication in both the Vision and Supplementary Specification (SS)—and in use cases. Rather, record them only in the SS or uses cases (if use case specific). In the Vision, direct the reader to these for the other requirements.

This is a minor documentation nuance on the standard RUP templates that may reduce complications. If one prefers the standard template approach, that is also fine.

Vision, Features, or Use Cases—Which First?

It is not useful to be rigid about the order of some artifacts. While collaborating to create different requirements artifacts, a synergy emerges in which working on one influences and helps clarify another. Nevertheless, a suggested sequence is:

1. Write a brief first draft of the Vision.

2. Identify user goals and the supporting use cases.

3. Write some use cases and start the Supplementary Specification.

4. Refine the Vision, summarizing information from these.

7.6   NextGen Example: A (Partial) Glossary

Glossary

Revision History

Version	Date	Description	Author
Inception draft	Jan 10, 2031	First draft. To be refined primarily during elaboration.	Craig Larman

Definitions

Term	Definition and Information	Aliases
item	A product or service for sale	
payment authorization	Validation by an external payment authorization service that they will make or guarantee the payment to the seller.	
payment authorization request	A composite of elements electronically sent to an authorization service, usually as a char array. Elements include: store ID, customer account number, amount, and timestamp.	
UPC	12 digit code that identifies a product. Usually symbolized with a bar code placed on products. See http://www.uc-council.org for details.	Universal Product Code
. . .	. . .	

7.7   Commentary: Glossary (Data Dictionary)

In its simplest form, the **Glossary** is a list of noteworthy terms and their definitions. It is surprisingly common that a term, often technical or particular to the domain, will be used in slightly different ways by different stakeholders; this needs to be resolved to reduce problems in communication and ambiguous requirements.

> *Suggestion*
>
> Start the Glossary early. I'm reminded of an experience working with simulation experts, in which the seemingly innocuous, but important, word "cell" was discovered to have slippery and varying meanings among the group members.

The goal is not to record all possible terms, but those that are unclear, ambiguous, or which require some kind of noteworthy elaboration, such as format information or validation rules.

Glossary as Data Dictionary

In the UP, the Glossary also plays the role of a **data dictionary**, a document that records data about the data—that is, **metadata**. During inception the glossary should be a simple document of terms and descriptions. During elaboration, it may expand into a data dictionary.

Term attributes could include:

- aliases
- description
- format (type, length, unit)
- relationships to other elements
- range of values
- validation rules

> Note that the range of values and validation rules in the Glossary constitute requirements with implications on the behavior of the system.

Units

As Martin Fowler underscores in *Analysis Patterns* [Fowler96], units (currency, measures, ...) must be considered, especially in this age of internationalized software applications. For example, in the NextGen system, which will hopefully be sold to many customers in different countries, *price* cannot be just a raw number. It must be in a *Money* or *Currency* unit that captures the notion of varying currencies.

Composite Terms

The Glossary is not only for atomic terms such as "product price." It can and should include composite elements such as "sale" (which includes other elements, such as date and location), and nicknames used to describe a collection of data transmitted between actors in the use cases. For example, in the *Process Sale* use case, consider the following statement:

> System sends <u>payment authorization request</u> to an external Payment Authorization Service, and requests payment approval.

"Payment authorization request" is a nickname for an aggregate of data, which needs to be explained in the Glossary.

7.8   Reliable Specifications: An Oxymoron?

Written requirements can promote the illusion that the real requirements are understood and well-defined, and can (early on) be used to reliably estimate and plan the project. This illusion is more strong for non-software developers; programmers know from painful experience how unreliable it is. This is part of the motivation for the opening quote by Goethe.

What really matters is building software that passes the acceptance tests defined by the users and stakeholders, and that meets their true goals (which are often not discovered until they are evaluating or working with the software).

Writing a Vision and Supplementary Specification is worthwhile as an exercise in clarifying a first approximation of what is wanted, the motivation for the product, and as a repository for the big ideas. But they are not—nor is any requirements artifact—a reliable specification. Only writing code, testing it, getting feedback, ongoing close collaboration with users and customers, and adapting, truly hit the mark.

This is not a call to abandon analysis and thinking, and just rushing to code, but a suggestion to treat written requirements lightly, and continually—indeed, daily—engage users.

7.9 Online Artifacts at the Project Website

Since this is a book, these examples and the preceding use cases have a static and perhaps paper-oriented feel. Nevertheless, these should be digital artifacts recorded only online at the project website. And instead of being plain static documents, they may be hyperlinked, or recorded in tools other than a word processor or spreadsheet. For example, the Glossary could be stored in a database table.

7.10 Not Much UML During Inception?

The purpose of inception is to collect just enough information to establish a common vision, decide if moving forward is feasible, and if the project is worth serious investigation in the elaboration phase. As such, beyond simple UML use case diagrams, not much diagramming is often motivated. There is more focus in inception on understanding the basic scope and 10% of the requirements, expressed in textual forms. In practice, and thus in this presentation, most UML diagramming will occur in the next phase—elaboration.

7.11 Other Requirement Artifacts Within the UP

As in the prior use case chapter, Table 7.1 summarizes a sample of artifacts and their timing. All requirements artifacts are started in inception, and primarily worked on through elaboration.

Discipline	Artifact	Incep.	Elab.	Const.	Trans.
	Iteration→	I1	E1..En	C1..Cn	T1..T2
Business Modeling	Domain Model		s		
Requirements	Use-Case Model	s	r		
	Vision	s	r		
	Supplementary Specification	s	r		
	Glossary	s	r		
Design	Design Model		s	r	
	SW Architecture Document		s		
	Data Model		s	r	
Implementation	Implementation Model		s	r	r
Project Management	SW Development Plan	s	r	r	r
Testing	Test Model		s	r	
Environment	Development Case	s	r		

Table 7.1 Sample UP artifacts and timing. s - start; r - refine

Inception

It should not be the case that these requirements artifacts are finalized in the inception phase. Indeed, they will barely be started.

Stakeholders need to decide if the project is worth serious investigation; that real investigation occurs during elaboration, not inception. During inception, the Vision summarizes the project idea in a form to help decision makers determine if it is worth continuing, and where to start.

Since most requirements work occurs during elaboration, the Supplementary Specification should be only lightly developed during inception, highlighting noteworthy quality attributes (for example, the NextGen POS must have recoverability when external services fail) that expose major risks and challenges.

Input into these artifacts could be generated during an inception phase requirements workshop, both through explicit consideration of its topics, and indirectly via use case analysis. Draft, readable artifacts will not get written in the workshop, but afterwards by the system analyst.

Elaboration

Through the elaboration iterations, the "vision" and the Vision are refined, based upon feedback from incrementally building parts of the system, adapting, and multiple requirements workshops over several development iterations.

Through ongoing requirements investigation and iterative development, the other requirements will become more clear and can be recorded in the SS. The quality attributes (for example, reliability) identified in the SS will be key drivers in shaping the core architecture that is designed and programmed during elaboration. They may also be key risk factors that influence what gets worked on in early iterations. For example, the NextGen POS quality requirement of client-side recoverability if external components fail will be explored during elaboration.

The majority of terms will be discovered and elaborated in the Glossary during this phase.

By the end of elaboration, it is feasible to have use cases, a Supplementary Specification, and a Vision that reasonably reflects the stabilized major features and other requirements to be completed for delivery. Nevertheless, the Supplementary Specification and Vision are not something to freeze and "sign off" on as a fixed specification; adaptation—not rigidity—is a core value of iterative development and the UP.

To clarify this "frozen sign off" comment: It is perfectly sensible—at the end of elaboration—to form an agreement with stakeholders about what will be done in the remainder of the project, and to make commitments (perhaps contractual) regarding requirements and schedule. At some point (the end of elaboration, in the UP), we need a reliable idea of "what, how much, and when." In that sense, a formal agreement on the requirements is normal and expected. It is also necessary to have a change control process (one of the explicit best practice in the UP) so that changes in requirements are formally considered and approved, rather than chaotic and uncontrolled change.

Rather, several ideas are implied by the "frozen sign off" comment:

- In iterative development and the UP it is understood that no matter how much due diligence is given to requirements specification, some change is inevitable, and should be acceptable. This change could be a late-breaking opportunistic improvement in the system that gives its owners a competitive advantage, or change due to improved insight.

- In iterative development, it is a core value to have continual engagement by the stakeholders to evaluate, provide feedback, and steer the project as they really want it. It does not benefit stakeholders to "wash their hands" of attentive engagement by signing off on a frozen set of requirements and waiting for the finished product, because they will seldom get what they really needed.

Construction

By construction, the major requirements—both functional and otherwise—should be stabilized—not finalized, but settled down to minor pertubation. Therefore, the SS and Vision are unlikely to experience much change in this phase.

7.12   Further Readings

Vision and Supplementary Specification-like documents are not new. They are used on many projects and described in many requirements books. Most such books implicitly assume the waterfall attitude that the objective is to get them detailed and correct at the beginning, and commit to them, before moving on to design and implementation. In that sense, their traditional descriptions are not helpful, although they otherwise provide good advice for possible sections and their content.

Most books on software architecture include discussion of requirements analysis for quality attributes of the application, since these quality requirements tend to strongly influence architectural design. One example is *Software Architecture in Practice* [BCK98].

Business rules get an exhaustive treatment in *The Business Rule Book* [Ross97]. The book presents a broad, deep, and thoroughly-considered theory of business rules, but the method is not well-connected to other modern requirements techniques such as use cases, or to iterative development.

7.13   UP Artifacts and Process Context

Artifact influence emphasizing the Vision, Supplementary Specification, and Glossary are show in Figure 7.1.

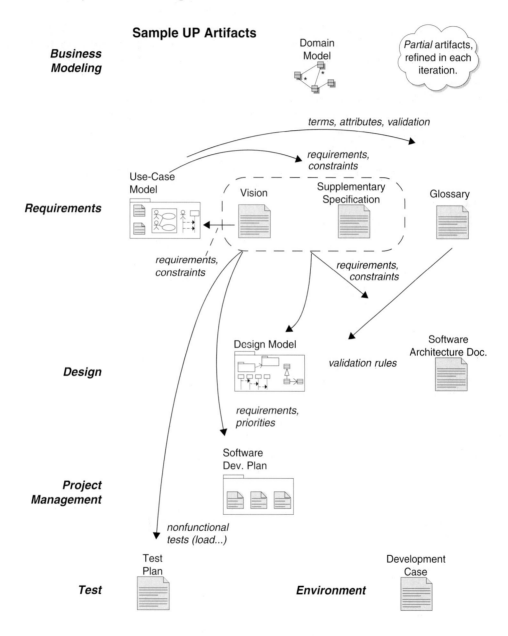

Figure 7.1 Sample UP artifact influence.

In the UP, Vision and Supplementary Specification work is a requirements discipline activity which could be initiated during a requirements workshop, along with use case analysis. Figure 7.2 offers suggestions on the time and space for doing this work.

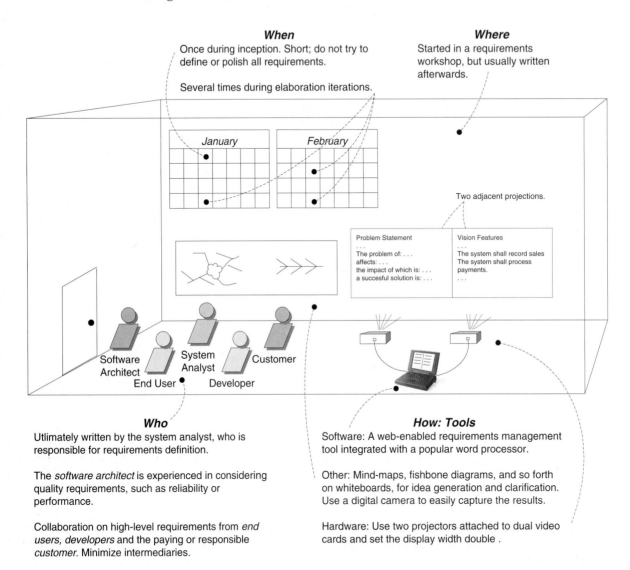

Figure 7.2 Process and setting context.

FROM INCEPTION TO ELABORATION

The hard and stiff breaks. The supple prevails.

—Tao Te Ching

Objectives

- Define the elaboration step.
- Motivate the following chapters in this section.

Introduction

Elaboration is the initial series of iterations during which:

- the majority of requirements are discovered and stabilized
- the major risks are mitigated or retired
- the core architectural elements are implemented and proven

Rarely, the architecture is not a risk—for example, if building a website like others the team has successfully built, with the same tools and similar requirements—in which case, it does not have to be a focus of these early iterations. In that case, critical but non-architecturally significant features or use cases may be implemented.

It is in this phase that the book emphasizes an introduction to OOA/D, applying the UML, patterns, and architecture.

8.1   Checkpoint: What Happened in Inception?

The inception step of the NextGen POS project may last only one week. The artifacts created should be brief and incomplete, the phase quick, and the investigation light.

It is not the requirements phase of the project, but a short step to determine basic feasibility, risk, and scope, and decide if the project is worth more serious investigation, which occurs in elaboration. Not all activities that could reasonably occur in inception have been covered; this exploration emphasizes requirements-oriented artifacts. Some likely activities and artifacts in inception include:

- a short requirements workshop
- most actors, goals, and use cases named
- most use cases written in brief format; 10-20% of the use cases are written in fully dressed detail to improve understanding of the scope and complexity
- most influential and risky quality requirements identified
- version one of the Vision and Supplementary Specification written
- risk list
  - For example, leadership really wants a demo at the POSWorld trade show in Hamburg, in 18 months. But the effort for a demo cannot yet be even roughly estimated until deeper investigation.
- technical proof-of-concept prototypes and other investigations to explore the technical feasibility of special requirements ("Does Java Swing work properly on touch-screen displays?")
- user interface-oriented prototypes to clarify the vision of functional requirements
- recommendations on what components to buy/build/reuse, to be refined in elaboration
  - For example, a recommendation to buy a tax calculation package.
- high-level *candidate* architecture and components proposed
  - This is not a detailed architectural description, and it is not meant to be final or correct. Rather, it is brief speculation to use as a starting point of investigation in elaboration. For example, "A Java client-side application, no application server, Oracle for the database, ..." In elaboration, it may be proven worthy, or discovered to be a poor idea and rejected.
- plan for the first iteration
- candidate tools list

8.2   On to Elaboration

Elaboration is the initial series of iterations during which the team does serious investigation, implements (programs and tests) the core architecture, clarifies most requirements, and tackles the high-risk issues. In the UP, "risk" includes business value. Therefore, early work may include implementing scenarios that are deemed important, but are not especially technically risky.

Elaboration often consists of between two and four iterations; each iteration is recommended to be between two and six weeks, unless the team size is massive. Each iteration is timeboxed, meaning its end date is fixed; if the team is not likely to meet the date, requirements are placed back on the future tasks list, so that the iteration can end on time with a stable and tested release.

Elaboration is not a design phase or a phase when the models are fully developed in preparation for implementation in the construction step—that would be an example of superimposing waterfall ideas on to iterative development and the UP.

During this phase, one is not creating throw-away prototypes; rather, the code and design are production-quality portions of the final system. In some UP descriptions, the potentially misunderstood term "**architectural prototype**" is used to describe the partial system. This is not meant to be a prototype in the sense of a discardable experiment; in the UP, it means a production subset of the final system. More commonly it is called the **executable architecture** or **architectural baseline**.

Elaboration in one sentence:

Build the core architecture, resolve the high-risk elements, define most requirements, and estimate the overall schedule and resources.

Some key ideas and best practices that will manifest in elaboration include:

- do short timeboxed risk-driven iterations

- start programming early

- adaptively design, implement, and test the core and risky parts of the architecture

- test early, often, realistically

- adapt based on feedback from tests, users, developers

- write most of the use cases and other requirements in detail, through a series of workshops, once per elaboration iteration

What Is Architecturally Significant in Elaboration?

Early iterations build and prove the core architecture. For the NextGen POS project—indeed, most—this will include:

- Employing "wide and shallow" design and implementation; or "designing at the seams" as Grady Booch has called it.

    o That is, identifying the separate processes, layers, packages, and subsystems, and their high-level responsibilities and interfaces. Partially implement these in order to connect them and clarify the interfaces. Modules may contain mostly "stubbed" code.

- Refining the inter-module local and remote interfaces (this includes the finest details of the parameters and return values).

    o For example, the interface to the object which will wrap access to third-party accounting systems.

    o Version one of an interface is seldom perfect. Early attention to stress testing, "breaking," and refining the interfaces supports later multi-team parallel work relying on stable interfaces.

- Integrating existing components.

    o For example, a tax calculator.

- Implementing simplified end-to-end scenarios that force design, implementation, and test across many major components.

    o For example, the main success scenario of *Process Sale*, using the credit payment extension scenario.

Elaboration phase testing is important, to obtain feedback, adapt, and prove that the core is robust. Early testing for the NextGen project will include:

- Usability testing of the user interface for *Process Sale*.

- Testing of recovery when remote services, such as the credit authorizer, fail.

- Testing of high load to remote services, such as load on the remote tax calculator.

8.3   Planning the Next Iteration

Planning and project management are important but large topics. Some key ideas are briefly presented here, and an introduction is given in Chapter 36.

Organize requirements and iterations by risk, coverage, and criticality.

- **Risk** includes both technical complexity and other factors, such as uncertainty of effort or usability.

- **Coverage** implies that all major parts of the system are at least touched on in early iterations—perhaps a "wide and shallow" implementation across many components.

- **Criticality** refers to functions of high business value.

These criteria are used to rank work across iterations. Use cases or use case scenarios are ranked for implementation—early iterations implement high ranking scenarios. In addition, some requirements are expressed as high-level features unrelated to a particular use case, such as a logging service. These are also ranked.

The ranking is done before Iteration 1, but then again before Iteration 2, and so forth, as new requirements and new insights influence the order. That is, the plan is adaptive, rather than speculatively frozen at the beginning of the project.

Usually based on some small-group collaborative ranking technique, a fuzzy grouping of requirements will emerge. For example:

Rank	Requirement (Use Case or Feature)	Comment
High	Process Sale Logging . . .	Scores high on all ranking criteria. Pervasive. Hard to add late. . . .
Medium	Maintain Users . . .	Affects security subdomain. . . .
Low	. . .	. . .

Based on this ranking, we see that some key architecturally significant scenarios of the *Process Sale* use case should be tackled in early iterations. This list is not exhaustive; other requirements will also be tacked. In addition, an implicit or explicit *Start Up* use case will be worked on in each iteration, to meet its initialization needs.

In terms of UP artifacts, a few comments on this planning information:

- The chosen requirements for the next iteration are briefly listed in an **Iteration Plan**. This is not a plan of all the iterations, only a plan of the next.

- If the short description in the Iteration Plan is insufficient, a task or requirement for the iteration may be written in greater detail in a separate **Change Request**, and given to the responsible party.

- The overall requirements ranking is recorded in the **Software Development Plan**.

8.4 Iteration 1 Requirements and Emphasis: Fundamental OOA/D Skills

In this case study, Iteration 1 of the elaboration phase emphasizes a range of fundamental and common OOA/D skills used in building object systems, such as assigning responsibilities to objects. Of course, many other skills and steps—such as database design, usability engineering, and UI design—are needed to build software, but they are out of scope in this introduction to OOA/D and the UP.

Iteration 1 Requirements

The requirements for the first iteration of the NextGen POS application follow:

- Implement a basic, key scenario of the *Process Sale* use case: entering items and receiving a cash payment.

- Implement a *Start Up* use case as necessary to support the initialization needs of the iteration.

- Nothing fancy or complex is handled, just a simple happy path scenario, and the design and implementation to support it.

- There is no collaboration with external services, such as a tax calculator or product database.

- No complex pricing rules are applied.

The design and implementation of the supporting UI would also be done, but is not covered.

Subsequent iterations will grow on this foundation.

Incremental Development for the Same Use Case Across Iterations

Note that not all requirements in the *Process Sale* use case are being handled in iteration 1. It is common to work on varying scenarios or features of the same use case over several iterations and gradually extend the system to ultimately handle all the functionality required (see Figure 8.1). On the other hand, short, simple use cases may be completed within one iteration.

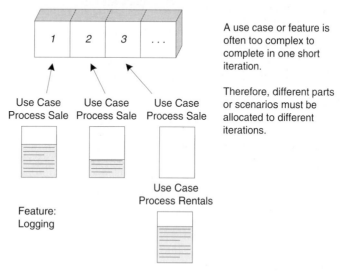

Figure 8.1 Use case implementation may be spread across iterations.

8.5 What Artifacts May Start in Elaboration?

Table 8.1 lists *sample* artifacts that may be started in elaboration, and indicates the issues they address. Subsequent chapters will examine some of these in greater detail, especially the Domain Model and Design Model. For brevity, the table excludes artifacts that may have begun in inception (and were listed in Chapter 4); it introduces artifacts that are more likely to start in elaboration. Note these will not be completed in one iteration; rather, they will be refined over a series of iterations.

Artifact	Comment
Domain Model	This is a visualization of the domain concepts; it is similar to a static information model of the domain entities.
Design Model	This is the set of diagrams that describes the logical design. This includes software class diagrams, object interaction diagrams, package diagrams, and so forth.

Artifact	Comment
Software Architecture Document	A learning aid that summarizes the key architectural issues and their resolution in the design. It is a summary of the outstanding design ideas and their motivation in the system.
Data Model	This includes the database schemas, and the mapping strategies between object and non-object representations.
Test Model	A description of what will be tested, and how.
Implementation Model	This is the actual implementation—the source code, executables, database, and so on.
Use-Case Storyboards, UI Prototypes	A description of the user interface, paths of navigation, usability models, and so forth.

Table 8.1 Sample elaboration artifacts, excluding those started in inception.

8.6   You Know You Didn't Understand Elaboration When...

- It is more than "a few" months long for most projects.

- It only has one iteration (with rare exceptions for well-understood problems)

- Most requirements were defined before elaboration.

- The risky elements and core architecture are not being tackled.

- It does not result in an *executable* architecture; there is no production-code programming.

- It is considered primarily a requirements phase, preceding an implementation phase in construction.

- There is an attempt to do a full and careful design before programming.

- There is minimal feedback and adaptation; users are not continually engaged in evaluation and feedback

- There is no early and realistic testing.

- The architecture is speculatively finalized before programming.

- It is considered a step to do the proof-of-concept programming, rather than programming the production core executable architecture.

- There are not multiple short requirements workshops that adapt and refine the requirements based on feedback from the prior and current iterations.

If a project exhibits these symptoms, the elaboration phase was not understood.

PART 3 ELABORATION ITERATION 1

USE-CASE MODEL: DRAWING SYSTEM SEQUENCE DIAGRAMS

In theory, there is no difference between theory and practice. But, in practice, there is.

—Jan L.A. van de Snepscheut

Objectives

- Identify system events.
- Create system sequence diagrams for use cases.

Moving on to Iteration 1

The NextGen POS project has entered the first real development iteration. Some light requirements work was done in inception to help decide if the project was worth more serious investigation. Planning for the first iteration has been completed, and it has been decided to tackle a simple cash-only success scenario of *Process Sale* (with no remote collaborations), with the goal of starting a "wide and shallow" design and implementation that touches on many major architectural elements of the new system. In the first iteration, many tasks related to establishing the environment (tools, people, process, and setting) occur; this will be skipped.

Rather, we turn our attention to use case and domain modeling analysis. Before starting iteration 1 design work, some further investigation of the problem domain is useful. Part of this investigation is the clarification of the input and output system events related to our system, which can be illustrated in UML sequence diagrams.

Introduction

A system sequence diagram is a fast and easily created artifact that illustrates input and output events related to the systems under discussion. The UML contains notation in the form of sequence diagrams to illustrate events from external actors to a system.

9.1 System Behavior

Before proceeding to a logical design of how a software application will work, it is useful to investigate and define its behavior as a "black box." **System behavior** is a description of *what* a system does, without explaining how it does it. One part of that description is a system sequence diagram. Other parts include the use cases, and system contracts (to be discussed later).

9.2 System Sequence Diagrams

Use cases describe how external actors interact with the software system we are interested in creating. During this interaction an actor generates events to a system, usually requesting some operation in response. For example, when a cashier enters an item's ID, the cashier is requesting the POS system to record that item's sale. That request event initiates an operation upon the system.

It is desirable to isolate and illustrate the operations that an external actor requests of a system, because they are an important part of understanding system behavior. The UML includes **sequence diagrams** as a notation that can illustrate actor interactions and the operations initiated by them.

A **system sequence diagram** (SSD) is a picture that shows, for a particular scenario of a use case, the events that external actors generate, their order, and inter-system events. All systems are treated as a black box; the emphasis of the diagram is events that cross the system boundary from actors to systems.

> An SSD should be done for the main success scenario of the use case, and frequent or complex alternative scenarios.

The UML does not define something called a "system" sequence diagram, but simply a sequence diagram. The qualification is used to emphasize its application to systems as black boxes. Later, sequence diagrams will be used in another context—to illustrate the design of interacting software objects to fulfill work.

9.3   Example of an SSD

An SSD shows, for a particular course of events within a use case, the external actors that interact directly with the system, the system (as a black box), and the system events that the actors generate (see Figure 9.1). Time proceeds downward, and the ordering of events should follow their order in the use case.

System events may include parameters.

This example is for the main success scenario of the *Process Sale* use case. It indicates that the cashier generates *makeNewSale, enterItem, endSale,* and *makePayment* system events.

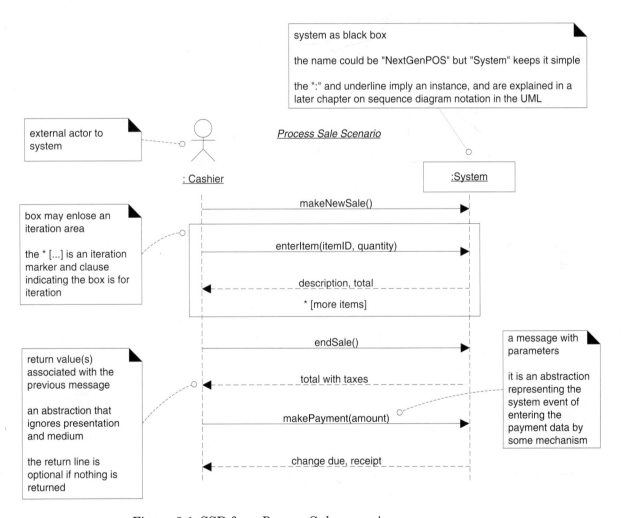

Figure 9.1 SSD for a *Process Sale* scenario.

9.4   Inter-System SSDs

SSDs can also be used to illustrate collaborations between systems, such as between the NextGen POS and the external credit payment authorizer. However, this is deferred until a later iteration in the case study, since this iteration does not include remote systems collaboration.

9.5   SSDs and Use Cases

An SSD shows system events for a scenario of a use case, therefore it is generated from inspection of a use case (see Figure 9.2).

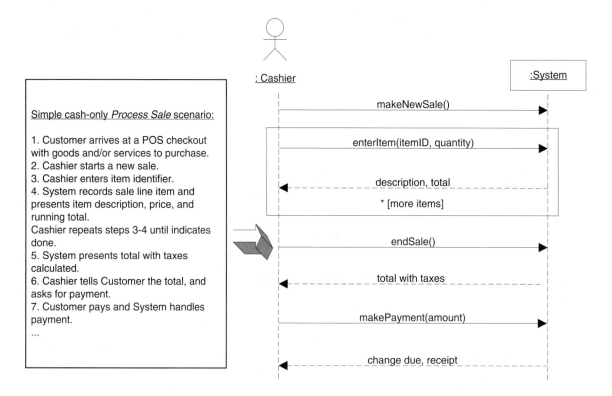

Figure 9.2 SSDs are derived from use cases.

9.6   System Events and the System Boundary

To identify system events, it is necessary to be clear on the choice of system boundary, as discussed in the prior chapter on use cases. For the purposes of software development, the system boundary is usually chosen to be the software (and possibly hardware) system itself; in this context, a system event is an external event that directly stimulates the software (see Figure 9.3).

Consider the *Process Sale* use case to identify system events. First, we must determine the actors that directly interact with the software system. The customer interacts with the cashier, but for this simple cash-only scenario, does not directly interact with the POS system—only the cashier does. Therefore, the customer is not a generator of system events; only the cashier is.

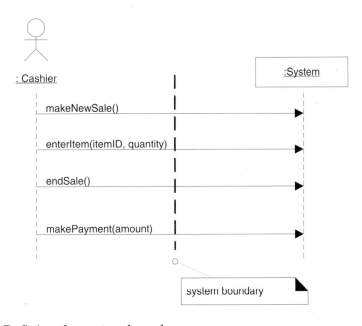

Figure 9.3 Defining the system boundary.

9.7   Naming System Events and Operations

System events (and their associated system operations) should be expressed at the level of intent rather than in terms of the physical input medium or interface widget level.

It also improves clarity to start the name of a system event with a verb (add..., enter..., end..., make...), as in Figure 9.4, since it emphasizes the command orientation of these events.

Thus "enterItem" is better than "scan" (that is, laser scan) because it captures the intent of the operation while remaining abstract and noncommittal with respect to design choices about what interface is used to capture the system event.

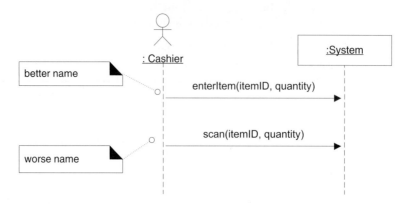

Figure 9.4 Choose event and operation names at an abstract level.

9.8   Showing Use Case Text

It is sometimes desirable to show at least fragments of use case text for the scenario, to clarify or enhance the two views (see Figure 9.5). The text provides the details and context; the diagram visually summarizes the interaction.

9.9   SSDs and the Glossary

The terms shown in SSDs (operations, parameters, return data) are terse. These may need proper explanation so that during design work it is clear what is coming in and going out. If this was not explicated in the use cases, the Glossary could be used.

However, as always when discussing the creation of artifacts other than code (the heart of the project), be suspicious. There should be some truly meaningful use or decision made with the Glossary data, otherwise it is simply low-value unnecessary work.

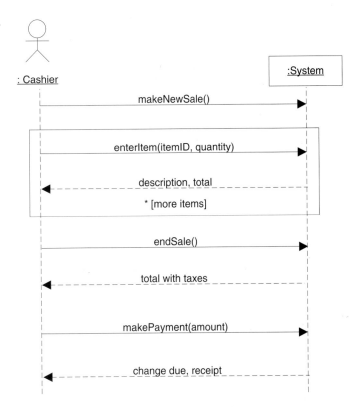

Simple cash-only *Process Sale* scenario:

1. Customer arrives at a POS checkout with goods and/or services to purchase.
2. Cashier starts a new sale.

3. Cashier enters item identifier.
4. System records sale line item and presents item description, price, and running total.

Cashier repeats steps 3-4 until indicates done.

5. System presents total with taxes calculated.

6. Cashier tells Customer the total, and asks for payment.
7. Customer pays and System handles payment.
...

Figure 9.5 SSD with use case text.

9.10   SSDs Within the UP

SSDs are part of the Use-Case Model—a visualization of the interactions implied in the use cases. SSDs were not explicitly mentioned in the original UP description, although the UP creators are aware of and understand the usefulness of such diagrams. SSDs are an example of the many possible skillful analysis and design artifacts or activities that the UP or RUP documents do not mention.

Phases

Inception—SSDs are not usually motivated in inception.

Elaboration—Most SSDs are created during elaboration, when it is useful to identify the details of the system events to clarify what major operations the system must be designed to handle, write system operation contracts (discussed in Chapter 13), and possibly support estimation (for example, macroestimation with unadjusted function points and COCOMO II).

Note that it is not necessary to create SSDs for all scenarios of all use cases—at least not at the same time. Rather, create them only for some chosen scenarios of the current iteration.

Finally, it should only take a few minutes or an half hour to create the SSDs.

Discipline	Artifact	Incep.	Elab.	Const.	Trans.
	Iteration→	I1	E1..En	C1..Cn	T1..T2
Business Modeling	Domain Model		s		
Requirements	*Use-Case Model (SSDs)*	s	r		
	Vision	s	r		
	Supplementary Specification	s	r		
	Glossary	s	r		
Design	Design Model		s	r	
	SW Architecture Document		s		
	Data Model		s	r	
Implementation	Implementation Model		s	r	r
Project Management	SW Development Plan	s	r	r	r
Testing	Test Model		s	r	
Environment	Development Case	s	r		

Table 9.1 Sample UP artifacts and timing. s - start; r - refine

9.11 Further Readings

Variations of diagrams that illustrate the I/O events for a system treated as a black box have been in widespread use for decades; for example, in telecommunications as call-flow diagrams. They were especially popularized in object-oriented methods via their use in the Fusion method [Coleman+94], which provided a detailed example of the relationship of SSDs and system operations to other analysis and design artifacts.

9.12   UP Artifacts

Sample relationships of SSDs to other artifacts are shown in Figure 9.6.

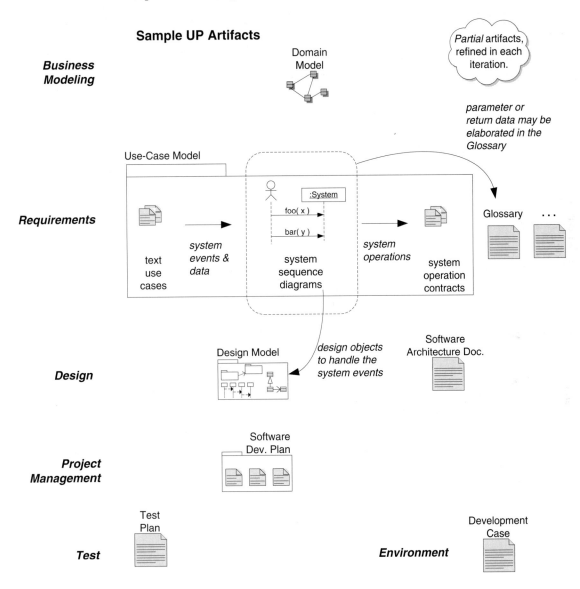

Figure 9.6 Sample UP artifact influence.

DOMAIN MODEL: VISUALIZING CONCEPTS

It's all very well in practice, but it will never work in theory.

—anonymous management maxim

Objectives

- Identify conceptual classes related to the current iteration requirements.
- Create an initial domain model.
- Distinguish between correct and incorrect attributes.
- Add *specification* conceptual classes, when appropriate.
- Compare and contrast conceptual and implementation views.

Introduction

A domain model is widely used as a source of inspiration for designing software objects, and will be a required input to several subsequent artifacts discussed in this book. Therefore, it is important to read this chapter if the subject of domain modeling is unfamiliar.

A domain model illustrates meaningful (to the modelers) conceptual classes in a problem domain; it is the most important artifact to create during object-oriented analysis.[1] This chapter explores introductory skills in creating domain

---

1. Use cases are an important requirements analysis artifact, but are not *object*-oriented. They emphasize a process view of the domain.

models. The following two chapters expand on domain modeling skills—adding attributes and associations.

Identifying a rich set of objects or conceptual classes is at the heart of object-oriented analysis, and well worth the effort in terms of payoff during the design and implementation work.

The identification of conceptual classes is part of an investigation of the problem domain. The UML contains notation in the form of class diagrams to illustrate domain models.

Key Idea

A domain model is a representation of real-world conceptual classes, not of software components. It is *not* a set of diagrams describing software classes, or software objects with responsibilities.

10.1 Domain Models

The quintessential *object*-oriented step in analysis or investigation is the decomposition of a domain of interest into individual conceptual classes or objects—the things we are aware of. A **domain model** is a *visual* representation of conceptual classes or real-world objects in a domain of interest [MO95, Fowler96]. They have also been called **conceptual models** (the term used in the first edition of this book), **domain object models**, and **analysis object models**.[2]

The UP defines a Domain Model[3] as one of the artifacts that may be created in the Business Modeling discipline.

Using UML notation, a domain model is illustrated with a set of **class diagrams** in which no operations are defined. It may show:

■ domain objects or conceptual classes

■ associations between conceptual classes

■ attributes of conceptual classes

For example, Figure 10.1 shows a partial domain model. It illustrates that the conceptual class of *Payment* and *Sale* are significant in this domain, that a *Pay-*

---

2. They are also related to conceptual entity relationship models, which are capable of showing purely conceptual views of domains, but that have been widely re-interpreted as data models for database design. Domain models are not data models.

3. Capitalization of Domain Model is used when I wish to emphasize it as an official model defined in the UP, vs. the general well-known concept of "domain models."

ment is related to a *Sale* in a way that is meaningful to note, and that a *Sale* has a date and time. The details of the notation are not important at this time.

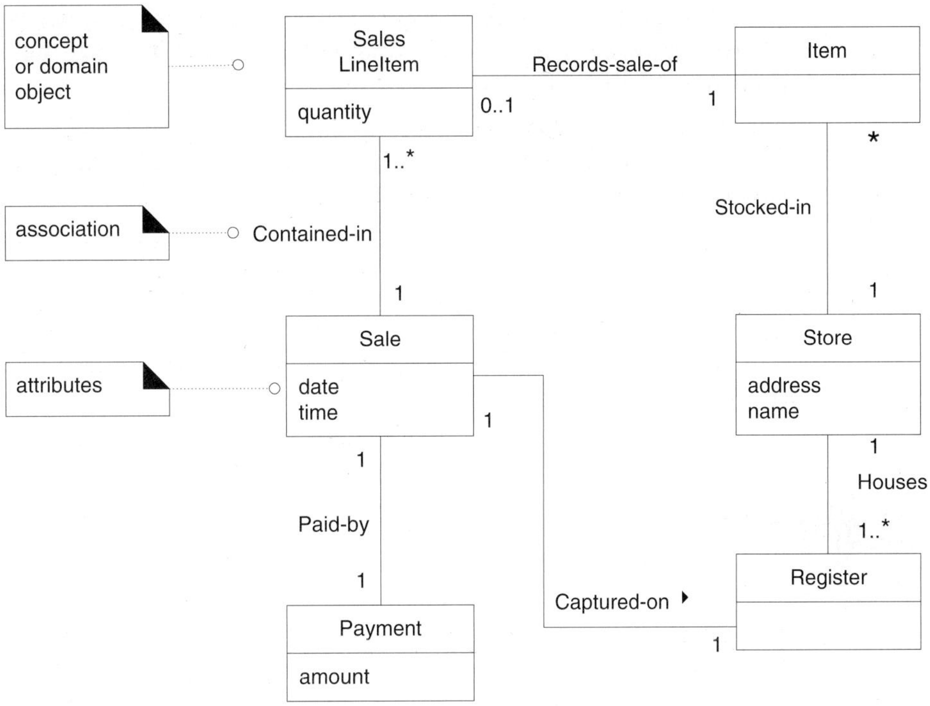

Figure 10.1 Partial domain model—a visual dictionary. The numbers at each end of the line indicate multiplicity, which is described in a subsequent chapter.

Key Idea: Domain Model—A Visual Dictionary of Abstractions

Please reflect on Figure 10.1 for a moment. It visualizes and relates some words or conceptual classes in the domain. It also depicts an *abstraction* of the conceptual classes, because there are many things one could communicate about registers, sales, and so forth. The model displays a partial view, or abstraction, and ignores uninteresting (to the modelers) details.

The information it illustrates (using UML notation) could alternatively have been conveyed in prose, in statements in the Glossary or elsewhere. But it is easy to comprehend the discrete elements and their relationships in this visual language, since a significant percentage of the brain participates in visual processing—it is a human strength.

Thus, the domain model may be considered a *visual dictionary* of the noteworthy abstractions, domain vocabulary, and information content of the domain.

Domain Models Are not Models of Software Components

A domain model, as shown in Figure 10.2, is a visualization of things in the real-world domain of interest, *not* of software components such as a Java or C++ class (see Figure 10.3), or software objects with responsibilities. Therefore, the following elements are not suitable in a domain model:

- Software artifacts, such as a window or a database, unless the domain being modeled is of software concepts, such as a model of graphical user interfaces.

- Responsibilities or methods.[4]

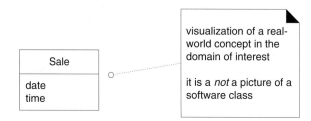

Figure 10.2 A domain model shows real-world conceptual classes, not software classes.

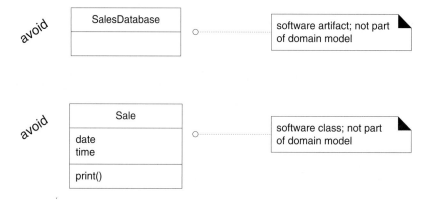

Figure 10.3 A domain model does not show software artifacts or classes.

---

4. In object modeling, we usually speak of responsibilities related to software components. And methods are purely a software concept. But, the domain model describes real-world concepts, not software components. Considering object responsibilities during *design* work is very important; it is just not part of this model. One valid case in which responsibilities may be shown in a domain model is if it includes human worker roles (such as Cashier), and the modeler wishes to record the responsibilities of these human workers.

Conceptual Classes

The domain model illustrates conceptual classes or vocabulary in the domain. Informally, a conceptual class is an idea, thing, or object. More formally, a conceptual class may be considered in terms of its symbol, intension, and extension [MO95] (see Figure 10.4).

- **Symbol**—words or images representing a conceptual class.

- **Intension**—the definition of a conceptual class.

- **Extension**—the set of examples to which the conceptual class applies.

For example, consider the conceptual class for the event of a purchase transaction. I may choose to name it by the symbol *Sale*. The intension of a *Sale* may state that it "represents the event of a purchase transaction, and has a date and time." The extension of *Sale* is all the examples of sales; in other words, the set of all sales.

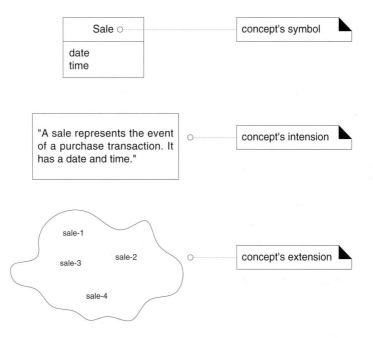

Figure 10.4 A conceptual class has a symbol, intension, and extension.

When creating a domain model, it is usually the symbol and intensional view of a conceptual class that are of most practical interest.

Domain Models and Decomposition

Software problems can be complex; decomposition—divide-and-conquer—is a common strategy to deal with this complexity by division of the problem space into comprehensible units. In **structured analysis**, the dimension of decomposition is by processes or *functions*. However, in object-oriented analysis, the dimension of decomposition is fundamentally by things or entities in the domain.

> A central distinction between object-oriented and structured analysis is: division by conceptual classes (objects) rather than division by functions.

Therefore, a primary analysis task is to identify different concepts in the problem domain and document the results in a domain model.

Conceptual Classes in the Sale Domain

For example, in the real-world domain of sales in a store, there are the conceptual classes of *Store, Register,* and *Sale.* Therefore, our domain model, shown in Figure 10.5, may include *Store, Register,* and *Sale.*

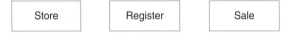

Figure 10.5 Partial domain model in the domain of the store.

10.2   Conceptual Class Identification

Our goal is to create a domain model of interesting or meaningful conceptual classes in the domain of interest (sales). In this case, that means concepts related to the use case *Process Sale*.

In iterative development, one incrementally builds a domain model over several iterations in the elaboration phase. In each, the domain model is limited to the prior and current scenarios under consideration, rather than a "big bang" model which early on attempts to capture all possible conceptual classes and relationships. For example, this iteration is limited to a simplified cash-only *Process Sale* scenario; therefore, a partial domain model will be created to reflect just that—not more.

The central task is therefore to identify conceptual classes related to the scenarios under design.

The following is a useful guideline in identifying conceptual classes:

> It is better to overspecify a domain model with lots of fine-grained conceptual classes than to underspecify it.

Do not think that a domain model is better if it has fewer conceptual classes; quite the opposite tends to be true.

It is common to miss conceptual classes during the initial identification step, and to discover them later during the consideration of attributes or associations, or during design work. When found, they may be added to the domain model.

Do not exclude a conceptual class simply because the requirements do not indicate any obvious need to remember information about it (a criterion common in data modeling for relational database design, but not relevant to domain modeling), or because the conceptual class has no attributes.

It is valid to have attributeless conceptual classes, or conceptual classes which have a purely behavioral role in the domain instead of an information role.

Strategies to Identify Conceptual Classes

Two techniques are presented in the following sections:

1. Use a conceptual class category list.

2. Identify noun phrases.

Another excellent technique for domain modeling is the use of **analysis patterns**, which are existing partial domain models created by experts, using published resources such as *Analysis Patterns* [Fowler96] and *Data Model Patterns* [Hay96].

Use a Conceptual Class Category List

Start the creation of a domain model by making a list of candidate conceptual classes. Table 10.1 contains many common categories that are usually worth considering, though not in any particular order of importance. Examples are drawn from the store and airline reservation domains.

Conceptual Class Category	Examples
physical or tangible objects	*Register* *Airplane*
specifications, designs, or descriptions of things	*ProductSpecification* *FlightDescription*
places	*Store* *Airport*
transactions	*Sale, Payment* *Reservation*
transaction line items	*SalesLineItem*
roles of people	*Cashier* *Pilot*
containers of other things	*Store, Bin* *Airplane*
things in a container	*Item* *Passenger*
other computer or electro-mechanical systems external to the system	*CreditPaymentAuthorizationSystem* *AirTrafficControl*
abstract noun concepts	*Hunger* *Acrophobia*
organizations	*SalesDepartment* *ObjectAirline*
events	*Sale, Payment, Meeting* *Flight, Crash, Landing*
processes (often *not* represented as a concept, but may be)	*SellingAProduct* *BookingASeat*
rules and policies	*RefundPolicy* *CancellationPolicy*
catalogs	*ProductCatalog* *PartsCatalog*

Conceptual Class Category	Examples
records of finance, work, contracts, legal matters	*Receipt, Ledger, EmploymentContract MaintenanceLog*
financial instruments and services	*LineOfCredit Stock*
manuals, documents, reference papers, books	*DailyPriceChangeList RepairManual*

Table 10.1 Conceptual Class Category List.

Finding Conceptual Classes with Noun Phrase Identification

Another useful technique (because of its simplicity) suggested in [Abbot83] is linguistic analysis: identify the nouns and noun phrases in textual descriptions of a domain, and consider them as candidate conceptual classes or attributes.

Care must be applied with this method; a mechanical noun-to-class mapping isn't possible, and words in natural languages are ambiguous.

Nevertheless, it is another source of inspiration. The fully dressed use cases are an excellent description to draw from for this analysis. For example, the current scenario of the *Process Sale* use case can be used.

Main Success Scenario (or Basic Flow):
1. **Customer** arrives at a **POS checkout** with **goods** and/or **services** to purchase.
2. **Cashier** starts a new **sale**.
3. **Cashier** enters **item identifier**.
4. System records **sale line item** and presents **item description**, **price**, and running **total**. Price calculated from a set of price rules.
Cashier repeats steps 2-3 until indicates done.
5. System presents total with **taxes** calculated.
6. Cashier tells Customer the total, and asks for **payment**.
7. Customer pays and System handles payment.
8. System logs the completed **sale** and sends sale and payment information to the external **Accounting** (for accounting and **commissions**) and **Inventory** systems (to update inventory).
9. System presents **receipt**.
10. Customer leaves with receipt and goods (if any).

Extensions (or Alternative Flows):
. . .
7a. Paying by cash:
   1. Cashier enters the cash **amount tendered**.

> 2. System presents the **balance due**, and releases the **cash drawer**.
> 3. Cashier deposits cash tendered and returns balance in cash to Customer.
> 4. System records the cash payment.

The domain model is a visualization of noteworthy domain concepts and vocabulary. Where are those terms found? In the use cases. Thus, they are a rich source to mine via noun phrase identification.

Some of these noun phrases are candidate conceptual classes, some may refer to conceptual classes that are ignored in this iteration (for example, "Accounting" and "commissions"), and some may be attributes of conceptual classes. Please see the subsequent section and chapter on attributes for advice on distinguishing between the two.

A weakness of this approach is the imprecision of natural language; different noun phrases may represent the same conceptual class or attribute, among other ambiguities. Nevertheless, it is recommended in combination with the *Conceptual Class Category List* technique.

10.3   Candidate Conceptual Classes for the Sales Domain

From the Conceptual Class Category List and noun phrase analysis, a list is generated of candidate conceptual classes for the domain. The list is constrained to the requirements and simplifications currently under consideration—the simplified scenario of *Process Sale*.

Register	*ProductSpecification*
Item	*SalesLineItem*
Store	*Cashier*
Sale	*Customer*
Payment	*Manager*
ProductCatalog	

There is no such thing as a "correct" list. It is a somewhat arbitrary collection of abstractions and domain vocabulary that the modelers consider noteworthy. Nevertheless, by following the identification strategies, similar lists will be produced by different modelers.

Report Objects—Include Receipt in the Model?

A receipt is a record of a sale and payment and a relatively prominent conceptual class in the domain, so should it be shown in the model?

Here are some factors to consider:

- A receipt is a report of a sale. In general, showing a report of other information in a domain model is not useful since all its information is derived from other sources; it duplicates information found elsewhere. This is one reason to exclude it.

- A receipt has a special role in terms of the business rules: it usually confers the right to the bearer of the receipt to return bought items. This is a reason to show it in the model.

Since item returns are not being considered in this iteration, *Receipt* will be excluded. During the iteration that tackles the *Handle Returns* use case, it would be justified to include it.

10.4   Domain Modeling Guidelines

How to Make a Domain Model

Apply the following steps to create a domain model:

---

1. List the candidate conceptual classes using the Conceptual Class Category List and noun phrase identification techniques related to the current requirements under consideration.

2. Draw them in a domain model.

3. Add the associations necessary to record relationships for which there is a need to preserve some memory (discussed in a subsequent chapter).

4. Add the attributes necessary to fulfill the information requirements (discussed in a subsequent chapter).

An adjunct useful method is to learn and copy analysis patterns, which are discussed in a later chapter.

On Naming and Modeling Things: The Mapmaker

The mapmaker strategy applies to both maps and domain models.

> Make a domain model in the spirit of how a cartographer or mapmaker works:
>
> ■ Use the existing names in the territory.
>
> ■ Exclude irrelevant features.
>
> ■ Do not add things that are not there.

A domain model is a kind of map of concepts or things in a domain. This spirit emphasizes the analytical role of a domain model, and suggests the following:

■ A mapmaker uses the names of the territory—they do not change the names of cities on a map. For a domain model, this means *use the vocabulary of the domain when naming conceptual classes and attributes*. For example, if developing a model for a library, name the customer a *"Borrower"* or *"Patron"*—the terms used by the library staff.

■ A mapmaker deletes things from a map if they are not considered relevant to the purpose of the map; for example, topography or populations need not be shown. Similarly, a domain model may exclude conceptual classes in the problem domain not pertinent to the requirements. For example, we may exclude *Pen* and *PaperBag* from our domain model (for the current set of requirements) since they do not have any obvious noteworthy role.

■ A mapmaker does not show things that are not there, such as a mountain that does not exist. Similarly, the domain model should exclude things *not* in the problem domain under consideration.

The principle is also named the *Use the Domain Vocabulary* strategy [Coad95].

A Common Mistake in Identifying Conceptual Classes

Perhaps the most common mistake when creating a domain model is to represent something as an attribute when it should have been a concept. A rule of thumb to help prevent this mistake is:

> If we do not think of some conceptual class X as a number or text in the real world, X is probably a conceptual class, not an attribute.

As an example, should *store* be an attribute of *Sale*, or a separate conceptual class *Store*?

In the real world, a store is not considered a number or text—the term suggests a legal entity, an organization, and something occupies space. Therefore, *Store* should be a concept.

As another example, consider the domain of airline reservations. Should *destination* be an attribute of *Flight*, or a separate conceptual class *Airport*?

Flight	or... ?	Flight	Airport
destination			name

In the real world, a destination airport is not considered a number or text—it is a massive thing that occupies space. Therefore, *Airport* should be a concept.

> If in doubt, make it a separate concept. Attributes should be fairly rare in a domain model.

10.5 Resolving Similar Conceptual Classes—Register vs. "POST"

POST stands for point-of-sale terminal. In computerese, a terminal is any endpoint device in a system, such as a client PC, a wireless networked PDA, and so forth. In earlier times, long before POSTs, a store maintained a *register*—a book that logged sales and payments. Eventually, this was automated in a mechanical "cash register." Today, a POST fulfills the role of the register (see Figure 10.6).

A register is a thing that records sales and payments, but so is a POST. However, the term *register* seems somewhat more abstract and less implementation oriented than *POST*. So, in the domain model, should the symbol *Register* be used instead of *POST*?

> First, as a rule of thumb, a domain model is not absolutely correct or wrong, but more or less useful; it is a tool of communication.

By the mapmaker principle, *"POST"* is a term familiar in the territory, so it is a useful symbol from the point of view of familiarity and communication. By the goal of creating models that represent abstractions and are implementation independent, *Register* is appealing and useful.[5] *Register* may be fairly considered to represent both the conceptual class of a place to register sales, and/or an abstraction of various kinds of terminals, such as a POST.

Both choices have merit; *Register* has been chosen in this case study somewhat arbitrarily, but *POST* would also have been understandable to the stakeholders.

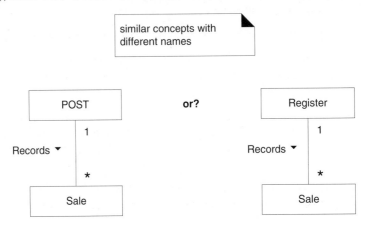

Figure 10.6 POST and register are similar conceptual classes.

10.6 Modeling the *Unreal* World

Some software systems are for domains that find very little analogy in natural or business domains; software for telecommunications is an example. It is still possible to create a domain model in these domains, but it requires a high degree of abstraction and stepping back from familiar designs.

For example, here are some candidate conceptual classes related to a telecommunication switch: *Message, Connection, Port, Dialog, Route, Protocol.*

10.7 Specification or Description Conceptual Classes

The following discussion may at first seem related to a rare, highly specialized issue. However, it turns out that the need for specification conceptual classes (as will be defined) is common in many domain models. Thus, it is emphasized.

---

5. Note that in earlier times a *register* was just one possible implementation of how to record sales. The term has acquired a generalized meaning over time.

Assume the following:

- An *Item* instance represents a physical item in a store; as such, it may even have a serial number.

- An *Item* has a description, price, and itemID, which are not recorded anywhere else.

- Everyone working in the store has amnesia.

- Every time a real physical item is sold, a corresponding software instance of *Item* is deleted from "software land."

With these assumptions, what happens in the following scenario?

There is strong demand for the popular new vegetarian burger—ObjectBurger. The store sells out, implying that all *Item* instances of ObjectBurgers are deleted from computer memory.

Now, here is the heart of the problem: If someone asks, "How much do Object-Burgers cost?", no one can answer, because the memory of their price was attached to inventoried instances, which were deleted as they were sold.

Notice also that the current model, if implemented in software as described, has duplicate data and is space-inefficient because the description, price, and itemID are duplicated for every *Item* instance of the same product.

The Need for Specification or Description Conceptual Classes

The preceding problem illustrates the need for a concept of objects that are specifications or descriptions of other things. To solve the *Item* problem, what is needed is a *ProductSpecification* (or *ItemSpecification, ProductDescription, ...*) conceptual class that records information about items. A *ProductSpecification* does not represent an *Item*, it represents a description of information *about* items. Note that even if all inventoried items are sold and their corresponding *Item* software instances are deleted, the *ProductSpecifications* still remain.

Description or specification objects are strongly related to the things they describe. In a domain model, it is common to state that an *XSpecification Describes an X* (see Figure 10.7).

The need for specification conceptual classes is common in sales and product domains. It is also common in manufacturing, where a *description* of a manufactured thing is required that is distinct from the thing itself. Time and space have been taken in motivating specification conceptual classes because they are very common; it is not a rare modeling concept.

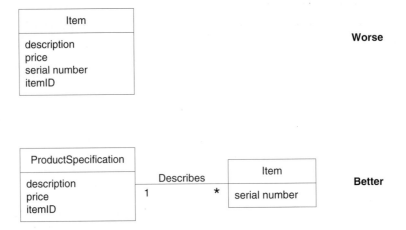

Figure 10.7 Specifications or descriptions about other things. The "*" means a multiplicity of "many." It indicates that one *ProductSpecification* may describe many (*) *Items*.

When Are Specification Conceptual Classes Required?

The following guideline suggests when to use specifications:

Add a specification or description conceptual class (for example, *ProductSpecification*) when:

- There needs to be a description about an item or service, independent of the current existence of any examples of those items or services.

- Deleting instances of things they describe (for example, *Item*) results in a loss of information that needs to be maintained, due to the incorrect association of information with the deleted thing.

- It reduces redundant or duplicated information.

Another Specification Example

As another example, consider an airline company that suffers a fatal crash of one of its planes. Assume that all the flights are cancelled for six months pending completion of an investigation. Also assume that when flights are cancelled, their corresponding *Flight* software objects are deleted from computer memory. Therefore, after the crash, all *Flight* software objects are deleted.

If the only record of what airport a flight goes to is in the *Flight* software instances, which represent specific flights for a particular date and time, then there is no longer a record of what flight routes the airline has.

To solve this problem, a *FlightDescription* (or *FlightSpecification*) is required that describes a flight and its route, even when a particular flight is not scheduled (see Figure 10.8).

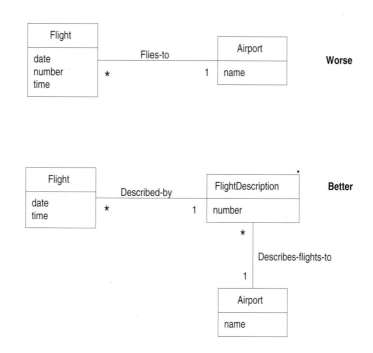

Figure 10.8 Specifications about other things.

Descriptions of Services

Note that the prior example is about a service (a flight) rather than a good (such as a veggieburger). Descriptions of services or service plans are commonly needed.

As another example, a mobile phone company sells packages such as "bronze," "gold," and so forth. It is necessary to have the concept of a description of the package (a kind of service plan describing rates per minute, wireless Internet content, the cost, and so forth) separate from the concept of an actual sold package (such as "gold package sold to Craig Larman on Jan 1, 2002 at $55 per month"). Marketing needs to define and record this service plan or *MobileCommunicationsPackageDescription* before any are sold.

10.8   UML Notation, Models, and Methods: Multiple Perspectives

The UP defines something called a Domain Model, which is illustrated with UML notation. However, there is no term "Domain Model" to be found in the official UML documentation. This points to an important insight:

> The UML simply describes raw diagram types, such as class diagrams and sequence diagrams. It does not superimpose a method or modeling perspective on these. Rather, a process (such as the UP) applies raw UML in the context of methodologist-defined models.

For example, raw UML class diagramming notation can be used to create pictures of domain conceptual classes (a domain model), software classes, relational database tables, and so forth.

Thus, do not confuse the basic UML diagram notation with its application to visualizing various kinds of models defined by methodologists (see Figure 10.9). This point applies not only to UML class diagrams, but to most UML notation.

As another example of raw diagrams being interpreted differently in different models, UML sequence diagrams can be used to illustrate messaging between software objects (as in the UP Design Model), or interaction between people and parties in the real world (as in the UP Business Object Model).

This insight was emphasized in the Syntropy object-oriented method [CD94], and reiterated by Martin Fowler in *UML Distilled* [FS00]. That is, the same diagramming notation may be used for three perspectives and types of models:

1. **Essential or conceptual perspective**—the diagrams are interpreted as describing things in the real world or domain of interest.

2. **Specification perspective**—the diagrams (using the same notation as for essential models) are interpreted as describing software abstractions or components with specifications and interfaces, but no commitment to a particular implementation (for example, not specifically a class in C# or Java).

3. **Implementation perspective**—the diagrams (using the same notation as for essential models) are interpreted as describing software implementations in a particular technology and language (such as Java).

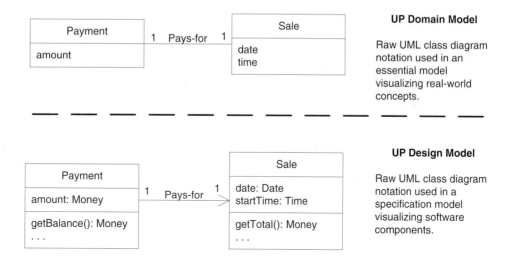

Figure 10.9 Raw UML notation is applied in different perspectives and models defined by a process or method.

Superimposing Terminology: UML vs. Methods

In the raw UML, the rectangular boxes shown in Figure 10.9 are called **classes**, but note that in the UML, this term encompasses a variety of phenomenon—physical things, software things, events, and so forth.[6] A process or method will superimpose alternative terminology on top of the UML. For example, in the UP, when the UML boxes are drawn in the Domain Model, they may be called **domain concepts** or **conceptual classes**; the Domain Model offers a conceptual perspective. In the UP, when UML boxes are drawn in the Design Model, they are officially called **design classes**; the Design Model offers a specification or implementation perspective, as desired by the modeler.

Regardless of the definition, the bottom line is that it is useful to distinguish between the perspective of an analyst looking at real-world concepts such as a sale (a conceptual perspective), and software designers specifying software components such as a *Sale* software class (a specification or implementation perspective).

The UML can be used to illustrate both perspectives with very similar notation and terminology, so it is important to bear in mind which perspective is being taken.

---

6. A UML class is a special case of the very general UML model element **classifier**—something with structural features and/or behavior, including classes, actors, interfaces, and use cases.

To keep things clear, this book will use class-related terms as follows, which is consistent with the UML and the UP:

- **Conceptual class**—real-world concept or thing. A conceptual or essential perspective. The UP Domain Model contains conceptual classes.

- **Software class**—a class representing a specification or implementation perspective of a software component, regardless of the process or method.

- **Design class**—a member of the UP Design Model. It is a synonym for software class, but for some reason I wish to emphasize that it is a class in the Design Model. The UP allows a design class to be either a specification or implementation perspective, as desired by the modeler.

- **Implementation class**—a class implemented in an object-oriented language such as Java.

- **Class**—as in the UML, the general term representing either a real-world thing (a conceptual class) or software thing (a software class).

10.9 Lowering the Representational Gap

Please consider Figure 10.10. Why do books and educators discussing object design common only show the use of software classes whose names reflect domain vocabulary? Why choose a software class name such as *Sale*, and what does a *Sale* do?

Simply, choosing names that reflect the domain vocabulary (*Sale*) enhances quick comprehension and provides a clue as to what to expect from the chunk of code in a *Sale* software class. We have a mental or domain model of the domain in question (for example, a store selling things). In the real world, we know that a sale has a date. Consequently, if we create a Java class named *Sale*, and give it the responsibility of knowing about a real sale and its date, then the Java class *Sale* somewhat corresponds to our mental or domain model of the real domain; that is, it appeals to our "intuitions" of the domain.

The Domain Model provides a visual dictionary of the domain vocabulary and concepts from which to draw inspiration for the naming of some things in the software design.

This relates to the issue of **representational gap** or semantic gap—the gap between our mental model of the domain and its representation in software.

UP Domain Model
Stakeholder's view of the noteworthy concepts in the domain.

A Payment in the Domain Model is a concept, but a Payment in the Design Model is a software class. They are not the same thing, but the former *inspired* the naming and definition of the latter.

This reduces the representational gap.

This is one of the big ideas in object technology.

Payment				Sale
amount	1	Pays-for	1	date
				time

inspires objects and names in

Payment				Sale
amount: Money	1	Pays-for	1	date: Date
				startTime: Time
getBalance(): Money				getTotal(): Money
				. . .

UP Design Model
The object-oriented developer has taken inspiration from the real world domain in creating software classes.

Therefore, the representational gap between how stakeholders conceive the domain, and its representation in software, has been lowered.

Figure 10.10 In object design and programming it is common to create software classes whose names and information is inspired from the real world domain.

At one extreme, we could directly program the NextGen POS application in raw binary code to invoke the processor instruction set. We understand that the gap in representations is huge, and there will be a real cost—albeit hard to quantify—in software with such a large representational gap because it is hard to comprehend or relate to the problem domain. Closer to the other end of the spectrum are object technologies that allow us to chunk code into classes whose names reflect the kind of chunking we perceive in the domain. In the real world we perceive a "chunk" (or event) called a sale, so in software land we have a software class called *Sale*. This closer one-to-one mapping between the domain vocabulary and our software vocabulary and its chunking reduces the representational gap. This speeds comprehension of existing code (because it works in ways we expect, knowing the domain) and suggests "natural" ways to extend the code in ways that similarly correspond to the domain, or appeal to our intuitions of the domain. Put simply, the software model reminds us of the conceptual or mental model, and works in predictable ways.

There is a practical advantage to software models that reduce the representational gap. Most software engineers know this is true, even if it is hard to quantify. Indeed, a proof of this is that Java obfuscators make source code hard to practically reverse-engineer from bytecode by changing the names of Java classes and methods so they are unintelligible, and thus no longer appeal to our intuitions of the domain, even though the control and data structures are unchanged.

Of course, object technology is also of value because it can support the design of elegant, loosely coupled systems that scale and extend easily, as will be explored in the remainder of the book. A lowered representational gap is useful, but arguably secondary to the advantage of objects to support ease of change and extension, and their support to manage and hide complexity.

10.10   Example: The NextGen POS Domain Model

The list of conceptual classes generated for the NextGen POS domain may be represented graphically (see Figure 10.11) to show the start of the Domain Model.

Figure 10.11 Initial Domain Model.

Consideration of attributes and associations for the Domain Model will be deferred to subsequent chapters.

10.11   Domain Models Within the UP

As suggested in the example of Table 10.2, a Domain Model is usually both started and completed in elaboration.

Inception

Domain models are not strongly motivated in inception, since inception's purpose is not to do a serious investigation, but rather to decide if the project is worth deeper investigation in an elaboration phase.

Discipline	Artifact Iteration→	Incep. I1	Elab. E1..En	Const. C1..Cn	Trans. T1..T2
Business Modeling	*Domain Model*		s		
Requirements	Use-Case Model (SSDs)	s	r		
	Vision	s	r		
	Supplementary Specification	s	r		
	Glossary	s	r		
Design	Design Model		s	r	
	SW Architecture Document		s		
	Data Model		s	r	
Implementation	Implementation Model		s	r	r
Project Management	SW Development Plan	s	r	r	r
Testing	Test Model		s	r	
Environment	Development Case	s	r		

Table 10.2 Sample UP artifacts and timing. s - start; r - refine

Elaboration

The Domain Model is primarily created during elaboration iterations, when the need is highest to understand the noteworthy concepts and map some to software classes during design work.

Although ironically a significant number of pages will be devoted to explaining domain object modeling, in experienced hands the development of a (partial, incrementally growing) domain model in each iteration should only take a few hours. This is further shortened by the use of predefined analysis patterns.

The UP Business Object Model vs. Domain Model

The UP Domain Model is an official variation of the less common UP Business Object Model (BOM). The UP BOM—not to be confused with how other people or methods may define a BOM, which is a widely used term with different meanings—is a kind of enterprise model used to describe the entire business. It may be used when doing business process engineering or reengineering, independent of any one software application (such as the NextGen POS). To quote:

> [The UP BOM] serves as an abstraction of how business workers and business entities need to be related and how they need to collaborate in order to perform the business. [RUP]

The BOM is represented with several different diagrams (class, activity, and sequence) that illustrate how the entire enterprise runs (or should run). It is most useful if doing enterprise-wide business process engineering, but that is a less common activity than creating a single software application.

Consequently, the UP defines the Domain Model as the more commonly created subset artifact or specialization of the BOM. To quote:

> You can choose to develop an "incomplete" business object model, focusing on explaining "things" and products important to a domain. ... This is often referred to as a domain model. [RUP]

10.12   Further Readings

Odell's *Object-Oriented Methods: A Foundation* provides a solid introduction to conceptual domain modeling. Cook and Daniel's *Designing Object Systems* is also useful.

Fowler's *Analysis Patterns* offers worthwhile patterns in domain models, and is definitely recommended. Another good book that describes patterns in domain models is Hay's *Data Model Patterns: Conventions of Thought*. Advice from data modeling experts who understand the distinction between pure conceptual models and database schema models can be very useful for domain object modeling.

Java Modeling in Color with UML [CDL99] has more relevant domain modeling advice than the title suggests. The authors identify common patterns in related types and their associations; the color aspect is really a visualization of the common categories of these types, such as *descriptions* (blue), *roles* (yellow), and *moment-intervals* (pink). Color is used to aid in seeing the patterns.

Since the original work by Abbot, linguistic analysis has acquired more sophisticated techniques for object-oriented analysis, generally called natural language modeling, or a variant. See [Moreno97] as an example.

10.13   UP Artifacts

Artifact influence emphasizing the Domain Model is shown in Figure 10.12.

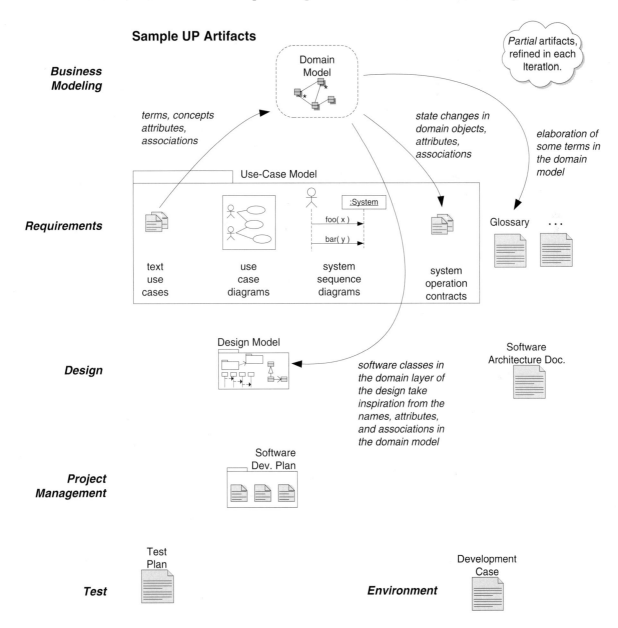

Figure 10.12 Sample UP artifact influence.

DOMAIN MODEL: ADDING ASSOCIATIONS

Objectives

- Identify associations for a domain model.
- Distinguish between need-to-know and comprehension-only associations.

Introduction

It is useful to identify those associations of conceptual classes that are needed to satisfy the information requirements of the current scenarios under development, and which aid in comprehending the domain model. This chapter explores the identification of suitable associations, and adds associations to the domain model for the NextGen case study.

11.1   Associations

An **association** is a relationship between types (or more specifically, instances of those types) that indicates some meaningful and interesting connection (see Figure 11.1).

In the UML associations are defined as "the semantic relationship between two or more classifiers that involve connections among their instances."

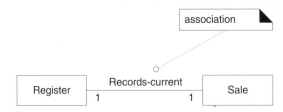

Figure 11.1 Associations.

Criteria for Useful Associations

Associations worth noting usually imply knowledge of a relationship that needs to be preserved for some duration—it could be milliseconds or years, depending on context. In other words, between what objects do we need to have some memory of a relationship? For example, do we need to remember what *SalesLineItem* instances are associated with a *Sale* instance? Definitely, otherwise it would not be possible to reconstruct a sale, print a receipt, or calculate a sale total.

Consider including the following associations in a domain model:

■ Associations for which knowledge of the relationship needs to be preserved for some duration ("need-to-know" associations).

■ Associations derived from the Common Associations List.

By contrast, do we need to have memory of a relationship between a current *Sale* and a *Manager*? No, the requirements do not suggest that any such relationship is needed. It is not wrong to show a relationship between a *Sale* and *Manager*, but it is not compelling or useful in the context of our requirements.

This is an important point. On a domain model with n different conceptual classes, there can be n·(n-1) associations to other conceptual classes—a potentially large number. Many lines on the diagram will add "visual noise" and make it less comprehensible. Therefore, be parsimonious about adding association lines. Use the criterion guidelines suggested in this chapter.

11.2   The UML Association Notation

An association is represented as a line between classes with an association name. The association is inherently bidirectional, meaning that from instances of either class, logical traversal to the other is possible.

This traversal is purely abstract; it is *not* a statement about connections between software entities.

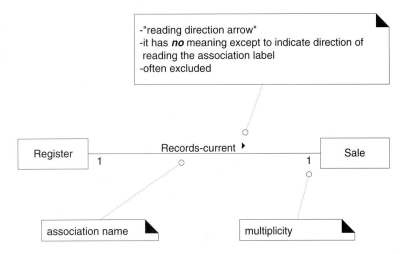

Figure 11.2 The UML notation for associations.

The ends of an association may contain a multiplicity expression indicating the numerical relationship between instances of the classes.

An optional "reading direction arrow" indicates the direction to read the association name; it does not indicate direction of visibility or navigation.

If not present, it is conventional to read the association from left to right or top to bottom, although the UML does not make this a rule (see Figure 11.2).

The reading direction arrow has no meaning in terms of the model; it is only an aid to the reader of the diagram.

11.3 Finding Associations—Common Associations List

Start the addition of associations by using the list in Table 11.1.

It contains common categories that are usually worth considering. Examples are drawn from the store and airline reservation domains.

Category	Examples
A is a physical part of B	*Drawer—Register (or more specifically, a POST)* *Wing—Airplane*
A is a logical part of B	*SalesLineItem—Sale* *FlightLeg—FlightRoute*
A is physically contained in/on B	*Register—Store, Item—Shelf* *Passenger—Airplane*
A is logically contained in B	*ItemDescription—Catalog* *Flight—FlightSchedule*
A is a description for B	*ItemDescription—Item* *FlightDescription—Flight*
A is a line item of a transaction or report B	*SalesLineItem—Sale* *MaintenanceJob—Maintenance-Log*
A is known/logged/recorded/reported/captured in B	*Sale—Register* *Reservation—FlightManifest*
A is a member of B	*Cashier—Store* *Pilot—Airline*
A is an organizational subunit of B	*Department—Store* *Maintenance—Airline*
A uses or manages B	*Cashier—Register* *Pilot—Airplane*
A communicates with B	*Customer—Cashier* *ReservationAgent—Passenger*
A is related to a transaction B	*Customer—Payment* *Passenger—Ticket*
A is a transaction related to another transaction B	*Payment—Sale* *Reservation—Cancellation*
A is next to B	*SalesLineItem—SalesLineItem* *City—City*

Category	Examples
A is owned by B	*Register—Store* *Plane—Airline*
A is an event related to B	*Sale—Customer, Sale—Store* *Departure—Flight*

Table 11.1 Common Associations List.

High-Priority Associations

Here are some high-priority association categories that are invariably useful to include in a domain model:

- A is a *physical or logical part* of B.
- A is *physically or logically contained* in/on B.
- A is *recorded in* B.

11.4 Association Guidelines

- Focus on those associations for which knowledge of the relationship needs to be preserved for some duration ("need-to-know" associations).
- It is more important to identify *conceptual classes* than to identify associations.
- Too many associations tend to confuse a domain model rather than illuminate it. Their discovery can be time-consuming, with marginal benefit.
- Avoid showing redundant or derivable associations.

11.5 Roles

Each end of an association is called a **role**. Roles may optionally have:

- name
- multiplicity expression
- navigability

Multiplicity is examined next, and the other two features are discussed in later chapters.

Multiplicity

Multiplicity defines how many instances of a class *A* can be associated with one instance of a class *B* (see Figure 11.3).

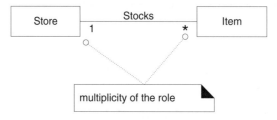

Figure 11.3 Multiplicity on an association.

For example, a single instance of a *Store* can be associated with "many" (zero or more, indicated by the *) *Item* instances.

Some examples of multiplicity expressions are shown in Figure 11.4.

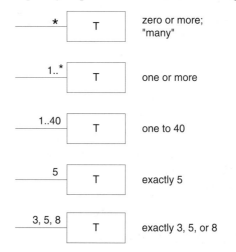

Figure 11.4 Multiplicity values.

The multiplicity value communicates how many instances can be validly associated with another, at a particular moment, rather than over a span of time. For example, it is possible that a used car could be repeatedly sold back to used car dealers over time. But at any particular moment, the car is only *Stocked-by* <u>one</u> dealer. The car is not *Stocked-by* <u>many</u> dealers at any particular moment. Similarly, in countries with monogamy laws, a person can be *Married-to* only <u>one</u> other person at any particular moment, even though over a span of time, they may be married to <u>many</u> persons.

The multiplicity value is dependent on our interest as a modeler and software developer, because it communicates a domain constraint that will be (or could be) reflected in software. See Figure 11.5 for an example and explanation.

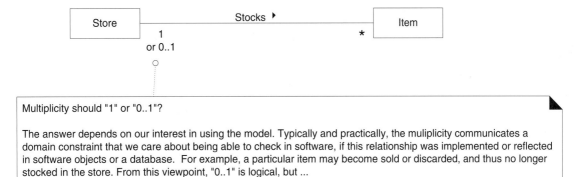

Multiplicity should "1" or "0..1"?

The answer depends on our interest in using the model. Typically and practically, the muliplicity communicates a domain constraint that we care about being able to check in software, if this relationship was implemented or reflected in software objects or a database. For example, a particular item may become sold or discarded, and thus no longer stocked in the store. From this viewpoint, "0..1" is logical, but ...

Do we care about that viewpoint? If this relationship was implemented in software, we would probably want to ensure that an *Item* software instance would always be related to 1 particular *Store* instance, otherwise it indicates a fault or corruption in the software elements or data.

This partial domain model does not represent software objects, but the multiplicities record constraints whose practical value is usually related to our interest in building software or databases (that reflect our real-world domain) with validity checks. From this viewpoint, "1" may be the desired value.

Figure 11.5 Multiplicity is context dependent.

Rumbaugh gives another example of *Person* and *Company* in the *Works-for* association [Rumbaugh91]. Indicating if a *Person* instance works for one or many *Company* instances is dependent on the context of the model; the tax department is interested in *many*; a union probably only *one*. The choice usually practically depends on whom we are building the software for, and thus the valid multiplicities in an implementation.

11.6   How Detailed Should Associations Be?

Associations are important, but a common pitfall in creating domain models is to spend too much time during investigation trying to discover them.

It is critical to appreciate the following:

> Finding *conceptual classes* is more important than finding associations. The majority of time spent in domain model creation should be devoted to identifying conceptual classes, not associations.

11.7   Naming Associations

> Name an association based on a *TypeName-VerbPhrase-TypeName* format where the verb phrase creates a sequence that is readable and meaningful in the model context.

Association names should start with a capital letter, since an association represents a classifier of links between instances; in the UML, classifiers should start with a capital letter. Two common and equally legal formats for a compound association name are:

■ *Paid-by*

■ *PaidBy*

In Figure 11.6, the default direction to read an association name is left to right or top to bottom. This is not a UML default, but a common convention.

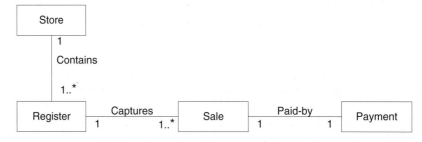

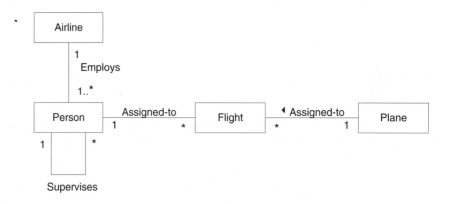

Figure 11.6 Association names.

11.8 Multiple Associations Between Two Types

Two types may have multiple associations between them; this is not uncommon. There is no outstanding example in our POS case study, but an example from the domain of the airline is the relationships between a *Flight* (or perhaps more precisely, a *FlightLeg*) and an *Airport* (see Figure 11.7); the flying-to and flying-from associations are distinctly different relationships, which should be shown separately.

Figure 11.7 Multiple associations.

11.9 Associations and Implementation

During domain modeling, an association is *not* a statement about data flows, instance variables, or object connections in a software solution; it is a statement that a relationship is meaningful in a purely conceptual sense—in the real world. Practically speaking, many of these relationships will typically be implemented in software as paths of navigation and visibility (both in the Design Model and Data Model), but their presence in a conceptual (or essential) view of a domain model does not require their implementation.

When creating a domain model, we may define associations that are not necessary during implementation. Conversely, we may discover associations that need to be implemented but were missed during domain modeling. In these cases, the domain model can be updated to reflect these discoveries.

Suggestion

Should prior investigative models such as a domain model be updated with insights (such as new associations) revealed during implementation work? Do not bother unless there is some future practical use for the model. If it is just (as is sometimes the case) a temporary artifact used to provide inspiration for a later step, and will not be meaningfully used later on, why update it? Avoid making or updating any documentation or model unless there is a concrete justification for future use.

Later on we will discuss ways to implement associations in an object-oriented programming language (the most common is to use an attribute that references an instance of the associated class), but for now, it is valuable to think of them as purely conceptual expressions, *not* statements about a database or software solution. As always, deferring design considerations frees us from extraneous information and decisions while doing pure "analysis" investigations and maximizes our design options later on.

11.10 NextGen POS Domain Model Associations

We can now add associations to our POS domain model. We should add those associations which the requirements (for example, use cases) suggest or imply a need to remember, or which otherwise are strongly suggested in our perception of the problem domain. When tackling a new problem, the common categories of associations presented earlier should be reviewed and considered, as they represent many of the relevant associations that typically need to be recorded.

Unforgettable Relationships in the Store

The following sample of associations is justified in terms of a need-to-know. It is based on the use cases currently under consideration.

Register Records Sale	To know the current sale, generate a total, print a receipt.
Sale Paid-by Payment	To know if the sale has been paid, relate the amount tendered to the sale total, and print a receipt.
ProductCatalog Records ProductSpecification	To retrieve an *ProductSpecification*, given an itemID.

Applying the Category of Associations Checklist

We will run through the checklist, based on previously identified types, considering the current use case requirements.

Category	System
A is a physical part of B	*Register—CashDrawer*
A is a logical part of B	*SalesLineItem—Sale*
A is physically contained in/on B	*Register—Store* *Item—Store*

Category	System
A is logically contained in B	*ProductSpecification—Product-Catalog* *ProductCatalog—Store*
A is a description for B	*ProductSpecification—Item*
A is a line item of a transaction or report B	*SalesLineItem—Sale*
A is logged/recorded/reported/captured in B	*(completed) Sales—Store* *(current) Sale—Register*
A is a member of B	*Cashier—Store*
A is an organizational subunit of B	*not applicable*
A uses or manages B	*Cashier—Register* *Manager—Register* *Manager—Cashier, but probably not applicable.*
A communicates with B	*Customer—Cashier*
A is related to a transaction B	*Customer—Payment* *Cashier—Payment*
A is a transaction related to another transaction B	*Payment—Sale*
A is next to B	*SalesLineItem—SalesLineItem*
A is owned by B	*Register—Store*

11.11 NextGen POS Domain Model

The domain model in Figure 11.8 shows a set of conceptual classes and associations that are candidates for our POS application. The associations were primarily derived from the candidate association checklist.

Preserve Only Need-to-Know Associations?

The set of associations shown in the domain model of Figure 11.8 were, for the most part, mechanically derived from the association checklist. However, it may be desirable to be more choosy in the associations included in our domain model. Viewed as a tool of communication, it is undesirable to overwhelm the domain model with associations that are not strongly required and which do not illuminate our understanding. Too many uncompelling associations obscure rather than clarify.

As previously suggested, the following criteria for showing associations is recommended:

- Focus on those associations for which knowledge of the relationship needs to be preserved for some duration ("need-to-know" associations).

- Avoid showing redundant or derivable associations.

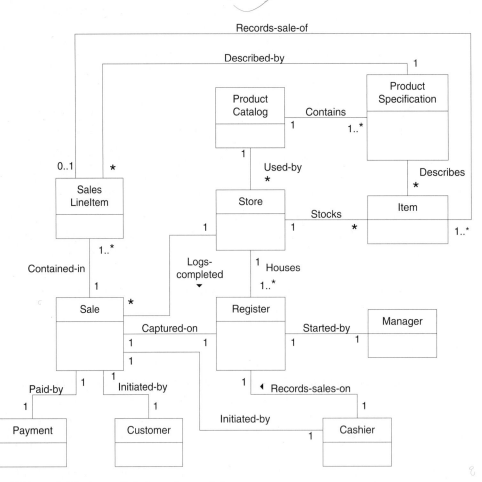

Figure 11.8 A partial domain model.

Based on this advice, not every association currently shown is compelling. Consider the following:

Association	Discussion
Sale Entered-by Cashier	The requirements do not indicate a need-to-know or record the current cashier. Also, it is derivable if the *Register Used-by Cashier* association is present.
Register Used-by Cashier	The requirements do not indicate a need-to-know or record the current cashier.
Register Started-by Manager	The requirements do not indicate a need-to-know or record the manager who starts up a *Register*.
Sale Initiated-by Customer	The requirements do not indicate a need-to-know or record the current customer who initiates a sale.
Store Stocks Item	The requirements do not indicate a need-to-know or maintain inventory information.
SalesLineItem Records-sale-of Item	The requirements do not indicate a need-to-know or maintain inventory information.

Note that the ability to justify an association in terms of need-to-know is dependent on the requirements; obviously a change in these—such as requiring that the cashier's ID show on a receipt—changes the need to remember a relationship.

Based on the above analysis, it *may* be justifiable to delete the associations in question.

Associations for Need-to-Know vs. Comprehension

A strict need-to-know criterion for maintaining associations will generate a minimal "information model" of what is needed to model the problem domain—bounded by the current requirements under consideration. However, this approach may create a model that does not convey (to us or anyone else) a full understanding of the domain.

In addition to being a need-to-know model of information about things, the domain model is a tool of communication in which we are trying to understand and communicate to others important concepts and their relationships. From this viewpoint, deleting some associations that are not strictly demanded on a need-to-know basis can create a model that misses the point—it does not communicate key ideas and relationships.

For example, in the POS application: although on a strict need-to-know basis it might not be necessary to record *Sale Initiated-by Customer*, its absence leaves out an important aspect in understanding the domain—that a customer generates sales.

In terms of associations, a good model is constructed somewhere between a minimal need-to-know model and one that illustrates every conceivable relationship. The basic criterion for judging its value?—Does it satisfy all need-to-know requirements and additionally clearly communicate an essential understanding of the important concepts in the problem domain?

Emphasize need-to-know associations, but add choice comprehension-only associations to enrich critical understanding of the domain.

DOMAIN MODEL: ADDING ATTRIBUTES

Any sufficiently advanced bug is indistinguishable from a feature.

—*Rich Kulawiec*

Objectives

- Identify attributes in a domain model.
- Distinguish between correct and incorrect attributes.

Introduction

It is useful to identify those attributes of conceptual classes that are needed to satisfy the information requirements of the current scenarios under development. This chapter explores the identification of suitable attributes, and adds attributes to the domain model for the NextGen domain model.

12.1 Attributes

An **attribute** is a logical data value of an object.

Include the following attributes in a domain model: Those for which the requirements (for example, use cases) suggest or imply a need to remember information.

167

For example, a receipt (which reports the information of a sale) normally includes a date and time, and management wants to know the dates and times of sales for a variety of reasons. Consequently, the *Sale* conceptual class needs a *date* and *time* attribute.

12.2 UML Attribute Notation

Attributes are shown in the second compartment of the class box (see Figure 12.1). Their type may optionally be shown.

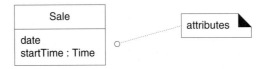

Figure 12.1 Class and attributes.

12.3 Valid Attribute Types

There are some things that should not be represented as attributes, but rather as associations. This section explores valid attributes.

Keep Attributes Simple

Intuitively, most simple attribute types are what are often thought of as primitive data types, such as numbers. The type of an attribute should not normally be a complex domain concept, such as a *Sale* or *Airport*. For example, the following *currentRegister* attribute in the *Cashier* class in Figure 12.2 is undesirable because its type is meant to be a *Register*, which is not a simple attribute type (such as *Number* or *String*). The most useful way to express that a *Cashier* uses a *Register* is with an association, not with an attribute..

> The attributes in a domain model should preferably be **simple attributes** or **data types**.
>
> Very common attribute data types include: *Boolean, Date, Number, String (Text), Time*
>
> Other common types include: *Address, Color, Geometrics (Point, Rectangle), Phone Number, Social Security Number, Universal Product Code (UPC), SKU, ZIP or postal codes, enumerated types*

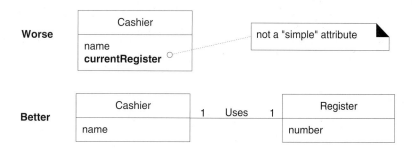

Figure 12.2 Relate with associations, not attributes.

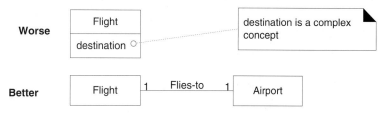

Figure 12.3 Avoid representing complex domain concepts as attributes; use associations.

To repeat an earlier example, a common confusion is modeling a complex domain concept as an attribute. To illustrate, a destination airport is not really a string; it is a complex thing that occupies many square kilometers of space. Therefore, *Flight* should be related to *Airport* via an association, not with an attribute, as shown in Figure 12.3.

> Relate conceptual classes with an association, not with an attribute.

Conceptual vs. Implementation Perspectives: What About Attributes in Code?

The restriction that attributes in the domain model be only of simple data types does *not* imply that C++ or Java attributes (data members, instance fields) must only be of simple, primitive data types. The domain model focuses on pure conceptual statements about a problem domain, not software components.

Later, during design and implementation work, it will be seen that the associations between objects expressed in the domain model will often be implemented as attributes that reference other complex software objects. However, this is but one of a number of possible design solutions to implement an association, and so the decision should be deferred during domain modeling.

Data Types

Attributes should generally be **data types**. This is a UML term that implies a set of values for which unique identity is not meaningful (in the context of our model or system) [RJB99]. For example, it is not (usually) meaningful to distinguish between:

- Separate instances of the *Number* 5.

- Separate instances of the *String* 'cat'.

- Separate instances of *PhoneNumber* that contain the same number.

- Separate instances of *Address* that contain the same address.

By contrast, it *is* meaningful to distinguish (by identity) between two separate instances of a *Person* whose names are both "Jill Smith" because the two instances can represent separate individuals with the same name.

In terms of software, there are few situations where one would compare the memory addresses of instances of *Number, String, PhoneNumber,* or *Address*; only value-based comparisons are relevant. By contrast, it is conceivable to compare the memory addresses of *Person* instances, and to distinguish them, even if they had the same attribute values, because their unique identity is important.

Thus, all primitive types (number, string) are UML data types, but not all data types are primitives. For example, *PhoneNumber* is a non-primitive data type.

These data type values are also known as **value objects**.

The notion of data types can get subtle. As a rule of thumb, stick to the basic test of "simple" attribute types: Make it an attribute if it is naturally thought of as number, string, boolean, date, or time (and so on); otherwise, represent it as a separate conceptual class.

> If in doubt, define something as a separate conceptual class rather than as an attribute.

12.4 Non-primitive Data Type Classes

The type of an attribute may be expressed as a non-primitive class in its own right in a domain model. For example, in the POS system there is an item identifier. It is typically viewed as just a number. So should it be represented as a non-primitive class? Apply this guideline:

Represent what may initially be considered a primitive data type (such as a number or string) as a non-primitive class if:

- It is composed of separate sections.
  - phone number, name of person
- There are operations usually associated with it, such as parsing or validation.
  - social security number
- It has other attributes.
  - promotional price could have a start (effective) date and end date
- It is a quantity with a unit.
  - payment amount has a unit of currency
- It is an abstraction of one or more types with some of these qualities.
  - item identifier in the sales domain is a generalization of types such as Universal Product Code (UPC) or European Article Number (EAN)

Applying these guidelines to the POS domain model attributes yields the following analysis:

- The item identifier is an abstraction of various common coding schemes, including UPC-A, UPC-E, and the family of EAN schemes. These numeric coding schemes have subparts identifying the manufacturer, product, country (for EAN), and a check-sum digit for validation. Therefore, there should be a non-primitive *ItemID* class, because it satisfies many of the guidelines above.

- The *price* and *amount* attributes should be non-primitive *Quantity* or *Money* classes because they are quantities in a unit of currency.

- The *address* attribute should be a non-primitive *Address* class because it has separate sections.

The classes *ItemID, Address,* and *Quantity* are data types (unique identity of instances is not meaningful) but they are worth considering as separate classes because of their qualities.

Where to Illustrate Data Type Classes?

Should the *ItemID* class be shown as a separate conceptual class in a domain model? It depends on what you want to emphasize in the diagram. Since *ItemID* is a *data type* (unique identity of instances is not important), it may be shown in the attribute compartment of the class box, as shown in Figure 12.4. But since it is a non-primitive class, with its own attributes and associations, it may be interesting to show it as a conceptual class in its own box. There is no correct answer; it depends on how the domain model is being used as a tool of communication, and the significance of the concept in the domain.

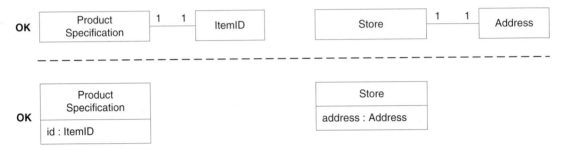

Figure 12.4 If the attribute class is a data type, it may be shown in the attribute box.

> A domain model is a tool of communication; choices about what is shown should be made with that consideration in mind.

12.5   Design Creep: No Attributes as Foreign Keys

Attributes should not be used to relate conceptual classes in the domain model. The most common violation of this principle is to add a kind of **foreign key attribute**, as is typically done in relational database designs, in order to associate two types. For example, in Figure 12.5 the *currentRegisterNumber* attribute in the *Cashier* class is undesirable because its purpose is to relate the *Cashier* to a *Register* object. The better way to express that a *Cashier* uses a *Register* is with an association, not with a foreign key attribute. Once again, relate types with an association, not with an attribute.

There are many ways to relate objects—foreign keys being one—and we will defer how to implement the relation until design, in order to avoid **design creep**.

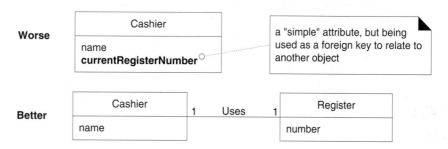

Figure 12.5 Do not use attributes as foreign keys.

12.6 Modeling Attribute Quantities and Units

Most numeric quantities should not be represented as plain numbers. Consider price or velocity. These are quantities with associated units, and it is common to require knowing the unit, and to support conversions. The NextGen POS software is for an international market and needs to support prices in multiple currencies. In the general case, the solution is to represent *Quantity* as a distinct conceptual class, with an associated *Unit* [Fowler96]. Since quantities are considered data types (unique identity of instances is not important), it is acceptable to collapse their illustration into the attribute section of the class box (see Figure 12.6). It is also common to show *Quantity* specializations. *Money* is a kind of quantity whose units are currencies. *Weight* is a quantity with units such as kilograms or pounds.

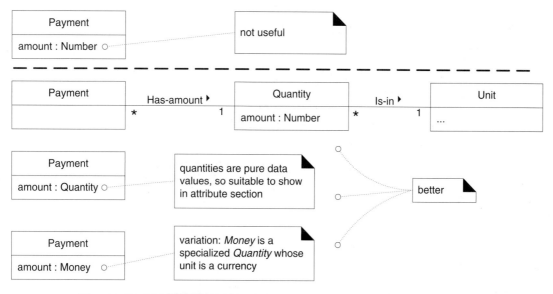

Figure 12.6 Modeling quantities.

12.7 Attributes in the NextGen Domain Model

The attributes chosen reflect the requirements for this iteration—the *Process Sale* scenarios of this iteration.

Payment	*amount*—To determine if sufficient payment was provided, and to calculate change, an amount (also known as "amount tendered") must be captured.
Product-Specification	*description*—To show the description on a display or receipt.
	id—To look up a *ProductSpecification*, given an entered itemID, it is necessary to relate them to a *id*.
	price—To calculate the sales total, and show the line item price.
Sale	*date, time*—A receipt is a paper report of a sale. It normally shows date and time of sale.
SalesLineItem	*quantity*—To record the quantity entered, when there is more than one item in a line item sale (for example, *five* packages of tofu).
Store	*address, name*—The receipt requires the name and address of the store.

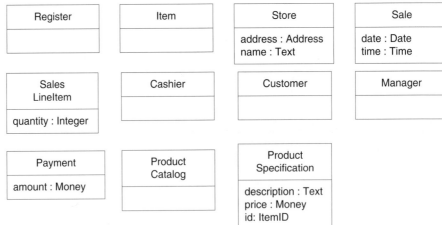

Figure 12.7 Domain model showing attributes.

12.8   Multiplicity From SalesLineItem to Item

It is possible for a cashier to receive a group of like items (for example, six tofu packages), enter the *itemID* once, and then enter a quantity (for example, six). Consequently, an individual *SalesLineItem* can be associated with more than one instance of an item.

The quantity that is entered by the cashier may be recorded as an attribute of the *SalesLineItem* (Figure 12.8). However, the quantity can be calculated from the actual multiplicity value of the relationship, so it may be characterized as a **derived attribute**—one that may be derived from other information. In the UML, a derived attribute is indicated with a "/" symbol.

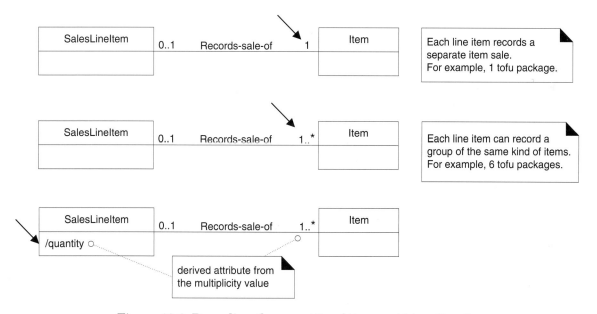

Figure 12.8 Recording the quantity of items sold in a line item.

12.9   Domain Model Conclusion

Combining the conceptual classes, associations, and attributes discovered in the previous investigation yields the model illustrated in Figure 12.9.

A relatively useful domain model for the domain of the POS application has been created. There is no such thing as a single correct model. All models are approximations of the domain we are attempting to understand. A good domain model captures the essential abstractions and information required to understand the domain in the context of the current requirements, and aids people in understanding the domain—its concepts, terminology, and relationships.

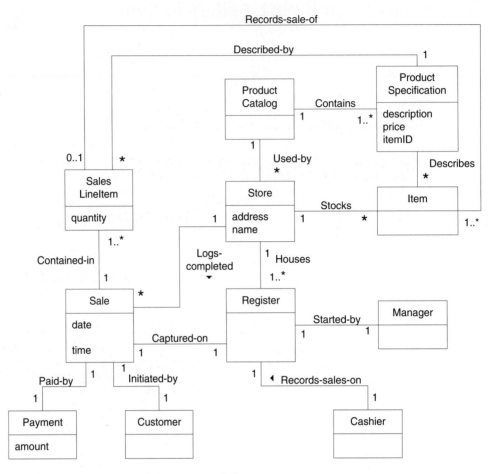

Figure 12.9 A partial domain model.

USE-CASE MODEL:
ADDING DETAIL WITH
OPERATION CONTRACTS

Fast, Cheap, Good: Choose any two.

—anonymous

Objectives

■ Create contracts for system operations.

Introduction

Contracts for operations can help define system behavior; they describe the outcome of executing system operation in terms of state changes to domain objects. This chapter explores their use.

13.1 Contracts

Use cases are the primary mechanism in the UP to describe system behavior, and are usually sufficient. However, sometimes a more detailed description of system behavior has value. Contracts describe detailed system behavior in terms of state changes to objects in the Domain Model, after a system operation has executed.

System Operations and the System Interface

Contracts may be defined for **system operations**—operations that the system as a black box offers in its public interface to handle incoming system events. System operations can be identified by discovering these system events, as shown in Figure 13.1.

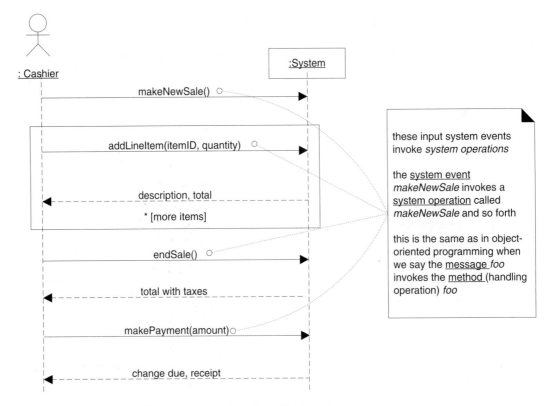

Figure 13.1 System operations handle input system events.

The entire set of system operations, across all use cases, defines the public system interface, viewing the system as a single component or class. In the UML, the system as a whole can be represented by a class.

13.2   Example Contract: enterItem

Before examining the reason to write a contract, an example is worthwhile. The following describes a contract for the *enterItem* system operation.

Contract CO2: enterItem

Operation:	enterItem(itemID : ItemID, quantity : integer)
Cross References:	Use Cases: Process Sale
Preconditions:	There is a sale underway.
Postconditions:	– A SalesLineItem instance sli was created (instance creation).
	– sli was associated with the current Sale (association formed).
	– sli.quantity became quantity (attribute modification).
	– sli was associated with a ProductSpecification, based on itemID match (association formed).

13.3   Contract Sections

A description of each section in a contract is shown in the following schema.

Operation:	Name of operation, and parameters
Cross References:	(optional) Use cases this operation can occur within
Preconditions:	Noteworthy *assumptions* about the state of the system or objects in the Domain Model before execution of the operation. These will not be tested within the logic of this operation, are assumed to be true, and are non-trivial assumptions the reader should know were made.
Postconditions:	– The state of objects in the Domain Model after completion of the operation. Discussed in detail in a following section.

13.4   Postconditions

Notice that each of the postconditions in the *enterItem* example included a categorization such as *instance creation* or *association formed*. Here is a key point:

> The postconditions describe changes in the state of objects in the Domain Model. Domain Model state changes include instances created, associations formed or broken, and attributes changed.

Postconditions are not actions to be performed during the operation; rather, they are declarations about the Domain Model objects that are true when the operation has finished—*after the smoke has cleared*.

To summarize, the postconditions fall into these categories:

- Instance creation and deletion.
- Attribute modification.
- Associations (to be precise, UML *links*) formed and broken.

As an example of a post-condition that breaks an association, consider an operation to allow the deletion of line items. The post-condition could read "The selected *SalesLineItem's* association with the *Sale* was broken." In other domains, when a loan is paid off or someone cancels their membership in something, associations are broken.

Instance deletion postconditions are most rare, because one does not usually care about explicitly enforcing the destruction of a thing in the real world. However, as an example: In many countries, after a person has declared bankruptcy and seven or ten years have passed, all records of their bankruptcy declaration must be destroyed, by law. Note that this is a conceptual perspective, not implementation. These are not statements about freeing up memory in a computer occupied by software objects.

The important quality is to be declarative and state change-oriented rather than action-oriented, since postconditions are declarations about states or outcomes rather than a description of actions to execute, or a design of a solution.

Postconditions Are Related to the Domain Model

These postconditions are expressed in the context of the Domain Model objects. What instances can be created?—those from the Domain Model; What associations can be formed?—those in the Domain Model; and so on.

An Advantage of Postconditions: Analytical Detail

Expressed in a declarative state-change fashion, the contract is an excellent tool for requirements analysis that describes the state changes required of a system operation (in terms of the Domain Model objects) without having to describe *how* they are to be achieved. In other words, the software design and solution can be deferred, and one can focus analytically on *what* must happen, rather than how it is to be accomplished. Furthermore, the postconditions support fine-grained detail and specificity in declaring what the outcome of the operation must be.

It is also possible to express this level of detail in the use cases, but usually undesirable, as they would then become overly verbose and detailed.

Consider the postconditions:

Postconditions:	– A SalesLineItem instance sli was created (instance creation).
	– sli was associated with the current Sale (association formed).
	– sli.quantity became quantity (attribute modification).
	– sli was associated with a ProductSpecification, based on itemID match (association formed).

No comment is made about how a *SalesLineItem* instance is created, or associated with a *Sale*. This could be a statement about writing on bits of paper and stapling them together, using Java technologies to create software objects and connect them, or inserting rows in a relational database.

The Spirit of Postconditions: The Stage and Curtain

Express postconditions in the past tense, to emphasize they are declarations about a state change in the past. For example:

- (better) A *SalesLineItem* **was** created.

rather than

- (worse) Create a *SalesLineItem*.

Think about postconditions using the following image:

The system and its objects are presented on a theatre stage.

1. Before the operation, take a picture of the stage.

2. Close the curtains on the stage, and apply the system operation (*background noise of clanging, screams, and screeches...*).

3. Open the curtains and take a second picture.

4. Compare the before and after pictures, and express as postconditions the changes in the state of the stage (*A SalesLineItem was created...*).

If Contracts Are Used, How Complete Should Postconditions Be?

First, contracts may not be needed. This question is discussed in a subsequent section. But assuming some contracts are desired, generating a complete and detailed set of postconditions for a system operation is not likely—or even necessary—during requirements work. Treat their creation as an initial best guess, with the understanding that the contracts will not be complete. Their early creation—even if incomplete—is certainly better than deferring this investigation until design work, when developers should be concerned with the design of a solution, rather than investigating *what* should be done.

Some of the fine details—and perhaps even larger ones—will be discovered during the design work. That is not necessarily a bad thing; there is a diminishing return on effort expended during requirements analysis if it is drawn out too long. Some discovery naturally arises during design work, which can then inform the requirements work of a later iteration. This is one of the advantages of iterative development: discoveries generated during a prior iteration can enhance the investigation and analysis work of the following one.

13.5   Discussion—enterItem Postconditions

The following section dissects the motivation for the postconditions of the *enterItem* system operation.

Instance Creation and Deletion

After the *itemID* and *quantity* of an item have been entered, what new object should have been created? A *SalesLineItem*. Thus:

■   A *SalesLineItem* instance *sli* was created (instance creation).

Note the naming of the instance. This name will simplify references to the new instance in other post-condition statements.

Attribute Modification

After the itemID and quantity of an item have been entered by the cashier, what attributes of new or existing objects should have been modified? The *quantity* of the *SalesLineItem* should have become equal to the *quantity* parameter. Thus:

■   *sli.quantity* became *quantity* (attribute modification).

Associations Formed and Broken

After the *itemID* and *quantity* of an item have been entered by the cashier, what associations between new or existing objects should have been formed or broken? The new *SalesLineItem* should have been related to its *Sale*, and related to its *ProductSpecification*. Thus:

■   *sli* was associated with the current *Sale* (association formed).

■   *sli* was associated with a *ProductSpecification*, based on *itemID* match (association formed).

Note the informal indication that it forms a relationship with a particular *ProductSpecification*—the one whose *itemID* matches the parameter. More fancy and formal language approaches are possible, such as using the Object Constraint Language (OCL). Recommendation: Keep it plain and simple.

13.6   Writing Contracts Leads to Domain Model Updates

It is common during the creation of the contracts to discover the need to record new conceptual classes, attributes, or associations in the Domain Model. Do not be limited to the prior definition of the Domain Model; enhance it as you make new discoveries while thinking through the operation contracts.

13.7   When Are Contracts Useful? Contracts vs. Use Cases?

The use cases are the main repository of requirements for the project. They may provide most or all of the detail necessary to know what to do in the design, in which case, contracts are not helpful. However, there are situations where the details and complexity of required state changes are awkward to capture in use cases.

For example, consider an airline reservation system and the system operation *addNewReservation*. The complexity is very high regarding all the domain objects that must be changed, created, and associated. These fine-grained details *can* be written up in the use case associated with this operation, but it will make the use case extremely detailed (for example, noting each attribute in all the objects that must change).

Observe that the contract post-condition format offers and encourages a very precise, analytical, exacting language that supports detailed thoroughness.

If, just based on the use cases and through ongoing (verbal) collaboration with a subject matter expert, the developers can comfortably understand what to do, then avoid writing contracts.

However, in those situations were there is high complexity and detailed precision adds value, contracts are another requirements tool.

They will not be practically motivated very often, so if a team is making contracts for every system operation of every use case, it is a warning that either the use cases are poorly done, there is not enough ongoing collaboration or access to a subject matter expert, or the team is doing too much unnecessary documentation.

This NextGen POS case study shows more contracts than are probably necessary, for educational reasons. In practice, most of the details they record are obviously inferable from the use case text. On the other hand, "obvious" is a very slippery concept.

13.8   Guidelines: Contracts

Apply the following advice to create contracts:

To make contracts:

1. Identify system operations from the SSDs.

2. For system operations that are complex and perhaps subtle in their results, or which are not clear in the use case, construct a contract.

3. To describe the postconditions, use the following categories:

    o   instance creation and deletion

    o   attribute modification

    o   associations formed and broken

Advice on Writing Contracts

■   State the postconditions in a declarative, passive past tense form (*was ...*) to emphasize the declaration of a state change rather than a design of how it is going to be achieved. For example:

    o   (better) A *SalesLineItem* **was** created.

    o   (worse) Create a *SalesLineItem*.

■   Remember to establish a memory between existing objects or those newly created by defining the forming of an association. For example, it is not enough that a new *SalesLineItem* instance is created when the *enterItem* operation occurs. After the operation is complete, it should also be true that the newly created instance was associated with *Sale*; thus:

    o   The *SalesLineItem* was associated with the *Sale* (association formed).

The Most Common Mistake in Creating Contracts

The most common problem is forgetting to include the *forming of associations*. Particularly when new instances are created, it is very likely that associations to several objects need be established. Don't forget!

13.9   NextGen POS Example: Contracts

System Operations of Process Sale

Contract CO1: makeNewSale

Operation:	makeNewSale()
Cross References:	Use Cases: Process Sale
Preconditions:	none
Postconditions:	– A Sale instance s was created (instance creation).
	– s was associated with the Register (association formed).
	– Attributes of s were initialized.

Note the vague description in the last post-condition. If sufficient, this is fine.

On a project, all these particular postconditions are so obvious from the use case that the *makeNewSale* contract should probably not be written.

Recall one of the guiding principles of healthy process and the UP: Keep it as light as possible, and avoid all artifacts unless they really add value.

Contract CO2: enterItem

Operation:	enterItem(itemID : ItemID, quantity : integer)
Cross References:	Use Cases: Process Sale
Preconditions:	There is a sale underway.
Postconditions:	– *A SalesLineItem instance sli was created (instance creation).*
	– *sli was associated with the current Sale (association formed).*
	– *sli.quantity became quantity (attribute modification).*
	– *sli was associated with a ProductSpecification, based on itemID match (association formed).*

Contract CO3: endSale

Operation:	endSale()
Cross References:	Use Cases: Process Sale
Preconditions:	There is a sale underway.
Postconditions:	– *Sale.isComplete became true (attribute modification).*

Contract CO4: makePayment

Operation:	makePayment(amount: Money)
Cross References:	Use Cases: Process Sale
Preconditions:	There is a sale underway.
Postconditions:	*– A Payment instance p was created (instance creation).*
	– p.amountTendered became amount (attribute modification).
	– p was associated with the current Sale (association formed).
	– The current Sale was associated with the Store (association formed); (to add it to the historical log of completed sales)

13.10 Changes to the Domain Model

There is one datum suggested by these contracts that is not yet represented in the domain model: completion of item entry to the sale. The *endSale* specification modifies it, and it is probably a good idea later during design work for the *makePayment* operation to test it, to disallow payments until a sale is complete.

One way to represent this information is with an *isComplete* attribute in the *Sale*, of boolean data type:

Sale
isComplete: Boolean date time

There are alternatives, especially considered during design work. One technique is called the **State pattern**, which is explored in Chapter 34. Another is the use of "session" objects that track the state of a session and disallow out-of-order operations; this too will be explored later.

13.11 Contracts, Operations, and the UML

Contracts in the UML: Operation Specifications

The UML formally defines **operations**. To quote:

> An operation is a specification of a transformation or query that an object may be called to execute [RJB99]

For example, the elements of an interface are operations, in UML terms. An operation is an abstraction, not an implementation. By contrast, a **method** (in the UML) is an implementation of an operation.

A UML operation has a **signature** (name and parameters), and also an **operation specification**, which describes the effects produced by executing the operation; that is, the postconditions. The UML operation specification format is flexible, and does not have be the contract format shown in this chapter. However, the UML documents give as examples the contract style with pre- and postconditions, as this is the most well-known approach to formal operation specifications.

To summarize: The UML defines operation specifications, which are specifiable in the pre- and post-condition contract style. Note that, as emphasized in this chapter, a UML operation specification may *not* show an algorithm or solution, but only the state changes or effects of the operation.

In addition to using contracts to specify public operations of the entire *System* (system operations), contracts can be applied to operations at any level of granularity: the public operations (or interface) of a subsystem, an abstract class, and so forth. The operations discussed in this chapter belong to a *System* class. In the UML operations belong to classes. Furthermore, in the UML, "subsystems" are modeled as classes (and simultaneously also as packages). In the UML, the overall "system" is the top-level subsystem, and modeled as a class named *System* (actually, any name is legal) with public operations and specifications.

Operation Contracts Expressed with the OCL

Associated with the UML is a formal language called the Object Constraint Language (**OCL**) [WK99], which can be used to express constraints in models. The OCL could be used instead of the informal natural language used in this chapter; the UML allows any format for an operation specification.

Suggestion

Unless there is a compelling practical reason to require people to learn and use the OCL, keep things simple and use natural language.

The OCL defines an official format for specifying pre- and postconditions for operations, as demonstrated in this fragment:

```
System::makeNewSale( )
    pre : <statements in OCL>
    post : ...
```

Further OCL details are beyond the scope of this introduction.

Contracts in Design by Contract

The pre- and post-condition contract form used for UML operation specifications has been promoted for many years by Bertrand Meyer, formalized in a design approach called **Design by Contract** [Meyer97 (first ed. 1989)], although its origin is from earlier work in the 1960s on formal specification languages. In Design by Contract, contracts are also written for operations of fine-grained classes, not only the public operations of systems or subsystems.

In addition, Design by Contract promotes the inclusion of an *invariant* section, as is common in thorough contract specifications. Invariants define things that must not change state before and after the operation has executed. Invariants have not been used in this chapter for the sake of simplicity.

Programming Language Support for Contracts

Some languages, such as Eiffel, have first-class support for invariants and pre- and postconditions. There are pre-processors that provide similar support in Java.

13.12 Operation Contracts Within the UP

A pre- and postcondition contract is a well-known style to specify an operation in the UML. In the UML, operations exists at many levels, from *System* down to fine-grained classes, such as *Sale*. Operation specification contracts for the *System* level are part of the Use-Case Model, although they were not formally highlighted in the original RUP or UP documentation; their inclusion in this model was verified with the RUP authors.[1]

Phases

Inception—Contracts are not motivated during inception—they are too detailed.

Elaboration—If used at all, most contracts will be written during elaboration, when most use cases are written. Only write contracts for the most complex and subtle system operations.

---

1. Private communication.

Artifacts Relationships

Relationships between contracts and other artifacts, at different levels of detail, are shown in Figure 13.2 and Figure 13.3.

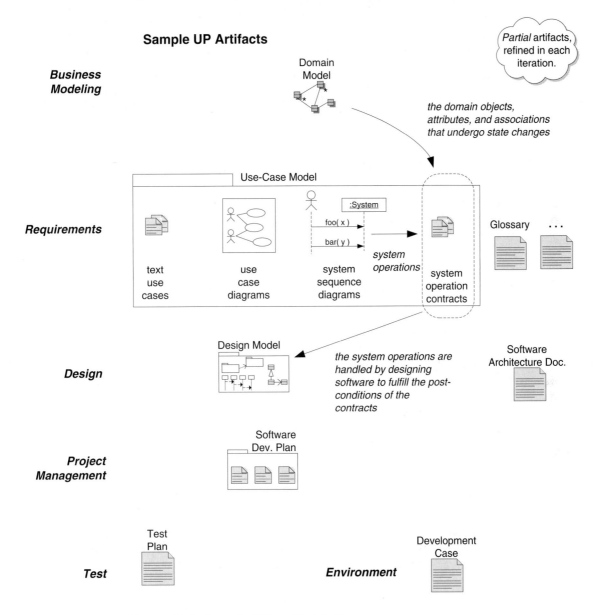

Figure 13.2 Sample UP artifact influence.

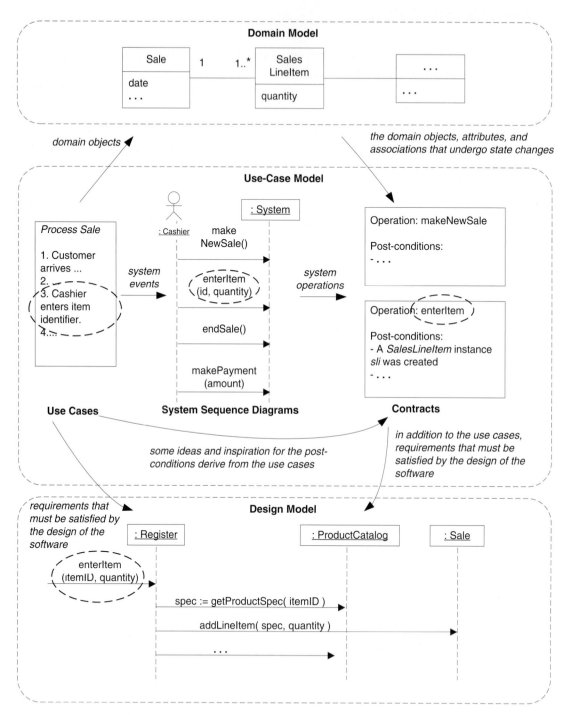

Figure 13.3 Contract relationship to other artifacts.

13.13   Further Readings

Operation contracts come out of the formal specifications area, and have been used and refined since the 1960s, such as in the Vienna Development Method (VDM) [BJ78]; there is a wealth of literature on VDM and other formal specification languages.

Bertrand Meyer contributed to a much wider awareness of formal specifications and contracts with the inclusion of pre- and postconditions within the Eiffel language; his *Object-Oriented Software Construction* provides details. He is responsible for the notion of **Design by Contract**.

Within the UML, operation contracts can also be specified more rigorously in the Object Constraint Language (OCL), for which Warmer and Kleppe's *The Object Constraint Language: Precise Modeling with UML* is required reading.

FROM REQUIREMENTS TO DESIGN IN THIS ITERATION

Hardware, n.: The parts of a computer system that can be kicked.

—anonymous

Objectives

- Motivate the transition to design activities.
- Contrast the importance of object design skill versus UML notation knowledge.

Introduction

So far, the case study has emphasized investigation of the requirements, concepts, and operations related to a system. Following the UP guidelines, perhaps 10% of the requirements were investigated in inception, and a slightly deeper investigation was started in this first iteration of elaboration. The following chapters are a shift in emphasis toward designing a solution for this iteration in terms of collaborating software objects.

14.1 Iteratively Do the Right Thing, Do the Thing Right

The requirements and object-oriented analysis has focused on learning to *do the right thing*; that is, understanding some of the outstanding goals for the Next-Gen POS, and related rules and constraints. By contrast, the following design work will stress *do the thing right*; that is, skillfully designing a solution to satisfy the requirements for this iteration.

In iterative development, a transition from primarily a requirements focus to primarily a design and implementation focus will occur in each iteration. Furthermore, it is natural and healthy to discover and change some requirements during the design and implementation work of the *early* iterations. These discoveries will both clarify the purpose of the design work of this iteration and refine the requirements understanding for future iterations. Over the course of these early elaboration iterations, the requirements discovery will stabilize, so that by the end of elaboration, perhaps 80% of the requirements are reliably defined in detail.

14.2   Didn't That Take Weeks To Do? No, Not Exactly.

After many chapters of detailed discussion, it must surely seem like the prior modeling would take weeks of effort. Not so. When one is comfortable with the skills of use case writing, domain modeling, and so forth, the duration to do all the actual modeling that has been explored so far is realistically just *a few* days.

However, that does not mean that only a few days have passed since the start of the project. Many other activities, such as proof-of-concept programming, finding resources (people, software, ...), planning, setting up the environment, and so on, could consume a few weeks of preparation.

14.3   On to Object Design

During object design, a logical solution based on the object-oriented paradigm is developed. The heart of this solution is the creation of **interaction diagrams**, which illustrate how objects collaborate to fulfill the requirements.

After—or in parallel with—drawing interaction diagrams, (design) **class diagrams** can be drawn. These summarize the definition of the software classes (and interfaces) that are to be implemented in software.

In terms of the UP, these artifacts are part of the **Design Model**.

> In practice, the creation of interaction and class diagrams happens in parallel and synergistically, but their introduction is linear in this case study, for simplicity and clarity.

The Importance of Object Design Skill vs. UML Notation Skill

The following chapters explore the creation of these artifacts, or more precisely, the object design skills underlying their creation. What is important is knowing how to think and design in objects, which is a very different and much more important ability than knowing UML diagramming notation. At the same time, a standard visual language is great, and thus the required UML notation to support the design work is presented.

Of the two artifacts that will be explored, interactions diagrams are the most important—from the point of view of developing a good design—and require the greatest degree of creative effort. The creation of interaction diagrams requires the application of principles for assigning **responsibilities** and the use of **design principles and patterns**. Therefore, the emphasis of the following chapters is on these principles and patterns in object design.

Object Design Skill vs. UML Notation Skill

Drawing UML interaction diagrams is a reflection of making decisions about the object design.

The object design skills are what really matter, rather than knowing how to draw UML diagrams.

Fundamental object design requires knowledge of:

■ principles of responsibility assignment

■ design patterns

INTERACTION DIAGRAM NOTATION

*Cats are smarter than dogs. You can't
get eight cats to pull a sled through snow.*

—Jeff Valdez

Objectives

■ Read basic UML interaction (sequence and collaboration) diagram notation.

Introduction

The following chapters explore object design. The language used to illustrate the designs is primarily interaction diagrams. Thus, it is advisable to at least skim the examples in this chapter and get familiar with the notation before moving on.

The UML includes **interaction diagrams** to illustrate how objects interact via messages. This chapter introduces the notation, while subsequent chapters focus on using them in the context of learning and doing object design for the NextGen POS case study.

Read the Following Chapters for Design Guidelines

This chapter introduces notation. To create well-designed objects, design principles must also be understood. After acquiring some familiarity with the notation of interaction diagrams, it is important to study the following chapters on these principles and how to apply them while drawing interaction diagrams.

15.1   Sequence and Collaboration Diagrams

The term *interaction diagram* is a generalization of two more specialized UML diagram types; both can be used to express similar message interactions:

- collaboration diagrams

- sequence diagrams

Throughout the book, both types will be used, to emphasize the flexibility in choice.

Collaboration diagrams illustrate object interactions in a graph or network format, in which objects can be placed anywhere on the diagram, as shown in Figure 15.1.

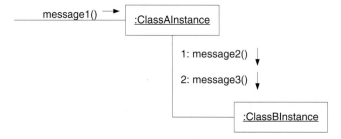

Figure 15.1 Collaboration diagram.

Sequence diagrams illustrate interactions in a kind of fence format, in which each new object is added to the right, as shown in Figure 15.2.

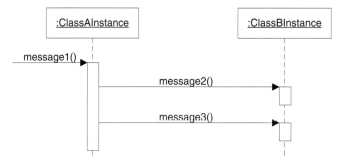

Figure 15.2 Sequence diagram.

Each type has strengths and weaknesses. When drawing diagrams to be published on pages of narrow width, collaboration diagrams have the advantage of allowing vertical expansion for new objects; additional objects in a sequence diagrams must extend to the right, which is limiting. On the other hand, collaboration diagram examples make it harder to easily see the sequence of messages.

Most prefer sequence diagrams when using a CASE tool to reverse engineer source code into an interaction diagram, as they clearly illustrate the sequence of messages.

Type	Strengths	Weaknesses
sequence	clearly shows sequence or time ordering of messages simple notation	forced to extend to the right when adding new objects; consumes horizontal space
collaboration	space economical—flexibility to add new objects in two dimensions better to illustrate complex branching, iteration, and concurrent behavior	difficult to see sequence of messages more complex notation

15.2   Example Collaboration Diagram: makePayment

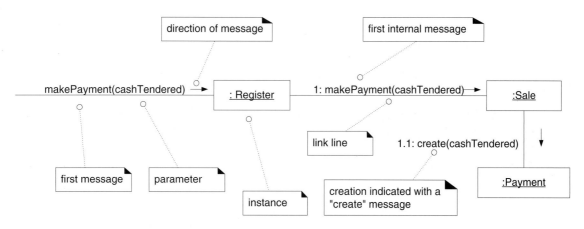

Figure 15.3 Collaboration diagram.

The collaboration diagram shown in Figure 15.3 is read as follows:

1. The message *makePayment* is sent to an instance of a *Register*. The sender is not identified.

2. The *Register* instance sends the *makePayment* message to a *Sale* instance.

3. The *Sale* instance creates an instance of a *Payment*.

15.3   Example Sequence Diagram: makePayment

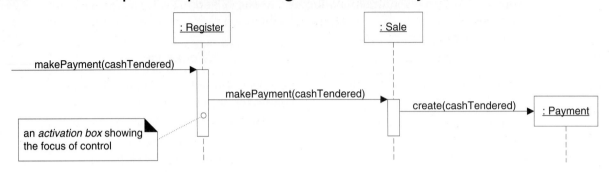

Figure 15.4 Sequence diagram.

The sequence diagram shown in Figure 15.4 has the same intent as the prior collaboration diagram.

15.4   Interaction Diagrams Are Valuable

A common problem in object technology projects is a lack of appreciation for the value of doing object design via the medium of interaction diagrams. A related problem is doing them in a vague way, such as showing messages to objects that actually require much further elaboration; for example, showing the message *runSimulation* to some *Simulation* object, but not continuing on with the more detailed design, as though by virtue of a well-named message the design is magically complete.

Some non-trivial time and effort should be spent in the creation of interaction diagrams, as a reflection of thinking through details of the object design. For example, if the length of the timeboxed iteration is two weeks, perhaps a half or full day near the start of the iteration should be spent on their creation (and in parallel, class diagrams), before proceeding to programming. Yes, the design illustrated in the diagrams will be imperfect and is speculative, and it will be modified during programming, but it will provide a thoughtful, cohesive, common starting point for inspiration during programming.

Suggestion

Create interaction diagrams in pairs, not alone. The collaborative design will be improved, and the partners will learn quickly from each other.

Note that it is primarily during this step that the application of design skill is required, in terms of patterns, idioms, and principles. Relatively speaking, the creation of use cases, domain models, and other artifacts is easier than the assignment of responsibilities and the creation of well-designed interaction diagrams. This is because there is a larger number of subtle design principles and "degrees of freedom" that underlie a well-designed interaction diagram than most other OOA/D artifacts.

Making interaction diagrams (in other words, deciding on the details of the object design) is a very creative step in OOA/D.

Codified patterns, principles, and idioms can be applied to improve the quality of their design.

The design principles necessary for the successful construction of interaction diagrams *can* be codified, explained, and applied in a methodical fashion. This approach to understanding and using design principles is based on **patterns**—structured guidelines and principles. Therefore, after introducing the syntax of interaction diagrams, attention (in subsequent chapters) will turn to design patterns and their application in interaction diagrams.

15.5 Common Interaction Diagram Notation

Illustrating Classes and Instances

The UML has adopted a simple and consistent approach to illustrate **instances** vs. classifiers (see Figure 15.5):

- For any kind of UML element (class, actor, ...), an instance uses the same graphic symbol as the type, but the designator string is <u>underlined</u>.

Figure 15.5 Class and instances.

Therefore, to show an instance of a class in an interaction diagram, the regular class box graphic symbol is used, but the name is underlined.

A name can be used to uniquely identify the instance. If none is used, note that a ":" precedes the class name.

Basic Message Expression Syntax

The UML has a standard syntax for message expressions:

```
return := message(parameter : parameterType) : returnType
```

Type information may be excluded if obvious or unimportant. For example:

```
spec := getProductSpect(id)
spec := getProductSpect(id:ItemID)
spec := getProductSpect(id:ItemID) : ProductSpecification
```

15.6   Basic Collaboration Diagram Notation

Links

A **link** is a connection path between two objects; it indicates some form of navigation and visibility between the objects is possible (see Figure 15.6). More formally, a link is an instance of an association. For example, there is a link—or path of navigation—from a *Register* to a *Sale*, along which messages may flow, such as the *makePayment* message.

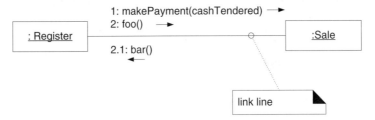

Figure 15.6 Link lines.

Note that multiple messages, and messages both ways, can flow along the same single link.

Messages

Each message between objects is represented with a message expression and small arrow indicating the direction of the message. Many messages may flow along this link (Figure 15.7). A sequence number is added to show the sequential order of messages in the current thread of control.

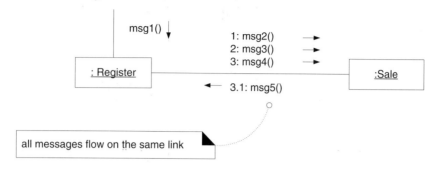

Figure 15.7 Messages.

Messages to "self" or "this"

A message can be sent from an object to itself (Figure 15.8). This is illustrated by a link to itself, with messages flowing along the link.

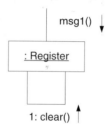

Figure 15.8 Messages to "this."

Creation of Instances

Any message can be used to create an instance, but there is a convention in the UML to use a message named *create* for this purpose. If another (perhaps less obvious) message name is used, the message may be annotated with a special feature called a UML stereotype, like so: «create».

The *create* message may include parameters, indicating the passing of initial values. This indicates, for example, a constructor call with parameters in Java.

Furthermore, the UML property *{new}* may optionally be added to the instance box to highlight the creation.

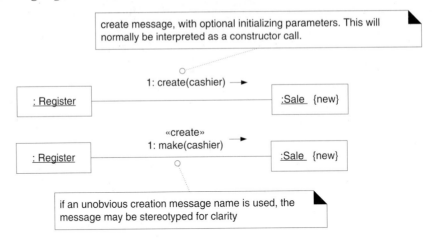

Figure 15.9 Instance creation.

Message Number Sequencing

The order of messages is illustrated with **sequence numbers**, as shown in Figure 15.10. The numbering scheme is:

1. The first message is not numbered. Thus, *msg1()* is unnumbered.

2. The order and nesting of subsequent messages is shown with a legal numbering scheme in which nested messages have a number appended to them. Nesting is denoted by prepending the incoming message number to the outgoing message number.

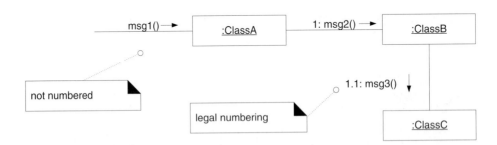

Figure 15.10 Sequence numbering.

In Figure 15.11 a more complex case is shown.

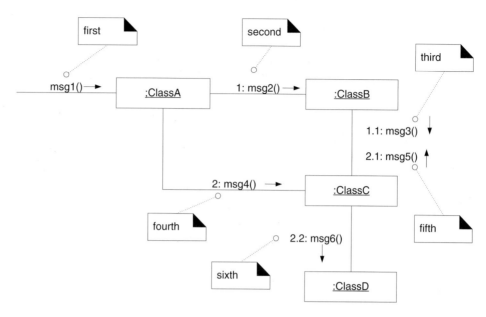

Figure 15.11 Complex sequence numbering.

Conditional Messages

A conditional message (Figure 15.12) is shown by following a sequence number with a conditional clause in square brackets, similar to an iteration clause. The message is only sent if the clause evaluates to *true*.

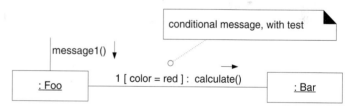

Figure 15.12 Conditional message.

Mutually Exclusive Conditional Paths

The example in Figure 15.13 illustrates the sequence numbers with mutually exclusive conditional paths.

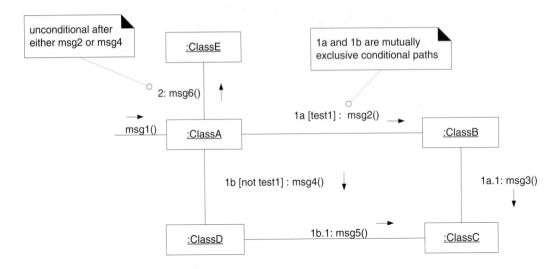

Figure 15.13 Mutually exclusive messages.

In this case it is necessary to modify the sequence expressions with a conditional path letter. The first letter used is **a** by convention. Figure 15.13 states that either *1a* or *1b* could execute after *msg1*. Both are sequence number 1 since either could be the first internal message.

Note that subsequent nested messages are still consistently prepended with their outer message sequence. Thus *1b.1* is nested message within *1b*.

Iteration or Looping

Iteration notation is shown in Figure 15.14. If the details of the iteration clause are not important to the modeler, a simple "*" can be used.

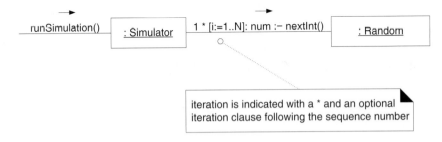

Figure 15.14 Iteration.

Iteration Over a Collection (Multiobject)

A common algorithm is to iterate over all members of a collection (such as a list or map), sending a message to each. Often, some kind of iterator object is ultimately used, such as an implementation of *java.util.Iterator* or a C++ standard library iterator. In the UML, the term **multiobject** is used to denote a set of instances—a collection. In collaboration diagrams, this can be summarized as shown in Figure 15.15.

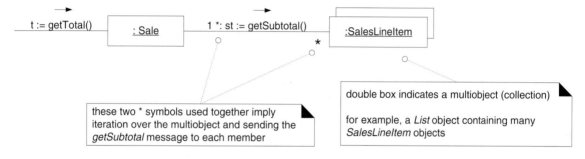

Figure 15.15 Iteration over a multiobject.

The "*" multiplicity marker at the end of the link is used to indicate that the message is being sent to each element of the collection, rather than being repeatedly sent to the collection object itself.

Messages to a Class Object

Messages may be sent to a class itself, rather than an instance, to invoke class or **static methods**. A message is shown to a class box whose name is not underlined, indicating the message is being sent to a class rather than an instance (see Figure 15.16).

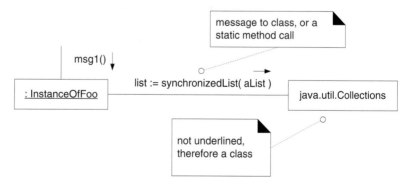

Figure 15.16 Messages to a class object (static method invocation).

Consequently, it is important to be consistent in underlining your instance names when an instance is intended, otherwise messages to instances versus classes may be incorrectly interpreted.

15.7   Basic Sequence Diagram Notation

Links

Unlike collaboration diagrams, sequence diagrams do not show links.

Messages

Each message between objects is represented with a message expression on an arrowed line between the objects (see Figure 15.17). The time ordering is organized from top to bottom.

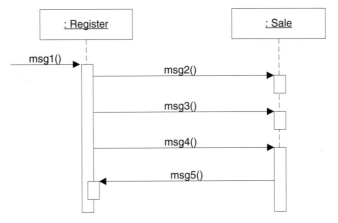

Figure 15.17 Messages and focus of control with activation boxes.

Focus of Control and Activation Boxes

As illustrated in Figure 15.17, sequence diagrams may also show the focus of control (that is, in a regular blocking call, the operation is on the call stack) using an **activation box**. The box is optional, but commonly used by UML practitioners.

Illustrating Returns

A sequence diagram may optionally show the return from a message as a dashed open-arrowed line at the end of an activation box (see Figure 15.18). Many practitioners exclude them. Some annotate the return line to describe what is being returned (if anything) from the message.

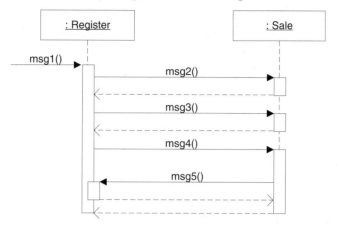

Figure 15.18 Showing returns.

Messages to "self" or "this"

A message can be illustrated as being sent from an object to itself by using a nested activation box (see Figure 15.19).

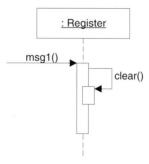

Figure 15.19 Messages to "this."

Creation of Instances

Object creation notation is shown in Figure 15.20.

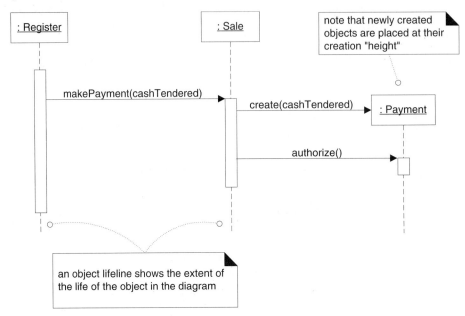

Figure 15.20 Instance creation and object lifelines.

Object Lifelines and Object Destruction

Figure 15.20 also illustrates **object lifelines**—the vertical dashed lines underneath the objects. These indicate the extent of the life of the object in the diagram. In some circumstances it is desirable to show explicit destruction of an object (as in C++, which does not have garbage collection); the UML lifeline notation provides a way to express this destruction (see Figure 15.21).

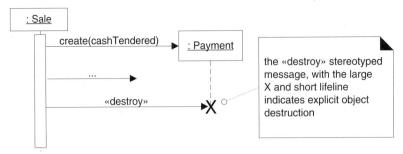

Figure 15.21 Object destruction.

Conditional Messages

A condition message is shown in Figure 15.22.

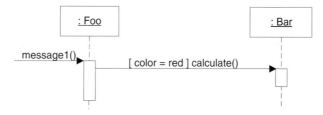

Figure 15.22 A conditional message.

Mutually Exclusive Conditional Messages

The notation for this case is a kind of angled message line emerging from a common point, as illustrated in Figure 15.23.

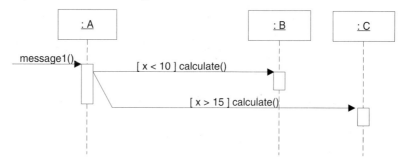

Figure 15.23 Mutually exclusive conditional messages.

Iteration for a Single Message

Iteration notation for one message is shown in Figure 15.24.

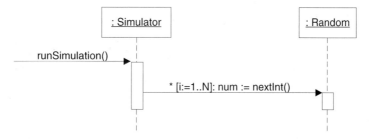

Figure 15.24 Iteration for one message.

Iteration of a Series of Messages

Notation to indicate iteration around a series of messages is shown in Figure 15.25.

Iteration Over a Collection (Multiobject)

In sequence diagrams, iteration over a collection is shown in Figure 15.26.

With collaboration diagrams the UML specifies a '*' multiplicity marker at the end of the role (next to the multiobject) to indicate sending a message to each element rather than repeatedly to the collection itself. However, the UML does not specify how to indicate this with sequence diagrams.

Messages to Class Objects

As in a collaboration diagram, class or static method calls are shown by not underlining the name of the classifier, which signifies a class object rather than an instance (see Figure 15.27).

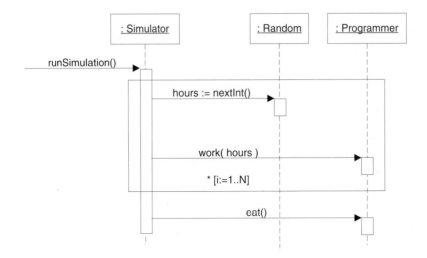

Figure 15.25 Iteration for a sequence of messages.

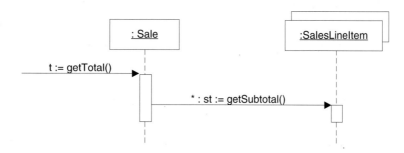

Figure 15.26 Iteration over a multiobject.

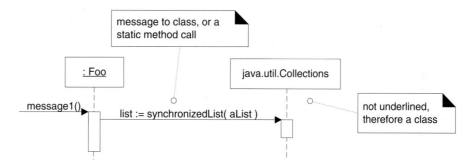

Figure 15.27 Invoking class or static methods.

GRASP: Designing Objects with Responsibilities

The most likely way for the world to be destroyed, most experts agree, is by accident. That's where we come in; we're computer professionals. We cause accidents.

—Nathaniel Borenstein

Objectives

- Define patterns.
- Learn to apply five of the GRASP patterns.

Introduction

Object design is sometimes described as some variation of the following:

> After identifying your requirements and creating a domain model, then add methods to the software classes, and define the messaging between the objects to fulfill the requirements.

Such terse advice is not especially helpful, because there are deep principles and issues involved in these steps. Deciding what methods belong where, and how the objects should interact, is terribly important and anything but trivial. It takes careful explanation, applicable while diagramming and programming.

And this is a critical step—this is at the heart of what it means to develop an object-oriented system, not drawing domain model diagrams, package diagrams, and so forth.

GRASP as a Methodical Approach to Learning Basic Object Design

It *is* possible to communicate the detailed principles and reasoning required to grasp basic object design, and to learn to apply these in a methodical approach that removes the magic and vagueness.

The GRASP patterns are a learning aid to help one understand essential object design, and apply design reasoning in a methodical, rational, explainable way. This approach to understanding and using design principles is based on *patterns of assigning responsibilities*.

16.1 Responsibilities and Methods

The UML defines a **responsibility** as "a contract or obligation of a classifier" [OMG01]. Responsibilities are related to the obligations of an object in terms of its behavior. Basically, these responsibilities are of the following two types:

- knowing
- doing

Doing responsibilities of an object include:

- ○ doing something itself, such as creating an object or doing a calculation
- ○ initiating action in other objects
- ○ controlling and coordinating activities in other objects

Knowing responsibilities of an object include:

- ○ knowing about private encapsulated data
- ○ knowing about related objects
- ○ knowing about things it can derive or calculate

Responsibilities are assigned to classes of objects during object design. For example, I may declare that "a *Sale* is responsible for creating *SalesLineItems*" (a doing), or "a *Sale* is responsible for knowing its total" (a knowing). Relevant responsibilities related to "knowing" are often inferable from the domain model, because of the attributes and associations it illustrates.

The translation of responsibilities into classes and methods is influenced by the granularity of the responsibility. The responsibility to "provide access to relational databases" may involve dozens of classes and hundreds of methods, packaged in a subsystem. By contrast, the responsibility to "create a *Sale*" may involve only one or few methods.

A responsibility is not the same thing as a method, but methods are implemented to fulfill responsibilities. Responsibilities are implemented using methods that either act alone or collaborate with other methods and objects. For example, the *Sale* class might define one or more methods to know its total; say, a method named *getTotal*. To fulfill that responsibility, the *Sale* may collaborate with other objects, such as sending a *getSubtotal* message to each *SalesLineItem* object asking for its subtotal.

16.2   Responsibilities and Interaction Diagrams

The purpose of this chapter is to help methodically apply fundamental principles for assigning responsibilities to objects. This will often be done while programming. Within the UML artifacts, a common context where these responsibilities (implemented as methods) are considered is during the creation of interaction diagrams (which are part of the UP Design Model), whose basic notation we examined in the previous chapter.

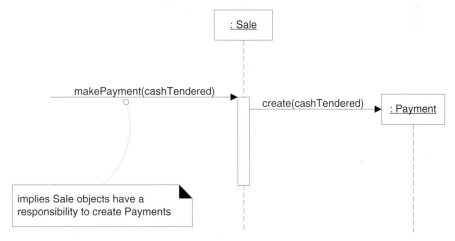

Figure 16.1 Responsibilities and methods are related.

Figure 16.1 indicates that *Sale* objects have been given a responsibility to create *Payments*, which is invoked with a *makePayment* message and handled with a corresponding *makePayment* method. Furthermore, the fulfillment of this responsibility requires collaboration to create the *SalesLineItem* object and invoke its constructor.

In summary, interaction diagrams show choices in assigning responsibilities to objects. When created, decisions in responsibility assignment are made, which are reflected in what messages are sent to different classes of objects. This chapter emphasizes fundamental principles—expressed in the GRASP patterns—to guide choices in where to assign responsibilities. These choices are reflected in interaction diagrams.

16.3   Patterns

Experienced object-oriented developers (and other software developers) build up a repertoire of both general principles and idiomatic solutions that guide them in the creation of software. These principles and idioms, if codified in a structured format describing the problem and solution, and given a name, may be called **patterns**. For example, here is a sample pattern:

Pattern Name:	Information Expert
Solution:	Assign a responsibility to the class that has the information needed to fulfill it.
Problem It Solves:	What is a basic principle by which to assign responsibilities to objects?

In object technology, a **pattern** is a named description of a problem and solution that can be applied to new contexts; ideally, it provides advice in how to apply it in varying circumstances, and considers the forces and trade-offs.[1] Many patterns provide guidance for how responsibilities should be assigned to objects, given a specific category of problem.

> Most simply, a **pattern** is a named problem/solution pair that can be applied in new contexts, with advice on how to apply it in novel situations and discussion of its trade-offs.

"One person's pattern is another person's primitive building block" is an object technology adage illustrating the vagueness of what can be called a pattern [GHJV94]. This treatment of patterns will bypass the issue of what is appropriate to label a pattern, and focus on the pragmatic value of using the pattern style as a vehicle for naming, presenting, learning, and remembering useful software engineering principles.

Repeating Patterns

New pattern could be considered an oxymoron, if it describes a new idea. The very term "pattern" is meant to suggest a repeating thing. The point of patterns is not to express new design ideas. Quite the opposite is true—patterns attempt to codify *existing* tried-and-true knowledge, idioms, and principles; the more honed and widely used, the better.

---

1. The formal notion of patterns originated with the (building) architectural patterns of Christopher Alexander [AIS77]. Patterns for software originated in the 1980s with Kent Beck, who became aware of Alexander's pattern work in architecture, and then were developed by Beck with Ward Cunningham [BC87, Beck94].

Consequently, the GRASP patterns—which will soon be introduced—do not state new ideas; they are a codification of widely used basic principles. To an object expert, the GRASP patterns—by idea if not by name—will appear very fundamental and familiar. That's the point!

Patterns Have Names

All patterns ideally have suggestive names. Naming a pattern, technique, or principle has the following advantages:

- It supports chunking and incorporating that concept into our understanding and memory.

- It facilitates communication.

Naming a complex idea such as a pattern is an example of the power of abstraction—reducing a complex form to a simple one by eliminating detail. Therefore, the GRASP patterns have concise names such as *Information Expert, Creator, Protected Variations*.

Naming Patterns Improves Communication

When a pattern is named, we can discuss with others a complex principle or design idea with a simple name. Consider the following discussion between two software designers, using a common vocabulary of patterns (*Creator, Factory,* and so on) to decide upon a design:

Fred: "Where do you think we should place the responsibility for creating a *SalesLineItem*? I think a *Factory*."

Wilma: "By *Creator,* I think *Sale* will be suitable."

Fred: "Oh, right—I agree."

Chunking design idioms and principles with commonly understood names facilitates communication and raises the level of inquiry to a higher degree of abstraction.

16.4   GRASP: Patterns of General Principles in Assigning Responsibilities

To summarize the preceding introduction:

- The skillful assignment of responsibilities is extremely important in object design.

- Determining the assignment of responsibilities often occurs during the creation of interaction diagrams, and certainly during programming.

- Patterns are named problem/solution pairs that codify good advice and principles often related to the assignment of responsibilities.

Question:	What are the GRASP patterns?
Answer:	They describe fundamental principles of object design and responsibility assignment, expressed as patterns.

Understanding and being able to apply these principles during the creation of interaction diagrams is important because a software developer new to object technology needs to master these basic principles as quickly as possible; they form the foundation of how a system will be designed.

GRASP is an acronym that stands for **G**eneral **R**esponsibility **A**ssignment **S**oftware **P**atterns.[2] The name was chosen to suggest the importance of *grasping* these principles to successfully design object-oriented software.

How to Apply the GRASP Patterns

The following sections present the first five GRASP patterns:

- Information Expert
- Creator
- High Cohesion
- Low Coupling
- Controller

There are others, introduced in a later chapter, but it is worthwhile mastering these five first because they address very basic, common questions and fundamental design issues.

Please study the following patterns, note how they are used in the example interaction diagrams, and then apply them during the creation of new interaction diagrams. Start by mastering *Information Expert, Creator, Controller, High Cohesion,* and *Low Coupling.* Later, learn the remaining patterns.

16.5   The UML Class Diagram Notation

A UML class box used to illustrate software classes often shows three compartments; the third illustrates the methods of the class, as shown in Figure 16.2.

---

2. Technically, one should write "GRAS Patterns" rather than "GRASP Patterns," but the latter sounds better.

Figure 16.2 Software classes illustrate method names.

The details of this notation are explored in a subsequent chapter. In the following discussion on patterns, this form of class box will occasionally be used.

16.6   Information Expert (or Expert)

Solution   Assign a responsibility to the information expert—the class that has the *information* necessary to fulfill the responsibility.

Problem   What is a general principle of assigning responsibilities to objects?

A Design Model may define hundreds or thousands of software classes, and an application may require hundreds or thousands of responsibilities to be fulfilled. During object design, when the interactions between objects are defined, we make choices about the assignment of responsibilities to software classes. Done well, systems tend to be easier to understand, maintain, and extend, and there is more opportunity to reuse components in future applications.

Example   In the NextGEN POS application, some class needs to know the grand total of a sale.

> Start assigning responsibilities by clearly stating the responsibility.

By this advice, the statement is:

> *Who should be responsible for knowing the grand total of a sale?*

By *Information Expert*, we should look for that class of objects that has the information needed to determine the total.

Now we come to a key question: Do we look in the Domain Model or the Design Model to analyze the classes that have the information needed? The Domain Model illustrates conceptual classes of the real-world domain; the Design Model illustrates software classes.

Answer:

1. If there are relevant classes in the Design Model, look there first.

2. Else, look in the Domain Model, and attempt to use (or expand) its representations to inspire the creation of corresponding design classes.

For example, assume we are just starting design work and there is no or a minimal Design Model. Therefore, we look to the Domain Model for information experts; perhaps the real-world *Sale* is one. Then, we add a software class to the Design Model similarly called *Sale*, and give it the responsibility of knowing its total, expressed with the method named *getTotal*. This approach supports *low representational gap* in which the software design of objects appeals to our concepts of how the real domain is organized.

To examine this case in detail, consider the partial Domain Model in Figure 16.3.

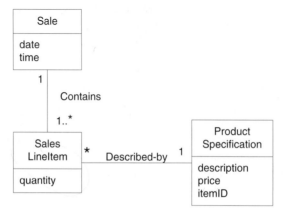

Figure 16.3 Associations of Sale.

What information is needed to determine the grand total? It is necessary to know about all the *SalesLineItem* instances of a sale and the sum of their subtotals. A *Sale* instance contains these; therefore, by the guideline of Information Expert, *Sale* is a suitable class of object for this responsibility; it is an *information expert* for the work.

As mentioned, it is in the context of the creation of interaction diagrams that these questions of responsibility often arise. Imagine we are starting to work through the drawing of diagrams in order to assign responsibilities to objects. A partial interaction diagram and class diagram in Figure 16.4 illustrate some decisions.

Figure 16.4 Partial interaction and class diagrams.

We are not done yet. What information is needed to determine the line item sub-total? *SalesLineItem.quantity* and *ProductSpecification.price* are needed. The *SalesLineItem* knows its quantity and its associated *ProductSpecification*; therefore, by Expert, *SalesLineItem* should determine the subtotal; it is the *information expert*.

In terms of an interaction diagram, this means that the *Sale* needs to send *get-Subtotal* messages to each of the *SalesLineItems* and sum the results; this design is shown in Figure 16.5.

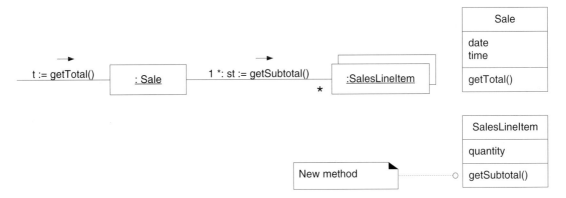

Figure 16.5 Calculating the Sale total.

To fulfill the responsibility of knowing and answering its subtotal, a *Sales-LineItem* needs to know the product price.

The *ProductSpecification* is an information expert on answering its price; there-fore, a message must be sent to it asking for its price.

The design is shown in Figure 16.6.

In conclusion, to fulfill the responsibility of knowing and answering the sale's total, three responsibilities were assigned to three design classes of objects as follows.

Design Class	Responsibility
Sale	knows sale total
SalesLineItem	knows line item subtotal
ProductSpecification	knows product price

The context in which these responsibilities were considered and decided upon was while drawing an interaction diagram. The method section of a class diagram can then summarize the methods.

The principle by which each responsibility was assigned was Information Expert—placing it with the object that had the information needed to fulfill it.

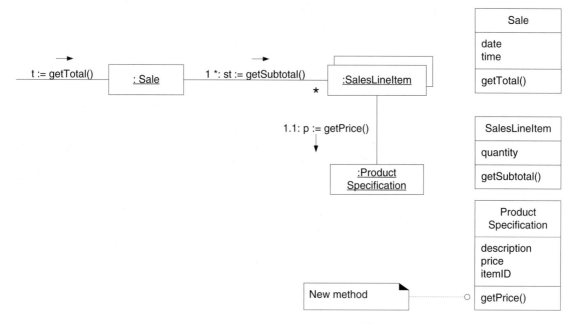

Figure 16.6 Calculating the *Sale* total.

Discussion Information Expert is frequently used in the assignment of responsibilities; it is a basic guiding principle used continuously in object design. Expert is not meant to be an obscure or fancy idea; it expresses the common "intuition" that objects do things related to the information they have.

Notice that the fulfillment of a responsibility often requires information that is spread across different classes of objects. This implies that there are many "partial" information experts who will collaborate in the task. For example, the sales total problem ultimately required the collaboration of three classes of objects.

Whenever information is spread across different objects, they will need to interact via messages to share the work.

Expert usually leads to designs where a software object does those operations that are normally done to the inanimate real-world thing it represents; Peter Coad calls this the "Do It Myself" strategy [Coad95]. For example, in the real world, without the use of electro-mechanical aids, a sale does not tell you its total; it is an inanimate thing. Someone calculates the total of the sale. But in object-oriented software land, all software objects are "alive" or "animated," and they can take on responsibilities and do things. Fundamentally, they do things related to the information they know. I call this the "animation" principle in object design; it is like being in a cartoon where everything is alive.

The Information Expert pattern—like many things in object technology—has a real-world analogy. We commonly give responsibility to individuals who have the information necessary to fulfill a task. For example, in a business, who should be responsible for creating a profit-and-loss statement? The person who has access to all the information necessary to create it—perhaps the chief financial officer. And just as software objects collaborate because the information is spread around, so it is with people. The company's chief financial officer may ask accountants to generate reports on credits and debits.

Contraindications
There are situations where a solution suggested by Expert is undesirable, usually because of problems in coupling and cohesion (these principles are discussed later in this chapter).

For example, who should be responsible for saving a *Sale* in a database? Certainly, much of the information to be saved is in the *Sale* object, and thus by Expert an argument could be made to put the responsibility in the *Sale* class. And the logical extension of this decision is that each class has its own services to save itself in a database. But this leads to problems in cohesion, coupling, and duplication. For example, the *Sale* class must now contain logic related to database handling, such as related to SQL and JDBC (Java Database Connectivity). The class is no longer focused on just the pure application logic of "being a sale;" it now has other kinds of responsibilities, which lowers its cohesion. The class must be coupled to the technical database services of another subsystem, such as JDBC services, rather than just being coupled to other objects in the domain layer of software objects, which raises its coupling. And it is likely that similar database logic would be duplicated in many persistent classes.

All these problems indicate violation of a basic architectural principle: design for a separation of major system concerns. Keep application logic in one place (such as the domain software objects), keep database logic in another place (such as a separate persistence services subsystem), and so forth, rather than intermingling different system concerns in the same component.[3]

---

3. See Chapter 32 for a discussion of separation of concerns.

Supporting a separation of major concerns improves coupling and cohesion in a design. Thus, even though by Expert there could be some justification to put the responsibility for database services in the *Sale* class, for other reasons (usually cohesion and coupling), it is a poor design.

Benefits
- Information encapsulation is maintained, since objects use their own information to fulfill tasks. This usually supports low coupling, which leads to more robust and maintainable systems. (Low Coupling is also a GRASP pattern that is discussed in a following section).

- Behavior is distributed across the classes that have the required information, thus encouraging more cohesive "lightweight" class definitions that are easier to understand and maintain. High cohesion is usually supported (another pattern discussed later).

Related Patterns or Principles
- Low Coupling
- High Cohesion

Also Known As; Similar To
"Place responsibilities with data," "That which knows, does," "Do It Myself," "Put Services with the Attributes They Work On."

16.7   Creator

Solution   Assign class B the responsibility to create an instance of class A if one or more of the following is true:

- B *aggregates* A objects.

- B *contains* A objects.

- B *records* instances of A objects.

- B *closely uses* A objects.

- B *has the initializing data* that will be passed to A when it is created (thus B is an Expert with respect to creating A).

B is a *creator* of A objects.

If more than one option applies, prefer a class B which *aggregates* or *contains* class A.

Problem   Who should be responsible for creating a new instance of some class?

The creation of objects is one of the most common activities in an object-oriented system. Consequently, it is useful to have a general principle for the assignment of creation responsibilities. Assigned well, the design can support low coupling, increased clarity, encapsulation, and reusability.

Example In the POS application, who should be responsible for creating a *SalesLineItem* instance? By Creator, we should look for a class that aggregates, contains, and so on, *SalesLineItem* instances. Consider the partial domain model in Figure 16.7.

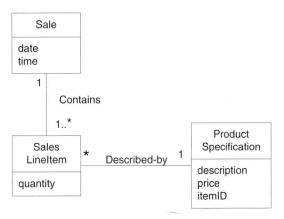

Figure 16.7 Partial domain model.

Since a *Sale* contains (in fact, aggregates) many *SalesLineItem* objects, the Creator pattern suggests that *Sale* is a good candidate to have the responsibility of creating *SalesLineItem* instances.

This leads to a design of object interactions as shown in Figure 16.8.

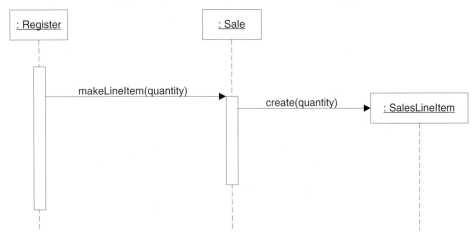

Figure 16.8 Creating a SalesLineItem.

This assignment of responsibilities requires that a *makeLineItem* method be defined in *Sale*.

Once again, the context in which these responsibilities were considered and decided upon was while drawing an interaction diagram. The method section of a class diagram can then summarize the responsibility assignment results, concretely realized as methods.

Discussion Creator guides assigning responsibilities related to the creation of objects, a very common task. The basic intent of the Creator pattern is to find a creator that needs to be connected to the created object in any event. Choosing it as the creator supports low coupling.

Aggregate *aggregates* Part, Container *contains* Content, and Recorder *records* Recorded are all very common relationships between classes in a class diagram. Creator suggests that the enclosing container or recorder class is a good candidate for the responsibility of creating the thing contained or recorded. Of course, this is only a guideline.

Note that the concept of **aggregation** has been used in considering the Creator pattern. Aggregation is discussed in Chapter 27; a brief definition is that aggregation involves things that are in a strong Whole-Part or Assembly-Part relationship, such as Body aggregates Leg or Paragraph aggregates Sentence.

Sometimes a creator is found by looking for the class that has the initializing data that will be passed in during creation. This is actually an example of the Expert pattern. Initializing data is passed in during creation via some kind of initialization method, such as a Java constructor that has parameters. For example, assume that a *Payment* instance needs to be initialized, when created, with the *Sale* total. Since *Sale* knows the total, *Sale* is a candidate creator of the *Payment*.

Contraindications Often, creation requires significant complexity, such as using recycled instances for performance reasons, conditionally creating an instance from one of a family of similar classes based upon some external property value, and so forth. In these cases, it is advisable to delegate creation to a helper class called a *Factory* [GHJV95] rather than use the class suggested by *Creator*. Factories are discussed in Chapter 23.

Benefits
- Low coupling (described next) is supported, which implies lower maintenance dependencies and higher opportunities for reuse. Coupling is probably not increased because the *created* class is likely already visible to the *creator* class, due to the existing associations that motivated its choice as creator.

Related Patterns or Principles
- Low Coupling
- Factory
- Whole-Part [BMRSS96] describes a pattern to define aggregate objects that support encapsulation of components.

16.8   Low Coupling

Solution   Assign a responsibility so that coupling remains low.

Problem   How to support low dependency, low change impact, and increased reuse?

Coupling is a measure of how strongly one element is connected to, has knowledge of, or relies on other elements. An element with low (or weak) coupling is not dependent on too many other elements; "too many" is context-dependent, but will be examined. These elements include classes, subsystems, systems, and so on.

A class with high (or strong) coupling relies on many other classes. Such classes may be undesirable; some suffer from the following problems:

- Changes in related classes force local changes.

- Harder to understand in isolation.

- Harder to reuse because its use requires the additional presence of the classes on which it is dependent.

Example   Consider the following partial class diagram from a NextGen case study:

Assume we have a need to create a *Payment* instance and associate it with the *Sale*. What class should be responsible for this? Since a *Register* "records" a *Payment* in the real-world domain, the Creator pattern suggests *Register* as a candidate for creating the *Payment*. The *Register* instance could then send an *addPayment* message to the *Sale*, passing along the new *Payment* as a parameter. A possible partial interaction diagram reflecting this is shown in Figure 16.9.

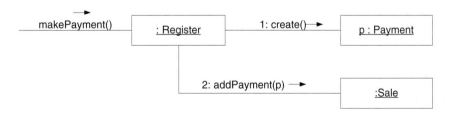

Figure 16.9 Register creates Payment.

This assignment of responsibilities couples the *Register* class to knowledge of the *Payment* class.

UML notation: Note that the *Payment* instance is explicitly named *p* so that in message 2 it can be referenced as a parameter.

An alternative solution to creating the *Payment* and associating it with the *Sale* is shown in Figure 16.10.

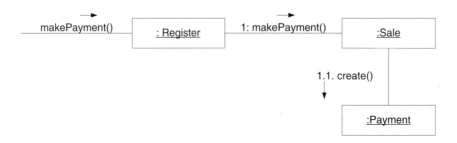

Figure 16.10 Sale creates Payment.

Which design, based on assignment of responsibilities, supports Low Coupling? In both cases we will assume the *Sale* must eventually be coupled to knowledge of a *Payment*. Design 1, in which the *Register* creates the *Payment,* adds coupling of *Register* to *Payment*, while Design 2, in which the *Sale* does the creation of a *Payment*, does not increase the coupling. Purely from the point of view of coupling, Design Two is preferable because overall lower coupling is maintained. This an example where two patterns—Low Coupling and Creator—may suggest different solutions.

In practice, the level of coupling alone can't be considered in isolation from other principles such as Expert and High Cohesion. Nevertheless, it is one factor to consider in improving a design.

Discussion   Low Coupling is a principle to keep in mind during all design decisions; it is an underlying goal to continually consider. It is an **evaluative principle** that a designer applies while evaluating all design decisions.

In object-oriented languages such as C++, Java, and C#, common forms of coupling from *TypeX* to *TypeY* include:

- *TypeX* has an attribute (data member or instance variable) that refers to a *TypeY* instance, or *TypeY* itself.

- A *TypeX* object calls on services of a *TypeY* object.

- *TypeX* has a method that references an instance of *TypeY*, or *TypeY* itself, by any means. These typically include a parameter or local variable of type *TypeY*, or the object returned from a message being an instance of *TypeY*.

- *TypeX* is a direct or indirect subclass of *TypeY*.

- *TypeY* is an interface, and *TypeX* implements that interface.

Low Coupling encourages assigning a responsibility so that its placement does not increase the coupling to such a level that it leads to the negative results that high coupling can produce.

Low Coupling supports the design of classes that are more independent, which reduces the impact of change. It can't be considered in isolation from other patterns such as Expert and High Cohesion, but rather needs to be included as one of several design principles that influence a choice in assigning a responsibility.

A subclass is strongly coupled to its superclass. The decision to derive from a superclass needs to be carefully considered since it is such a strong form of coupling. For example, suppose that objects need to be stored persistently in a relational or object database. In this case it is a relatively common design to create an abstract superclass called *PersistentObject* from which other classes derive. The disadvantage of this subclassing is that it highly couples domain objects to a particular technical service and mixes different architectural concerns, whereas the advantage is automatic inheritance of persistence behavior.

There is no absolute measure of when coupling is too high. What is important is that a developer can gauge the current degree of coupling, and assess if increasing it will lead to problems. In general, classes that are inherently very generic in nature, and with a high probability for reuse, should have especially low coupling.

The extreme case of Low Coupling is when there is no coupling between classes. This is not desirable because a central metaphor of object technology is a system of connected objects that communicate via messages. If Low Coupling is taken to excess, it yields a poor design because it leads to a few incohesive, bloated, and complex active objects that do all the work, with many very passive zero-coupled objects that act as simple data repositories. Some moderate degree of coupling between classes is normal and necessary to create an object-oriented system in which tasks are fulfilled by a collaboration between connected objects.

Contraindications High coupling to stable elements and to pervasive elements is seldom a problem. For example, a Java J2EE application can safely couple itself to the Java libraries (*java.util,* and so on), because they are stable and widespread.

Pick Your Battles

It is not high coupling per se that is the problem; it is high coupling to elements that are unstable in some dimension, such as their interface, implementation, or mere presence.

This is an important point: As designers, we can add flexibility, encapsulate details and implementations, and in general design for lower coupling in many areas of the system. But, if we put effort into "future proofing" or lowering the coupling at some point where in fact there is no realistic motivation, this is not time well spent.

Designers have to pick their battles in lowering coupling and encapsulating things. Focus on the points of realistic high instability or evolution. For example, in the NextGen project, it is known that different third-party tax calculators (with unique interfaces) need to be connected to the system. Therefore, designing for low coupling at this variation point is practical.

Benefits
- not affected by changes in other components
- simple to understand in isolation
- convenient to reuse

Background   Coupling and cohesion (described next) are truly fundamental principles in design, and should be appreciated and applied as such by all software developers. Larry Constantine, also a founder of structured design in the 1970s and a current advocate of more attention to usability engineering [CL99], was primarily responsible in the 1960s for identifying and communicating coupling and cohesion as critical principles [Constantine68, CMS74].

Related Patterns
- Protected Variation

16.9   High Cohesion

Solution   Assign a responsibility so that cohesion remains high.

Problem   How to keep complexity manageable?

In terms of object design, **cohesion** (or more specifically, functional cohesion) is a measure of how strongly related and focused the responsibilities of an element are. An element with highly related responsibilities, and which does not do a tremendous amount of work, has high cohesion. These elements include classes, subsystems, and so on.

A class with low cohesion does many unrelated things, or does too much work. Such classes are undesirable; they suffer from the following problems:

- hard to comprehend
- hard to reuse
- hard to maintain
- delicate; constantly effected by change

Low cohesion classes often represent a very "large grain" of abstraction, or have taken on responsibilities that should have been delegated to other objects.

Example   The same example problem used in the Low Coupling pattern can be analyzed for High Cohesion.

Assume we have a need to create a (cash) *Payment* instance and associate it with the *Sale*. What class should be responsible for this? Since *Register* records a *Payment* in the real-world domain, the Creator pattern suggests *Register* as a candidate for creating the *Payment*. The *Register* instance could then send an *addPayment* message to the *Sale*, passing along the new *Payment* as a parameter, as shown in Figure 16.11.

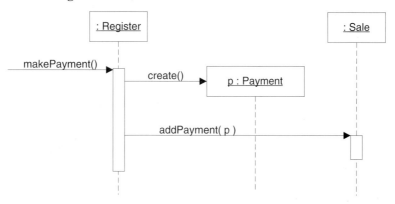

Figure 16.11 Register creates Payment.

This assignment of responsibilities places the responsibility for making a payment in the *Register*. The *Register* is taking on part of the responsibility for fulfilling the *makePayment* system operation.

In this isolated example, this is acceptable; but if we continue to make the *Register* class responsible for doing some or most of the work related to more and more system operations, it will become increasingly burdened with tasks and become incohesive.

Imagine that there were fifty system operations, all received by *Register*. If it did the work related to each, it would become a "bloated" incohesive object. The point is not that this single *Payment* creation task in itself makes the *Register* incohesive, but as part of a larger picture of overall responsibility assignment, it may suggest a trend toward low cohesion.

And most important in terms of developing skills as an object designer, regardless of the final design choice, the valuable thing is that at least a developer knows to consider the impact on cohesion.

By contrast, as shown in Figure 16.12, the second design delegates the payment creation responsibility to the *Sale*, which supports higher cohesion in the *Register*.

Since the second design supports both high cohesion and low coupling, it is desirable.

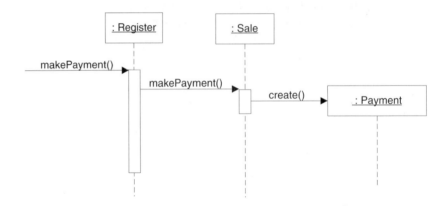

Figure 16.12 Sale creates Payment.

> In practice, the level of cohesion alone can't be considered in isolation from other responsibilities and other principles such as Expert and Low Coupling.

Discussion Like Low Coupling, High Cohesion is a principle to keep in mind during all design decisions; it is an underlying goal to continually consider. It is an evaluative principle that a designer applies while evaluating all design decisions.

Grady Booch describes high functional cohesion as existing when the elements of a component (such as a class) "all work together to provide some well-bounded behavior" [Booch94].

Here are some scenarios that illustrate varying degrees of functional cohesion:

1. *Very low cohesion*—A class is solely responsible for many things in very different functional areas.

    ○ Assume a class exists called *RDB-RPC-Interface* which is completely responsible for interacting with relational databases and for handling remote procedure calls. These are two vastly different functional areas, and each requires lots of supporting code. The responsibilities should be split into a family of classes related to RDB access and a family related to RPC support.

2. *Low cohesion*—A class has sole responsibility for a complex task in one functional area.

    ○ Assume a class exists called *RDBInterface* which is completely responsible for interacting with relational databases. The methods of the class are all related, but there are lots of them, and a tremendous amount of supporting code; there may be hundreds or thousands of methods. The class should split into a family of lightweight classes sharing the work to provide RDB access.

3. *High cohesion*—A class has moderate responsibilities in one functional area and collaborates with other classes to fulfill tasks.

   ○ Assume a class exists called *RDBInterface* which is only partially responsible for interacting with relational databases. It interacts with a dozen other classes related to RDB access in order to retrieve and save objects.

4. *Moderate cohesion*—A class has lightweight and sole responsibilities in a few different areas that are logically related to the class concept, but not to each other.

   ○ Assume a class exists called *Company* which is completely responsible for (a) knowing its employees and (b) knowing its financial information. These two areas are not strongly related to each other, although both are logically related to the concept of a company. In addition, the total number of public methods is small, as is the amount of supporting code.

As a rule of thumb, a class with high cohesion has a relatively small number of methods, with highly related functionality, and does not do too much work. It collaborates with other objects to share the effort if the task is large.

A class with high cohesion is advantageous because it is relatively easy to maintain, understand, and reuse. The high degree of related functionality, combined with a small number of operations, also simplifies maintenance and enhancements. The fine grain of highly related functionality also supports increased reuse potential.

The High Cohesion pattern—like many things in object technology—has a real-world analogy. It is a common observation that if a person takes on too many unrelated responsibilities—especially ones that should properly be delegated to others—then the person is not effective. This is observed in some managers who have not learned how to delegate. These people suffer from low cohesion; they are ready to become "unglued."

Another Classic Principle: Modular Design

Coupling and cohesion are old principles in software design; designing with objects does not imply ignoring well-established fundamentals. Another of these—which is strongly related to coupling and cohesion—is to promote **modular design**. To quote:

> Modularity is the property of a system that has been decomposed into a set of cohesive and loosely coupled modules [Booch94].

We promote a modular design by creating methods and classes with high cohesion. At the basic object level, modularity is achieved by designing each method with a clear, single purpose, and grouping a related set of concerns into a class.

Cohesion and Coupling; Yin and Yang

Bad cohesion usually begets bad coupling, and vice versa. I call cohesion and coupling the *yin and yang of software engineering* because of their interdependent influence. For example, consider a GUI widget class that represents and paints a widget, saves data to a database, and invokes remote object services. Not only is it profoundly incohesive, but it is coupled to many (and disparate) elements.

Contraindications   There are a few cases in which accepting lower cohesion is justified.

One case is the grouping of responsibilities or code into one class or component to simplify maintenance by one person—although be warned that such grouping may also make maintenance worse. But for example, suppose an application contains embedded SQL statements that by other good design principles should be distributed across ten classes, such as ten "database mapper" classes. Now, it is common that only one or two SQL experts know how to best define and maintain this SQL, even if there are dozens of object-oriented (OO) programmers on the project; few OO programmers may have strong SQL skills. Suppose the SQL expert is not even a comfortable OO programmer. The software architect may decide to group all the SQL statements into one class, *RDBOperations*, so that it is easy for the SQL expert to work on the SQL in one location.

Another case for components with lower cohesion is with distributed server objects. Because of overhead and performance implications associated with remote objects and remote communication, it is sometimes desirable to create fewer and larger, less cohesive server objects that provide an interface for many operations. This is also related to the pattern called **Coarse-Grained Remote Interface**, in which the remote operations are made more coarse-grained in order to do or request more work in remote operation call, because of the performance penalty of remote calls over a network. As a simple example, instead of a remote object with three fine-grained operations *setName*, *setSalary*, and *setHireDate*, there is one remote operation *setData* which receives a set of data. This results in less remote calls, and better performance.

Benefits   ■   Clarity and ease of comprehension of the design is increased.

■   Maintenance and enhancements are simplified.

■   Low coupling is often supported.

■   The fine grain of highly related functionality supports increased reuse because a cohesive class can be used for a very specific purpose.

16.10   Controller

Solution   Assign the responsibility for receiving or handling a system event message to a class representing one of the following choices:

- Represents the overall system, device, or subsystem (*facade controller*).

- Represents a use case scenario within which the system event occurs, often named <UseCaseName>Handler, <UseCaseName>Coordinator, or <Use-CaseName>Session (*use-case or session controller*).

  ○ Use the same controller class for all system events in the same use case scenario.

  ○ Informally, a session is an instance of a conversation with an actor. Sessions can be of any length, but are often organized in terms of use cases (use case sessions).

Corollary: Note that "window," "applet," "widget," "view," and "document" classes are not on this list. Such classes should *not* fulfill the tasks associated with system events, they typically receive these events and delegate them to a controller.

Problem   Who should be responsible for handling an input system event?

An input **system event** is an event generated by an external actor. They are associated with **system operations**—operations of the system in response to system events, just as messages and methods are related.

For example, when a cashier using a POS terminal presses the "End Sale" button, he is generating a system event indicating "the sale has ended." Similarly, when a writer using a word processor presses the "spell check" button, he is generating a system event indicating "perform a spell check."

A **Controller** is a non-user interface object responsible for receiving or handling a system event. A Controller defines the method for the system operation.

Example   In the NextGen application, there are several system operations, as illustrated in Figure 16.13, showing the system itself as a class or component (which is legal in the UML).

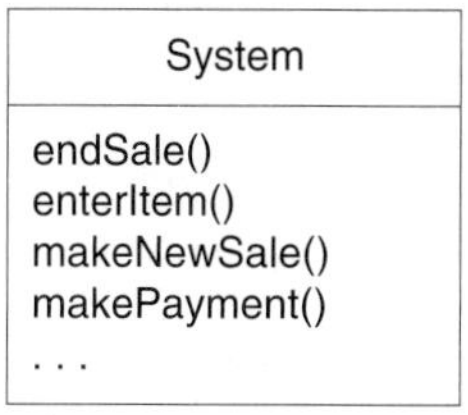

System
endSale() enterItem() makeNewSale() makePayment() . . .

Figure 16.13 System operations associated with the system events.

During analysis, system operations may be assigned to the class *System*, to indicate they are system operations. However, this does *not* mean that a software class named *System* fulfills them during design. Rather, during design, a Controller class is assigned the responsibility for system operations (see Figure 16.14).

Who should be the controller for system events such as *enterItem* and *endSale*?

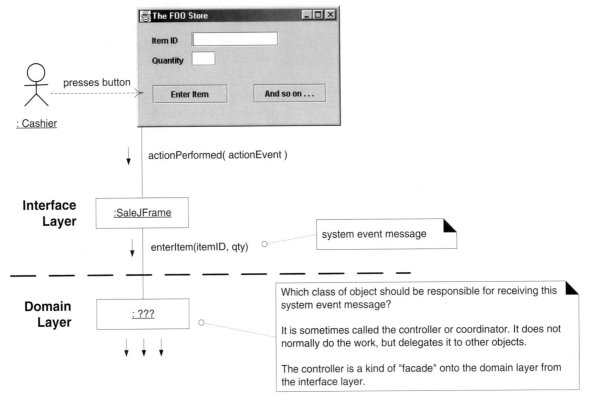

Figure 16.14 Controller for enterItem?

By the Controller pattern, here are some choices:

represents the overall "system," device, or subsystem	*Register, POSSystem*
represents a receiver or handler of all system events of a use case scenario	*ProcessSaleHandler, ProcessSaleSession*

In terms of interaction diagrams, it means that one of the examples in Figure 16.15 may be useful.

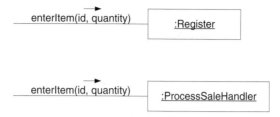

Figure 16.15 Controller choices.

The choice of which of these classes is the most appropriate controller is influenced by other factors, which the following section explores.

During design, the system operations identified during system behavior analysis are assigned to one or more controller classes, such as *Register*, as shown in Figure 16.16.

Discussion Systems receive external input events, typically involving a GUI operated by a person. Other mediums of input include external messages such as in a call processing telecommunications switch, or signals from sensors such as in process control systems.

In all cases, if an object design is used, some handler for these events must be chosen. The Controller pattern provides guidance for generally accepted, suitable choices. As illustrated in Figure 16.14, the controller is a kind of facade into the domain layer from the interface layer.

It is often desirable to use the same controller class for all the system events of one use case so that it is possible to maintain information about the state of the use case in the controller. Such information is useful, for example, to identify out-of-sequence system events (for example, a *makePayment* operation before an *endSale* operation). Different controllers may be used for different use cases.

A common defect in the design of controllers is to give them too much responsibility.

> Normally, a controller should *delegate* to other objects the work that needs to be done; it coordinates or controls the activity. It does not do much work itself.

Please see the "Issues and Solutions" section later for elaboration.

The first category of controller is a facade controller representing the overall system, device, or a subsystem. The idea is to choose some class name that suggests a cover, or facade, over the other layers of the application, and that provides the main point of service calls from the UI layer down to other layers. It could be an abstraction of the overall physical unit, such as a *Register*[4], *TelecommSwitch, Phone,* or *Robot*; a class representing the entire software system, such as *POSSystem,* or any other concept which the designer chooses to represent the overall system or a subsystem, even, for example, *ChessGame* if it was game software.

Facade controllers are suitable when there are not "too many" system events, or it is not possible for the user interface (UI) to redirect system event messages to alternating controllers, such as in a message processing system.

If a use-case controller is chosen, then there is a different controller for each use case. Note that this is not a domain object; it is an artificial construct to support the system (a *Pure Fabrication* in terms of the GRASP patterns). For example, if the NextGen application contains use cases such as *Process Sale* and *Handle Returns*, then there may be a *ProcessSaleHandler* class and so forth.

When should you choose a use-case controller? It is an alternative to consider when placing the responsibilities in a facade controller leads to designs with low cohesion or high coupling, typically when the facade controller is becoming "bloated" with excessive responsibilities. A use-case controller is a good choice when there are many system events across different processes; it factors their handling into manageable separate classes, and also provides a basis for knowing and reasoning about the state of the current scenario in progress.

In the UP and Jacobson's older Objectory method [Jacobson92], there are the (optional) concepts of boundary, control, and entity classes. **Boundary objects** are abstractions of the interfaces, **entity objects** are the application-independent (and typically persistent) domain software objects, and **control objects** are use case handlers as described in this Controller pattern.

A important corollary of the Controller pattern is that interface objects (for example, window objects or widgets) and the presentation layer should not have responsibility for fulfilling system events. In other words, system operations should be handled in the application logic or domain layers of objects rather than in the interface layer of a system. See the "Issues and Solutions" section for an example.

The Controller object is typically a client-side object within the same process as the UI (for example, an application with a Java Swing GUI), and so is not exactly applicable when the UI is a Web client in a browser, and there is server-side software involved. In the latter case, there are various common patterns of handling the system events that are strongly influenced by the chosen server-side technical framework, such as Java servlets. Nevertheless, it is a common idiom to create server-side use-case controllers with either a servlet for each use case or an Enterprise JavaBeans (EJB) session bean for each use case. The

---

4. Various terms are used for a physical POS unit, including register, point-of-sale terminal (POST), and so forth. Over time, "register" has come to embody the notion of both a physical unit, and the logical abstraction of the thing that registers sales and payments.

server-side session object represents a "session" of interaction with an external actor.

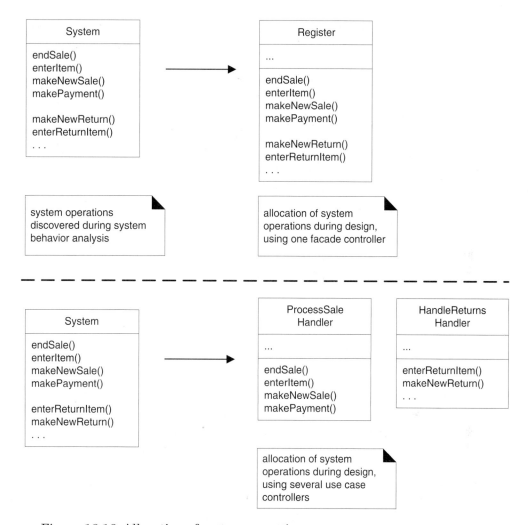

Figure 16.16 Allocation of system operations.

If the UI is not a web client (for example, it is a Swing or Windows GUI), but the application calls on remote services, it is still common to use the Controller pattern. The UI forwards the request to the local client-side Controller, and the Controller may forward all or part of the request handling on to remote services. This design lowers the coupling of the UI to remote services, and makes it easier, for example, to provide the services either locally or remotely, through the indirection of the client-side Controller.

To summarize, the Controller receives the service requests from the UI layer and coordinates their fulfillment, usually by delegation to other objects.

Benefits
- *Increased potential for reuse,* and *pluggable interfaces*—It ensures that application logic is *not* handled in the interface layer. The responsibilities of a controller could technically be handled in an interface object, but the implication of such a design is that program code and logic related the fulfillment of application logic would be embedded in interface or window objects. An interface-as-controller design reduces the opportunity to reuse logic in future applications, since it is bound to a particular interface (for example, window-like objects) that is seldom applicable in other applications. By contrast, delegating a system operation responsibility to a controller supports the reuse of the logic in future applications. And since the application logic is not bound to the interface layer, it can be replaced with a different interface.

- *Reason about the state of the use case*—It is sometimes necessary to ensure that system operations occur in a legal sequence, or to be able to reason about the current state of activity and operations within the use case that is underway. For example, it may be necessary to guarantee that the *makePayment* operation can not occur until the *endSale* operation has occurred. If so, this state information needs to be captured somewhere; the controller is one reasonable choice, especially if the same controller is used throughout the use case (which is recommended).

Issues and Solutions

Bloated Controllers

Poorly designed, a controller class will have low cohesion—unfocused and handling too many areas of responsibility; this is called a **bloated controller**. Signs of bloating include:

- There is only a *single* controller class receiving *all* system events in the system, and there are many of them. This sometimes happens if a facade controller is chosen.

- The controller itself performs many of the tasks necessary to fulfill the system event, without delegating the work. This usually involves a violation of Information Expert and High Cohesion.

- A controller has many attributes, and maintains significant information about the system or domain, which should have been distributed to other objects, or duplicates information found elsewhere.

There are several cures to a bloated controller, including:

1. Add more controllers—a system does not have to have only one. Instead of facade controllers, use use-case controllers. For example, consider an application with many system events, such as an airline reservation system.

It may contain the following controllers:

Use-case controllers
MakeReservationHandler
ManageSchedulesHandler
ManageFaresHandler

2. Design the controller so that it primarily delegates the fulfillment of each system operation responsibility on to other objects.

Interface Layer Does Not Handle System Events

To reiterate: an important corollary of the Controller pattern is that interface objects (for example, window objects) and the interface layer should not have responsibility for handling system events. As an example, consider a design in Java that uses a *JFrame* to display the information.

Assume the NextGen application has a window that displays sale information and captures cashier operations. Using the Controller pattern, Figure 16.17 illustrates an acceptable relationship between the *JFrame* and Controller and other objects in a portion of the POS system (with simplifications).

Notice that the *SaleJFrame* class—part of the interface layer—passes the *enterItem* message to the *Register* object. It did not get involved in processing the operation or deciding how to handle it; the window only delegated it to another layer.

Assigning the responsibility for system operations to objects in the application or domain layer—using the Controller pattern rather than the interface layer supports increased reuse potential. If an interface layer object (like the *SaleJFrame*) handles a system operation—which represents part of a business process—then business process logic would be contained in an interface (for example, window-like) object, which has low opportunity for reuse because of its coupling to a particular interface and application.

Consequently, the design in Figure 16.18 is undesirable.

Placing system operation responsibility in a domain object controller makes it easier to reuse the program logic supporting the associated business process in future applications. It also makes it easier to unplug the interface layer and use a different interface framework or technology, or to run the system in an offline "batch" mode.

Message Handling Systems and the Command Pattern

Some applications are message-handling systems or servers that receive requests from other processes. A telecommunications switch is a common example. In such systems, the design of the interface and controller is somewhat different. The details are explored in a later chapter, but in essence, a common solution is to use the Command pattern [GHJV95] and Command Processor pattern [BMRSS96], introduced in Chapter 34.

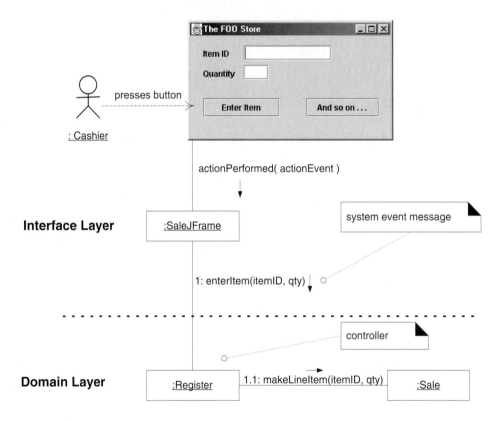

Figure 16.17 Desirable coupling of interface layer to domain layer.

Related Patterns

- **Command**—In a message-handling system, each message may be represented and handled by a separate Command object [GHJV95].

- **Facade**—A facade controller is a kind of Facade [GHJV95].

- **Layers**—This is a POSA pattern [BMRSS96]. Placing domain logic in the domain layer rather than the presentation layer is part of the Layers pattern.

■ **Pure Fabrication**—This is another GRASP pattern. A Pure Fabrication is an arbitrary creation of the designer, not a software class whose name is inspired by the Domain Model. A use-case controller is a kind of Pure Fabrication.

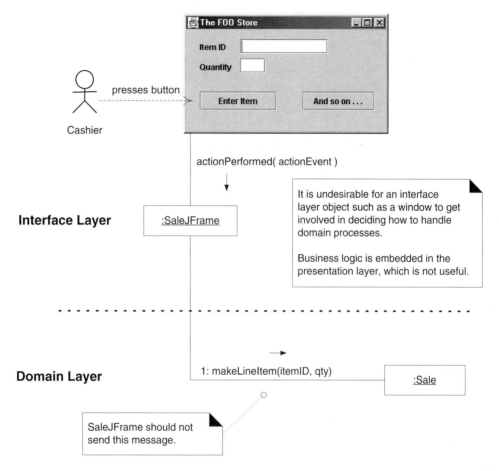

Figure 16.18 Less desirable coupling of interface layer to domain layer.

16.11 Object Design and CRC Cards

Although not formally part of the UML, another device sometimes used to help assign responsibilities and indicate collaboration with other objects are **CRC cards** (Class-Responsibility-Collaborator cards) [BC89]. These were pioneered by Kent Beck and Ward Cunningham, who are largely responsible for encouraging objects designers to think more abstractly in terms of responsibility assignment and collaborations, and also for the use of patterns.

CRC cards are index cards, one for each class, upon which the responsibilities of the class are briefly written, and a list of collaborator objects to fulfill those responsibilities. They are usually developed in a small group session. The GRASP patterns may be applied when considering the design while using CRC cards.

CRC cards are one approach to recording the results of responsibility assignment and collaborations. The recording can be enhanced with the use of interaction and class diagrams. The real value is not the cards or the diagrams, but the consideration of responsibility assignment.

16.12   Further Readings

The metaphor of collaborating objects with responsibilities, or **Responsibility-Driven Design**, especially emerged from the influential object work in Smalltalk at Tektronix in Portland, from Kent Beck, Ward Cunningham, Rebecca Wirfs-Brock, and others. *Designing Object-Oriented Software* [WWW90] is the landmark text, and as relevant today as when it was written.

Two other recommended texts emphasizing fundamental object design principles are *Object-Oriented Design Heuristics* by Riel, and *Object Models* by Coad.

DESIGN MODEL: USE-CASE REALIZATIONS WITH GRASP PATTERNS

To invent, you need a good imagination and a pile of junk.

—Thomas Edison

Objectives

- Design use-case realizations.
- Apply the GRASP patterns to assign responsibilities to classes.
- Use the UML interaction diagram notation to illustrate the design of objects.

Introduction

This chapter explores how to create a design of collaborating objects with responsibilities. Particular attention is given to the application of the GRASP patterns to develop a well-designed solution. Please note that the GRASP patterns as such or by name are not the important thing; they are just a learning aid to help talk about and methodically do fundamental object design.

This chapter communicates the principles, using the NextGen POS example, by which an object-oriented designer assigns responsibilities and establishes object interactions—a core skill in object-oriented development.

Note:

> The assignment of responsibilities and design of collaborations are very important and creative steps during design, either while diagraming or while programming.

The material is intentionally detailed; it attempts to exhaustively illustrate that there is no "magic" or unjustifiable decisions in object design—assignment of responsibilities and the choice of object interactions can be rationally explained and learned.

17.1 Use-Case Realizations

To quote, "A use-case realization describes how a particular use case is realized within the design model, in terms of collaborating objects" [RUP]. More precisely, a designer can describe the design of one or more *scenarios* of a use case; each of these is called a use-case realization. Use-case realization is a UP term or concept used to remind us of the connection between the requirements expressed as use cases, and the object design that satisfies the requirements.

UML interaction diagrams are a common language to illustrate use-case realizations. And as was explored in the prior chapter, there are principles and patterns of object design, such as Information Expert and Low Coupling, that can be applied during this design work.

To review, Figure 17.20 (near the end of this chapter) illustrates the relationship between some UP artifacts:

■ The use case suggests the system events that are explicitly shown in system sequence diagrams.

■ Details of the effect of the system events in terms of changes to domain objects may optionally be described in system operation contracts.

■ The system events represent messages that initiate interaction diagrams, which illustrate how objects interact to fulfill the required tasks—the use case realization.

■ The interaction diagrams involve message interaction between software objects whose names are sometimes inspired by the names of conceptual classes in the Domain Model, plus other classes of objects.

17.2 Artifact Comments

Interaction Diagrams and Use-Case Realizations

In the current iteration we are considering various scenarios and system events such as:

- *Process Sale: makeNewSale, enterItem, endSale, makePayment*

If collaboration diagrams are used to illustrate the use-case realizations, a different collaboration diagram will be required to show the handling of each system event message. For example (Figure 17.1):

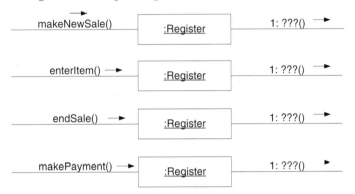

Figure 17.1 Collaboration diagrams and system event message handling.

On the other hand, if sequence diagrams are used, it *may* be possible to fit all system event messages on the same diagram, as in Figure 17.2.

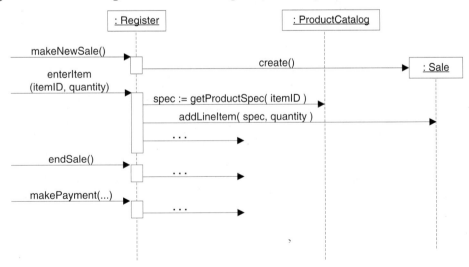

Figure 17.2 One sequence diagram and system event message handling.

However, it is often the case that the sequence diagram is then too complex or long. It is legal, as with interaction diagrams, to use a sequence diagram for each system event message, as in Figure 17.3.

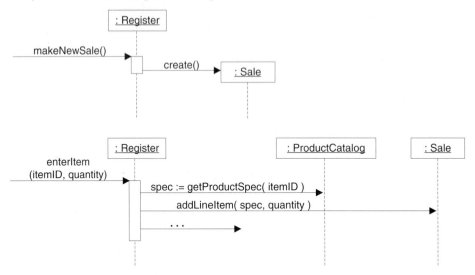

Figure 17.3 Multiple sequence diagrams and system event message handling.

Contracts and Use-Case Realizations

To reiterate, it may be possible to design use-case realizations directly from the use case text. In addition, for some system operations, contracts may have been written that add greater detail or specificity. For example:

Contract CO2: enterItem

Operation:	enterItem(itemID : ItemID, quantity : integer)
Cross References:	Use Cases: Process Sale
Preconditions:	There is a sale underway.
Postconditions:	– A SalesLineItem instance sli was created (instance creation). – ...

In conjunction with contemplating the use case text, for each contract, we work through the postcondition state changes and design message interactions to satisfy the requirements. For example, given this partial *enterItem* system operation, a partial interaction diagram is shown in Figure 17.4 that satisfies the state change of *SalesLineItem* instance creation.

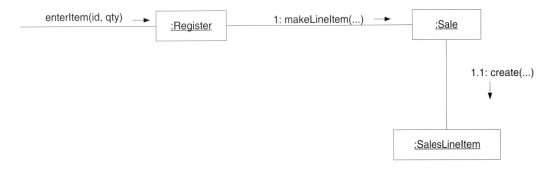

Figure 17.4 Partial interaction diagram.

Caution: The Requirements Are Not Perfect

It is useful to bear in mind that previously written use cases and contracts are only a guess of what must be achieved. The history of software development is one of invariably discovering that the requirements are not perfect, or have changed. This is not an excuse to ignore trying to do a good requirements job, but a recognition of the need to continuously engage customers and subject matter experts in review and feedback on the growing system's behavior.

An advantage of iterative development is that it naturally supports the discovery of new analysis and design results during design and implementation work. The spirit of iterative development is to capture a "reasonable" degree of information during requirements analysis, filling in details during design and implementation.

The Domain Model and Use-Case Realizations

Some of the software objects that interact via messages in the interaction diagrams are inspired from the Domain Model, such as a *Sale* conceptual class and *Sale* design class. The choice of appropriate responsibility placement using the GRASP patterns relies, in part, upon information in the Domain Model. As mentioned, the existing Domain Model is not likely to be perfect; errors and omissions are to be expected. You will discover new concepts that were previously missed, ignore concepts that were previously identified, and do likewise with associations and attributes.

Conceptual vs. Design Classes

Recall that the UP Domain Model does not illustrate software classes, but may be used to inspire the presence and names of some software classes in the

Design Model. During interaction diagramming or programming, the developers may look to the Domain Model to name some design classes, thus creating a design with lower representational gap between the software design and our concepts of the real domain to which the software is related (see Figure 17.5).

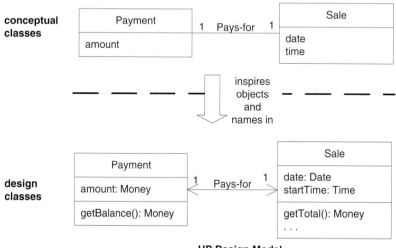

UP Domain Model

Stakeholder's view of the noteworthy concepts in the domain.

UP Design Model

The object developer has taken inspiration from the real-world domain in creating software classes. Therefore, the representational gap between how stakeholders conceive the domain, and its representation in software, has been lowered.

Figure 17.5 Lowering representational gap with design classes named from conceptual classes.

Must the design classes in the Design Model be limited to classes with names inspired from the Domain Model? Not at all; it is appropriate to discover new conceptual classes during this design work that were missed during earlier domain analysis, and also to make up software classes whose names and purpose is completely unrelated to the Domain Model.

17.3   Use-Case Realizations for the NextGen Iteration

The following sections explore the choices and decisions made while designing a use-case realization with objects based on the GRASP patterns. The explanations are intentionally detailed, in an attempt to illustrate that there does not have be any "hand waving" in the creation of well-designed interaction diagrams; their construction is based on justifiable principles.

Notationally, the design of objects for each system event message will be shown in a separate diagram, to focus on the design issues of each. However, they could have been grouped together on one sequence diagram.

17.4 Object Design: makeNewSale

The *makeNewSale* system operation occurs when a cashier requests to start a new sale, after a customer has arrived with things to buy. The use case may have been sufficient to decide what was necessary, but for this case study we wrote contracts for all the system events, for explanation and completeness.

Contract CO1: makeNewSale

Operation:	makeNewSale()
Cross References:	Use Cases: Process Sale
Preconditions:	none
Postconditions:	– A Sale instance s was created (instance creation).
	– s was associated with the Register (association formed).
	– Attributes of s were initialized.

Choosing the Controller Class

Our first design choice involves choosing the controller for the system operation message *enterItem*. By the Controller pattern, here are some choices:

represents the overall "system," device, or subsystem	*Register, POSSystem*
represents a receiver or handler of all system events of a use case scenario.	*ProcessSaleHandler, ProcessSaleSession*

Choosing a facade controller like *Register* is satisfactory if there are only a few system operations and the facade controller is not taking on too many responsibilities (in other words, if it is becoming incohesive). Choosing a use-case controller is suitable when there are many system operations and we wish to distribute responsibilities in order to keep each controller class lightweight and focused (in other words, cohesive). In this case, *Register* will suffice, since there are only a few system operations.

> This *Register* is a software object in the Design Model. It is not a real physical register but a software abstraction whose name was chosen to lower the representational gap between our concept of the domain and the software.

Thus, the interaction diagram shown in Figure 17.6 begins by sending the *makeNewSale* message to a *Register* software object.

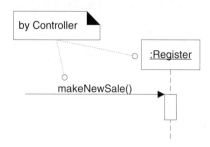

Figure 17.6 Applying the GRASP Controller pattern.

Creating a New Sale

A software *Sale* object must be created, and the GRASP Creator pattern suggests assigning the responsibility for creation to a class that aggregates, contains, or records the object to be created.

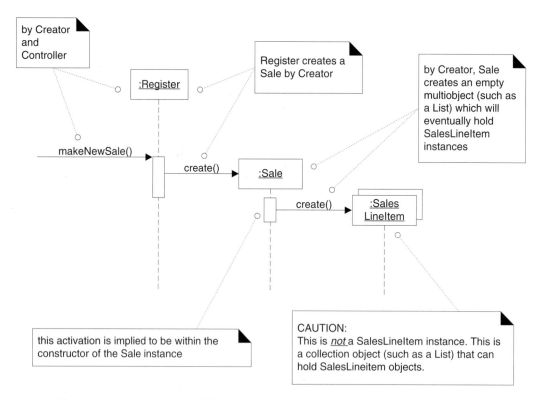

Figure 17.7 Sale and multiobject creation.

Analyzing the Domain Model reveals that a *Register* may be thought of as recording a *Sale*; indeed, the word "register" in business has for many years meant the thing that recorded (or registered) account transactions, such as sales.

Thus, *Register* is a reasonable candidate for creating a *Sale*. And by having the *Register* create the *Sale*, the *Register* can easily be associated with it over time, so that during future operations within the session, the *Register* will have a reference to the current *Sale* instance.

In addition to the above, when the *Sale* is created, it must create an empty collection (container, such as a Java *List*) to record all the future *SalesLineItem* instances that will be added. This collection will be contained within and maintained by the *Sale* instance, which implies by Creator that the *Sale* is a good candidate for creating it.

Therefore, the *Register* creates the *Sale*, and the *Sale* creates an empty collection, represented by a multiobject in the interaction diagram.

Hence, the interaction diagram in Figure 17.7 illustrates the design.

Conclusion

The design was not difficult, but the point of its careful explanation in terms of Controller and Creator was to illustrate that the details of a design can be rationally and methodically decided and explained in terms of principles and patterns, such as GRASP.

17.5   Object Design: enterItem

The *enterItem* system operation occurs when a cashier enters the *itemID* and (optionally) the quantity of something to be purchased. Here is the complete contract:

Contract CO2: enterItem

Operation:	enterItem(itemID : ItemID, quantity : integer)
Cross References:	Use Cases: Process Sale
Preconditions:	There is an underway sale.
Postconditions:	– A SalesLineItem instance sli was created (instance creation).
	– sli was associated with the current Sale (association formed).
	– sli.quantity became quantity (attribute modification).
	– sli was associated with a ProductSpecification, based on itemID match (association formed).

An interaction diagram will be constructed to satisfy the postconditions of *enter-Item*, using the GRASP patterns to help with the design decisions.

Choosing the Controller Class

Our first choice involves handling the responsibility for the system operation message *enterItem*. Based on the Controller pattern, as for *makeNewSale*, we will continue to use *Register* as a controller.

Display Item Description and Price?

Because of a design principle called **Model-View Separation**, it is not the responsibility of non-GUI objects (such as a *Register* or *Sale*) to get involved in output tasks. Therefore, although the use case states that the description and price are displayed after this operation, the design will be ignored at this time.

All that is required with respect to responsibilities for the display of information is that the information is known, which it is in this case.

Creating a New SalesLineItem

The *enterItem* contract postconditions indicate the creation, initialization, and association of a *SalesLineItem*. Analyzing the Domain Model reveals that a *Sale* contains *SalesLineItem* objects. Taking inspiration from the domain, a software *Sale* may similarly contain software *SalesLineItem*. Hence, by Creator, a software *Sale* is an appropriate candidate to create a *SalesLineItem*.

The *Sale* can be associated with the newly created *SalesLineItem* by storing the new instance in its collection of line items. The postconditions indicate that the new *SalesLineItem* needs a quantity, when created; therefore, the *Register* must pass it along to the *Sale*, which must pass it along as a parameter in the *create* message (in Java, that would be implemented as a constructor call with a parameter).

Therefore, by Creator, a *makeLineItem* message is sent to a *Sale* for it to create a *SalesLineItem*. The *Sale* creates a *SalesLineItem*, and then stores the new instance in its permanent collection.

The parameters to the *makeLineItem* message include the *quantity*, so that the *SalesLineItem* can record it, and likewise the *ProductSpecification* which matches the itemID.

Finding a ProductSpecification

The *SalesLineItem* needs to be associated with the *ProductSpecification* that matches the incoming *itemID*. This implies it is necessary to retrieve a *Product-Specification,* based on an *itemID* match.

Before considering *how* to achieve the lookup, it is useful to consider *who* should be responsible for it. Thus, a first step is:

> Start assigning responsibilities by clearly stating the responsibility.

To restate the problem:

> Who should be responsible for knowing a *ProductSpecification*, based on an *itemID* match?

This is neither a creation problem nor one of choosing a controller for a system event. Now we see our first application of Information Expert in the design.

In many cases, the Expert pattern is the principal one to apply. Information Expert suggests that the object that has the information required to fulfill the responsibility should do it. Who knows about all the *ProductSpecification* objects?

Analyzing the Domain Model reveals that the *ProductCatalog* logically contains all the *ProductSpecifications*. Once again, taking inspiration from the domain, we design software classes with similar organization: a software *ProductCatalog* will contain software *ProductSpecifications*.

With that decided, then by Information Expert *ProductCatalog* is a good candidate for this lookup responsibility since it knows all the *ProductSpecification* objects.

This may be implemented, for example, with a method called *getSpecification.*[1]

Visibility to a ProductCatalog

Who should send the *getSpecification* message to the *ProductCatalog* to ask for a *ProductSpecification*?

It is reasonable to assume that a *Register* and *ProductCatalog* instance were created during the initial *Start Up* use case, and that there is a permanent connection from the *Register* object to the *ProductCatalog* object. With that assump-

---

[1]. The naming of accessing methods is of course idiomatic to each language. Java always uses the *object.getFoo()* form, C++ tends to use *object.foo()*, and C# uses *object.Foo,* which hides (like Eiffel and Ada) if it is a method call or direct access of a public attribute. The Java style is used in the examples.

tion (which we might record on a task list of things to ensure in the design when we get to designing the initialization), then it is possible for the *Register* to send the *getSpecification* message to the *ProductCatalog*.

This implies another concept in object design: visibility. **Visibility** is the ability of one object to "see" or have a reference to another object.

> For an object to send a message to another object it must have visibility to it.

Since we will assume that the *Register* has a permanent connection—or reference—to the *ProductCatalog*, it has visibility to it, and hence can send it messages such as *getSpecification*.

The following chapter will explore the question of visibility more closely.

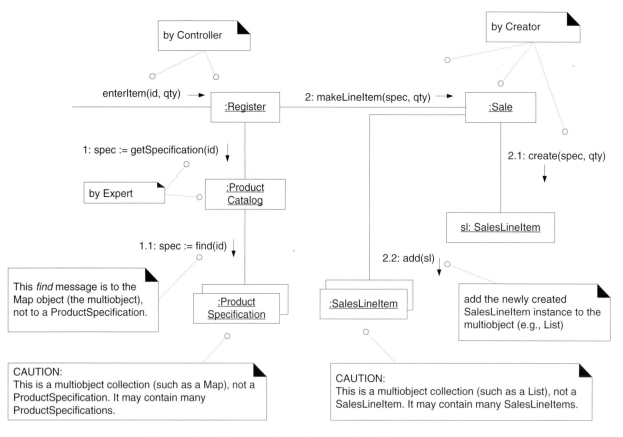

Figure 17.8 The enterItem interaction diagram.

Retrieving ProductSpecifications from a Database

In the final version of the NextGen POS application, it is unlikely that all the *ProductSpecifications* will actually be in memory. They will most likely be stored in a relational or object database and retrieved on demand; some may be cached in the client process for performance or fault-tolerance reasons. However, the issues surrounding retrieval from a database will be deferred for now in the interest of simplicity. It will be assumed that all the *ProductSpecifications* are in memory.

Chapter 34 explores the topic of database access of persistent objects, which is a large topic usually influenced by the choice of technologies, such as J2EE, .NET, and so forth.

The enterItem Object Design

Given the above discussion, the interaction diagram in Figure 17.8 reflects the decisions regarding the assignment of responsibilities and how objects should interact. Observe that considerable reflection was done to arrive at this design, based on the GRASP patterns; the design of object interactions and responsibility assignment require some deliberation.

Messages to Multiobjects

Notice that the interpretation of a message sent to a multiobject in the UML is that it is a message to the collection object itself, rather than an implicit broadcast to the collection's members. This is especially obvious for generic collection operations such as *find* and *add*.

For example, in the *enterItem* interaction diagram:

- The *find* message sent to the *ProductSpecification* multiobject is a message being sent once to the collection data structure represented by the multiobject (such as a Java *Map*).

  ○ The language-independent and generic *find* message will, during programming, be translated for a specific language and library. Perhaps it will actually be *Map.get* in Java. The message *get* could have been used in the diagram; *find* was used to make the point that design diagrams may require some mapping to different languages and libraries.

- The *add* message sent to the *SalesLineItem* multiobject is to add an element to the collection data structure represented by the multiobject (such as a Java *List*).

17.6   Object Design: endSale

The *endSale* system operation occurs when a cashier presses a button indicating the end of a sale. Here is the contract:

Contract CO3: endSale

Operation:	endSale()
Cross References:	Use Cases: Process Sale
Preconditions:	There is an underway sale.
Postconditions:	Sale.isComplete became true (attribute modification).

Choosing the Controller Class

Our first choice involves handling the responsibility for the system operation message *endSale*. Based on the Controller GRASP pattern, as for *enterItem*, we will continue to use *Register* as a controller.

Setting the Sale.isComplete Attribute

The contract postconditions state:

■ *Sale.isComplete* became *true* (attribute modification).

As always, Expert should be the first pattern considered unless it is a controller or creation problem (which it is not).

Who should be responsible for setting the *isComplete* attribute of the *Sale* to true?

By Expert, it should be the *Sale* itself, since it owns and maintains the *isComplete* attribute. Thus the *Register* will send a *becomeComplete* message to the *Sale* to set it to *true*.

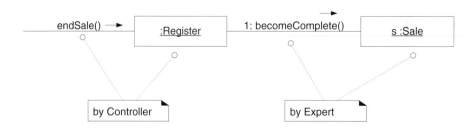

Figure 17.9   Completion of item entry.

UML Notation to Show Constraints, Notes, and Algorithms

Figure 17.9 shows the *becomeComplete* message, but does not communicate the details of what happens in the *becomeComplete* method (although it is admittedly trivial in this case). Sometimes in the UML we wish to use text to describe the algorithm of a method, or specify some constraint.

For these needs, the UML provides both **constraints** and **notes**. A UML constraint is some semantically meaningfully information attached to a model element. UML constraints are text enclosed in { } braces; for example, { x > 20 }. Any informal or formal language can be used for the constraint, and the UML especially includes the **OCL** (object constraint language) [WK99] if one desires to use that.

A UML note is a comment that has no semantic impact, such as date of creation or author.

A note is always shown in a **note box** (a dog-eared text box).

A constraint may be shown as simple text with braces, which is suitable for short statements. However, long constraints may be also placed within a "note box," in which case the so-called note box actually holds a constraint rather than a note. The text in the box is within braces, to indicate it is a constraint.

In Figure 17.10 both styles are used. Note that the simple constraint style (in braces but not in a box) just shows a statement which must hold true (the classic meaning of a constraint in logic). On the other hand, the "constraint" in the note box shows a Java method implementation of the constraint. Both styles are legal in the UML for a constraint.

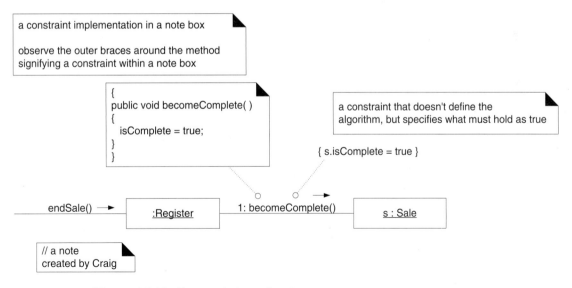

Figure 17.10 Constraints and notes.

Calculating the Sale Total

Consider this fragment of the *Process Sale* use case:

Main Success Scenario:
1. Customer arrives ...
2. Cashier tells System to create a new sale.
3. Cashier enters item identifier.
4. System records sale line item and ...
Cashier repeats steps 3-4 until indicates done.
5. System presents total with taxes calculated.

In step 5, a total is presented (or displayed). Because of the Model-View Separation principle, we should not concern ourselves with the design of how the sale total will be displayed, but it is necessary to ensure that the total is known. Note that no design class currently knows the sale total, so we need to create a design of object interactions that satisfies this requirement.

As always, Information Expert should be a pattern to consider unless it is a controller or creation problem (which it is not).

It is probably obvious the *Sale* itself should be responsible for knowing its total, but just to make the reasoning process to find an Expert crystal clear—with a simple example—please consider the following analysis.

1. State the responsibility:

    ❍   Who should be responsible for knowing the sale total?

2. Summarize the information required:

    ❍   The sale total is the sum of the subtotals of all the sales line-items.

    ❍   sales line-item subtotal := line-item quantity * product description price

3. List the information required to fulfill this responsibility and the classes that know this information.

Information Required for Sale Total	Information Expert
ProductSpecification.price	*ProductSpecification*
SalesLineItem.quantity	*SalesLineItem*
all the *SalesLineItems* in the current Sale	*Sale*

A detailed analysis follows:

- Who should be responsible for calculating the *Sale* total? By Expert, it should be the *Sale* itself, since it knows about all the *SalesLineItem* instances whose subtotals must be summed to calculate the sale total. Therefore, *Sale* will have the responsibility of knowing its total, implemented as a *getTotal* method.

- For a *Sale* to calculate its total, it needs the subtotal for each *SalesLineItem*. Who should be responsible for calculating the *SalesLineItem* subtotal? By Expert, it should be the *SalesLineItem* itself, since it knows the quantity and the *ProductSpecification* it is associated with. Therefore, *SalesLineItem* will have the responsibility of knowing its subtotal, implemented as a *getSubtotal* method.

- For the *SalesLineItem* to calculate its subtotal, it needs the price of the *ProductSpecification*. Who should be responsible for providing the *ProductSpecification* price? By Expert, it should be the *ProductSpecification* itself, since it encapsulates the price as an attribute. Therefore, *ProductSpecification* will have the responsibility of knowing its price, implemented as a *getPrice* operation.

> Although the above analysis is trivial in this case, and the degree of excruciating elaboration presented is uncalled for in actual design practice, the same reasoning strategy to find an Expert can and should be applied in more difficult situations. You will find that once you learn these principles you can quickly perform this kind of reasoning mentally.

The Sale--getTotal Design

Given the above discussion, it is now desirable to construct an interaction diagram that illustrates what happens when a *Sale* is sent a *getTotal* message. The first message in this diagram is *getTotal*, but observe that the *getTotal* message is not a system event.

This leads to the following observation:

> Not every interaction diagram starts with a system event message; they can start with any message for which the designer wishes to show interactions.

The interaction diagram is shown in Figure 17.11. First, the *getTotal* message is sent to a *Sale* instance. The *Sale* will then send a *getSubtotal* message to each related *SalesLineItem* instance. The *SalesLineItem* will in turn send a *getPrice* message to its associated *ProductSpecifications*.

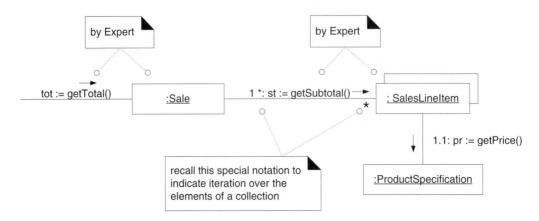

Figure 17.11 Sale--getTotal interaction diagram.

Since arithmetic is not (usually) illustrated via messages, the details of the calculations can be illustrated by attaching algorithms or constraints to the diagram that defines the calculations.

Who will send the *getTotal* message to the *Sale*? Most likely, it will be an object in the UI layer, such as a Java *JFrame*.

Observe in Figure 17.12 the use of algorithm notes and constraints, to communicate details of *getTotal* and *getSubtotal*.

17.7   Object Design: makePayment

The *makePayment* system operation occurs when a cashier enters the amount of cash tendered for payment. Here is the complete contract:

Contract CO4: makePayment

Operation:	makePayment(amount: Money)
Cross References:	Use Cases: Process Sale
Preconditions:	There is an underway sale.
Postconditions:	– A Payment instance p was created (instance creation).
	– p.amountTendered became amount (attribute modification).
	– p was associated with the current Sale (association formed).
	– The current Sale was associated with the Store (association formed); (to add it to the historical log of completed sales).

A design will be constructed to satisfy the postconditions of *makePayment*.

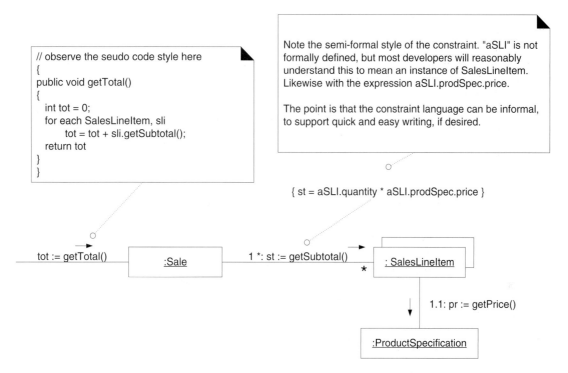

Figure 17.12 Algorithm notes and constraints.

Creating the Payment

One of the contract postconditions states:

■ A *Payment* instance p was created (instance creation).

This is a creation responsibility, so the Creator GRASP pattern should be applied.

Who records, aggregates, most closely uses, or contains a *Payment*? There is some appeal in stating that a *Register* logically records a *Payment*, because in the real domain a "register" records account information, so it is a candidate by the goal of reducing the representational gap in the software design. Additionally, it is reasonable to expect that a *Sale* software will closely use a *Payment*; thus, it may be a candidate.

Another way to find a creator is to use the Expert pattern in terms of who is the Information Expert with respect to initializing data—the amount tendered in this case. The *Register* is the controller which receives the system operation *makePayment* message, so it will initially have the amount tendered. Consequently the *Register* is again a candidate.

In summary, there are two candidates:

- *Register*

- *Sale*

Now, this leads a key design idea:

> When there are alternative design choices, take a closer look at the cohesion and coupling implications of the alternatives, and possibly at the future evolution pressures on the alternatives. Choose an alternative with good cohesion, coupling, and stability in the presence of likely future changes.

Consider some of the implications of these choices in terms of the High Cohesion and Low Coupling GRASP patterns. If the *Sale* is chosen to create the *Payment*, the work (or responsibilities) of the *Register* is lighter—leading to a simpler *Register* definition. Also, the *Register* does not need to know about the existence of a *Payment* instance because it can be recorded indirectly via the *Sale*—leading to lower coupling in the *Register*. This leads to the design shown in Figure 17.13.

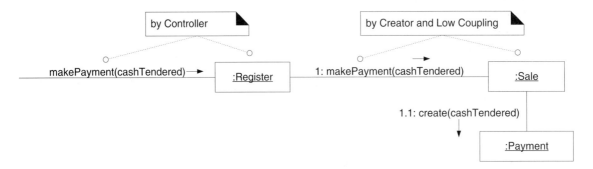

Figure 17.13 Register--makePayment interaction diagram.

This interaction diagram satisfies the postconditions of the contract: the *Payment* has been created, associated with the *Sale*, and its *amountTendered* has been set.

Logging a Sale

Once complete, the requirements state that the sale should be placed in an historical log. As always, Information Expert should be an early pattern considered unless it is a controller or creation problem (which it is not), and the responsibility should be stated:

> Who is responsible for knowing all the logged sales, and doing the logging?

By the goal of low representational gap in the software design (in relation to our concepts of the domain) it is reasonable for a *Store* to know all the logged sales, since they are strongly related to its finances. Other alternatives include classic accounting concepts, such as a *SalesLedger*. Using a *SalesLedger* object makes sense as the design grows and the *Store* becomes incohesive (see Figure 17.14).

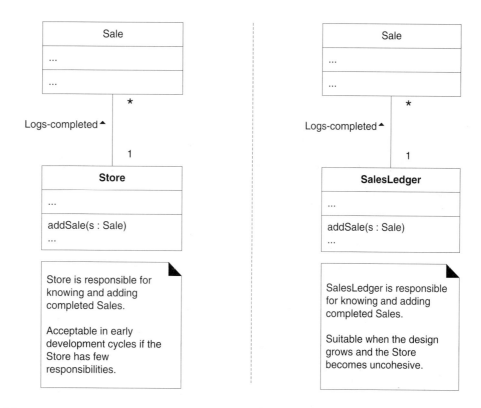

Figure 17.14 Who should be responsible for knowing the completed sales?

Note also that the postconditions of the contract indicate relating the *Sale* to the *Store*. This is an example where the postconditions may not be what we want to actually achieve in the design. Perhaps we didn't think of a *SalesLedger* earlier, but now that we have, we choose to use it instead of a *Store*. If this were the case, *SalesLedger* would ideally be added to the Domain Model as well, as it is a name of a concept in the real-world domain. This kind of discovery and change during design work is to be expected.

In this case, we will stick with the original plan of using the *Store* (see Figure 17.15).

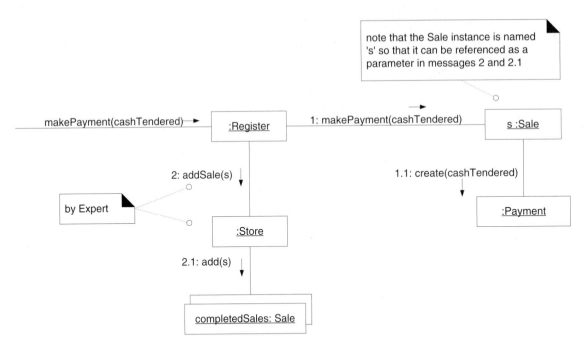

Figure 17.15 Logging a completed sale.

Calculating the Balance

The *Process Sale* use case implies that the balance due from a payment be printed on a receipt and displayed somehow.

Because of the Model-View Separation principle, we should not concern ourselves with how the balance will be displayed or printed, but it is necessary to ensure that it is known. Note that no class currently knows the balance, so we need to create a design of object interactions that satisfies this requirement.

As always, Information Expert should be considered unless it is a controller or creation problem (which it is not), and the responsibility should be stated:

> Who is responsible for knowing the balance?

To calculate the balance, the sale total and payment cash tendered are required. Therefore, *Sale* and *Payment* are partial Experts on solving this problem.

If the *Payment* is primarily responsible for knowing the balance, it would need visibility to the *Sale*, in order to ask the *Sale* for its total. Since it does not currently know about the *Sale*, this approach would increase the overall coupling in the design—it would not support the Low Coupling pattern.

In contrast, if the *Sale* is primarily responsible for knowing the balance, it needs visibility to the *Payment*, in order to ask it for its cash tendered. Since the *Sale* already has visibility to the *Payment*—as its creator—this approach does not increase the overall coupling, and is therefore a preferable design.

Consequently, the interaction diagram in Figure 17.16 provides a solution for knowing the balance.

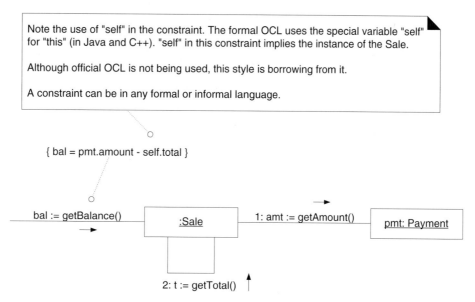

Figure 17.16 Sale--getBalance interaction diagram.

17.8   Object Design: startUp

When to Create the startUp Design?

Most, if not all, systems have a *Start Up* use case, and some initial system operation related to the starting up of the application. Although this *startUp* system operation is the earliest one to execute, delay the development of an interaction diagram for it until after all other system operations have been considered. This ensures that information has been discovered concerning the initialization activities required to support the later system operation interaction diagrams.

Do the initialization design last.

How Applications Start Up

The *startUp* operation abstractly represents the initialization phase of execution when an application is launched. To understand how to design an interaction diagram for this operation, it is helpful to understand the contexts in which initialization can occur. How an application starts and initializes is dependent on the programming language and operating system.

In all cases, a common design idiom is to ultimately create an **initial domain object**, which is the first software "domain" object created.

A note on terminology: As will be explored, applications are organized into logical layers that separate the major concerns of the application. These include a UI layer (for UI concerns) and a "domain" layer (for domain logic concerns). The domain layer of the Design Model is composed of software classes whose names are inspired from the domain vocabulary, and which contain application logic. Virtually all the design objects we have considered, such as *Sale* and *Register*, are domain objects in the domain layer of the Design Model.

The initial domain object, once created, is responsible for the creation of its direct child domain objects. For example, if a *Store* is chosen as the initial domain object, it may be responsible for the creation of a *Register* object.

The place where this initial domain object is created is dependent on the object technology chosen. For example, in a Java application, the *main* method may create it, or delegate the work to a *factory* object that creates it.

```
public class Main
{

public static void main( String[] args )
{
    // Store is the initial domain object.
    // The Store creates some other domain objects.

    Store store = new Store();

    Register register = store.getRegister();

    ProcessSaleJFrame frame = new ProcessSaleJFrame( register );
    ...
}

}
```

Interpretation of the startUp System Operation

The preceding discussion illustrates that the *startUp* system operation is a language-independent abstraction. During design, there is variation in where the initial object is created, and whether or not it takes control of the process. The initial domain object does not usually take control if there is a GUI; otherwise, it often does.

The interaction diagrams for the *startUp* operation represent what happens when the initial problem domain object is created, and optionally what happens if it takes control. They do not include any prior or subsequent activity in the GUI layer of objects, if one exists.

Hence, the *startUp* operation may be reinterpreted as:

1. In one interaction diagram, send a *create()* message to create the initial domain object.

2. (optional) If the initial object is taking control of the process, in a second interaction diagram, send a *run* message (or something equivalent) to the initial object.

The POS Application startUp Operation

The *startUp* system operation occurs when a manager powers on the POS system and the software loads. Assume that the initial domain object is *not* responsible for taking control of the process; control will remain in the UI layer (such as a Java *JFrame*) after the initial domain object is created. Therefore, the interaction diagram for the *startUp* operation may be reinterpreted solely as a *create()* message sent to create the initial object.

Choosing the Initial Domain Object

What should the class of the initial domain object be?

Choose as an initial domain object a class at or near the root of the containment or aggregation hierarchy of domain objects. This may be a facade controller, such as *Register*, or some other object considered to contain all or most other objects, such as a *Store*.

Choosing between these alternatives may be influenced by High Cohesion and Low Coupling considerations. In this application, the *Store* is chosen as the initial object.

Persistent Objects: ProductSpecification

The *ProductSpecification* instances will reside in a persistent storage medium, such as relational or object database. During the *startUp* operation, if there are only a few of these objects, they may all be loaded into the computer's direct memory. However, if there are many, loading them all would consume too much memory or time. Alternately—and more likely—individual instances will be loaded on demand into memory as they are required.

The design of how to dynamically on-demand load objects from a database into memory is simple if an object database is used, but difficult for a relational database. This problem is deferred for now and makes a simplifying assumption that all the *ProductSpecification* instances can be "magically" created in memory by the *ProductCatalog* object.

Chapter 34 explores the question of persistent objects and one way to load them into memory.

Store--create() Design

The tasks of creation and initialization derive from the needs of the prior design work, such as the design for handling *enterItem* and so on. By reflecting on the prior interaction designs, the following initialization work can be identified:

- A *Store, Register, ProductCatalog* and *ProductSpecifications* need to be created.

- The *ProductCatalog* needs to be associated with *ProductSpecifications*.

- *Store* needs to be associated with *ProductCatalog*.

- *Store* needs to be associated with *Register*.

- *Register* needs to be associated with *ProductCatalog*.

Figure 17.17 shows a design. The *Store* was chosen to create the *ProductCatalog* and *Register* by the Creator pattern. *ProductCatalog* was likewise chosen to create the *ProductSpecifications*. Recall that this approach to creating the specifications is temporary. In the final design, they will be materialized from a database, as needed.

UML notation: Observe that the creation of all the *ProductSpecification* instances and their addition to a container happens in a repeating section, indicated by the "*" following the sequence numbers.

An interesting deviation between modeling the real-world domain and the design is illustrated in the fact that the software *Store* object only creates *one Register* object. A real store may house *many* real registers or POS terminals. However, we are considering a software design, not real life. In our current requirements, our software *Store* only needs to create a single instance of a software *Register*.

> Multiplicity between classes of objects in the Domain Model and Design Model may not be the same.

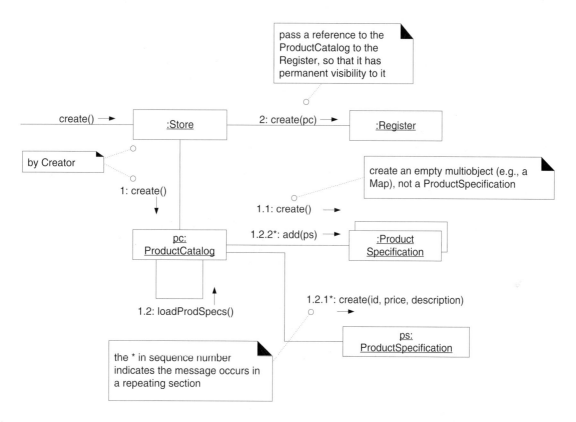

Figure 17.17 Creation of the initial domain object and subsequent objects.

17.9 Connecting the UI Layer to the Domain Layer

As has been briefly discussed, applications are organized into logical layers that separate the major concerns of the application, such as the UI layer (for UI concerns) and a "domain" layer (for domain logic concerns).

Common designs by which objects in the UI layer obtain visibility to objects in the domain layer include the following:

- An initializing routine (for example, a Java *main* method) creates both a UI and a domain object, and passes the domain object to the UI.

- A UI object retrieves the domain object from a well-known source, such as a factory object that is responsible for creating domain objects.

The sample code shown before is an example of the first approach:

```
public class Main
{
```

```
public static void main( String[] args )
{
    Store store = new Store();
    Register register = store.getRegister();
    ProcessSaleJFrame frame = new ProcessSaleJFrame( register );
    ...
}

}
```

Once the UI object has a connection to the *Register* instance (the facade controller in this design), it can forward system event messages to it, such as the *enterItem* and *endSale* message (see Figure 17.18).

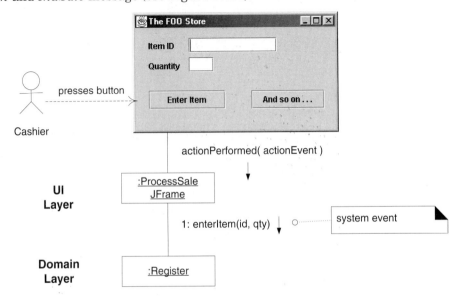

Figure 17.18 Connecting the UI and domain layers.

In the case of the *enterItem* message, the window needs to show the running total after each entry. There are several design solutions:

■ Add a *getTotal* method to the *Register*. The UI sends the *getTotal* message to the *Register*, which forwards it to the *Sale*. This has the possible advantage of maintaining lower coupling from the UI to the domain layer—the UI only knows of the *Register* object. But it starts to expand the interface of the Register object, making it less cohesive.

■ A UI asks for a reference to the current *Sale* object, and then when it needs the total (or any other information related to the sale), it directly sends messages to the *Sale*. This design increases the coupling from the UI to the domain layer. However, as was explored in the Low Coupling GRASP pattern discussion, higher coupling in and of itself is not a problem; rather, it is especially coupling to unstable things that is a problem. Assume we decide the *Sale* is a stable object that will be an integral part of the design—which is very reasonable. Then, coupling to the *Sale* is not a problem.

As illustrated in Figure 17.19, this design follows the second approach.

Notice in these diagrams that the Java window (*ProcessSaleJFrame*), which is part of the UI layer, is not responsible for handling the logic of the application. It forwards requests for work (the system operations) to the domain layer, via the *Register*. This leads to the following design principle:

Interface and Domain Layer Responsibilities

The UI layer should not have any domain logic responsibilities. It should only be responsible for user interface tasks, such as updating widgets.

The UI layer should forward requests for all domain-oriented tasks on to the domain layer, which is responsible for handling them.

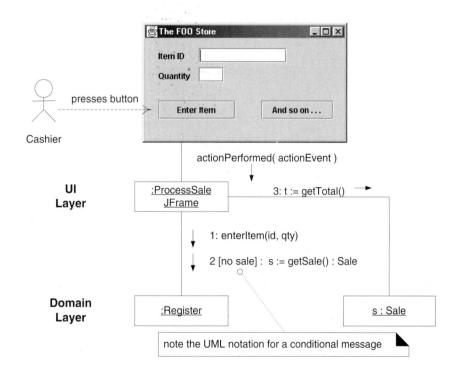

Figure 17.19 Connecting the UI and domain layers.

17.10   Use-Case Realizations Within the UP

Use-case realizations are part of the UP Design Model. This chapter has empha-sized drawing interaction diagrams, but it is common and recommended to draw class diagrams in parallel. Class diagrams are examined in Chapter 19.

| Discipline | Artifact | Incep. | Elab. | Const. | Trans. |
	Iteration→	I1	E1..En	C1..Cn	T1..T2
Business Modeling	Domain Model		s		
Requirements	Use-Case Model (SSDs)	s	r		
	Vision	s	r		
	Supplementary Specification	s	r		
	Glossary	s	r		
Design	*Design Model*		s	r	
	SW Architecture Document		s		
	Data Model		s	r	
Implementation	Implementation Model		s	r	r
Project Management	SW Development Plan	s	r	r	r
Testing	Test Model		s	r	
Environment	Development Case	s	r		

Table 17.1 Sample UP artifacts and timing. s - start; r - refine

Phases

Inception—The Design Model and use-case realizations will not usually be started until elaboration because it involves detailed design decisions which are premature during inception.

Elaboration—During this phase, use-case realizations may be created for the most architecturally significant or risky scenarios of the design. However, UML diagramming will not be done for every scenario, and not necessarily in com-plete and fine-grained detail. The idea is to do interaction diagrams for the key use-case realizations that benefit from some forethought and exploration of alternatives, focusing on the major design decisions.

Construction—Use-case realizations are created for remaining design problems.

UP Artifacts and Process Context

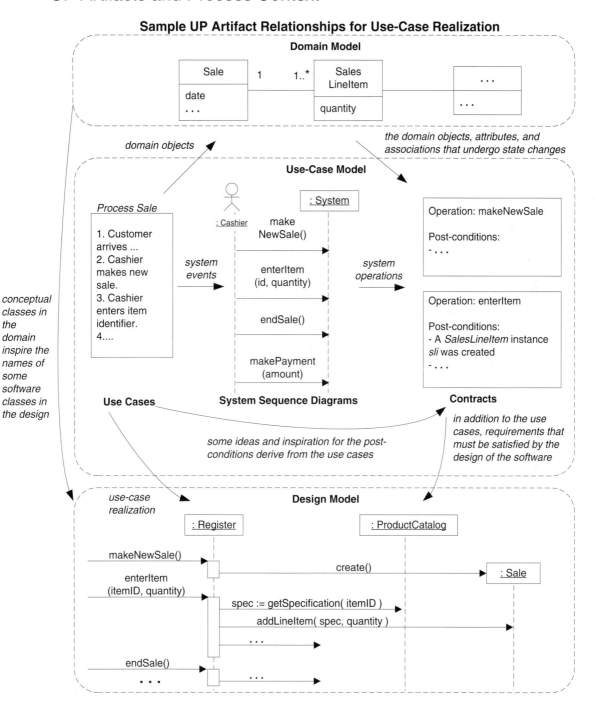

Figure 17.20 Sample UP artifact influence.

In the UP, use-case realization work is a design activity. Figure 17.21 offers suggestions on the time and space for doing this work.

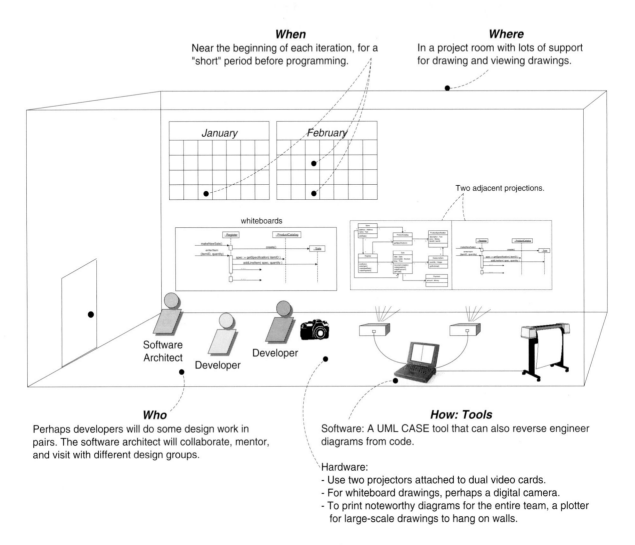

When
Near the beginning of each iteration, for a "short" period before programming.

Where
In a project room with lots of support for drawing and viewing drawings.

Two adjacent projections.

whiteboards

Software Architect

Developer

Developer

Who
Perhaps developers will do some design work in pairs. The software architect will collaborate, mentor, and visit with different design groups.

How: Tools
Software: A UML CASE tool that can also reverse engineer diagrams from code.

Hardware:
- Use two projectors attached to dual video cards.
- For whiteboard drawings, perhaps a digital camera.
- To print noteworthy diagrams for the entire team, a plotter for large-scale drawings to hang on walls.

Figure 17.21 Sample process and setting context.

17.11 Summary

Designing object interactions and assigning responsibilities is at the heart of object design. These choices have can have a profound impact on the extensibility, clarity, and maintainability of an object software system, plus on the degree and quality of reusable components. There are principles by which the choices of responsibility assignment can be made; the GRASP patterns summarize some of the most general and common used by object-oriented designers.

DESIGN MODEL: DETERMINING VISIBILITY

A mathematician is a device for turning coffee into theorems.

—Paul Erdös

Objectives

- Identify four kinds of visibility.
- Design to establish visibility.
- Illustrate kinds of visibility in the UML notation.

Introduction

Visibility is the ability of one object to see or have reference to another. This chapter explores design issues related to visibility.

18.1 Visibility Between Objects

The designs created for the system events (*enterItem*, and so on) illustrate messages between objects. For a sender object to send a message to a receiver object, the sender must be visible to the receiver—the sender must have some kind of reference or pointer to the receiver object.

For example, the *getSpecification* message sent from a *Register* to a *ProductCatalog* implies that the *ProductCatalog* instance is visible to the *Register* instance, as shown in Figure 18.1.

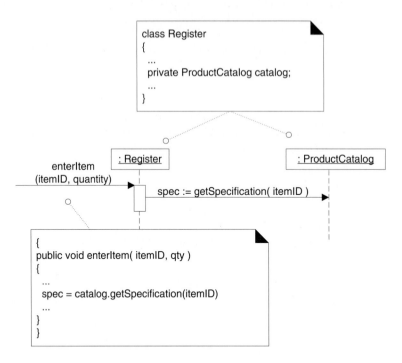

Figure 18.1 Visibility from the Register to ProductCatalog is required.[1]

When creating a design of interacting objects, it is necessary to ensure that the necessary visibility is present to support message interaction.

The UML has special notation for illustrating visibility; this chapter explores various kinds of visibility and their depiction.

18.2   Visibility

In common usage, **visibility** is the ability of an object to "see" or have a reference to another object. More generally, it is related to the issue of scope: Is one resource (such as an instance) within the scope of another? There are four common ways that visibility can be achieved from object A to object B:

- **Attribute visibility**—B is an attribute of A.

- **Parameter visibility**—B is a parameter of a method of A.

- **Local visibility**—B is a (non-parameter) local object in a method of A.

- **Global visibility**—B is in some way globally visible.

---

1. In this and subsequent code examples, language simplifications may be made for the sake of brevity and clarity.

The motivation to consider visibility is this:

> For an object A to send a message to an object B, B must be visible to A.

For example, to create an interaction diagram in which a message is sent from a *Register* instance to a *ProductCatalog* instance, the *Register* must have visibility to the *ProductCatalog*. A typical visibility solution is that a reference to the *ProductCatalog* instance is maintained as an attribute of the *Register*.

Attribute Visibility

Attribute visibility from A to B exists when B is an attribute of A. It is a relatively permanent visibility because it persists as long as A and B exist. This is a very common form of visibility in object-oriented systems.

To illustrate, in a Java class definition for *Register*, a *Register* instance may have attribute visibility to a *ProductCatalog*, since it is an attribute (Java instance variable) of the *Register*.

```
public class Register
{
...
private ProductCatalog catalog;
...
}
```

This visibility is required because in the *enterItem* diagram shown in Figure 18.2, a *Register* needs to send the *getSpecification* message to a *ProductCatalog*:

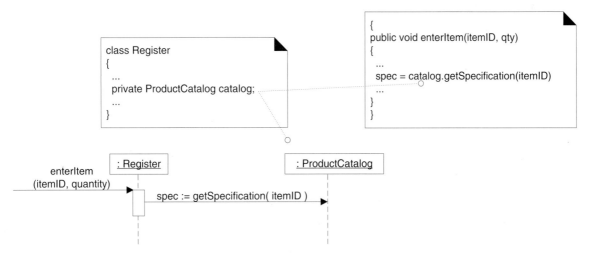

Figure 18.2 Attribute visibility.

Parameter Visibility

Parameter visibility from A to B exists when B is passed as a parameter to a method of A. It is a relatively temporary visibility because it persists only within the scope of the method. After attribute visibility, it is the second most common form of visibility in object-oriented systems.

To illustrate, when the *makeLineItem* message is sent to a *Sale* instance, a *ProductSpecification* instance is passed as a parameter. Within the scope of the *makeLineItem* method, the *Sale* has parameter visibility to a *ProductSpecification* (see Figure 18.3).

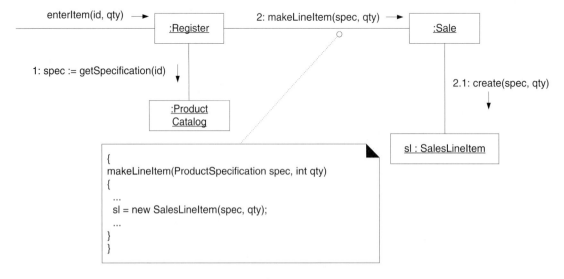

Figure 18.3 Parameter visibility.

It is common to transform parameter visibility into attribute visibility. For example, when the *Sale* creates a new *SalesLineItem*, it passes a *ProductSpecification* in to its initializing method (in C++ or Java, this would be its **constructor**). Within the initializing method, the parameter is assigned to an attribute, thus establishing attribute visibility (Figure 18.4).

Local Visibility

Local visibility from A to B exists when B is declared as a local object within a method of A. It is a relatively temporary visibility because it persists only within the scope of the method. After parameter visibility, it is the third most common form of visibility in object-oriented systems.

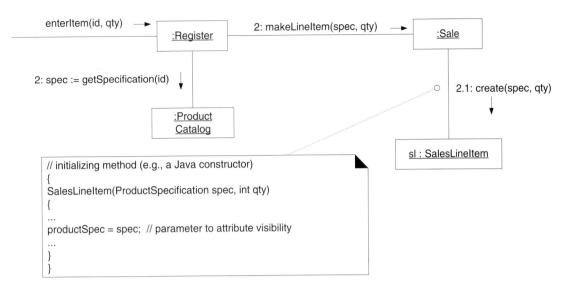

Figure 18.4 Parameter to attribute visibility.

Two common means by which local visibility is achieved are:

- Create a new local instance and assign it to a local variable.
- Assign the returning object from a method invocation to a local variable.

As with parameter visibility, it is common to transform locally declared visibility into attribute visibility.

An example of the second variation (assigning the returning object to a local variable) can be found in the *enterItem* method of class *Register* (Figure 18.5).

A subtle version on the second variation is when the method does not explicitly declare a variable, but one implicitly exists as the result of a returning object from a method invocation. For example:

```
// there is implicit local visibility to the foo object
// returned via the getFoo call

anObject.getFoo().doBar();
```

Global Visibility

Global visibility from A to B exists when B is global to A. It is a relatively permanent visibility because it persists as long as A and B exist. It is the least common form of visibility in object-oriented systems.

One way to achieve global visibility is to assign an instance to a global variable, which is possible in some languages, such as C++, but not others, such as Java.

The preferred method to achieve global visibility is to use the **Singleton** pattern [GHJV95], which is discussed in a later chapter.

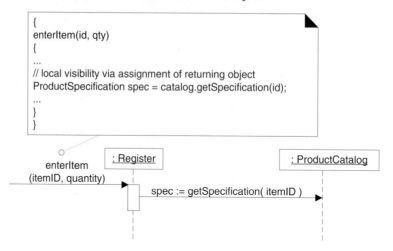

Figure 18.5 Local visibility.

18.3   Illustrating Visibility in the UML

The UML includes notation to show the kind of visibility in a collaboration diagram (see Figure 18.6). These adornments are optional and not normally called for; they are useful when clarification is needed.

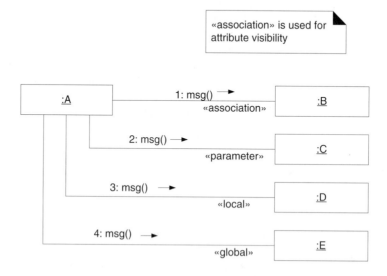

Figure 18.6 Implementation stereotypes for visibility.

DESIGN MODEL: CREATING DESIGN CLASS DIAGRAMS

To iterate is human, to recurse, divine.

—anonymous

Objectives

- Create design class diagrams (DCDs).
- Identify the classes, methods, and associations to show in a DCD.

Introduction

With the completion of interaction diagrams for use-case realizations for the current iteration of the NextGen POS application, it is possible to identify the specification for the software classes (and interfaces) that participate in the software solution, and annotate them with design details, such as methods.

The UML has notation for showing design details in class diagrams; in this chapter, we explore it and create DCDs.

19.1 When to Create DCDs

Although this presentation of DCDs *follows* the creation of interaction diagrams, in practice they are usually created in parallel. Many classes, method names and relationships may be sketched out very early in design by applying responsibility assignment patterns, prior to the drawing of interaction diagrams. It is possible and desirable to do a little interaction diagramming, then update the DCDs, then extend the interaction diagrams some more, and so on.

These class diagrams may be used as an alternative, more graphical notation over CRC cards in order to record responsibilities and collaborators.

19.2   Example DCD

The DCD in Figure 19.1 illustrates a partial software definition of the *Register* and *Sale* classes.

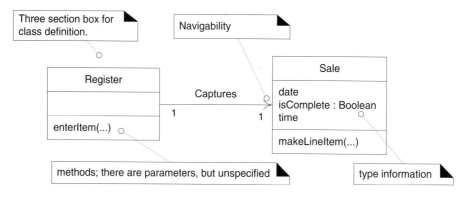

Figure 19.1 Sample design class diagram.

In addition to basic associations and attributes, the diagram is extended to illustrate, for example, the methods of each class, attribute type information, and attribute visibility and navigation between objects.

19.3   DCD and UP Terminology

A **design class diagram** (DCD) illustrates the specifications for software classes and interfaces (for example, Java interfaces) in an application. Typical information includes:

- classes, associations and attributes
- interfaces, with their operations and constants
- methods
- attribute type information
- navigability
- dependencies

In contrast to conceptual classes in the Domain Model, design classes in the DCDs show definitions for software classes rather than real-world concepts.

The UP does not specifically define an artifact called a "design class diagram." The UP defines the Design Model, which contains several diagram types, including interaction, package, and class diagrams. The class diagrams in the UP Design Model contain "design classes" in UP terms. Hence, it is common to speak of "design class diagrams," that is shorter than, and implies, "class diagrams in the Design Model."

19.4 Domain Model vs. Design Model Classes

To reiterate, in the UP Domain Model, a *Sale* does not represent a software definition; rather, it is an abstraction of a real-world concept about which we are interested in making a statement. By contrast, DCDs express—for the software application—the definition of classes as software components. In these diagrams, a *Sale* represents a software class (see Figure 19.2).

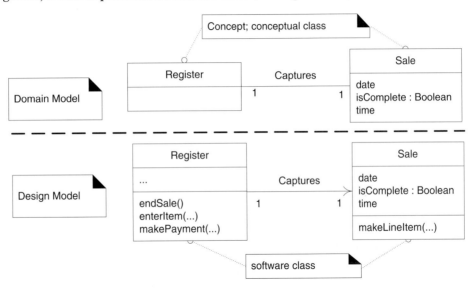

Figure 19.2 Domain model vs. Design Model classes.

19.5 Creating a NextGen POS DCD

Identify Software Classes and Illustrate Them

The first step in the creation of DCDs as part of the solution model is to identify those classes that participate in the software solution. These can be found by scanning all the interaction diagrams and listing the classes mentioned.

For the POS application, these are:

Register	Sale
ProductCatalog	ProductSpecification
Store	SalesLineItem
Payment	

The next step is to draw a class diagram for these classes and include the attributes previously identified in the Domain Model that are also used in the design (see Figure 19.3).

Note that some of the concepts in the Domain Model, such as *Cashier*, are not present in the design. There is no need—for the current iteration—to represent them in software. However, in later iterations, as new requirements and use cases are tackled, they may enter into the design. For example, when security and log-in requirements are implemented, it is likely that a software class named *Cashier* will be relevant.

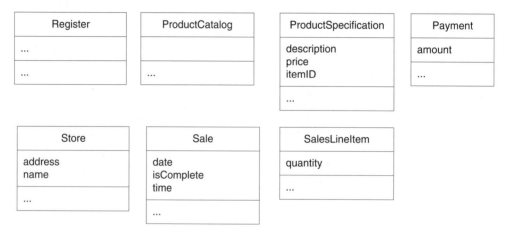

Figure 19.3 Software classes in the application.

Add Method Names

The methods of each class can be identified by analyzing the interaction diagrams. For example, if the message *makeLineItem* is sent to an instance of class *Sale*, then class *Sale* must define a *makeLineItem* method (see Figure 19.4).

In general, the set of all messages sent to a class X across all interaction diagrams indicates the majority of methods that class X must define.

Inspection of all the interaction diagrams for the POS application yields the allocation of methods shown in Figure 19.5.

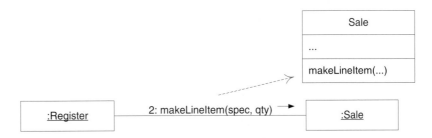

Figure 19.4 Method names from interaction diagrams.

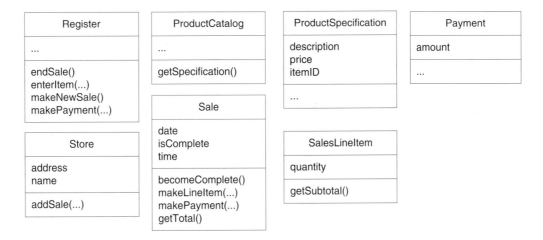

Figure 19.5 Methods in the application.

Method Name Issues

The following special issues must be considered with respect to method names:

■ interpretation of the *create* message

■ depiction of accessing methods

■ interpretation of messages to multiobjects

■ language-dependent syntax

Method Names—create

The *create* message is a possible UML language independent form to indicate instantiation and initialization. When translating the design to an object-oriented programming language, it must be expressed in terms of its idioms for instantiation and initialization. There is no actual *create* method in C++, Java, or Smalltalk. For example, in C++, it implies automatic allocation, or free store allocation with the *new* operator, followed by a constructor call. In Java, it implies the invocation of the *new* operator, followed by a constructor call.

Because of its multiple interpretations, and also because initialization is a very common activity, it is common to omit creation-related methods and constructors from a DCD.

Method Names—Accessing Methods

Accessing methods retrieve (accessor method) or set (mutator method) attributes. In some languages (such as Java) it is a common idiom to have an accessor and mutator for each attribute, and to declare all attributes private (to enforce data encapsulation). These methods are usually excluded from depiction in the class diagram because of the high noise-to-value ratio they generate; for n attributes, there are 2n uninteresting methods. For example, the *Product-Specification's getPrice* (or *price*) method is not shown, although present, because *getPrice* is a simple accessor method.

Method Names—Multiobjects

A message to a multiobject is interpreted as a message to the container/collection object itself. For example, the following *find* message to the multiobject is meant be interpreted as a message to the container/collection object, such as to a Java *Map,* a C++ *map* or a Smalltalk *Dictionary* (see Figure 19.6).

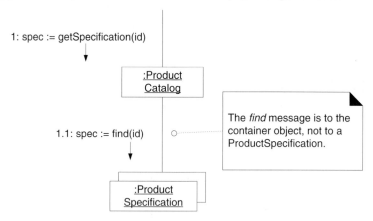

Figure 19.6 Message to a multiobject.

Therefore, the *find* method is not part of the *ProductSpecification* class; rather, it is part of the multiobject's interface. Consequently, it is incorrect to add *find* as a method to the *ProductSpecification* class.

These container/collection interfaces or classes (such as the interface *java.util.Map*) are usually predefined library elements, and it is not useful to show these classes explicitly in the DCD, since they add noise, but little new information.

Method Names—Language-Dependent Syntax

Some languages, such as Smalltalk, have a syntax that is very different from the basic UML format of *methodName(parameterList)*. It is recommended that the basic UML format be used, even if the planned implementation language uses a different syntax. The translation should ideally take place during code generation time, instead of during the creation of the class diagrams. However, the UML does allow other syntax for method specification.

Adding More Type Information

The types of the attributes, method parameters, and method return values may all optionally be shown. The question as to whether to show this information or not should be considered in the following context:

> The DCD should be created by considering the audience.
>
> - If it is being created in a CASE tool with automatic code generation, full and exhaustive details are necessary.
>
> - If it is being created for software developers to read, exhaustive low-level detail may adversely affect the noise-to-value ratio.

For example, is it necessary to show all the parameters and their type information? It depends on how obvious the information is to the intended audience.

The design class diagram in Figure 19.7 shows more type information.

Adding Associations and Navigability

Each end of an association is called a role, and in the DCDs the role may be decorated with a navigability arrow. **Navigability** is a property of the role that indicates that it is possible to navigate uni-directionally across the association from objects of the source to target class. Navigability implies visibility—usually attribute visibility (see Figure 19.8).

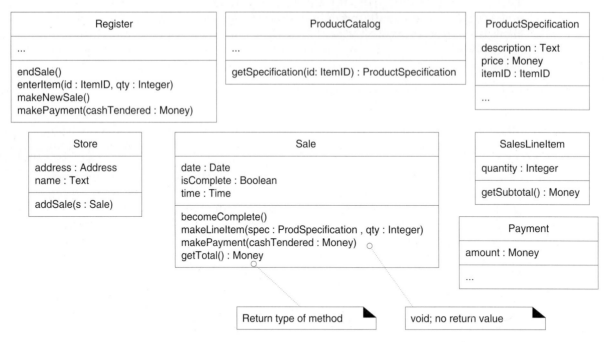

Figure 19.7 Adding type information.

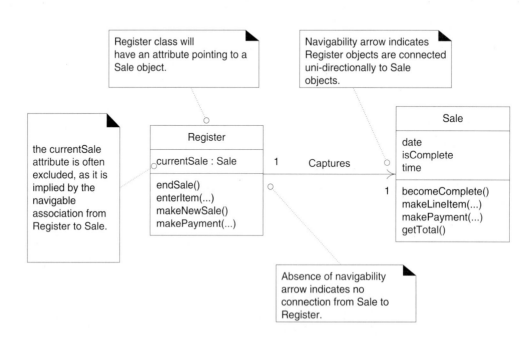

Figure 19.8 Showing navigability, or attribute visibility.

The usual interpretation of an association with a navigability arrow is attribute visibility from the source to target class. During implementation in an object-oriented programming language it is usually translated as the source class having an attribute that refers to an instance of the target class. For instance, the *Register* class will define an attribute that references a *Sale* instance.

Most, if not all, associations in DCDs should be adorned with the necessary navigability arrows.

In a DCD, associations are chosen by a spartan software-oriented, need-to-know criterion—what associations are required to satisfy the visibility and ongoing memory needs indicated by the interaction diagrams? This is in contrast with associations in the Domain Model, which may be justified by the intention to enhance comprehension of the problem domain. Once again, we see a distinction between the goals of the Design Model and the Domain Model: one is analytical, the other a description of software components.

The required visibility and associations between classes are indicated by the interaction diagrams. Here are common situations suggesting a need to define an association with a navigability adornment from A to B:

- A sends a message to B.

- A creates an instance B.

- A needs to maintain a connection to B.

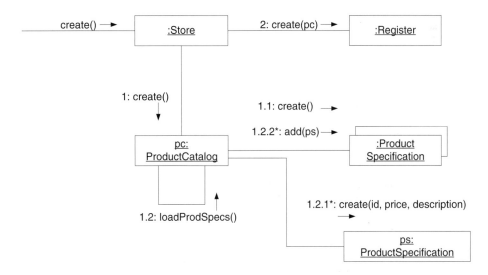

Figure 19.9 Navigability is identified from interaction diagrams.

For example, from the interaction diagram in Figure 19.9 starting with the *create* message to a *Store*, and from the larger context of the other interaction diagrams, it is discernible that the *Store* should probably have an ongoing connection to the *Register* and *ProductCatalog* instances that it created. It is also reasonable that the *ProductCatalog* needs an ongoing connection to the collection of *ProductSpecifications* it created. In fact, the creator of another object very typically requires an ongoing connection to it. The implied connections will therefore be present as associations in the class diagram.

Based on the above criterion for associations and navigability, analysis of all the interaction diagrams generated for the NextGen POS application will yield a class diagram (seen in Figure 19.10) with the following associations (exhaustive type information is hidden for the sake of clarity).

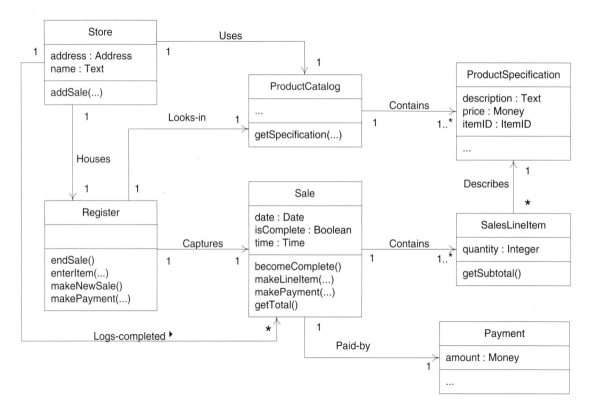

Figure 19.10 Associations with navigability adornments.

Note that this is not exactly the same set of associations that was generated for the class diagrams in the Domain Model. For instance, there was no *Looks-in* association between *Register* and *ProductCatalog* in the domain model—it was not discovered as an important lasting relationship at that time. But during the creation of the interaction diagrams, it was decided that a *Register* software object should have a lasting connection to a software *ProductCatalog* in order to look up *ProductSpecifications*.

Adding Dependency Relationships

The UML includes a general **dependency relationship**, which indicates that one element (of any kind, including classes, use cases, and so on) has knowledge of another element. It is illustrated with a dashed arrow line. In class diagrams the dependency relationship is useful to depict non-attribute visibility between classes; in other words, parameter, global, or locally declared visibility. By contrast, plain attribute visibility is shown with a regular association line and a navigability arrow. For example, the *Register* software object receives a return object of type *ProductSpecification* from the specification message it sent to a *ProductCatalog*. Thus *Register* has a short-term locally declared visibility to *ProductSpecifications*. And *Sale* receives a *ProductSpecification* as a parameter in the *makeLineItem* message; it has parameter visibility to one.

These non-attribute visibilities may be illustrated with the dashed arrow line indicating a dependency relationship (see Figure 19.11). There is no significance in the curving of the dependency lines; it is graphically convenient.

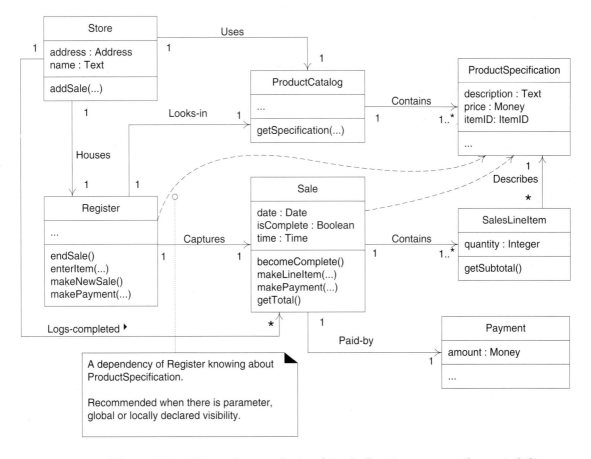

Figure 19.11 Dependency relationships indicating non-attribute visibility.

19.6   Notation for Member Details

The UML provides a rich notation to describe features of class and interface members, such as visibility, initial values, and so on. An example is shown in Figure 19.12.

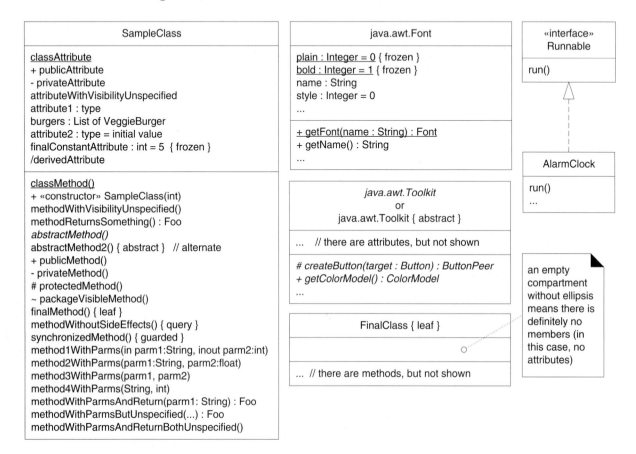

Figure 19.12 Some UML class diagram member notation details.

Visibility Defaults in the UML?

If no explicit visibility marker is shown for an attribute or method, what is the default? Answer: there isn't a default. If none is shown, it implies "not specified" in the UML. However, there is a common convention to assume that attributes are private and methods public, unless otherwise noted.

The current iteration of the NextGen POS design class diagram (see Figure 19.13) does not have many interesting member details; all attributes are private and all methods public.

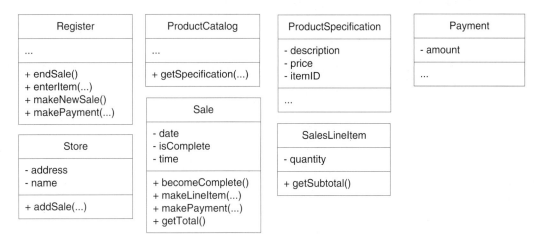

Figure 19.13 Member details in the POS class diagram.

Notation for Method Bodies in DCDs (and Interaction Diagrams)

A method body can be shown as illustrated in Figure 19.14 in both a DCD and an interaction diagram.

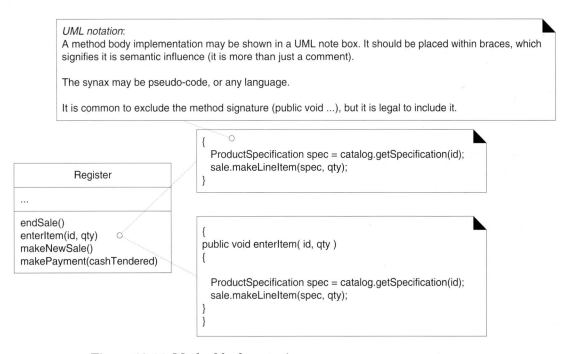

Figure 19.14 Method body notation.

19.7   DCDs, Drawing, and CASE Tools

CASE tools can reverse-engineer (generate) DCDs from source code. In Chapter 35 on drawing and CASE tools, there is a brief discussion on the process context and the practice of drawing DCDs.

19.8   DCDs Within the UP

DCDs are part of the use-case realizations and thus members of the UP Design Model.

Discipline	Artifact	Incep.	Elab.	Const.	Trans.
	Iteration→	I1	E1..En	C1..Cn	T1..T2
Business Modeling	Domain Model		s		
Requirements	Use-Case Model (SSDs)	s	r		
	Vision	s	r		
	Supplementary Specifications	s	r		
	Glossary	s	r		
Design	*Design Model*		s	r	
	SW Architecture Document		s		
	Data Model		s	r	
Implementation	Implementation Model		s	r	r
Project Management	SW Development Plan	s	r	r	r
Testing	Test Model		s	r	
Environment	Development Case	s	r		

Table 19.1 Sample UP artifacts and timing. s - start; r - refine

Phases

Inception—The Design Model and DCDs will not usually be started until elaboration because it involves detailed design decisions, which are premature during inception.

Elaboration—During this phase, DCDs will accompany the use-case realization interaction diagrams; they may be created for the most architecturally significant classes of the design.

Note that CASE tools can reverse-engineer (generate) DCDs from source code. It is recommended to generate DCDs regularly from the source code, to visualize the static structure of the system.

Construction—DCDs will continue to be generated from the source code as an aid in visualizing the static structure of the system.

19.9   UP Artifacts

Artifact influence emphasizing the DCDs is shown in Figure 19.15.

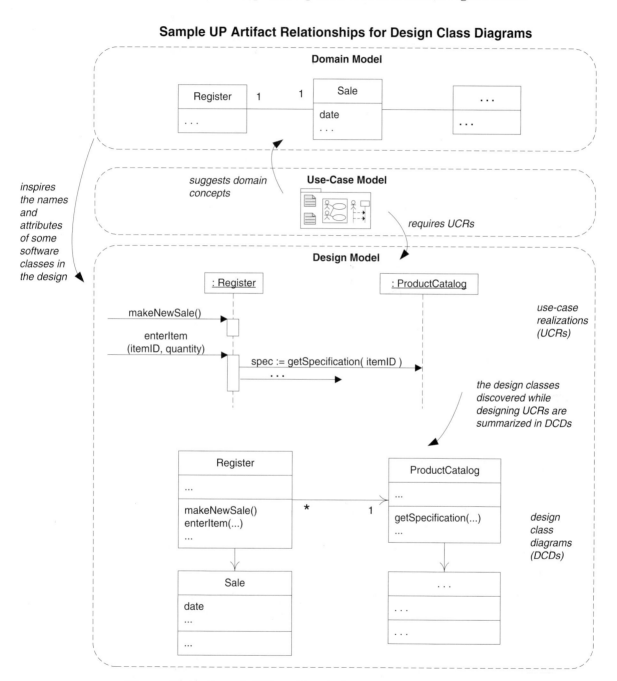

Figure 19.15 Sample UP artifact influence.

IMPLEMENTATION MODEL: MAPPING DESIGNS TO CODE

> *Beware of bugs in the above code;*
> *I have only proved it correct, not tried it.*
>
> —*Donald Knuth*

Objectives

■ Map design artifacts to code in an object-oriented language.

Introduction

With the completion of interaction diagrams and DCDs for the current iteration of the NextGen application, there is sufficient detail to generate code for the domain layer of objects.

The UML artifacts created during the design work—the interaction diagrams and DCDs—will be used as input to the code generation process.

The UP defines the Implementation Model. This contains the implementation artifacts such as the source code, database definitions, JSP/XML/HTML pages, and so forth. Thus, the code being created in this chapter is part of the Implementation Model.

Language Samples

Java is used for the examples because of its widespread use and familiarity. However, this is not meant to imply a special endorsement of Java; C#, Visual Basic, C++, Smalltalk, Python, and many more languages are amenable to the object design principles and mapping to code presented in this case study.

20.1   Programming and the Development Process

The prior design work should not be taken to imply that there is no prototyping or design while programming; modern development tools provide an excellent environment to quickly explore alternate approaches, and some (or even lots) design-while-programming is usually worthwhile.

However, some developers find that a little forethought with visual modeling before programming is helpful, especially those who are comfortable with visual thinking or diagrammatic languages.

<hr>

Suggestion

For a two-week iteration, consider spending at least a half-day near the start of the iteration doing some visual modeling design work, before moving on to programming. Use simple "tools" that support quick creative diagramming, such as a whiteboard and digital camera. If you find a UML computer-aided software engineering (CASE) tool that is equally fast, easy, and convenient, excellent.

<hr>

The creation of code in an object-oriented programming language—such as Java or C#—is not part of OOA/D; it is an end goal. The artifacts created in the UP Design Model provide some of the information necessary to generate the code.

A strength of OOA/D and OO programming—when used with the UP—is that they provide an end-to-end roadmap from requirements through to code. The various artifacts feed into later artifacts in a traceable and useful manner, ultimately culminating in a running application. This is not to suggest that the road will be smooth, or can simply be mechanically followed—there are too many variables. But having a roadmap provides a starting point for experimentation and discussion.

Creativity and Change During Implementation

Some decision-making and creative work was accomplished during design work. It will be seen during the following discussion that the generation of the code—in this example—is a relatively mechanical translation process.

However, in general, the programming work is not a trivial code generation step—quite the opposite. Realistically, the results generated during design are an incomplete first step; during programming and testing, myriad changes will be made and detailed problems will be uncovered and resolved.

Done well, the design artifacts will provide a resilient core that scales up with elegance and robustness to meet the new problems encountered during programming. Consequently, expect and plan for change and deviation from the design during programming.

Code Changes and the Iterative Process

A strength of an iterative and incremental development process is that the results of a prior iteration can feed into the beginning of the next iteration (see Figure 20.1). Thus, subsequent analysis and design results are continually being refined and enhanced from prior implementation work. For example, when the code in iteration N deviates from the design of iteration N (which it inevitably will), the final design based on the implementation can be input to the analysis and design models of iteration N+1.

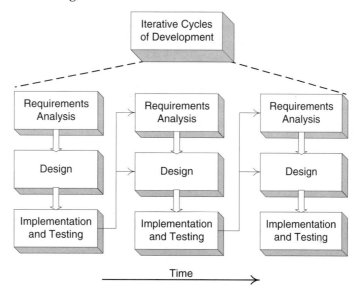

Figure 20.1 Implementation in an iteration influences later design.

An early activity within an iteration is to synchronize the design diagrams; the earlier diagrams of iteration N will not match the final code of iteration N, and they need to be synchronized before being extended with new design results.

Code Changes, CASE Tools, and Reverse-Engineering

It is desirable for the diagrams generated during design to be semi-automatically updated to reflect changes in the subsequent coding work. Ideally this should be done with a CASE tool that can read source code and automatically generate, for example, package, class, and sequence diagrams. This is an aspect of **reverse-engineering**—the activity of generating diagrams from source (or sometimes, executable) code.

20.2   Mapping Designs to Code

Implementation in an object-oriented programming language requires writing source code for:

■ class and interface definitions

■ method definitions

The following sections discuss their generation in Java (as a typical case).

20.3   Creating Class Definitions from DCDs

At the very least, DCDs depict the class or interface name, superclasses, method signatures, and simple attributes of a class. This is sufficient to create a basic class definition in an object-oriented programming language. Later discussion will explore the addition of interface and namespace (or package) information, among other details.

Defining a Class with Methods and Simple Attributes

From the DCD, a mapping to the basic attribute definitions (simple Java instance fields) and method signatures for the Java definition of *SalesLineItem* is straightforward, as shown in Figure 20.2.

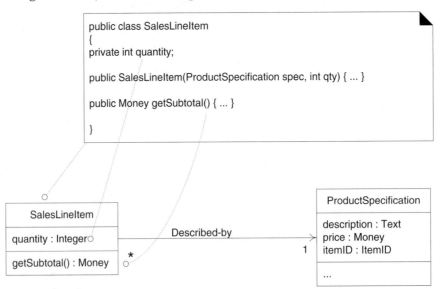

Figure 20.2 SalesLineItem in Java.

Note the addition in the source code of the Java constructor *SalesLineItem(...)*. It is derived from the *create(spec, qty)* message sent to a *SalesLineItem* in the *enterItem* interaction diagram. This indicates, in Java, that a constructor supporting these parameters is required. The *create* method is often excluded from the class diagram because of its commonality and multiple interpretations, depending on the target language.

Adding Reference Attributes

A **reference attribute** is an attribute that refers to another complex object, not to a primitive type such as a String, Number, and so on.

> The reference attributes of a class are suggested by the associations and navigability in a class diagram.

For example, a *SalesLineItem* has an association to a *ProductSpecification*, with navigability to it. It is common to interpret this as a reference attribute in class *SalesLineItem* that refers to a *ProductSpecification* instance (see Figure 20.3).

In Java, this means that an instance field referring to a *ProductSpecification* instance is suggested.

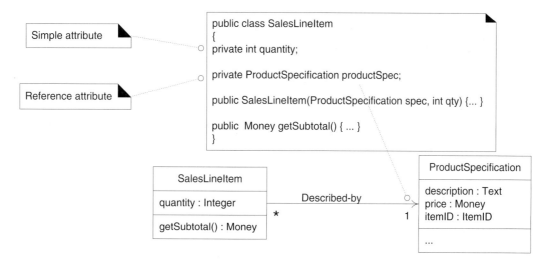

Figure 20.3 Adding reference attributes.

> Note that reference attributes of a class are often implied, rather than explicit, in a DCD.

For example, although we have added an instance field to the Java definition of *SalesLineItem* to point to a *ProductSpecification*, it is not explicitly declared as an attribute in the attribute section of the class box. There is a *suggested* attribute visibility—indicated by the association and navigability—which is explicitly defined as an attribute during the code generation phase.

Reference Attributes and Role Names

The next iteration will explore the concept of role names in static structure diagrams. Each end of an association is called a role. Briefly, a **role name** is a name that identifies the role and often provides some semantic context as to the nature of the role.

If a role name is present in a class diagram, use it as the basis for the name of the reference attribute during code generation, as shown in Figure 20.4.

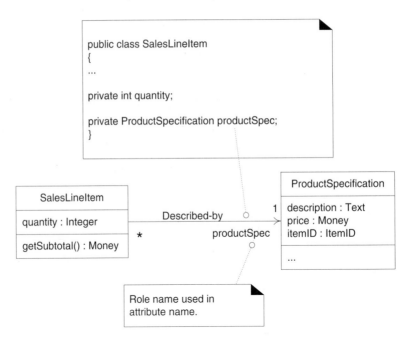

Figure 20.4 Role names may be used to generate instance variable names.

Mapping Attributes

The *Sale* class illustrates that in some cases one must consider the mapping of attributes from the design to the code in different languages. Figure 20.5 illustrates the problem and its resolution.

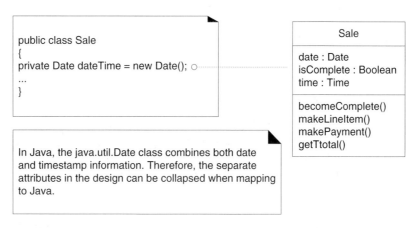

In Java, the java.util.Date class combines both date and timestamp information. Therefore, the separate attributes in the design can be collapsed when mapping to Java.

Figure 20.5 Mapping date and time to Java.

20.4   Creating Methods from Interaction Diagrams

An interaction diagram shows the messages that are sent in response to a method invocation. The sequence of these messages translates to a series of statements in the method definition. The *enterItem* interaction diagram in Figure 20.6 illustrates the Java definition of the *enterItem* method.

In this example, the *Register* class will be used. A Java definition is shown in Figure 20.7.

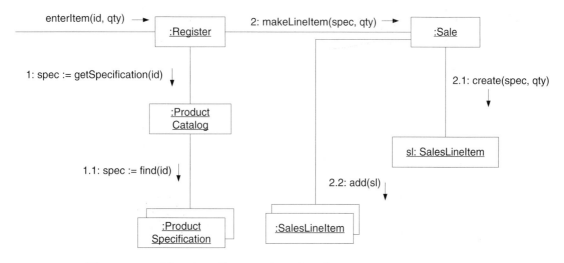

Figure 20.6 The enterItem interaction diagram.

The Register--enterItem Method

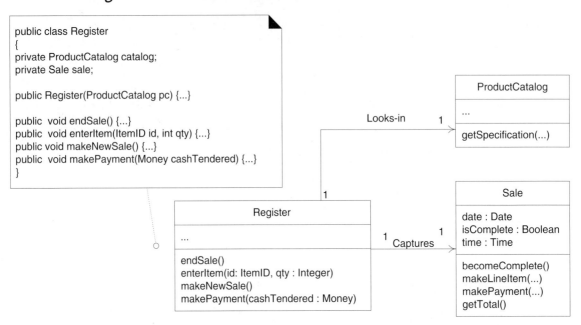

```
public class Register
{
private ProductCatalog catalog;
private Sale sale;

public Register(ProductCatalog pc) {...}

public  void endSale() {...}
public  void enterItem(ItemID id, int qty) {...}
public void makeNewSale() {...}
public  void makePayment(Money cashTendered) {...}
}
```

Figure 20.7 The Register class.

The *enterItem* message is sent to a *Register* instance; therefore, the *enterItem* method is defined in class *Register*.

```
public void enterItem(ItemID itemID, int qty)
```

Message 1: A *getSpecification* message is sent to the *ProductCatalog* to retrieve a *ProductSpecification*.

```
ProductSpecification spec = catalog.getSpecification( itemID );
```

Message 2: The *makeLineItem* message is sent to the *Sale*.

```
sale.makeLineItem(spec, qty);
```

In summary, each sequenced message within a method, as shown on the interaction diagram, is mapped to a statement in the Java method.

The complete *enterItem* method and its relationship to the interaction diagram is shown in Figure 20.8.

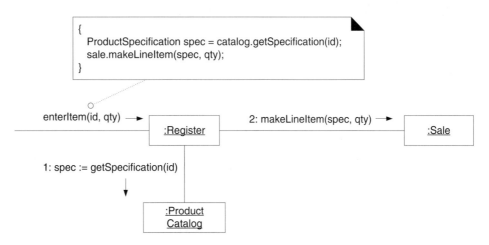

{
    ProductSpecification spec = catalog.getSpecification(id);
    sale.makeLineItem(spec, qty);
}

enterItem(id, qty) →   :Register   2: makeLineItem(spec, qty) →   :Sale

1: spec := getSpecification(id)

:Product
Catalog

Figure 20.8 The enterItem method.

20.5   Container/Collection Classes in Code

It is often necessary for an object to maintain visibility to a group of other objects; the need for this is usually evident from the multiplicity value in a class diagram—it may be greater than one. For example, a *Sale* must maintain visibility to a group of *SalesLineItem* instances, as shown in Figure 20.9.

In OO programming languages, these relationships are often implemented with the introduction of a intermediate container or collection. The one-side class defines a reference attribute pointing to a container/collection instance, which contains instances of the many-side class.

For example, the Java libraries contain collection classes such as *ArrayList* and *HashMap*, which implement the *List* and *Map* interfaces, respectively. Using *ArrayList*, the *Sale* class can define an attribute that maintains an ordered list of *SalesLineItem* instances.

The choice of collection class is of course influenced by the requirements; key-based lookup requires the use of a *Map*, a growing ordered list requires a *List*, and so on.

20.6   Exceptions and Error Handling

Exception handling has been ignored so far in the development of a solution. This was intentional to focus on the basic questions of responsibility assignment and object design. However, in application development, it is wise to consider exception handling during design work, and certainly during implementation.

Briefly, in the UML, exceptions are illustrated as asynchronous messages in interaction diagrams. This is examined in Chapter 33.

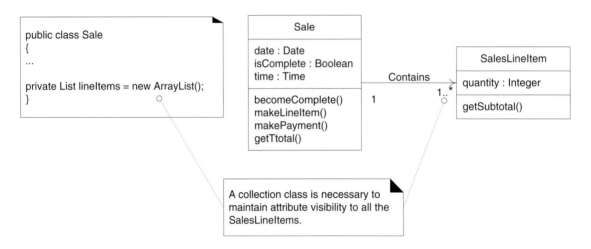

Figure 20.9 Adding a collection.

20.7 Defining the Sale--makeLineItem Method

As a final example, the *makeLineItem* method of class *Sale* can also be written by inspecting the *enterItem* collaboration diagram. An abridged version of the interaction diagram, with the accompanying Java method, is shown in Figure 20.10.

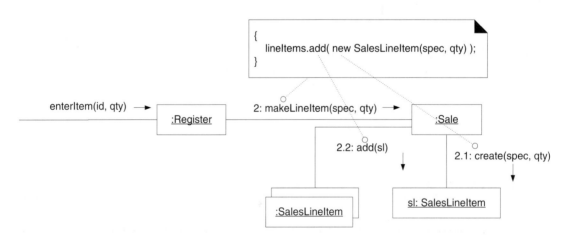

Figure 20.10 Sale--makeLineItem method.

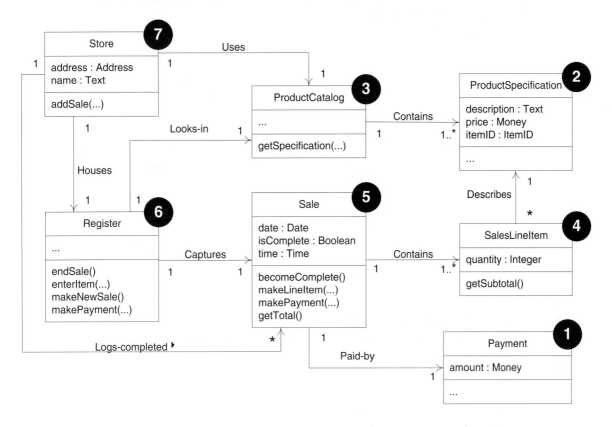

Figure 20.11 Possible order of class implementation and testing.

20.8 Order of Implementation

Classes need to be implemented (and ideally, fully unit tested) from least-coupled to most-coupled (see Figure 20.11). For example, possible first classes to implement are either *Payment* or *ProductSpecification*; next are classes only dependent on the prior implementations—*ProductCatalog* or *SalesLineItem*.

20.9 Test-First Programming

An excellent practice promoted by the Extreme Programming (XP) method [Beck00], and applicable to the UP (as most XP practices are), is **test-first programming**. In this practice, unit testing code is written *before* the code to be tested, and the developer writes unit testing code for *all* production code. The basic rhythm is to write a little test code, then write a little production code, make it pass the test, then write some more test code, and so forth.

Advantages include:

- **The unit tests actually get written**—Human (or at least programmer) nature is such that avoidance of writing unit tests is very common, if left as an afterthought.

- **Programmer satisfaction**—If a developer writes the production code, informally debugs it, and then as an afterthought adds unit tests, it does not feel very satisfying. However, if the tests are written first, and then production code is created and refined to pass the tests, there is some feeling of accomplishment—of passing a test. The psychological aspects of development can't be ignored—programming is a human endeavor.

- **Clarification of interface and behavior**—Often, the exact public interface and behavior of a class is not perfectly clear until programming it. By writing the unit test for it first, one clarifies the design of the class.

- **Provable verification**—Obviously, having hundreds or thousands of unit tests provides some meaningful verification of correctness.

- **The confidence to change things**—In test-first programming, there are hundreds or thousands of unit tests, and a unit test class for each production class. When a developer needs to change existing code—written by themselves or others—there is a unit test suite that can be run, providing immediate feedback if the change caused an error.

As an example, a popular, simple and free unit testing framework is JUnit (www.junit.org) for Java. Suppose we are using JUnit and test-first programming to create the *Sale* class. *Before* programming the *Sale* class, we write a unit testing method in a *SaleTest* class that does the following:

1. Set up a new sale.

2. Add some line items to it.

3. Ask for the total, and verify it is the expected value.

For example:

```
public class SaleTest extends TestCase
{
    // ...

  public void testTotal()
  {
    // set up the test
    Money total = new Money( 7.5 );
    Money price = new Money( 2.5 );
    ItemID id = new ItemID( 1 );
    ProductSpecification spec;
    spec = new ProductSpecification( id, price, "product 1" );
    Sale sale = new Sale();

    // add the items
    sale.makeLineItem( spec, 1 );
    sale.makeLineItem( spec, 2 );

    // verify the total is 7.5
```

```
    assertEquals( sale.getTotal(), total);
  }
}
```

Only after this *SaleTest* class is created do we then write the *Sale* class to pass this test. However, not all unit testing methods need to be written beforehand. A developer writes one testing method, then the production code to satisfy it, then another testing method, and so on.

20.10   Summary of Mapping Designs to Code

The translation process from DCDs to class definitions, and from interaction diagrams to methods, is relatively straightforward. There is still lots of room for decision-making, design changes, and exploration during programming work, but some of the big design ideas have been considered prior to the programming.

20.11   Introduction to the Program Solution

This section presents a sample domain object layer program solution in Java for this iteration. The code generation is largely derived from the design class diagrams and interaction diagrams defined in the design work, based on the principles of mapping designs to code as previously explored.

> The main point of this listing is to show that there is a translation from design artifacts to a foundation of code. This code defines a simple case; it is not meant to illustrate a robust, fully developed Java program with synchronization, exception handling, and so on.

Class Payment

```
public class Payment
{
    private Money amount;
    public Payment( Money cashTendered ){ amount = cashTendered; }
    public Money getAmount() { return amount; }
}
```

Class ProductCatalog

```
public class ProductCatalog
{
    private Map productSpecifications = new HashMap();
```

```java
    public ProductCatalog()
    {
        // sample data
        ItemID id1 = new ItemID( 100 );
        ItemID id2 = new ItemID( 200 );
        Money price = new Money( 3 );

        ProductSpecification ps;
        ps = new ProductSpecification( id1, price, "product 1" );
        productSpecifications.put( id1, ps );
        ps = new ProductSpecification( id2, price, "product 2" );
        productSpecifications.put( id2, ps );
    }

    public ProductSpecification getSpecification( ItemID id )
    {
        return (ProductSpecification)productSpecifications.get( id );
    }
}
```

Class Register

```java
public class Register
{
    private ProductCatalog catalog;
    private Sale sale;

    public Register( ProductCatalog catalog )
    {
        this.catalog = catalog;
    }

    public void endSale()
    {
        sale.becomeComplete();
    }

    public void enterItem( ItemID id, int quantity )
    {
        ProductSpecification spec = catalog.getSpecification( id );

        sale.makeLineItem( spec, quantity );
    }

    public void makeNewSale()
    {
        sale = new Sale();
    }

    public void makePayment( Money cashTendered )
    {
        sale.makePayment( cashTendered );
    }

}
```

Class ProductSpecification

```
public class ProductSpecification
{
    private ItemID id;
    private Money price;
    private String description;

    public ProductSpecification
        ( ItemID id, Money price, String description )
    {
        this.id = id;
        this.price = price;
        this.description = description;
    }

    public ItemID getItemID() { return id;}

    public Money getPrice() { return price; }

    public String getDescription() { return description; }
}
```

Class Sale

```
public class Sale
{
    private List lineItems = new ArrayList();
    private Date date = new Date();
    private boolean isComplete = false;
    private Payment payment;

    public Money getBalance()
    {
        return payment.getAmount().minus( getTotal() );
    }

    public void becomeComplete() { isComplete = true; }

    public boolean isComplete() { return isComplete; }

    public void makeLineItem
        ( ProductSpecification spec, int quantity )
    {
        lineItems.add( new SalesLineItem( spec, quantity ) );
    }

    public Money getTotal()
    {
        Money total = new Money();
        Iterator i = lineItems.iterator();
        while( i.hasNext() )
        {
         SalesLineItem sli = (SalesLineItem) i.next();
         total.add( sli.getSubtotal() );
        }
        return total;
    }
```

```
    public void makePayment( Money cashTendered )
    {
        payment = new Payment( cashTendered );
    }
}
```

Class SalesLineItem

```
public class SalesLineItem
{
    private int quantity;
    private ProductSpecification productSpec;

    public SalesLineItem (ProductSpecification spec, int quantity )
    {
        this.productSpec = spec;
        this.quantity = quantity;
    }

    public Money getSubtotal()
    {
        return productSpec.getPrice().times( quantity );
    }
}
```

Class Store

```
public class Store
{
    private ProductCatalog catalog = new ProductCatalog();
    private Register register = new Register( catalog );

    public Register getRegister() { return register; }
}
```

PART 4 ELABORATION
ITERATION 2

ITERATION 2 AND ITS REQUIREMENTS

21.1 Iteration 2 Emphasis: Object Design and Patterns

The inception phase chapters and those for iteration 1 in the elaboration phase emphasized a range of fundamental analysis and object design skills, in order to share information on a breadth of common steps in building object systems.

In this iteration, the case study just emphasizes:

■ essential object design

■ the use of patterns to create a solid design

■ application of the UML to visualize the models

These are primary objectives of the book, and critical skills.

There is minimal discussion of requirements analysis or domain modeling, and the explanation of the design is more succinct, now that (in iteration 1) a detailed explanation of the basics of how to think in objects has been presented.

Many other analysis, design, and implementation activities would of course occur in this iteration, but these are de-emphasized in favor of sharing information about how to do object design.

21.2 From Iteration 1 to 2

When iteration 1 ends, the following should be accomplished:

■ All the software has been vigorously tested: unit, acceptance, load, usability, and so on. The idea in the UP is to do early, realistic, and continuous verification of quality and correctness, so that early feedback guides the developers to adapt and improve the system, finding its "true path."

- Customers have been regularly engaged in evaluating the partial system, to obtain feedback for adaptation and clarification of requirements. And the customers get to see early visible progress with the system.

- The system, across all subsystems, has been completely integrated and stabilized as a baselined internal release.

In the interest of brevity, many activities concluding iteration 1 and initiating iteration 2 are skipped, since the emphasis of this presentation is an introduction to OOA/D. Comments on a few of the myriad activities that are skipped include:

- At the start of the new iteration, use a CASE tool to reverse-engineer UML diagrams from the source code of the last iteration (the results are part of the UP Design Model). These can be printed in large size on a plotter and posted on the walls of the project room, as a communication aid to illustrate the starting point of the logical design for the next iteration.

- Usability analysis and engineering for the UI is underway. This is an extraordinarily important skill and activity for the success of many systems. However, the subject is detailed and non-trivial, and outside the scope of this book.

- Database modeling and implementation is underway.

- Near the end of the prior iteration, requirements for the next are chosen.

- Another two-day (for example) requirements workshop occurs, in which more use cases are written in their fully dressed format. During elaboration, while perhaps 10% of the most risky requirements are being designed and implemented, there is a *parallel* activity to deeply explore and define perhaps 80% of the use cases for the system, even though most of these requirements won't be implemented until construction.

  ○ Participants will include a few developers (such as the software architect) from the first iteration, so that the investigation and questioning during this workshop is informed from the insights (and confusions) gained from actually quickly building some software. There's nothing like building some software to discover what we really don't know about the requirements—this is a key idea in the UP and iterative development.

Simplifications in the Case Study

In a skillful UP project, the requirements chosen for the early iterations are organized by risk and high business value, so that the high-risk issues are identified and resolved early. However, if this case study exactly followed that strategy, it would not be possible to help explain fundamental ideas and principles of OOA/D in the early iterations. Therefore, some license is taken with the prioritization of requirements, preferring those that support the educational goals, rather than project risk goals.

21.3   Iteration 2 Requirements

Iteration 2 of the NextGen POS application handles several interesting requirements:

1. Support for variations in third-party external services. For example, different tax calculators must be connectable to the system, and each has a unique interface. Likewise with different accounting systems and so forth. Each will offer a different API and protocol for a core of common functions.

2. Complex pricing rules.

3. Pluggable business rules.

4. A design to refresh a GUI window when the sale total changes.

These requirements will only be considered (for this iteration) in the context of scenarios of the *Process Sale* use case.

Note that these are not newly discovered requirements; they were identified during inception. For example, the original *Process Sale* use case indicates the pricing problem:

Main Success Scenario:
1. Customer arrives at a POS checkout with goods and/or services to purchase.
2. Cashier tells System to create a new sale.
3. Cashier enters item identifier.
4. System records sale line item and presents item description, price, and running total.
   Price calculated from a set of price rules.
   ...

Furthermore, sections in the Supplementary Specification record details of the domain rules for pricing, and indicate the need to support varying external systems:

Supplementary Specification

...

Interfaces

Software Interfaces

For most external collaborating systems (tax calculator, accounting, inventory, ...) we need to be able to plug in varying systems and thus varying interfaces.

...

Domain (Business) Rules

ID	Rule	Changeability	Source
RULE4	Purchaser discount rules. Examples: Employee—20% off. Preferred Customer—10% off. Senior—15% off.	High. Each retailer uses different rules.	Retailer policy.
...	...	...	...

Information in Domains of Interest

Pricing

In addition to the pricing rules described in the domain rules section, note that products have an *original price*, and optionally a *permanent markdown price*. A product's price (before further discounts) is the permanent markdown price, if present. Organizations maintain the original price even if there is a permanent markdown price, for accounting and tax reasons.

...

Incremental Development for the Same Use Case Across Iterations

Because of these requirements, we are revisiting the *Process Sale* use case in iteration 2, but implementing more scenarios, so that the system incrementally grows. It is common to work on varying scenarios or features of the same use case over several iterations and gradually extend the system to ultimately handle all the functionality required. On the other hand, short, simple use cases may be completely implemented within one iteration.

Iteration 1 made simplifications so that the problem and solution were not overly complex to explore. Once again—for the same reason—a relatively small amount of additional functionality is considered.

In a development project the requirements chosen for this iteration in the book would not be the undisputed choice—another possibility is updating inventory, credit payment handling, or a completely different use case. However, this choice is rich with valuable learning opportunities.

21.4 Refinement of Analysis-oriented Artifacts in this Iteration

Use-Case Model: Use Cases

No refinement is required of the use cases as a result of the chosen requirements for this iteration, although they may change as a result of other insights.

However, in addition to object design and programming, a parallel activity of a second short requirements workshop will occur in this iteration, within which more use cases will be investigated and written in detail. The previously fully dressed use cases (for example, *Process Sale*) will be revisited and probably refined based on insights gained from iteration 1. Some of these use case updates may be considered for the next elaboration phase iteration, but many will be deferred until construction (because they are not architecturally significant or risky).

Use-Case Model: SSDs

This iteration includes adding support for third-party external systems with varying interfaces, such as a tax calculator. The NextGen POS system will be remotely communicating with external systems. Consequently, the SSDs should be updated to reflect at least some of the inter-system collaborations, in order to clarify what the new system-level events are.

Figure 21.1 illustrates an SSD for one scenario of paying by credit, which requires collaboration with several external systems. Even though the design of paying by credit is not handled in this iteration, the designer (me) has drawn an SSD based on it (and probably several others as well), to better understand the inter-system collaboration, and thus the required support for varying interfaces in the external systems.

Domain Model

After a little experience in domain modeling, a modeler can estimate if a set of new requirements will have a minor or major impact on the Domain Model in terms of many new concepts, associations, and attributes. In contrast to the prior iteration, the requirements being tackled this time do not involve many new domain concepts. A brief survey of the new requirements suggests something like *PriceRule* as a domain concept, but there are probably not dozens of new things.

In this situation, it is quite reasonable to skip refining the Domain Model, move quickly on to design work, and let the discovery of new domain concepts occur during object design, when the designers are thinking through a solution. A sign of process maturity with the UP is understanding when creating an artifact will add significant value, or is a kind of mechanical "make work" step, and better skipped.

This flexibility is a double-edged sword. All too often, the flexibility to skip pre-programming activities occurs out of an overly optimistic belief that the problem can be solved simply by rushing to code. If it truly can, great, because programming is the work that really matters, not drawing domain models. On the other hand, most developers have stories where a little reflection, investigation, and forethought before programming would have reduced pain and suffering.

Use-Case Model: System Operation Contracts

No new system operations are being considered in this iteration, and thus contracts are not required. In any event, contracts are just an option to consider when the detailed precision they offer is an improvement over the descriptions in the use cases.

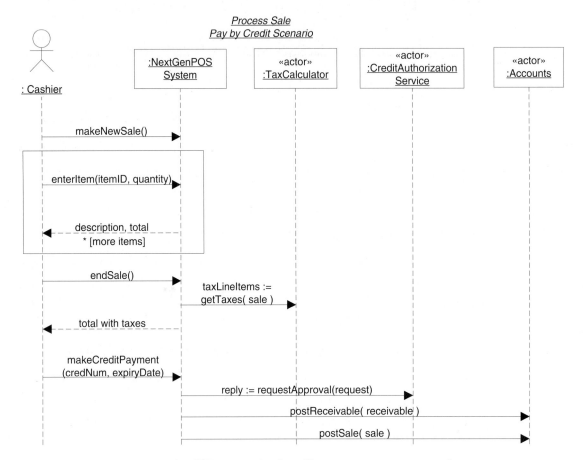

Figure 21.1 An SSD scenario that illustrates some external systems.

GRASP: MORE PATTERNS FOR ASSIGNING RESPONSIBILITIES

Luck is the residue of design.

—Branch Rickey

Objectives

■ Learn to apply the remaining GRASP patterns.

Introduction

Previously, we explored the application of the first five GRASP patterns:

■ Information Expert, Creator, High Cohesion, Low Coupling, and Controller

The final four GRASP patterns are:

■ Polymorphism

■ Indirection

■ Pure Fabrication

■ Protected Variations

Once these have been explained, we will have a rich and shared vocabulary with which to discuss designs. And as some of the "gang-of-four" (GoF) design patterns (such as Strategy and Factory) are also introduced (in subsequent chapters), that vocabulary will grow. A short sentence such as, "I suggest a Strategy generated from a Factory to support Protected Variations and low coupling with respect to <X>" communicates lots of information about the design, since pattern names tersely convey a complex design concept.

This chapter introduces the remaining GRASP patterns, a learning aid of fundamental principles by which responsibilities are assigned to objects and objects are designed.

Subsequent chapters introduce other useful patterns and apply them to the development of the second iteration of the NextGen POS application.

22.1   Polymorphism

Solution   When related alternatives or behaviors vary by type (class), assign responsibility for the behavior—using polymorphic operations—to the types for which the behavior varies.[1]

Corollary: Do not test for the type of an object and use conditional logic to perform varying alternatives based on type.

Problem   How to handle alternatives based on type? How to create pluggable software components?

Alternatives based on type—Conditional variation is a fundamental theme in programs. If a program is designed using if-then-else or case statement conditional logic, then if a new variation arises, it requires modification of the case logic. This approach makes it difficult to easily extend a program with new variations because changes tend to be required in several places—wherever the conditional logic exists.

Pluggable software components—Viewing components in client-server relationships, how can you replace one server component with another, without affecting the client?

Example   In the NextGen POS application, there are multiple external third-party tax calculators that must be supported (such as Tax-Master and Good-As-Gold Tax-Pro); the system needs to be able to integrate with different ones. Each tax calculator has a different interface, and so there is similar but varying behavior to adapt to each of these external fixed interfaces or APIs. One product may support a raw TCP socket protocol, another may offer a SOAP interface, and a third may offer a Java RMI interface.

What objects should be responsible for handling these varying external tax calculator interfaces?

---

1. **Polymorphism** has several related meanings. In this context, it means "giving the same name to services in different objects" [Coad95] when the services are similar or related. The different object types usually implement a common interface or are related in an implementation hierarchy with a common superclass, but this is language-dependent; for example, dynamic binding languages such as Smalltalk do not require this.

Since the behavior of calculator adaptation varies by the type of calculator, by Polymorphism we should assign the responsibility for adaptation to different calculator (or calculator adapter) objects themselves, implemented with a polymorphic *getTaxes* operation (see Figure 22.1).

These calculator adapter objects are not the external calculators, but rather, local software objects that represent the external calculators, or the adapter for the calculator. By sending a message to the local object, a call will ultimately be made on the external calculator in its native API.

Each *getTaxes* method takes the *Sale* object as a parameter, so that the calculator can analyze the sale. The implementation of each *getTaxes* method will be different: *TaxMasterAdapter* will adapt the request to the API of Tax-Master, and so on.

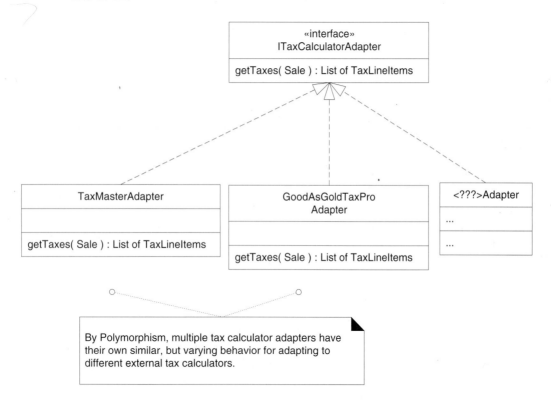

Figure 22.1 Polymorphism in adapting to different external tax calculators.

UML notation—Figure 22.1 introduces some new UML notation for specifying **interfaces** (a descriptor of operations without implementation), interface implementation, and for "collection" return types; Figure 22.2 elaborates. A UML **stereotype** is used to indicate an interface; a stereotype is a mechanism to categorize an element in some way. A stereotype name is surrounded by guillemets symbols, as in «interface». Guillemets are special *single*-character brackets most widely known by their use in French typography to indicate a quote; but to quote Rumbaugh, "the typographically challenged could substitute two angle brackets (<< >>) if necessary" [RJB99].

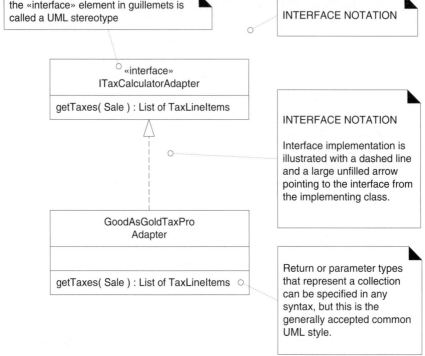

Figure 22.2 UML notation for interfaces and return types.

Discussion Polymorphism is a fundamental principle in designing how a system is organized to handle similar variations. A design based on assigning responsibilities by Polymorphism can be easily extended to handle new variations. For example, adding a new calculator adapter class with its own polymorphic *getTaxes* method will have minor impact on the existing design.

Contraindications Sometimes, developers design systems with interfaces and polymorphism for speculative "future-proofing" against an unknown possible variation. If the variation point is definitely motivated by an immediate or very probable variability, then the effort of adding the flexibility through polymorphism is of course rational. But critical evaluation is required, because it is not uncommon to see unnecessary effort being applied to future-proofing a design with polymorphism at variation points that in fact are improbable and will never actually arise. Be realistic about the true likelihood of variability before investing in increased flexibility.

Benefits ■ Extensions required for new variations are easy to add.

■ New implementations can be introduced without affecting clients.

Related Patterns	■	Protected Variations
	■	A number of popular GoF design patterns [GHJV95], which will be discussed in this book rely on polymorphism, including Adapter, Command, Composite, Proxy, State, and Strategy.

Also Known As; Similar To	Choosing Message, Don't Ask "What Kind?"

22.2   Pure Fabrication

Solution   Assign a highly cohesive set of responsibilities to an artificial or convenience class that does not represent a problem domain concept—something made up, to support high cohesion, low coupling, and reuse.

Such a class is a *fabrication* of the imagination. Ideally, the responsibilities assigned to this fabrication support high cohesion and low coupling, so that the design of the fabrication is very clean, or *pure*—hence a pure fabrication.

Finally, a pure fabrication implies making something up, which we do when we're desperate!

Problem   What object should have the responsibility, when you do not want to violate High Cohesion and Low Coupling, or other goals, but solutions offered by Expert (for example) are not appropriate?

Object-oriented designs are sometimes characterized by implementing as software classes representations of concepts in the real-world problem domain to lower the representational gap; for example a *Sale* and *Customer* class. However, there are many situations in which assigning responsibilities only to domain layer software classes leads to problems in terms of poor cohesion or coupling, or low reuse potential.

Example   For example, suppose that support is needed to save *Sale* instances in a relational database. By Information Expert, there is some justification to assign this responsibility to the *Sale* class itself, because the sale has the data that needs to be saved. But consider the following implications:

■   The task requires a relatively large number of supporting database-oriented operations, none related to the concept of sale-ness, so the *Sale* class becomes incohesive.

■   The *Sale* class has to be coupled to the relational database interface (such as JDBC in Java technologies), so its coupling goes up. And the coupling is not even to another domain object, but to a particular kind of database interface.

- Saving objects in a relational database is a very general task for which many classes need support. Placing these responsibilities in the *Sale* class suggests there is going to be poor reuse or lots of duplication in other classes that do the same thing.

Thus, even though *Sale* is a logical candidate by virtue of Information Expert to save itself in a database, it leads to a design with low cohesion, high coupling, and low reuse potential—exactly the kind of desperate situation that calls for making something up.

A reasonable solution is to create a new class that is solely responsible for saving objects in some kind of persistent storage medium, such as a relational database; call it the *PersistentStorage*.[2] This class is a Pure Fabrication—a figment of the imagination.

Notice the name: *PersistentStorage*. This is an understandable concept, yet the name or concept "persistent storage" is not something one would find in the Domain Model. And if a designer asked a business-person in a store, "Do you work with persistent storage objects?" they would not understand. They understand concepts such as "sale" and "payment." *PersistentStorage* is not a domain concept, but something made up or fabricated for the convenience of the software developer.

This Pure Fabrication solves the following design problems:

- The *Sale* remains well-designed, with high cohesion and low coupling.

- The *PersistentStorage* class is itself relatively cohesive, having the sole purpose of storing or inserting objects in a persistent storage medium.

- The *PersistentStorage* class is a very generic and reusable object.

Creating a pure fabrication in this example is exactly the situation in which their use is called for—eliminating a bad design based on Expert, with poor cohesion and coupling, with a good design in which there is greater potential for reuse.

Note that, as with all the GRASP patterns, the emphasis is on where responsibilities should be placed. In this example the responsibilities are shifted from the *Sale* class (motivated by Expert) to a Pure Fabrication.

---

2. In a real persistence framework, more than a single pure fabrication class is ultimately necessary to create a reasonable design. This object will be a front-end facade on to a large number of back-end helper objects.

Discussion   The design of objects can be broadly divided into two groups:

1. Those chosen by **representational decomposition**.
2. Those chosen by **behavioral decomposition**.

For example, the creation of a software class such as *Sale* is by representational decomposition; the software class is related to or represents a thing in a domain. Representational decomposition is a common strategy in object design and supports the goal of reduced representational gap. But sometimes, we desire to assign responsibilities by grouping behaviors or by algorithm, without any concern for creating a class with a name or purpose that is related to a real-world domain concept.

A good example is an "algorithm" object such as a *TableOfContentsGenerator*, whose purpose is (surprise) to generate a table of contents and was created as a helper or convenience class by a developer, without any concern for choosing a name from the domain vocabulary of books and documents. It exists as a convenience class conceived by the developer to group together some related behavior or methods, and is thus motivated by *behavioral decomposition*.

To contrast, a software class named *TableOfContents* is inspired by *representational decomposition*, and should contain information consistent with our concept of the real domain (such as chapter names).

Identifying a class as a Pure Fabrication is not critical. It is an educational concept to communicate the general idea that some software classes are inspired by representations of the domain, and some are simply "made up" as a convenience for the object designer. These convenience classes are usually designed to group together some common behavior, and are thus inspired by behavioral rather than representational decomposition.

Said another way, a Pure Fabrication is usually partitioned based on related functionality, and so is a kind of function-centric or behavioral object.

Many existing object-oriented design patterns are examples of Pure Fabrications: Adapter, Strategy, Command, and so on [GHJV95].

As a final comment worth reiterating: Sometimes a solution offered by Information Expert is not desirable. Even though the object is a candidate for the responsibility by virtue of having much of the information related to the responsibility, in other ways, its choice leads to a poor design, usually due to problems in cohesion or coupling.

Benefits   ■   High Cohesion is supported because responsibilities are factored into a fine-grained class that only focuses on a very specific set of related tasks.

■   Reuse potential may increase because of the presence of fine-grained Pure Fabrication classes whose responsibilities have applicability in other applications.

Contraindications   Behavioral decomposition into Pure Fabrication objects is sometimes overused by those new to object design and more familiar with decomposing or organizing software in terms of functions. To exaggerate, functions just become objects. There is nothing inherently wrong with creating "function" or "algorithm" objects, but it needs to be balanced with the ability to design with representational decomposition, such as the ability to apply Information Expert so that a representational class such as *Sale* also has responsibilities. Information Expert supports the goal of co-locating responsibilities with the objects that know the information needed for those responsibilities, which tends to support lower coupling. If overused, Pure Fabrication could lead to too many behavior objects that have responsibilities *not* co-located with the information required for their fulfillment, which can adversely affect coupling. The usual symptom is that most of the data inside the objects is being passed to other objects to reason with it.

Related Patterns and Principles

- Low Coupling.

- High Cohesion.

- A Pure Fabrication usually takes on responsibilities from the domain class that would be assigned those responsibilities based on the Expert pattern.

- All GoF design patterns [GHJV95], such as Adapter, Command, Strategy, and so on, are Pure Fabrications.

- Virtually all other design patterns are Pure Fabrications.

22.3 Indirection

Solution Assign the responsibility to an intermediate object to mediate between other components or services so that they are not directly coupled.

The intermediary creates an *indirection* between the other components.

Problem Where to assign a responsibility, to avoid direct coupling between two (or more) things? How to de-couple objects so that low coupling is supported and reuse potential remains higher?

Examples **TaxCalculatorAdapter**

These objects act as intermediaries to the external tax calculators. Via polymorphism, they provide a consistent interface to the inner objects and hide the variations in the external APIs. By adding a level of indirection and adding polymorphism, the adapter objects protect the inner design against variations in the external interfaces (see Figure 22.3).

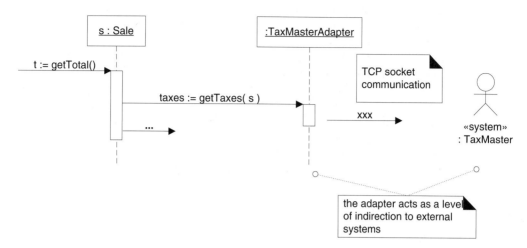

Figure 22.3 Indirection via the adapter.

PersistentStorage

The Pure Fabrication example of decoupling the *Sale* from the relational database services through the introduction of a *PersistentStorage* class is also an example of assigning responsibilities to support Indirection. The *PersistentStorage* acts as a intermediary between the *Sale* and the database.

Discussion "Most problems in computer science can be solved by another level of indirection" is an old adage with particular relevance to object-oriented designs. [3]

Just as many existing design patterns are specializations of Pure Fabrication, many are also specializations of Indirection. Adapter, Facade, and Observer are examples [GHJV95]. In addition, many Pure Fabrications are generated because of Indirection. The motivation for Indirection is usually Low Coupling; an intermediary is added to decouple other components or services.

Benefits ■ Lower coupling between components.

Related Patterns and Principles
■ Protected Variations

■ Low Coupling

■ Many GoF patterns, such as Adapter, Bridge, Facade, Observer, and Mediator [GHJV95].

■ Many Indirection intermediaries are Pure Fabrications.

---

3. If any adage is old in computer science! I have forgotten the source (Parnas?). Note there is also the counter-adage: "Most problems in performance can be solved by removing another layer of indirection!"

22.4   Protected Variations

Solution   Identify points of predicted variation or instability; assign responsibilities to create a stable interface around them.

Note: The term "interface" is used in the broadest sense of an access view; it does not literally only mean something like a Java or COM interface.

Problem   How to design objects, subsystems, and systems so that the variations or instability in these elements does not have an undesirable impact on other elements?

Example   For example, the prior external tax calculator problem and its solution with Polymorphism illustrate Protected Variations (Figure 22.1). The point of instability or variation is the different interfaces or APIs of external tax calculators. The POS system needs to be able to integrate with many existing tax calculator systems, and also with future third-party calculators not yet in existence.

By adding a level of indirection, an interface, and using polymorphism with various *ITaxCalculatorAdapter* implementations, protection within the system from variations in external APIs is achieved. Internal objects collaborate with a stable interface; the various adapter implementations hide the variations to the external systems.

Discussion   Protected Variations (PV) was first published as a pattern by Cockburn in [VCK96], although this very fundamental design principle has been around for decades under various terms.

Mechanisms Motivated by PV

PV is a root principle motivating most of the mechanisms and patterns in programming and design to provide flexibility and protection from variations.

At one level, the maturation of a developer or architect can be seen in their growing knowledge of ever-wider mechanisms to achieve PV, to pick the appropriate PV battles worth fighting, and their ability to choose a suitable PV solution. In the early stages, one learns about data encapsulation, interfaces, and polymorphism—all core mechanisms to achieve PV. Later, one learns techniques such as rule-based languages, rule interpreters, reflective and metadata designs, virtual machines, and so forth—all of which can be applied to protect against some variation.

For example:

Core Protected Variations Mechanisms

Data encapsulation, interfaces, polymorphism, indirection, and standards are motivated by PV. Note that components such as brokers and virtual machines are complex examples of indirection to achieve PV.

Data-Driven Designs

Data-driven designs cover a broad family of techniques include reading codes, values, class file paths, class names, and so forth, from an external source in order to change the behavior of, or "parameterize" a system in some way at runtime. Other variants include style sheets, metadata for object-relational mapping, property files, reading in window layouts, and much more. The system is protected from the impact of data, metadata, or declarative variations by externalizing the variant, reading it in, and reasoning with it.

Service Lookup

Service lookup includes techniques such as using naming services (for example, Java's JNDI) or traders to obtain a service (for example, Java's Jini, or UDDI for Web services). Clients are protected from variations in the location of services, using the stable interface of the lookup service. It is a special case of data-driven design.

Interpreter-Driven Designs

Interpreter-driven designs include rule interpreters that execute rules read from an external source, script or language interpreters that read and run programs, virtual machines, neural network engines that execute nets, constraint logic engines that read and reason with constraint sets, and so forth. This approach allows changing or parameterizing the behavior of a system via external logic expressions. The system is protected from the impact of logic variations by externalizing the logic, reading it in, and using an interpreter.

Reflective or Meta-Level Designs

An example of this approach is using the *java.beans.Introspector* to obtain a *BeanInfo* object, asking for the getter *Method* object for bean property X, and calling *Method.invoke*. The system is protected from the impact of logic or external code variations by reflective algorithms that use introspection and meta-language services. It may be considered a special case of data-driven designs.

Uniform Access

Some languages, such as Ada, Eiffel, and C#, support a syntactic construct so that both a method and field access are expressed the same way. For example, *aCircle.radius* may invoke a *radius():float* method or directly refer to a public field, depending on the definition of the class. We can change from public fields to access methods, without changing the client code.

The Liskov Substitution Principle (LSP)

LSP [Liskov88] formalizes the principle of protection against variations in different implementations of an interface, or subclass extensions of a superclass.

To quote:

What is wanted here is something like the following substitution property: If for each object *o1* of type *S* there is an object *o2* of type *T* such that for all programs *P* defined in terms of *T*, the behavior of *P* is unchanged when o1 is substituted for o2 then S is a subtype of *T* [Liskov88].

Informally, software (methods, classes, ...) that refers to a type *T* (some interface or abstract superclass) should work properly or as expected with any substituted implementation or subclass of *T*—call it *S*. For example:

```
public void addTaxes( ITaxCalculatorAdapter calculator, Sale sale )
{
    List taxLineItems = calculator.getTaxes( sale );
    // ...
}
```

For this method *addTaxes*, no matter what implementation of *ITaxCalculatorAdapter* is passed in as an actual parameter, the method should continue to work "as expected." LSP is a simple idea, intuitive to most object developers, that formalizes this intuition.

Structure-Hiding Designs

In the first edition of this book, an important object design principle called **Don't Talk to Strangers** or the **Law of Demeter** [Lieberherr88] was expressed as one of the nine GRASP patterns. Briefly, it means to avoid creating designs that traverse long object structure paths and send messages (or talk) to distant, indirect (stranger) objects. Such designs are fragile with respect to changes in the object structures—a common point of instability. But in the second edition the more general PV replaced Don't Talk to Strangers, because the latter is a special case of the former. That is, a mechanism to achieve protection from structure changes is to apply the Don't Talk to Strangers rules.

Don't Talk to Strangers places constraints on what objects you should send messages to within a method. It states that within a method, messages should only be sent to the following objects:

1. The *this* object (or *self*).

2. A parameter of the method.

3. An attribute of *this*.

4. An element of a collection which is an attribute of *this*.

5. An object created within the method.

The intent is to avoid coupling a client to knowledge of indirect objects and the object connections between objects.

Direct objects are a client's "familiars," indirect objects are "strangers." A client should talk to familiars, and avoid talking to strangers.

Here is an example that (mildly) violates Don't Talk to Strangers. The comments explain the violation.

```
class Register
{
private Sale sale;

public void slightlyFragileMethod()
{
    // sale.getPayment() sends a message to a "familiar" (passes #3)

    // but in sale.getPayment().getTenderedAmount()
    // the getTenderedAmount() message is to a "stranger" Payment

    Money amount = sale.getPayment().getTenderedAmount();

    // ...
}
    // ...
}
```

This code traverses structural connections from a familiar object (the *Sale*) to a stranger object (the *Payment*), and then sends it a message. It is very slightly fragile, as it depends on the fact that *Sale* objects are connected to *Payment* objects. Realistically, this is unlikely to be a problem.

But, consider this next fragment, which traverses farther along the structural path:

```
public void moreFragileMethod()
{
    AccountHolder holder =
        sale.getPayment().getAccount().getAccountHolder();

    // ...
}
```

The example is contrived, but you see the pattern: Traversing farther along a path of object connections in order to send a message to a distant, indirect object—talking to a distant stranger. The design is coupled to a particular structure of how objects are connected. The farther along a path the program traverses, the more fragile it is.

Karl Lieberherr and his colleagues have done research into good object design principles, under the umbrella of the Demeter project. This Law of Demeter (Don't Talk to Strangers) was identified because of the frequency with which they saw change and instability in object structure, and thus frequent breakage in code that was coupled to knowledge of object connections.

Yet, as will be examined in the following "Speculative PV and Picking your Battles" section, it is not always necessary to protect against this; it depends on the instability of the object structure. In standard libraries (such as the Java libraries) the structural connections between classes of objects are relatively stable. In mature systems, the structure is more stable. In new systems in early iteration, it isn't stable.

In general, the farther along a path one traverses, the more fragile it is, and thus it is more useful to conform to Don't Talk to Strangers.

Strictly obeying this law—protection against structural variations—requires adding new public operations to the "familiars" of an object; these operations provide the ultimately desired information, and hide how it was obtained. For example, to support Don't Talk to Strangers for the previous two cases:

```
// case 1
Money amount = sale.getTenderedAmountOfPayment();

// case 2
AccountHolder holder = sale.getAccountHolderOfPayment();
```

Contraindications *Caution: Speculative PV and Picking Your Battles*

First, two points of change are worth defining:

- **variation point**—Variations in the existing, current system or requirements, such as the multiple tax calculator interfaces that must be supported.

- **evolution point**—Speculative points of variation that may arise in the future, but which are not present in the existing requirements.[4]

PV is applied to both variation and evolution points.

A caution: Sometimes the cost of speculative "future-proofing" at evolution points outweighs the cost incurred by a simple, more "brittle" design that is reworked as necessary in response to the true change pressures. That is, the cost of engineering protection at evolution points can be higher than reworking a simple design.

For example, I recall a pager message handling system where the architect added a scripting language and interpreter to support flexibility and protected variation at an evolution point. However, during rework in an incremental release, the complex (and inefficient) scripting was removed—it simply wasn't needed. And when I started OO programming (in the early 1980s) I suffered the disease of "generalize-itis" in which I tended to spend many hours creating superclasses of the classes I really needed to write. I would make everything very general and flexible (and protected against variations), for that future situation when it would really pay off—which never came. I was a poor judge of when it was worth the effort.

The point is not to advocate rework and brittle designs. If the need for flexibility and protection from change is realistic, then applying PV is motivated. But if it is for speculative future-proofing or speculative "reuse" with very uncertain probabilities, then restraint and critical thinking is called for.

---

4. In the UP, evolution points can be formally documented in **Change Cases**; each describes relevant aspects of an evolution point for the benefit of a future architect.

Novice developers tend toward brittle designs, intermediate developers tend toward overly fancy and flexible, generalized ones (in ways that never get used). Expert designers choose with insight; perhaps a simple and brittle design whose cost of change is balanced against its likelihood.

Benefits
- Extensions required for new variations are easy to add.
- New implementations can be introduced without affecting clients.
- Coupling is lowered.
- The impact or cost of changes can be lowered.

Related Patterns and Principles
- Most design principles and patterns are mechanisms for protected variation, including polymorphism, interfaces, indirection, data encapsulation, most of the GoF design patterns, and so on.
- In [Pree95] variation and evolution points are called "hot spots."

Also Known As; Similar To
PV is essentially the same as the information hiding and open-closed principles, which are older terms. As an "official" pattern in the pattern community, it was named "Protected Variations" in 1996 by Cockburn in [VCK96].

Information Hiding

David Parnas's famous paper *On the Criteria To Be Used in Decomposing Systems Into Modules* [Parnas72] is an example of classics often cited but seldom read. In it, Parnas introduces the concept of **information hiding**. Perhaps because the term sounds like the idea of data encapsulation, it has been misinterpreted as that, and some books erroneously define the concepts as synonyms. Rather, Parnas intended information hiding to mean hide information about the design from other modules, at the points of difficultly or likely change. To quote his discussion of information hiding as a guiding design principle:

> We propose instead that one begins with a list of difficult design decisions or design decisions which are likely to change. Each module is then designed to hide such a decision from the others.

That is, Parnas's information hiding is the same principle expressed in PV, and not simply data encapsulation—which is but one of many techniques to hide information about the design. However, the term has been so widely reinterpreted as a synonym for data encapsulation that it is no longer possible to use it in its original sense without misunderstanding.

Open-Closed Principle

The **Open-Closed Principle** (OCP), described by Bertrand Meyer in [Meyer88] is essentially equivalent to the PV pattern and to information hiding. A definition of OCP is:

> Modules should be both open (for extension; adaptable) and closed (the module is closed to modification in ways that affect clients).

OCP and PV are essentially two expressions of the same principle, with different emphasis: protection at variation and evolution points. In OCP, "module" includes all discrete software elements, including methods, classes, subsystems, applications, and so forth.

In the context of OCP, the phrase "closed with respect to X" means that clients are not affected if X changes. For example, "the class is closed with respect to instance field definitions" through the mechanism of data encapsulation with private fields and public accessing methods. At the same time, they are open to modifying the definitions of the private data, because outside clients are not directly coupled to the private data.

As another example, "the tax calculator adapters are closed with respect to their public interface" through implementing the stable *ITaxCalculatorAdapter* interface. However, the adapters are open to extension by being privately modified in response to changes in the APIs of the external tax calculators, in ways that do not break their clients.

DESIGNING USE-CASE REALIZATIONS WITH GOF DESIGN PATTERNS

Anything you can do, I can do meta.

—Daniel Dennett

Objectives

- Apply GRASP and GoF design patterns to the design of the NextGen case study.

Introduction

This chapter explores object design for use-case realizations for the next iteration of the NextGen case study, which tackles support for external third-party services whose interfaces may vary, more complex product pricing rules, and pluggable business rules.

In the context of the design problems that will be discussed, new high-use UML notation will also be introduced.

The emphasis is to show how to apply the GoF and more basic GRASP patterns. It attempts to illustrate that object design and the assignment of responsibilities can be explained and learned based on the application of patterns—a vocabulary of principles and idioms that can be combined to design objects.

The Gang-of-Four Patterns

The additional patterns presented in this chapter are drawn from *Design Patterns* [GHJV95], a seminal and extremely popular work that presents 23 patterns useful during object design. Since the book was written by four authors, these patterns have become known as the "Gang-of-Four"—or "GoF"—patterns.[1]

This chapter provides an introduction to some of the high-use GoF patterns; subsequent chapters present more.[2] A thorough study of the *Design Patterns* book is recommended to grow as an object designer, although that book assumes the reader is already a designer with some experience; this book offers an introduction.

A Shared Vocabulary

In addition to the visual vocabulary of UML notation, by the end of this chapter we will have a richer shared vocabulary of design, in terms of pattern names. Thus, it will be possible to increasingly communicate software design ideas primarily in UML diagrams, with some attached notes that indicate the patterns (Indirection, Strategy, ...) being applied.

23.1 Adapter (GoF)

The problem explored in the previous chapter to motivate the Polymorphism pattern, and its solution, is more specifically an example of the GoF **Adapter** pattern.

Adapter

Context / Problem

How to resolve incompatible interfaces, or provide a stable interface to similar components with different interfaces?

Solution

Convert the original interface of a component into another interface, through an intermediate adapter object.

To review: The NextGen POS system needs to support several kinds of external third-party services, including tax calculators, credit authorization services,

---

1. With a tangential reference to Chinese politics.
2. In practice, perhaps approximately 15 of these 23 patterns are frequently used.

inventory systems, and accounting systems, among others. Each has a different API, which can't be changed.

A solution is to add a level of indirection with objects that adapt the varying external interfaces to a consistent interface used within the application. The solution is illustrated in Figure 23.1.

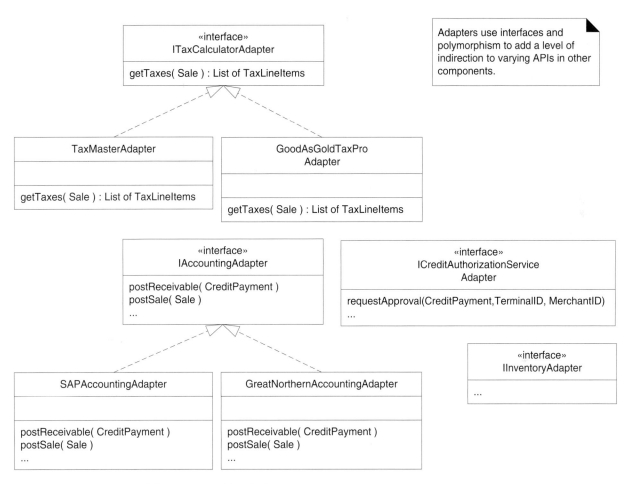

Figure 23.1 The Adapter pattern.

As illustrated in Figure 23.2, a particular adapter instance will be instantiated for the chosen external service[3], such as SAP for accounting, and will adapt the *postSale* request to the external interface, such as a SOAP XML interface over HTTPS for an intranet Web service offered by SAP.

---

3. In the J2EE Connector Architecture, these adapters to external services are more specifically called **resource adapters**.

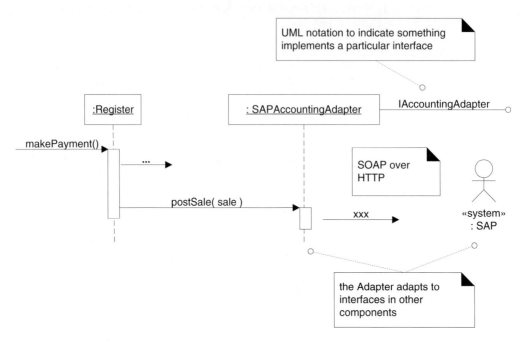

Figure 23.2 Using an Adapter.

UML notation—Note in Figure 23.2 the use of an interface "lollipop" to indicate that the *SAPAccountingAdapter* instance implements a noteworthy interface.

Polymorphism, Indirection, and Protected Variations (GRASP)

The previous application of the Adapter pattern is a specialization of the GRASP building blocks. It offers Protected Variations from changing external interfaces or third-party packages through the use of an Indirection object that applies interfaces and Polymorphism.

Note that most more complex or specialized patterns can be analyzed in terms of the basic GRASP family. There are hundreds of published design patterns, and although it is helpful to study these to accelerate learning, understanding their underlying basic themes (Protected Variations, Low Coupling, Polymorphism, Indirection, ...) helps us to cut through the myriad details and see the essential "alphabet" of design techniques being applied.

Naming Convention: Embed Pattern Name in Type Name?

Notice that the type names include the pattern name "Adapter." This is a relatively common style and has the advantage of easily communicating to others reading the code or diagrams what design patterns are being used.

23.2 "Analysis" Discoveries During Design: Domain Model

Observe that in the Adapter design in Figure 23.1, the *getTaxes* operation returns a list of *TaxLineItems*. That is, on deeper reflection and investigation of how taxes are handled and tax calculators work, the designer (me) realized that a list of tax line items are associated with a sale, such as state tax, federal tax, and so forth (there is always the chance governments will invent new taxes!).

In addition to being a newly created software class in the Design Model, this is a domain concept. It is normal and common to discover noteworthy domain concepts and refined understanding of the requirements during design or programming—iterative development supports this kind of incremental discovery.

Should this discovery be reflected in the Domain Model (or Glossary)? If the Domain Model will be used in the future as a source of inspiration for later design work, or as a visual learning aid to communicate the key domain concepts, then adding it could have value. Figure 23.3 illustrates an updated Domain Model.

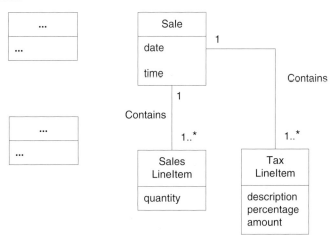

Figure 23.3 Updated partial Domain Model.

Maintain the Domain Model?

To put a finer point on the above comment about updating the Domain Model: Note that the architecture of the Design Model will usually be organized into layers (which is discussed in greater detail in a subsequent chapter). One of these layers of design classes will be called the **domain layer**; it will contain software classes whose names and structure take inspiration from the domain vocabulary and concepts (*Sale*, *TaxLineItem*, and so forth).

Suggestion

After some number of iterations, the Domain Model—as an early source of inspiration for the design classes in the domain layer of the Design Model—may outlive its usefulness. If updating the Domain Model to reflect changes in the Design Model does not continue to have practical value, consider eliminating it.

Rather, just reverse-engineer (with a UML CASE tool) a class diagram of the domain layer of design classes of the Design Model. Although these are software classes rather than pure domain conceptual classes, they reflect the noteworthy domain vocabulary that has emerged in the software design, and thus a UML class diagram of the design classes in the domain layer of the Design Model can be a useful "proxy" for a true Domain Model.

Please do not misunderstand: This is not a suggestion to definitely discard a Domain Model, but rather to consider if it is worth maintaining, or is just make-work documentation, and to know what alternatives can be helpful.

Related Patterns   A resource adapter that hides an external system may also be considered a Facade object (another GoF pattern discussed in this chapter), as it wraps access to the subsystem or system with a single object (which is the essence of Facade). However, the motivation to call it a resource adapter especially exists when the wrapping object provides adaptation to varying external interfaces.

23.3   Factory (GoF)

The adapter raises a new problem in the design: In the prior Adapter pattern solution for external services with varying interfaces, who creates the adapters? And how to determine which class of adapter to create, such as *TaxMasterAdapter* or *GoodAsGoldTaxProAdapter*?

If some domain object creates them, the responsibilities of the domain object are going beyond pure application logic (such as sales total calculations) and into other concerns related to connectivity with external software components.

This point underscores another fundamental design principle (usually considered an architectural design principle): Design to maintain a **separation of concerns**. That is, modularize or separate distinct concerns into different areas, so that each has a cohesive purpose. For example, the domain layer of software objects emphasizes relatively pure application logic responsibilities, whereas a different group of objects is responsible for the concern of connectivity to external systems.

Therefore, choosing a domain object (such as a *Register*) to create the adapters does not support the goal of a separation of concerns, and lowers its cohesion.

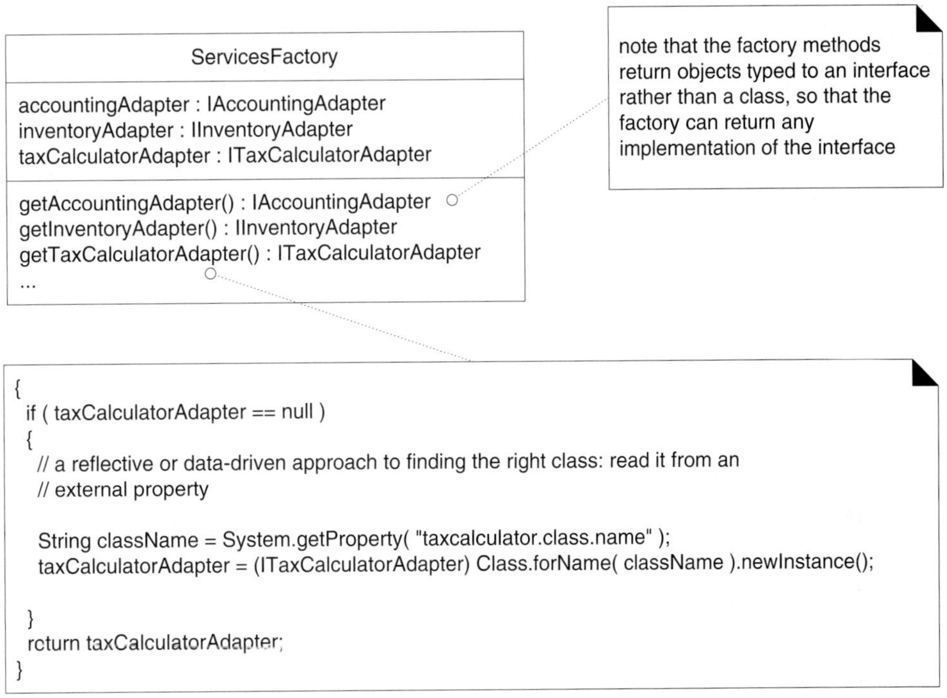

```
ServicesFactory

accountingAdapter : IAccountingAdapter
inventoryAdapter : IInventoryAdapter
taxCalculatorAdapter : ITaxCalculatorAdapter

getAccountingAdapter() : IAccountingAdapter     ○
getInventoryAdapter() : IInventoryAdapter
getTaxCalculatorAdapter() : ITaxCalculatorAdapter
...                                    ○
```

note that the factory methods return objects typed to an interface rather than a class, so that the factory can return any implementation of the interface

```
{
  if ( taxCalculatorAdapter == null )
  {
    // a reflective or data-driven approach to finding the right class: read it from an
    // external property

    String className = System.getProperty( "taxcalculator.class.name" );
    taxCalculatorAdapter = (ITaxCalculatorAdapter) Class.forName( className ).newInstance();

  }
  return taxCalculatorAdapter;
}
```

Figure 23.4 The Factory pattern.

UML notation—Observe the style in the UML diagram of Figure 23.4 that includes a note showing detailed pseudocode for the *getTaxCalculatorAdapter*. This style allows one to include dynamic algorithm details on a static class diagram such that it may lessen the need for interaction diagrams.

A common alternative in this case is to apply the **Factory** (or **Concrete Factory**) pattern, in which a Pure Fabrication "factory" object is defined to create objects.

Factory objects have several advantages:

- Separate the responsibility of complex creation into cohesive helper objects.

- Hide potentially complex creation logic.

- Allow introduction of performance-enhancing memory management strategies, such as object caching or recycling.

(Concrete) Factory

Context / Problem

Who should be responsible for creating objects when there are special considerations, such as complex creation logic, a desire to separate the creation responsibilities for better cohesion, and so forth?

Solution

Create a Pure Fabrication object called a Factory that handles the creation.

A Factory solution is illustrated in Figure 23.4.

Note that in the *ServicesFactory*, the logic to decide which class to create is resolved by reading in the class name from an external source (for example, via a system property if Java is used) and then dynamically loading the class. This is an example of a partial **data-driven design**. This design achieves Protected Variations with respect to changes in the implementation class of the adapter. Without changing the source code in this factory class, we can create instances of new adapter classes by changing the property value and ensuring the new class is visible in the Java class path for loading.

Related Patterns Factories are often accessed with the Singleton pattern.

23.4   Singleton (GoF)

The *ServicesFactory* raises another new problem in the design: who creates the factory itself, and how is it accessed?

First, observe that only one instance of the factory is needed within the process. Second, quick reflection suggests that the methods of this factory may need to be called from various places in the code, as different places need access to the adapters for calling on the external services. Thus, there is a visibility problem: how to get visibility to this single *ServicesFactory* instance?

One solution is pass the *ServicesFactory* instance around as a parameter to wherever a visibility need is discovered for it, or to initialize the objects that need visibility to it, with a permanent reference. This is possible but inconvenient; an alternative is the **Singleton** pattern.

Occasionally, it is desirable to support global visibility or a single access point to a single instance of a class rather than some other form of visibility. This is true for the *ServicesFactory* instance.

> *Singleton*
>
> *Context / Problem*
>
> Exactly one instance of a class is allowed—it is a "singleton." Objects need a global and single point of access.
>
> *Solution*
>
> Define a static method of the class that returns the singleton.

For example, Figure 23.5 shows an implementation of the Singleton pattern.

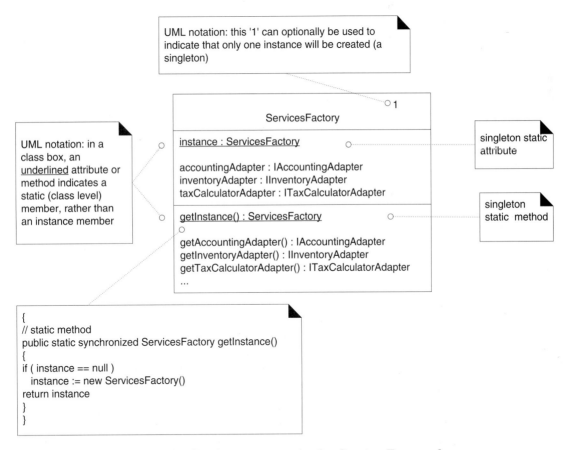

Figure 23.5 The Singleton pattern in the *ServicesFactory* class.

Thus, the key idea is that class X defines a static method *getInstance* that itself provides a single instance of X.

With this approach, a developer has global visibility to this single instance, via the static *getInstance* method of the class, as in this example:

```
public class Register
{

public void initialize()
{
    ... do some work ...

    // accessing the singleton Factory via the getInstance call
    accountingAdapter =
        ServicesFactory.getInstance().getAccountingAdapter();

    ... do some work ...
}

// other methods...

}
```

Since visibility to public classes is global in scope (in most languages), at any point in the code, in any method of any class, one can write *SingletonClass.getInstance()* in order to obtain visibility to the singleton instance, and then send it a message, such as *SingletonClass.getInstance().doFoo()*. It's hard to beat the feeling of being able to globally *doFoo*.

UML Shorthand for Singleton Access in Interaction Diagrams

A UML notation that implies—but does not explicitly show—the *getInstance* message in an interaction diagram is to add a «singleton» stereotype to the instance, as in Figure 23.6. This approach avoids having to explicitly show the (uninteresting) *getInstance* message to the class before sending a message to the singleton instance.

Implementation and Design Issues

A Singleton *getInstance* method is often frequently called. In multi-threaded applications, the creation step of the **lazy initialization** logic is a critical section requiring thread concurrency control. Thus, assuming the instance is lazy initialized, it is common to wrap the method with concurrency control. In Java, for example:

```
public static synchronized ServicesFactory getInstance()
{
    if ( instance == null )
    {
        // critical section if multithreaded application
        instance = new ServicesFactory();
    }
    return instance;
}
```

On the subject of lazy initialization, why not prefer **eager initialization**, as in this example?

```
public class ServicesFactory
{

// eager initialization
private static ServicesFactory instance =
    new ServicesFactory();


public static ServicesFactory getInstance()
{
    return instance;
}

// other methods...

}
```

The first approach of lazy initialization is usually preferred for at least these reasons:

- Creation work (and perhaps holding on to "expensive" resources) is avoided, if the instance is never actually accessed.

- The *getInstance* lazy initialization sometimes contains complex and conditional creation logic.

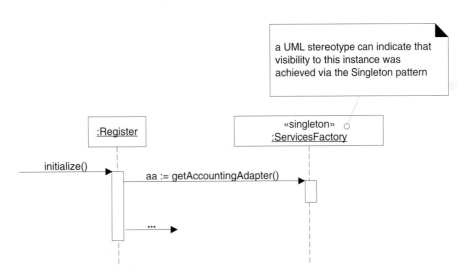

Figure 23.6 Implicit *getInstance* Singleton pattern message indicated in the UML with a stereotype.

Another common Singleton implementation question is: Why not make all the service methods *static* methods of the class itself, instead of using an instance object with instance-side methods? For example, what if we add a *static* method called *getAccountingAdapter* to *ServicesFactory*. But, an instance and instance-side methods are usually preferred for these reasons:

- Instance-side methods permit subclassing and refinement of the singleton class into subclasses; static methods are not polymorphic (virtual) and don't permit overriding in subclasses in most languages (Smalltalk excluded).

- Most object-oriented remote communication mechanisms (for example, Java's RMI) only support remote-enabling of instance methods, not static methods. A singleton instance could be remote-enabled, although that is admittedly rarely done.

- A class is not always a singleton in all application contexts. In application X, it may be a singleton, but it may be a "multi-ton" in application Y. It is also not uncommon to start off a design thinking the object will be a singleton, and then discovering a need for multiple instances in the same process. Thus, the instance-side solution offers flexibility.

Related Patterns The Singleton pattern is often used for Factory objects and Facade objects—another GoF pattern that will be discussed.

23.5   Conclusion of the External Services with Varying Interfaces Problem

A combination of Adapter, Factory, and Singleton patterns have been used to provide Protected Variations from the varying interfaces of external tax calculators, accounting systems, and so forth. Figure 23.7 illustrates a larger context of using these in the use-case realization.

This design may not be ideal, and there is always room for improvement. But one of the goals strived for in this case study is to illustrate that at least a design can be constructed from a set of principles or pattern "building blocks," and that there is a methodical approach to doing and explaining a design. It is my sincere hope that it is possible to see how the design in Figure 23.7 arose from reasoning based on Controller, Creator, Protected Variations, Low Coupling, High Cohesion, Indirection, Polymorphism, Adapter, Factory, and Singleton.

Note how succinct a designer can be in conversation or documentation when there is a shared understanding of patterns. I can say, "To handle the problem of varying interfaces for external services, let's use Adapters generated from a Singleton Factory." Object designers really do have conversations that sound like this; using patterns and pattern names supports raising the level of abstraction in design communication.

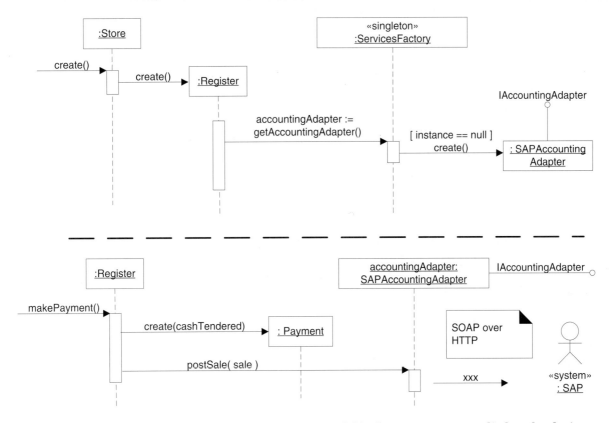

Figure 23.7 Adapter, Factory, and Singleton patterns applied to the design.

23.6 Strategy (GoF)

The next design problem to be resolved is to provide more complex pricing logic, such as a store-wide discount for the day, senior citizen discounts, and so forth.

The pricing strategy (which may also be called a rule, policy, or algorithm) for a sale can vary. During one period it may be 10% off all sales, later it may be $10 off if the sale total is greater than $200, and myriad other variations. How do we design for these varying pricing algorithms?

Strategy

Context / Problem

How to design for varying, but related, algorithms or policies? How to design for the ability to change these algorithms or policies?

Solution

Define each algorithm/policy/strategy in a separate class, with a common interface.

Since the behavior of pricing varies by the strategy (or algorithm), we create multiple *SalePricingStrategy* classes, each with a polymorphic *getTotal* method (see Figure 23.8). Each *getTotal* method takes the *Sale* object as a parameter, so that the pricing strategy object can find the pre-discount price from the *Sale*, and then apply the discounting rule. The implementation of each *getTotal* method will be different: *PercentDiscountPricingStrategy* will discount by a percentage, and so on.

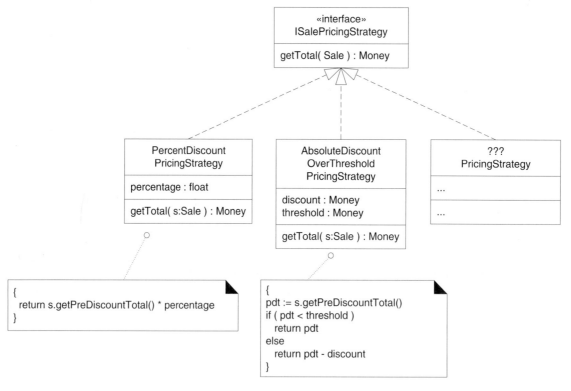

Figure 23.8 Pricing Strategy classes.

A strategy object is attached to a **context object**—the object to which it applies the algorithm. In this example, the context object is a *Sale*. When a *getTotal* message is sent to a *Sale*, it delegates some of the work to its strategy object, as illustrated in Figure 23.9. It is not required that the message to the context object and the strategy object have the same name, as in this example (for example, *getTotal* and *getTotal*), but it is common. However, it is common—indeed, usually required—that the context object pass a reference to itself (*this*) on to the strategy object, so that the strategy has parameter visibility to the context object, for further collaboration.

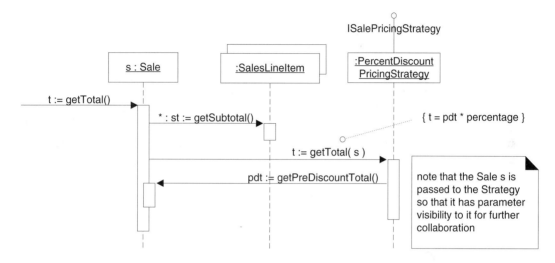

Figure 23.9 Strategy in collaboration.

Observe that the context object (*Sale*) needs attribute visibility to its strategy. This is reflected in the DCD in Figure 23.10.

Creating a Strategy with a Factory

There are different pricing algorithms or strategies, and they change over time. Who should create the strategy? A straightforward approach is to apply the Factory pattern again: a *PricingStrategyFactory* can be responsible for creating all strategies (all the pluggable or changing algorithms or policies) needed by the application. As with the *ServicesFactory*, it can read the name of the implementation class of the pricing strategy from a system property (or some external data source), and then make an instance of it. With this partial *data-driven design* (or reflective design) one can dynamically change at any time—while the NextGen POS application is running—the pricing policy, by specifying a different class of Strategy to create.

Observe that a new factory was used for the strategies; that is, different than the *ServicesFactory*. This supports the goal of High Cohesion—each factory is cohesively focused on creating a related family of objects.

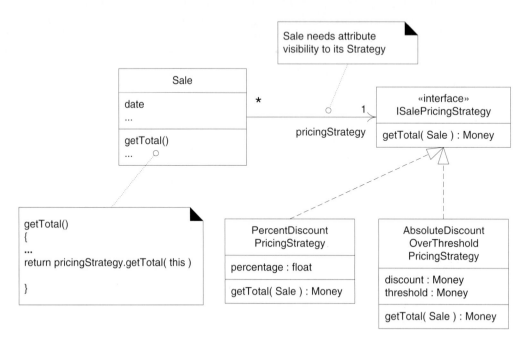

Figure 23.10 Context object needs attribute visibility to its strategy.

UML notation—Observe that in Figure 23.10 the reference via a directed association is to the interface *ISalePricingStrategy*, not to a concrete class. This indicates that the reference attribute in the *Sale* will be declared in terms of the interface, not a class, so that any implementation of the interface can be bound to the attribute.

Note that because of the frequently changing pricing policy (it could be every hour), it is *not* desirable to cache the created strategy instance in a field of the *PricingStrategyFactory*, but rather to re-create one each time, by reading the external property for its class name, and then instantiating the strategy.

And as with most factories, the *PricingStrategyFactory* will be a singleton (one instance) and accessed via the Singleton pattern (see Figure 23.11).

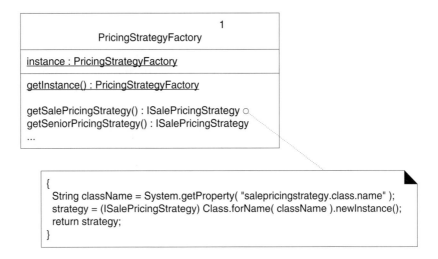

Figure 23.11 Factory for strategies.

When a *Sale* instance is created, it can ask the factory for its pricing strategy, as shown in Figure 23.12.

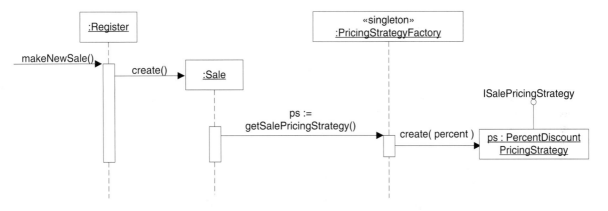

Figure 23.12 Creating a strategy.

Reading and Initializing the Percentage Value

Finally, a design problem that has been ignored until now is the issue of how to find the different numbers for the percentage or absolute discounts. For example, on Monday, the *PercentageDiscountPricingStrategy* may have a percentage value of 10%, but 20% on Tuesday.

Note also that a percentage discount may be related to the type of buyer, such as a senior citizen, rather than to a time period.

These numbers will be stored in some external data store, such as a relational database, so they can be easily changed. So, what object will read them and ensure they are assigned to the strategy? A reasonable choice is the *Strategy-Factory* itself, since it is creating the pricing strategy, and can know which percentage to read from a data store ("current store discount," "senior discount," and so forth).

Designs to read these numbers from external data stores vary from the simple to the complex, such as a plain JDBC SQL call (if Java technologies, as an example) or collaborating with objects that add levels of indirection in order to hide the particular location, data query language, or type of data store. Analyzing the variation and evolution points with respect to the data store will reveal if there is a need for protected variation. For example, we could ask, "Are we all comfortable with a long-term commitment to using a relational database that understands SQL?". If so, a simple JDBC call from within the *StrategyFactory* may suffice.

Summary

Protected Variations with respect to dynamically changing pricing policies has been achieved with the Strategy and Factory patterns. Strategy builds on Polymorphism and interfaces to allow pluggable algorithms in an object design.

Related Patterns   Strategy is based on Polymorphism, and provides Protected Variations with respect to changing algorithms. Strategies are often created by a Factory.

23.7   Composite (GoF) and Other Design Principles

To raise yet another interesting requirements and design problem: How do we handle the case of multiple, conflicting pricing policies? For example, suppose a store has the following policies in effect today (Monday):

- 20% senior discount policy
- preferred customer discount of 15% off sales over $400
- on Monday, there is $50 off purchases over $500
- buy 1 case of Darjeeling tea, get 15% discount off of everything

Suppose a senior who is also a preferred customer buys 1 case of Darjeeling tea, and $600 of veggieburgers (clearly an enthusiastic vegetarian who loves chai). What pricing policy should be applied?

To clarify: There are now pricing strategies that attach to the sale by virtue of three factors:

1. time period (Monday)

2. customer type (senior)

3. a particular line item product (Darjeeling tea)

Another point of clarification: Three of the four example policies are really just "percentage discount" strategies, which simplifies our view of the problem.

Part of the answer to this problem requires defining the store's **conflict resolution strategy**. Usually, a store applies the "best for the customer" (lowest price) conflict resolution strategy, but this is not required, and it could change. For example, during a difficult financial period, the store may have to use a "highest price" conflict resolution strategy.

The first point to note is that there can exist multiple co-existing strategies, that is, one sale may have several pricing strategies. Another point to note is that a pricing strategy can be related to the type of customer (for example, a senior). This has creation design implications: The customer type must be known by the *StrategyFactory* at the time of creation of a pricing strategy for the customer.

Similarly, a pricing strategy can be related to the type of product being bought (for example, Darjeeling tea). This likewise has creation design implications: The *ProductSpecification* must be known by the *StrategyFactory* at the time of creation of a pricing strategy influenced by the product.

Is there a way to change the design so that the *Sale* object does not know if it is dealing with one or many pricing strategies, and also offer a design for the conflict resolution? Yes, with the Composite pattern.

Composite

Context / Problem

How to treat a group or composition structure of objects the same way (polymorphically) as a non-composite (atomic) object?

Solution

Define classes for composite and atomic objects so that they implement the same interface.

For example, a new class called *CompositeBestForCustomerPricingStrategy* (well, at least it's descriptive) can implement the *ISalesPricingStrategy* and itself contain other *ISalesPricingStrategy* objects. Figure 23.13 explains the design idea in detail.

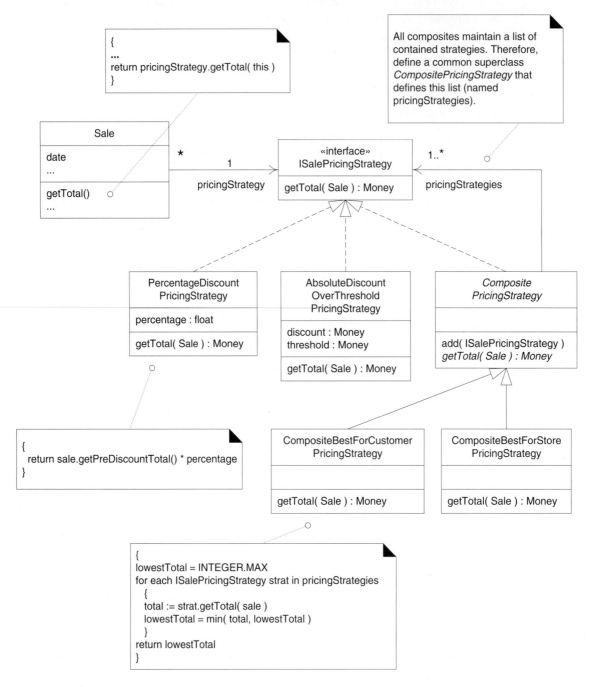

Figure 23.13 The Composite pattern.

Observe that in this design, the composite classes such as *CompositeBestForCustomerPricingStrategy* inherit an attribute *pricingStrategies* that contains a list of more *ISalePricingStrategy* objects. This is a signature feature of a composite object: The outer composite object contains a list of inner objects, and both the outer and inner objects implement the same interface. That is, the composite class itself implements the *ISalePricingStrategy* interface.

Thus, we can attach either a composite *CompositeBestForCustomerPricingStrategy* object (which contains other strategies inside of it) or an atomic *PercentDiscountPricingStrategy* object to the *Sale* object, and the *Sale* does not know or care if its pricing strategy is an atomic or composite strategy—it looks the same to the *Sale* object. It is just another object that implements the *ISalePricingStrategy* interface and understands the *getTotal* message (Figure 23.14).

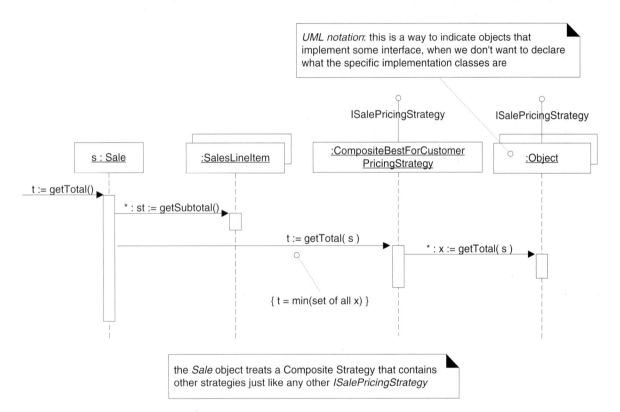

Figure 23.14 Collaboration with a Composite.

UML notation—In Figure 23.14, please note a way to indicate objects that implement an interface, when we don't care to specify the exact implementation class. Simply specifying the implementation class as *Object* communicates "no comment" on the specific class. This is a common need when diagramming.

To clarify with some sample code in Java, the *CompositePricingStrategy* and one of its subclasses are defined as follows:

```
// superclass so all subclasses can inherit a List of strategies

public abstract class CompositePricingStrategy
    implements ISalePricingStrategy
{

protected List pricingStrategies = new ArrayList();

public add( ISalePricingStrategy s )
{
    pricingStrategies.add( s );
}

public abstract Money getTotal( Sale sale );

} // end of class




// a Composite Strategy that returns the lowest total
// of its inner SalePricingStrategies

public class CompositeBestForCustomerPricingStrategy
    extends CompositePricingStrategy
{

public Money getTotal( Sale sale )
{
    Money lowestTotal = new Money( Integer.MAX_VALUE );

    // iterate over all the inner strategies

    for( Iterator i = pricingStrategies.iterator(); i.hasNext(); )
    {
        ISalePricingStrategy strategy =
                            (ISalePricingStrategy)i.next();
        Money total = strategy.getTotal( sale );
        lowestTotal = total.min( lowestTotal );
    }
return lowestTotal;
}


} // end of class
```

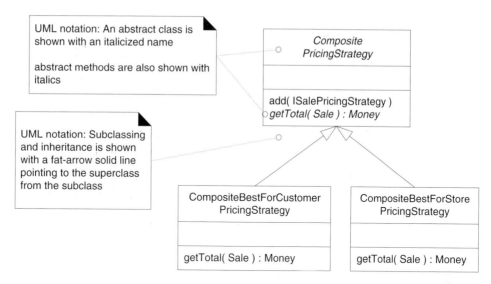

Figure 23.15 Abstract superclasses, abstract methods, and inheritance in the UML.

UML notation—Figure 23.13 introduced some new UML notation for class hierarchies and inheritance, which is explained in Figure 23.15.

Creating Multiple SalePricingStrategies

With the Composite pattern, we have made a group of multiple (and conflicting) pricing strategies look to the *Sale* object like a single pricing strategy. The composite object that contains the group also implements the *ISalePricingStrategy* interface. The more challenging (and interesting) part of this design problem is: When do we create these strategies?

A desirable design will start by creating a Composite that contains the present moment's store discount policy (which could be set to 0% discount if none is active), such as some *PercentageDiscountPricingStrategy*. Then, if at a later step in the scenario, another pricing strategy is discovered to also apply (such as senior discount), it will be easy to add it to the composite, using the inherited *CompositePricingStrategy.add* method.

There are three points in the scenario where pricing strategies may be added to the composite:

1. Current store-defined discount, added when the sale is created.

2. Customer type discount, added when the customer type is communicated to the POS.

3. Product type discount (if bought Darjeeling tea, 15% off the overall sale), added when the product is entered to the sale.

The design of the first case is shown in Figure 23.16. As in the original design discussed earlier, the strategy class name to instantiate could be read as a system property, and a percentage value could be read from an external data store.

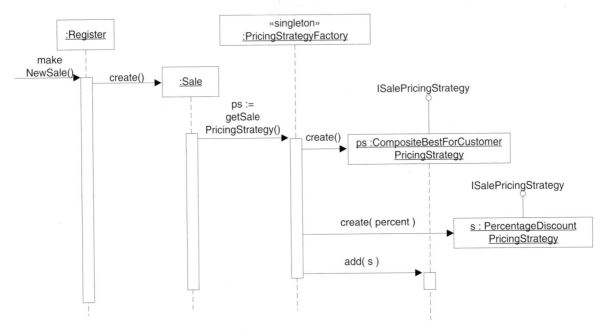

Figure 23.16 Creating a composite strategy.

For the second case of a customer type discount, first recall the use case extension which previously recognized this requirement:

Use Case UC1: Process Sale

...
Extensions (or Alternative Flows):
5b. Customer says they are eligible for a discount (e.g., employee, preferred customer)
    1. Cashier signals discount request.
    2. Cashier enters Customer identification.
    3. System presents discount total, based on discount rules.

This indicates a new system operation on the POS system, in addition to *makeNewSale*, *enterItem*, *endSale*, and *makePayment*. We will call this fifth system operation *enterCustomerForDiscount*; it may optionally occur after the *endSale* operation. It implies that some form of customer identification will have to come in through the user interface, the *customerID*. Perhaps it can be captured from a card reader, or via the keyboard.

The design of the second case is shown in Figure 23.17 and Figure 23.18. Not surprisingly, the factory object is responsible for the creation of the additional pricing strategy. It may make another *PercentageDiscountPricingStrategy* that represents, for example, a senior discount. But as with the original creation design, the choice of class will be read in as a system property, as will the specific percentage for the customer type, to provide Protected Variations with respect to changing the class or values. Note that by virtue of the Composite pattern, the *Sale* may have two or three conflicting pricing strategies attached to it, but it continues to look like a single strategy to the *Sale* object.

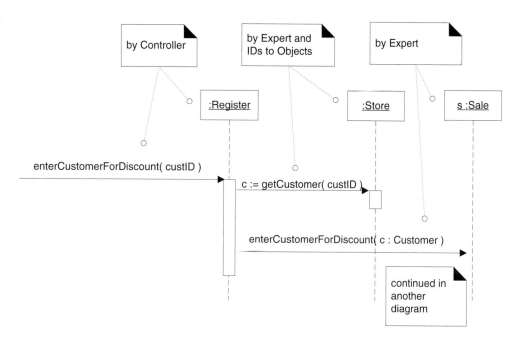

Figure 23.17 Creating the pricing strategy for a customer discount, part 1.

UML notation—Figure 23.17 and Figure 23.18 show an important UML idea in interaction diagrams: splitting one diagram into two, to keep each more readable.

Considering GRASP and Other Principles in the Design

To review thinking in terms of some basic GRASP patterns: For this second case, why not have the *Register* send a message to the *PricingStrategyFactory*, to create this new pricing strategy and then pass it to the *Sale*? One reason is to support Low Coupling. The *Sale* is already coupled to the factory; by making the *Register* also collaborate with it, the coupling in the design would increase. Furthermore, the *Sale* is the Information Expert that knows its current pricing strategy (which is going to be modified); so by Expert, it is also justified to delegate to the *Sale*.

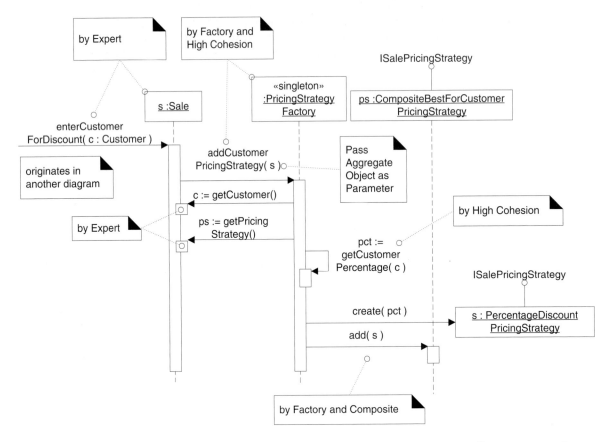

Figure 23.18 Creating the pricing strategy for a customer discount, part 2.

Observe in the design that *customerID* is transformed into a *Customer* object via the *Register* asking the *Store* for a *Customer*, given an ID. First, it is justifiable to give the *getCustomer* responsibility to the *Store*; by Information Expert and the goal of low representational gap, the *Store* can know all the *Customers*. And the *Register* asks the *Store*, because the *Register* already has attribute visibility to the *Store* (from earlier design work); if the *Sale* had to ask the *Store*, the *Sale* would need a reference to the *Store*, increasing the coupling beyond its current levels, and therefore not supporting Low Coupling.

IDs to Objects

Second, why transform the *customerID* (an "ID"—perhaps a number) into a *Customer* object? This is a common practice in object design—to transform keys and IDs for things into true objects. This transformation often takes place shortly after an ID or key enters the domain layer of the Design Model from the UI layer. It doesn't have a pattern name, but it could be a candidate for a pattern because it is such a common idiom among experienced object designers—perhaps *IDs to Objects*. Why bother? Having a true *Customer* object that encapsulates a set of information about the customer, and which can have behavior (related to Information Expert, for example), frequently becomes beneficial and flexible as the design grows, even if the designer does not originally perceive a need for a true object and thought instead that a plain number or ID would be sufficient. Note that in the earlier design, the transformation of the *itemID* into a *ProductSpecification* object is another example of this *IDs to Objects* pattern.

Pass Aggregate Object as Parameter

Finally, note that in the *addCustomerPricingStrategy(s:Sale)* message we pass a *Sale* to the factory, and then the factory turns around and asks for the *Customer* and *PricingStrategy* from the *Sale*.

Why not just extract these two objects from the *Sale*, and instead pass in the *Customer* and *PricingStrategy* to the factory? The answer is another common object design idiom: Avoid extracting child objects out of parent or aggregate objects, and then passing around the child objects. Rather, pass around the aggregate object that contains child objects.

Following this principle increases flexibility, because then the factory can collaborate with the entire *Sale* in ways we may not have previously anticipated as necessary (which is very common), and as a corollary, it reduces the need to anticipate what the factory object needs; the designer just passes as a parameter the entire *Sale*, without knowing what more particular objects the factory may need. Although this idiom does not have a name, it is related to Low Coupling and Protected Variations. Perhaps it could be called the *Pass Aggregate Object as Parameter* pattern.

Summary

This design problem was squeezed for many tips in object design. A skilled object designer has many of these patterns committed to memory through studying their published explanations, and has internalized core principles, such as those described in the GRASP family.

Please note that although this application of Composite was to a Strategy family, the Composite pattern can be applied to other kinds of objects, not just strategies. For example, it is common to create "macro commands"—commands that contain other commands—through the use of Composite. The Command pattern is described in a subsequent chapter.

Exercise Challenges

Exercise 1:

Buying a particular product causes a new discount to the entire sale. For example, if bought Darjeeling tea, 15% off the overall sale.

Exercise 2:

All the pricing policies considered so far apply to the overall sale total, sometimes called transaction level discounts. But the most interesting design challenge is to handle line item level discounts. For example:

- Buy two suits, get one free.

- Buy three X-computers, get the Y-printer at 50% off.

Is there an elegant way to design this with Strategy objects?

Related Patterns   Composite is often used with the Strategy and Command patterns. Composite is based on Polymorphism and provides Protected Variations to a client so that it is not impacted if its related objects are atomic or composite.

23.8   Facade (GoF)

Another requirement chosen for this iteration is *pluggable business rules*. That is, at predictable points in the scenarios, such as when *makeNewSale* or *enterItem* occurs in the *Process Sale* use case, or when a cashier starts cashing in, different customers who wish to purchase the NextGen POS would like to customize its behavior slightly.

To be more precise, assume that rules are desired that can invalidate an action. For example:

- Suppose when a new sale is created, it is possible to identify that it will be paid by a gift certificate (this is possible and common). Then, a store may have a rule to only allow one item to be purchased if a gift certificate is used. Consequently, subsequent *enterItem* operations, after the first, should be invalidated.

- If the sale is paid by a gift certificate, invalidate all payment types of change due back to the customer except for another gift certificate. For example, if the cashier requested change in the form of cash, or as a credit to the customer's store account, invalidate those requests.

- Suppose when a new sale is created, it is possible to identify that it is for a charitable donation (from the store to the charity). A store may also have a rule to only allow item entries less than $250 each, and also to only add items to the sale if the currently logged in "cashier" is a manager.

In terms of requirements analysis, the specific scenario points across all use cases (*enterItem*, *chooseCashChange*, ...) must be identified. For this exploration, only the *enterItem* point will be considered, but the same solution applies equally to all points.

Suppose that the software architect wants a design that has low impact on the existing software components. That is, she or he wants to design for a separation of concerns, and factor out this rule handling into a separate concern. Furthermore, suppose that the architect is unsure of the best implementation for this pluggable rule handling, and may want to experiment with different solutions for representing, loading, and evaluating the rules. For example, rules can be implemented with the Strategy pattern, or with free open-source rule interpreters that read and interpret a set of IF-THEN rules, or with commercial, purchased rule interpreters, among other solutions.

To solve this design problem, the Facade pattern can be used.

Facade

Context / Problem

A common, unified interface to a disparate set of implementations or interfaces—such as within a subsystem—is required. There may be undesirable coupling to many things in the subsystem, or the implementation of the subsystem may change. What to do?

Solution

Define a single point of contact to the subsystem—a facade object that wraps the subsystem. This facade object presents a single unified interface and is responsible for collaborating with the subsystem components.

A Facade is a "front-end" object that is the single point of entry for the services of a subsystem;[4] the implementation and other components of the subsystem are private and can't be seen by external components. Facade provides Protected Variations from changes in the implementation of a subsystem.

For example, we will define a "rule engine" subsystem, whose specific implementation is not yet known. It will be responsible for evaluating a set of rules against an operation (by some hidden implementation), and then indicating if any of the rules invalidated the operation.

---

4. "Subsystem" is here used in an informal sense to indicate a separate grouping of related components, not exactly as defined in the UML.

The facade object to this subsystem will be called *POSRuleEngineFacade*. The designer decides to place calls to this facade near the start of the methods that have been defined as the points for pluggable rules, as in this example:

```
public class Sale
{

public void makeLineItem( ProductSpecification spec, int quantity )
{
    SalesLineItem sli = new SalesLineItem( spec, quantity );

        // call to the Facade
    if ( POSRuleEngineFacade.getInstance().isInvalid( sli, this ) )
        return;

    lineItems.add( sli );
}

// ...

} // end of class
```

Note the use of the Singleton pattern. Facades are often accessed via Singleton.

With this design, the complexity and implementation of how rules will be represented and evaluated are hidden in the "rules engine" subsystem, accessed via the *POSRuleEngineFacade* facade. Observe that the subsystem hidden by the facade object could contain dozens or hundreds of classes of objects, or even a non-object-oriented solution, yet as a client to the subsystem, we see only its one public access point.

And a separation of concerns has been achieved to some degree—all the rule-handling concerns have been delegated to another subsystem.

Summary

The Facade pattern is simple, and widely used. It hides a subsystem behind an object.

Exercise Challenges

Exercise 1:

Design rule handling with the Strategy pattern, whose class names are dynamically discovered by reading from an external source.

Exercise 2:

If implementing in Java, design rule handling with Jess, a free-for-academic-use rule interpreter available at http://herzberg.ca.sandia.gov/jess/

Related Patterns Facades are usually accessed via the Singleton pattern. They provide Protected Variations from the implementation of a subsystem, by adding an Indirection object to help support Low Coupling. External objects are coupled to one point in a subsystem: the facade object.

As described in the Adapter pattern, an adapter object may be used to wrap access to external systems with varying interfaces. This is a kind of facade, but the emphasis is to provide adaptation to varying interfaces, and thus it is more specifically called an adapter.

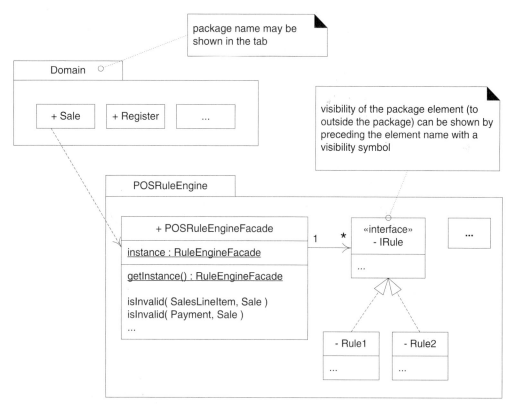

Figure 23.19 UML package notation.

UML notation—The UML provides a general purpose grouping notation called a **package**, which is a kind of tabbed folder icon. Packages can be used to show logical groupings of objects; they may correspond to something like Java packages or C++ namespaces, or to other logically distinct aggregate components or subsystems. Note that in Figure 23.19, only the *POSRuleEngineFacade* is public with respect to its package.

There is more complex UML notation available to illustrate subsystems, but the notation in Figure 23.19 will suffice for now. Designing with packages is explored in greater detail in the next iteration.

23.9   Observer/Publish-Subscribe/Delegation Event Model (GoF)

Another requirement for the iteration is adding the ability for a GUI window to refresh its display of the sale total when the total changes (see Figure 23.20). The idea is to solve the problem for this one case, and then in later iterations, extend the solution to refreshing the GUI display for other changing data as well.

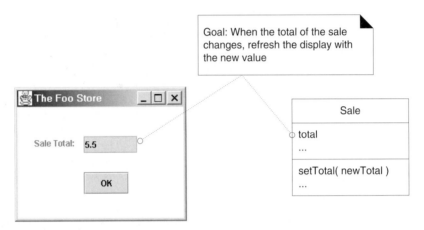

Figure 23.20 Updating the interface when the sale total changes.

Why not do the following as a solution? When the *Sale* changes its total, the *Sale* object sends a message to a window, asking it to refresh its display.

To review, the Model-View Separation principle discourages such solutions. It states that "model" objects (non-UI objects such as a *Sale*) should not know about view or presentation objects such as a window. It promotes Low Coupling from other layers to the presentation (UI) layer of objects.

A consequence of supporting this low coupling is that it allows the replacement of the view or presentation layer by a new one, or of particular windows by new windows, without impacting the non-UI objects. If model objects do not know about Java Swing objects (for example), then it is possible to unplug a Swing interface, or unplug a particular window, and plug in something else.

Thus, Model-View Separation supports Protected Variations with respect to a changing user interface.

To solve this design problem, the Observer pattern can be used.

Observer (Publish-Subscribe)

Context / Problem

Different kinds of subscriber objects are interested in the state changes or events of a publisher object, and want to react in their own unique way when the publisher generates an event. Moreover, the publisher wants to maintain low coupling to the subscribers. What to do?

Solution

Define a "subscriber" or "listener" interface. Subscribers implement this interface. The publisher can dynamically register subscribers who are interested in an event, and notify them when an event occurs.

An example solution is described in detail in Figure 23.21.

The major ideas and steps in this example:

1. An interface is defined; in this case, *PropertyListener* with the operation *onPropertyEvent*.

2. Define the window to implement the interface.

   ❍ *SaleFrame1* will implement the method *onPropertyEvent*.

3. When the *SaleFrame1* window is initialized, pass it the *Sale* instance from which it is displaying the total.

4. The *SaleFrame1* window registers or *subscribes* to the *Sale* instance for notification of "property events," via the *addPropertyListener* message. That is, when a property (such as total) changes, the window wants to be notified.

5. Note that the *Sale* does not know about *SaleFrame1* objects; rather, it only knows about objects that implement the *PropertyListener* interface. This lowers the coupling of the *Sale* to the window—the coupling is only to an interface, not to a GUI class.

6. The *Sale* instance is thus a *publisher* of "property events." When the total changes, it iterates across all subscribing *PropertyListeners*, notifying each.

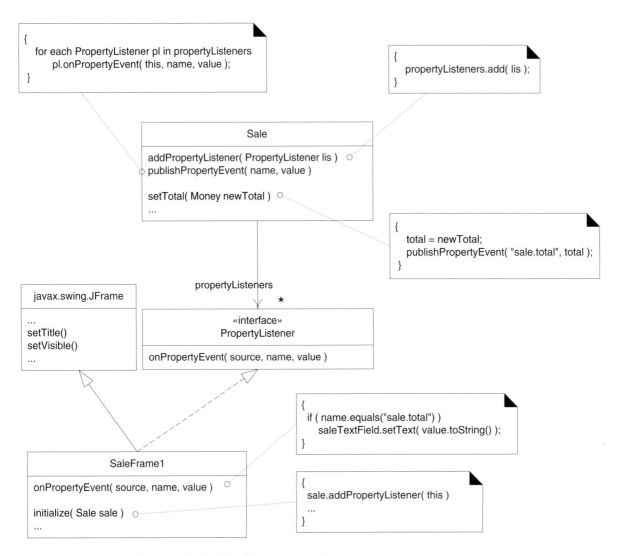

Figure 23.21 The Observer pattern.

UML notation—Observe in Figure 23.21 that the interesting methods are annotated with notes that indicate the implementation. These notes add dynamic behavior information to a diagram of static types. In some cases, a class diagram with these notes can replace the need for additional interaction diagrams. This is not an encouragement to avoid interaction diagrams, but an indicator of alternate notational approaches.

The *SaleFrame1* object is the observer/subscriber/listener. In Figure 23.22, it *subscribes* to interest in property events of the *Sale*, which is a *publisher* of property events. The *Sale* adds the object to its list of *PropertyListener* subscribers. Note that the *Sale* does not know about the *SaleFrame1* as a *SaleFrame1* object, but only as a *PropertyListener* object; this lowers the coupling from the model up to the view layer.

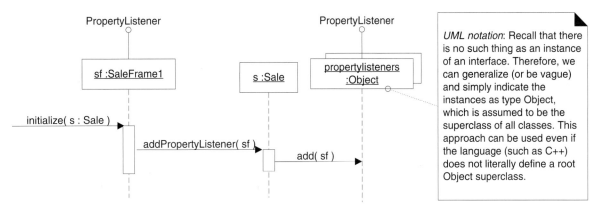

Figure 23.22 The observer *SaleFrame1* subscribes to the publisher *Sale*.

As illustrated in Figure 23.23, when the Sale total changes, it iterates across all its registered subscribers, and "publishes an event" by sending the *onPropertyEvent* message to each.

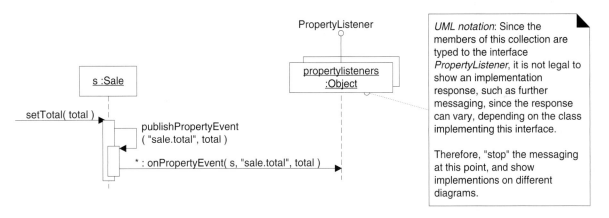

Figure 23.23 The Sale publishes a property event to all its subscribers.

UML notation: Note the approach to handing polymorphic messages in an interaction diagram, in Figure 23.23.

SaleFrame1, which implements the *PropertyListener* interface, thus implements an *onPropertyEvent* method. When the *SaleFrame1* receives the message, it sends a message to its *JTextField* GUI widget object to refresh with the new sale total. See Figure 23.24.

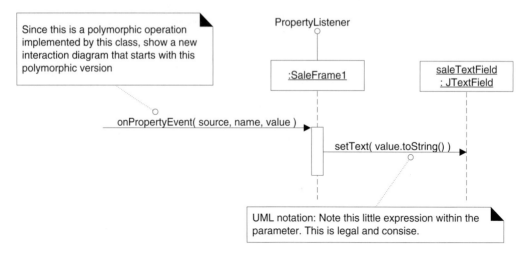

Figure 23.24 The subscriber SaleFrame1 receives notification of a published event.

In this pattern, there is still some coupling from the model object (the *Sale*) to the view object (the *SaleFrame1*). But it is a loose coupling to an interface independent of the presentation layer—the *PropertyListener* interface. And the design does not require any subscriber objects to actually be registered with the publisher (no objects have to be listening). That is, the list of registered *PropertyListeners* in the *Sale* can be empty. In summary, coupling to a generic interface of objects that do not need to be present, and which can be dynamically added (or removed), supports low coupling. Therefore, Protected Variations with respect to a changing user interface has been achieved through the use of an interface and polymorphism.

Why Is It Called Observer, Publish-Subscribe, or Delegation Event Model?

Originally, this idiom was called publish-subscribe, and it is still widely known by that name. One object "publishes events," such as the *Sale* publishing the "property event" when the total changes. No object may be interested in this event, in which case, the *Sale* has no registered subscribers. But objects that are interested, "subscribe" or register to interest in an event by asking the publishing to notify them. This was done with the *Sale--addPropertyListener* message. When the event happens, the registered subscribers are notified by a message.

It has been called Observer because the listener or subscriber is observing the event; that term was popularized in Smalltalk in the early 1980s.

It has also been called the Delegation Event Model (in Java) because the publisher delegates handling of events to "listeners" (subscribers; see Figure 23.25).

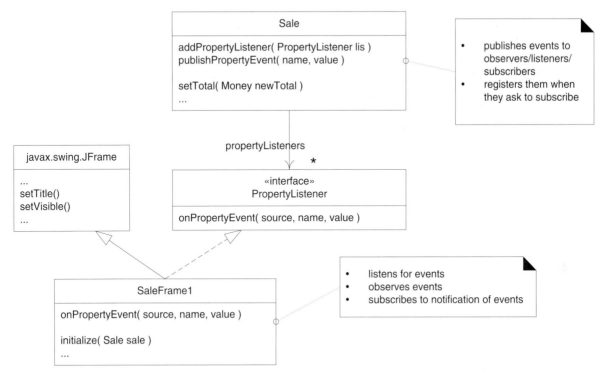

Figure 23.25 Who is the observer, listener, subscriber, and publisher?

Observer Is Not Only for Connecting UIs and Model Objects

The previous example illustrated connecting a non-UI object to a UI object with Observer. However, other uses are common.

The most prevalent use of this pattern is for GUI widget event handling, in both Java technologies (AWT and Swing) and in Microsoft's .NET. Each widget is a publisher of GUI-related events, and other objects can subscribe to interest in these. For example, a Swing *JButton* publishes an "action event" when it is pressed. Another object will register with the button so that when it is pressed, the object is sent a message and can take some action.

As another example, Figure 23.26 illustrates an *AlarmClock,* which is a publisher of alarm events and various subscribers. This example is illustrative in that it emphasizes that many classes can implement the *AlarmListener* interface, many objects can simultaneously be registered listeners, and all can react to the "alarm event" in their own unique way.

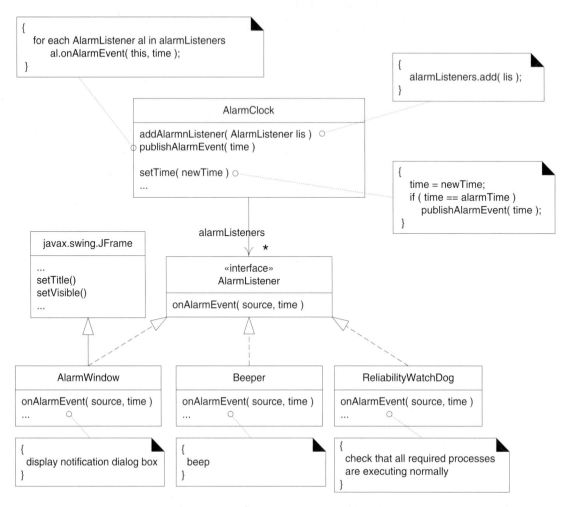

Figure 23.26 Observer applied to alarm events, with different subscribers.

One Publisher Can Have Many Subscribers for an Event

As suggested in Figure 23.26, one publisher instance could have from zero to many registered subscribers. For example, one instance of an *AlarmClock* could have three registered *AlarmWindows*, four *Beepers*, and one *ReliabilityWatch-Dog*. When an alarm event happens, all eight of these *AlarmListeners* are notified via an *onAlarmEvent*.

Implementation

Events

In both the Java and C# .NET implementations of Observer, an "event" is communicated via a regular message, such as *onPropertyEvent*. Moreover, in both cases, the event is more formally defined as a class, and filled with appropriate event data. The event is then passed as a parameter in the event message.

For example:

```
class PropertyEvent extends Event
{
    private Object sourceOfEvent;
    private String propertyName;
    private Object oldValue;
    private Object newValue;
    //...
}

//...

class Sale
{
    private void publishPropertyEvent(
        String name, Object old, Object new )
    {
        PropertyEvent evt =
         new PropertyEvent( this, "sale.total", old, new);

        for each AlarmListener al in alarmListeners
         al.onPropertyEvent( evt );
    }

    //...
}
```

Java

When the JDK 1.0 was released in January 1996, it contained a weak publish-subscribe implementation based on a class and interface called *Observable* and *Observer*, respectively. This was essentially copied without improvement from an early 1980s approach to publish-subscribe implemented in Smalltalk.

Therefore, in late 1996, as part of the JDK 1.1 effort, the Observable-Observer design was effectively replaced by the more robust Java Delegation Event Model (DEM) version of publish-subscribe, although the original design was kept for backward-compatibility (but in general to be avoided).

The designs that have been described in this chapter are consistent with the DEM, but slightly simplified to emphasize the core ideas.

Summary

Observer provides a way to loosely couple objects in terms of communication. Publishers know about subscribers only through an interface, and subscribers can register (or de-register) dynamically with the publisher.

Related Patterns   Observer is based on Polymorphism, and provides Protected Variations in terms of protecting the publisher from knowing the specific class of object, and number of objects, that it communicates with when the publisher generates an event.

23.10   Conclusion

The main lesson to draw from this exposition is that objects can be designed and responsibilities assigned with the support of patterns. These provide an explainable set of idioms by which well-designed object-oriented systems can be built.

23.11   Further Readings

Design Patterns by Gamma, Helm, Johnson, and Vlissides is the seminal patterns text, and essential reading for all object designers.

Each year there is a "Pattern Languages of Programs" (PLOP) conference, from which is published an annual compendium of patterns, in the series *Pattern Languages of Program Design*, volumes 1, 2, and so forth. The entire series is recommended.

Pattern-Oriented Software Architecture, volumes 1 and 2, furthered the discussion of patterns to larger-scale architectural concerns. Volume 1 presented a taxonomy of patterns.

There are hundreds of published patterns. *The Pattern Almanac* by Rising summarizes a respectable percentage of them.

PART 5 ELABORATION ITERATION 3

ITERATION 3 AND ITS REQUIREMENTS

24.1   Iteration 3 Requirements

- Provide failover to local services when the remote services cannot be accessed. For example, if the remote product database can't be accessed, use a local version with cached data.
- Provide support for POS device handling, such as the cash drawer and coin dispenser.
- Handle credit payment authorization.
- Support for persistent objects.

24.2   Iteration 3 Emphasis

Inception and iteration 1 explored a variety of fundamental issues in requirements analysis and OOA/D. Iteration 2 narrowly emphasized object design. This third iteration takes a broader view again, exploring a wide variety of analysis and design topics, including:

- relating use cases
- generalization and specialization
- state modeling
- layered architectures
- the design of packages
- architectural analysis
- more GoF design patterns
- the design of frameworks—in particular, a persistence framework

RELATING USE CASES

Why do programmers get Halloween and
Christmas mixed up? Because OCT(31) = DEC(25)

Objectives

■ Relate use cases with *include* and *extend* associations.

Introduction

Use cases can be related to each other. For example, a subfunction use case such as *Handle Credit Payment* may be part of several regular use cases, such as *Process Sale* and *Process Rental*. Organizing use cases into relationships has no impact on the behavior or requirements of the system. Rather, it is simply an organization mechanism to (ideally) improve communication and comprehension of the use cases, reduce duplication of text, and improve management of the use case documents.

A Caution

In some organizations working with use cases, unproductive time has been spent debating how to relate use cases in a use case diagram, rather than the important use case work: writing text. Consequently, although this chapter discusses relating use cases, the subject and its effort should be put in perspective: It has some value, but the important work is writing use case text. Specifying the requirements is done by writing, not by organizing use cases, which is an optional step to possibly improve their comprehension or reduce duplication. If a team starts off use-case modeling by spending hours (or worse, days) discussing a use case diagram and use case relationships ("Should that be an include or an extend relationship? Should we specialize this use case?"), rather than quickly focusing on writing the key use case text, relative effort was misplaced.

Furthermore, the organization of use cases into relationships can iteratively evolve in small steps over the elaboration phase; it is not helpful to attempt a waterfall-like effort of fully defining and refining a complete use case diagram and set of relationships in one step near the start of a project.

25.1   The include Relationship

This is the most common and important relationship.

It is common to have some partial behavior that is common across several use cases. For example, the description of paying by credit occurs in several use cases, including *Process Sale, Process Rental, Contribute to Lay-away Plan*, and so forth. Rather than duplicate this text, it is desirable to separate it into its own subfunction use case, and indicate its inclusion. This is simply refactoring and linking text to avoid duplication.[1]

For example:

UC1: Process Sale

> ...
>
> **Main Success Scenario:**
> 1. Customer arrives at a POS checkout with goods and/or services to purchase.
> ...
> 7. Customer pays and System handles payment.
> ...
>
> **Extensions:**
> 7b. Paying by credit: Include *Handle Credit Payment*.
> 7c. Paying by check: Include *Handle Check Payment*.
> ...

UC7: Process Rental

> ...
> **Extensions:**
> 6b. Paying by credit: Include *Handle Credit Payment*.
> ...

UC12: Handle Credit Payment

> ...
> **Level:** Subfunction
> **Main Success Scenario:**
> 1. Customer enters their credit account information.
> 2. System sends payment authorization request to an external Payment Authorization Service System, and requests payment approval.

---

1. It is helpful if the links are implemented with navigable hyperlinks as well.

3. System receives payment approval and signals approval to Cashier.
4. ...
Extensions:
2a. System detects failure to collaborate with external system:
    1. System signals error to Cashier.
    2. Cashier asks Customer for alternate payment.
...

This is the **include** relationship.

A slightly shorter (and thus perhaps preferred) notation to indicate an included use case is simply to underline it or highlight it in some fashion. For example:

UC1: Process Sale

...
Extensions:
7b. Paying by credit: *Handle Credit Payment*.
7c. Paying by check: *Handle Check Payment*.
...

Notice that the *Handle Credit Payment* subfunction use case was originally in the *Extensions* section of the *Process Sale* use case, but was factored out to avoid duplication. Also note that the same *Main Success* and *Extensions* structures are used in the subfunction use case as in the regular elementary business process use cases such as *Process Sale*.

A simple, practical guideline of when to use the include relationship is offered by Fowler [FS00]:

> Use *include* when you are repeating yourself in two or more separate use cases and you want to avoid repetition.

Another motivation is simply to decompose an overwhelmingly long use case into subunits to improve comprehension.

Using include with Asynchronous Event Handling

Yet another use of the include relationship is to describe the handling of an asynchronous event, such as when a user is able to, at any time, select or branch to a particular window, function, or web page, or within a range of steps.

In fact, the use case notation to support this asynchronous branching was already explored in the introduction to use cases in Chapter 6, but at that time the addition of calling out to an included sub-use case was not discussed.

The basic notation is to use the a^*, b^*, ... style labels in the Extensions section. Recall that these imply an extension or event that can happen at any time. A minor variation is a range label, such as *3-9*, to be used when the asynchronous event can occur within a relatively large range of the use case steps, but not all.

UC1: Process FooBars

> ...
> **Main Success Scenario:**
> 1. ...
> **Extensions:**
> a*. At any time, Customer selects to edit personal information: _Edit Personal Information_.
> b*. At any time, Customer selects printing help: _Present Printing Help_.
> 2-11. Customer cancels: _Cancel Transaction Confirmation_.
> ...

Summary

The include relationship can be used for most use case relationship problems. To summarize:

> Factor out subfunction use cases and use the _include_ relationship when:
>
> - They are duplicated in other use cases.
>
> - A use case is _very_ complex and long, and separating it into subunits aids comprehension.

As will be explained, there are other relationships: extend and generalization. But Cockburn, an expert use-case modeler, advises to prefer the include relationship over extend or generalization:

> As a first rule of thumb, always use the _include_ relationship between use cases. People who follow this rule report they and their readers have less confusion with their writing than people who mix _include_ with _extend_ and _generalizes_ [Cockburn01].

25.2 Terminology: Concrete, Abstract, Base, and Addition Use Cases

A **concrete use case** is initiated by an actor and performs the entire behavior desired by the actor [RUP]. These are the elementary business process use cases. For example, _Process Sale_ is a concrete use case. By contrast, an **abstract use case** is never instantiated by itself; it is a subfunction use case that is part of another use case. _Handle Credit Payment_ is abstract; it doesn't stand on its own, but is always part of another story, such as _Process Sale_.

A use case that includes another use case, or that is extended or specialized by another use case is called a **base use case**. _Process Sale_ is a base use case with respect to the included *Handle Credit Payment* subfunction use case. On the other hand, the use case that is an inclusion, extension, or specialization is called an **addition use case**. *Handle Credit Payment* is the addition use case in the include relationship to *Process Sale*. Addition use cases are usually abstract. Base use cases are usually concrete.

25.3 The extend Relationship

Suppose a use case's text should not be modified (at least not significantly) for some reason. Perhaps continually modifying the use case with myriad new extensions and conditional steps is a maintenance headache, or the use case has been baselined as a stable artifact, and can't be touched. How to append to the use case without modifying its original text?

The **extend** relationship provides an answer. The idea is to create an extending or addition use case, and within it, describe where and under what condition it extends the behavior of some base use case. For example:

UC1: Process Sale (the base use case)

...
Extension Points: *VIP Customer*, step 1. *Payment*, step 7.
Main Success Scenario:
1. Customer arrives at a POS checkout with goods and/or services to purchase.
...
7. Customer pays and System handles payment.
...

UC15: Handle Gift Certificate Payment (the extending use case)

...
Trigger: Customer wants to pay with gift certificate.
Extension Points: Payment in Process Sale.
Level: Subfunction
Main Success Scenario:
1. Customer gives gift certificate to Cashier.
2. Cashier enters gift certificate ID.
...

This is an example of an **extend** relationship. Note the use of an **extension point**, and that the extending use case is triggered by some condition. Extension points are labels in the base use case which the extending use case references as the point of extension, so that the step numbering of the base use case can change without affecting the extending use case—indirection yet again.

Sometimes, the extension point is simply "At any point in use case X." This is especially common in systems with many asynchronous events, such as a word processor ("do a spell check now," "do a thesaurus lookup now"), or reactive control systems. Note however, as described in the prior include relationship section, that include can also be used to describe asynchronous event handling. The extend alternative is an option when the base use case is closed to modification.

Note that a signature quality of the extend relationship is that the base use case (*Process Sale*) has no reference to the extending use case (*Handle Gift Certificate Payment*), and therefore, does not define or control the conditions under which the extensions trigger. *Process Sale* is complete and whole by itself, without knowing about the extending use case.

Observe that this *Handle Gift Certificate Payment* addition use case could alternatively have been referenced within *Process Sale* with an include relationship, as with *Handle Credit Payment*. That is often suitable. But this example was motivated by the constraint that the *Process Sale* use case was not to be modified, which is the situation in which to use extend rather than include.

Further, note that this gift certificate scenario could simply have been recorded by adding it as an extension in the *Extensions* section of *Process Sale*. This approach avoids both the include and extend relationships, and the creation of a separate subfunction use case.

> Indeed, just updating the *Extensions* section is usually the preferred solution, rather than creating complex use case relationships.

Some use case guidelines recommend using extending use cases and the extend relationship to model conditional or optional behavior inserted into the base use case. This is not inaccurate, but it misses the point that optional and conditional behavior can simply be recorded as text in the *Extensions* section of the base use case. The complication of using the extend relationship and more use cases is not motivated only by optional behavior.

What most practically motivates using the extend technique is when it is undesirable for some reason to modify the base use case.

25.4   The generalize Relationship

Discussion of the generalize relationship is outside the scope of this introduction. However, note that use case experts have been successfully doing use case work without this optional relationship, which adds another level of complexity to use cases, and there is not yet agreement by practitioners on the best-practice guidelines of how to get value from this idea. A common observation by use case consultants is that complications result and unproductive time is spent on the addition of many use case relationships.

25.5   Use Case Diagrams

Figure 25.1 illustrates the UML notation for the include relationship, which is the only one being used in the case study, following the advice of use-case experts to keep things simple and prefer the include relationship.

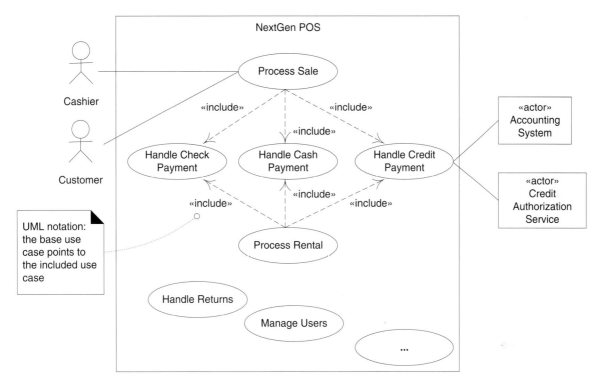

Figure 25.1 Use case include relationship in the Use-Case Model.

The extend relationship notation is illustrated in Figure 25.2.

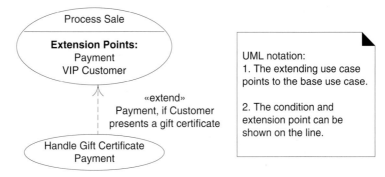

Figure 25.2 The extend relationship.

MODELING GENERALIZATION

*Crude classifications and false generalizations
are the curse of the organized life.*

—A generalization by H.G. Wells

Objectives

- Create generalization-specialization hierarchies.
- Identify when showing a subclass is worthwhile.
- Apply the "100%" and "Is-a" tests to validate subclasses.

Introduction

Generalization and specialization are fundamental concepts in domain modeling that support an economy of expression; further, conceptual class hierarchies are often the basis of inspiration for software class hierarchies that exploit inheritance and reduce duplication of code.

26.1 New Concepts for the Domain Model

As in iteration 1, the UP Domain Model may be incrementally developed by considering the concepts in the requirements for this iteration. Techniques such as the *Concept Category List* and noun phrase identification will help. An effective approach to developing a robust and rich domain model is to study the work of other authors on this subject, such as {Fowler96}. The myriad subtle modeling issues they explore are beyond the scope of this book.

Concepts Category List

Table 26.1 shows some noteworthy concepts being considered in this iteration.

Table 26.1 Category Concepts List

Category	Examples
physical or tangible objects	*CreditCard, Check*
specifications, designs or descriptions of things	
places	
transactions	*CashPayment, CreditPayment, CheckPayment*
transaction line items	
roles of people	
containers of other things	
things in a container	
other computer or electro-mechanical systems external to our system	*CreditAuthorizationService, CheckAuthorizationService*
abstract noun concepts	
organizations	*CreditAuthorizationService, CheckAuthorizationService*
events	
rules and policies	
catalogs	
records of finance, work, contracts, legal matters	*AccountsReceivable*
financial instruments and services	
manuals, books	

Noun Phrase Identification from the Use Cases

To reiterate, noun phrase identification cannot be mechanically applied to identify relevant concepts to include in the domain model. Judgement must be applied and suitable abstractions developed, since natural language is ambiguous and relevant concepts are not always explicit or clear in existing text. However, it is a practical technique in domain modeling since it is straightforward.

This iteration handles the scenarios of the *Process Sale* use case for credit and check payments. The following shows some noun phrase identification from these extensions:

Use Case UC1: Process Sale

...
Extensions:
7b. Paying by credit:
1. Customer enters their **credit account information**.
2. System sends **payment authorization request** to an external **Payment Authorization Service** System, and requests **payment approval**.
    2a. System detects failure to collaborate with external system:
        1. System signals error to Cashier.
        2. Cashier asks Customer for alternate payment.
3. System receives **payment approval** and signals approval to Cashier.
    3a. System receives **payment denial**:
        1. System signals denial to Cashier.
        2. Cashier asks Customer for alternate payment.
4. System records the **credit payment**, which includes the payment approval.
5. System presents credit payment signature input mechanism.
6. Cashier asks Customer for a credit payment signature. Customer enters signature.
7c. Paying by check:
1. The Customer writes a **check**, and gives it and their **driver's license** to the Cashier.
2. Cashier writes the driver's license number on the check, enters it, and requests **check payment authorization**.
3. Generates a **check payment request** and sends it to an external **Check Authorization Service**.
4. Receives a check payment approval and signals approval to Cashier.
5. System records the **check payment**, which includes the payment approval.
...

Authorization Service Transactions

The noun phrase identification reveals concepts such as *CreditPaymentRequest* and *CreditApprovalReply*. These may in fact be viewed as types of transactions with external services, and in general, it is useful to identify such transactions because activities and processes tend to revolve around them.

These transactions do not have to represent computer records or bits travelling over a line. They represent the abstraction of the transaction independent of its means of execution. For example, a credit payment request may be executed by people talking on the phone, by two computers sending records or messages to each other, and so on.

26.2   Generalization

The concepts *CashPayment*, *CreditPayment,* and *CheckPayment* are all very similar. In this situation, it is possible (and useful[1]) to organize them (as in Figure 26.1) into a **generalization-specialization class hierarchy** (or simply **class hierarchy**) in which the **superclass** *Payment* represents a more general concept, and the **subclasses** more specialized ones.

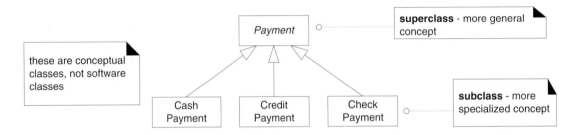

Figure 26.1 Generalization-specialization hierarchy.

Note that the discussion of classes in this chapter refers to *conceptual* classes, not software classes.

Generalization is the activity of identifying commonality among concepts and defining superclass (general concept) and subclass (specialized concept) relationships. It is a way to construct taxonomic classifications among concepts which are then illustrated in class hierarchies.

Identifying a superclass and subclasses is of value in a domain model because their presence allows us to understand concepts in more general, refined and abstract terms. It leads to economy of expression, improved comprehension and a reduction in repeated information. And although we are focusing now on the UP Domain Model and not the software Design Model, the later design and implementation of super- and subclass as software classes that use inheritance yields better software.

---

1. Later in the chapter, we will investigate reasons to define class hierarchies.

Thus:

> Identify domain superclasses and subclasses relevant to the current investigation, and illustrate them in the Domain Model.

UML notation—To review the generalization notation introduced in a prior chapter, in the UML the generalization relationship between elements is indicated with a large hollow triangle pointing to the more general element from the more specialized one (see Figure 26.2). Either a separate target or shared target arrow style may be used.

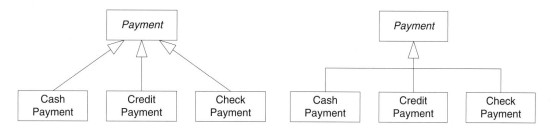

Figure 26.2 Class hierarchy with separate and shared arrow notations.

26.3   Defining Conceptual Superclasses and Subclasses

Since it is valuable to identify conceptual super- and subclasses, it is useful to clearly and precisely understand generalization, superclasses, and subclasses in terms of class definition and class sets.[2] This following sections explore these.

Generalization and Conceptual Class Definition

What is the relationship of a conceptual superclass to a subclass?

> A conceptual superclass definition is more general or encompassing than a subclass definition.

For example, consider the superclass *Payment* and its subclasses (*CashPayment*, and so on). Assume the definition of *Payment* is that it represents the transaction of transferring money (not necessarily cash) for a purchase from one party

---

2. That is, a class's intension and extension. This discussion was inspired by [MO95].

to another, and that all payments have an amount of money transferred. The model corresponding to this is shown in Figure 26.3.

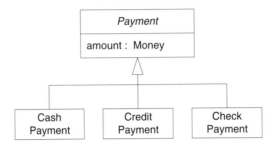

Figure 26.3 Payment class hierarchy.

A *CreditPayment* is a transfer of money via a credit institution which needs to be authorized. My definition of *Payment* encompasses and is more general than my definition of *CreditPayment*.

Generalization and Class Sets

Conceptual subclasses and superclasses are related in terms of set membership.

> All the members of a conceptual subclass set are members of their superclass set.

For example, in terms of set membership, all instances of the set *CreditPayment* are also members of the set *Payment*. In a Venn diagram, this is shown as in Figure 26.4.

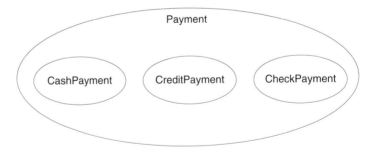

Figure 26.4 Venn diagram of set relationships.

Conceptual Subclass Definition Conformance

When a class hierarchy is created, statements about superclasses that apply to subclasses are made. For example, Figure 26.5 states that all *Payments* have an *amount* and are associated with a *Sale*.

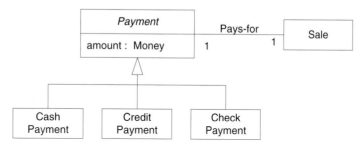

Figure 26.5 Subclass conformance.

All *Payment* subclasses must conform to having an amount and paying for a *Sale*. In general, this rule of conformance to a superclass definition is the *100% Rule*:

100% Rule

100% of the conceptual superclass's definition should be applicable to the subclass. The subclass must conform to 100% of the superclass's:

- attributes
- associations

Conceptual Subclass Set Conformance

A conceptual subclass should be a member of the set of the superclass. Thus, *CreditPayment* should be a member of the set of *Payments*.

Informally, this expresses the notion that the conceptual subclass *is a kind of* superclass. *CreditPayment is a kind of Payment*. More tersely, *is-a-kind-of* is called *is-a*.

This kind of conformance is the *Is-a Rule*:

Is-a Rule

All the members of a subclass set must be members of their superclass set.

In natural language, this can usually be informally tested by forming the statement: *Subclass **is a** Superclass*

For instance, the statement *CreditPayment is a Payment* makes sense, and conveys the notion of set membership conformance.

What Is a Correct Conceptual Subclass?

From the above discussion, apply the following tests[3] to define a correct subclass when constructing a domain model:

A potential subclass should conform to the:

- 100% Rule (definition conformance)
- Is-a Rule (set membership conformance)

26.4   When to Define a Conceptual Subclass

Rules to ensure that a subclass is correct have been examined (the Is-a and 100% rules). However, *when* should we even bother to define a subclass? First, a definition: A **conceptual class partition** is a division of a conceptual class into disjoint subclasses (or **types** in Odell's terminology) [MO95].

The question may be restated as:

"When is it useful to show a conceptual class partition?"

For example, in the POS domain, *Customer* may be correctly partitioned (or subclassed) into *MaleCustomer* and *FemaleCustomer*. But, is it relevant or useful to show this in our model (see Figure 26.6)?

---

3. These rule names have been chosen for their mnemonic support rather than precision.

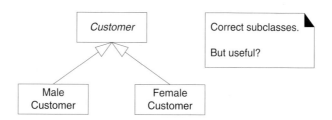

Figure 26.6 Legal conceptual class partition, but is it useful in our domain?

This partition is not useful for our domain; the next section explains why.

Motivations to Partition a Conceptual Class into Subclasses

The following are strong motivations to partition a class into subclass:

> Create a conceptual subclass of a superclass when:
>
> 1. The subclass has additional attributes of interest.
>
> 2. The subclass has additional associations of interest.
>
> 3. The subclass concept is operated on, handled, reacted to, or manipulated differently than the superclass or other subclasses, in ways that are of interest.
>
> 4. The subclass concept represents an animate thing (for example, animal, robot) that behaves differently than the superclass or other subclasses, in ways that are of interest.

Based on the above criteria, it is not compelling to partition *Customer* into the subclasses *MaleCustomer* and *FemaleCustomer* because they have no additional attributes or associations, are not operated on (treated) differently, and do not behave differently in ways that are of interest[4].

Table 26.2 shows some examples of class partitions from the domain of payments and other areas, using these criteria.

---

4. Men and women do exhibit different shopping habits. However, these are not relevant to our current use case requirements—the criterion that bounds our investigation.

Table 26.2 Example subclass partitions.

Conceptual Subclass Motivation	Examples
The subclass has additional attributes of interest.	Payments—not applicable. Library—*Book*, subclass of *LoanableResource*, has an *ISBN* attribute.
The subclass has additional associations of interest.	Payments—*CreditPayment*, subclass of *Payment*, is associated with a *CreditCard*. Library—*Video*, subclass of *LoanableResource*, is associated with *Director*.
The subclass concept is operated upon, handled, reacted to, or manipulated differently than the superclass or other subclasses, in ways that are of interest.	Payments—*CreditPayment*, subclass of *Payment*, is handled differently than other kinds of payments in how it is authorized. Library—*Software*, subclass of *LoanableResource*, requires a deposit before it may be loaned.
The subclass concept represents an animate thing (for example, animal, robot) that behaves differently than the superclass or other subclasses, in ways that are of interest.	Payments—not applicable. Library—not applicable. Market Research—*MaleHuman*, subclass of *Human*, behaves differently than *FemaleHuman* with respect to shopping habits.

26.5   When to Define a Conceptual Superclass

Generalization into a common superclass is usually advised when commonality is identified among potential subclasses. The following are motivations to generalize and define a superclass:

> Create a conceptual superclass in a generalization relationship to subclasses when:
>
> - The potential conceptual subclasses represent variations of a similar concept.
>
> - The subclasses will conform to the 100% and Is-a rules.
>
> - All subclasses have the same attribute which can be factored out and expressed in the superclass.
>
> - All subclasses have the same association which can be factored out and related to the superclass.

The following sections illustrate these points.

26.6   NextGen POS Conceptual Class Hierarchies

Payment Classes

Based on the above criteria for partitioning the *Payment* class, it is useful to create a class hierarchy of various kinds of payments. The justification for the superclass and subclasses is shown in Figure 26.7.

Authorization Service Classes

Credit and check authorization services are variations on a similar concept, and have common attributes of interest. This leads to the class hierarchy in Figure 26.8.

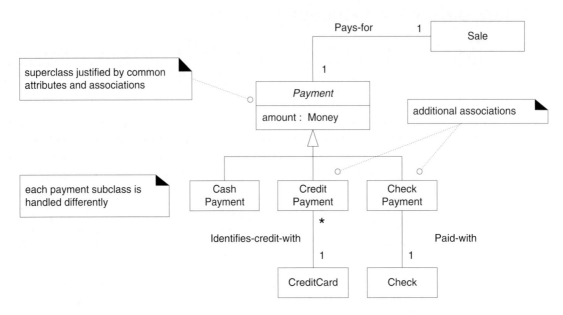

Figure 26.7 Justifying *Payment* subclasses.

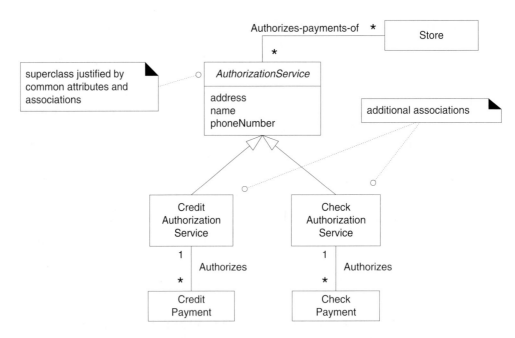

Figure 26.8 Justifying the AuthorizationService hierarchy.

Authorization Transaction Classes

Modeling the various kinds of authorization service transactions (requests and replies) presents an interesting case. In general, transactions with external services are useful to show in a domain model because activities and processes tend to revolve around them. They are important concepts.

Should the modeler illustrate *every* variation of an external service transaction? It depends. As mentioned, domain models are not necessarily correct or wrong, but rather more or less useful. They are useful, because each transaction class is related to different concepts, processes, and business rules.[5]

A second interesting question is the degree of generalization that is useful to show in the model. For argument's sake, let us assume that every transaction has a date and time. These common attributes, plus the desire to create an ultimate generalization for this family of related concepts, justifies the creation of *PaymentAuthorizationTransaction*.

But is it useful to generalize a reply into a *CreditPaymentAuthorizationReply* and *CheckPaymentAuthorizationReply,* as shown in Figure 26.9, or is it sufficient to show less generalization, as depicted in Figure 26.10?

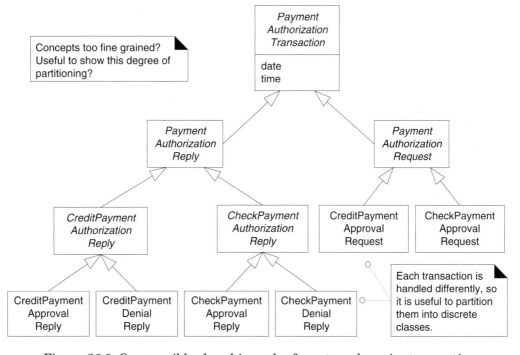

Figure 26.9 One possible class hierarchy for external service transactions.

---

5. In telecommunications domain models, it is similarly useful to identify each kind of exchange or switch message.

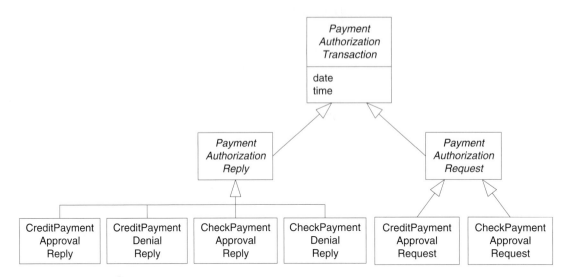

Figure 26.10 An alternate transaction class hierarchy.

The class hierarchy shown in Figure 26.10 is sufficiently useful in terms of generalization, because the additional generalizations do not add obvious value. The hierarchy of Figure 26.9 expresses a finer granularity of generalization that does not significantly enhance our understanding of the concepts and business rules, but it does make the model more complex—and added complexity is undesirable unless it confers other benefits.

26.7   Abstract Conceptual Classes

It is useful to identify abstract classes in the domain model because they constrain what classes it is possible to have concrete instances of, thus clarifying the rules of the problem domain.

> If every member of a class C must also be a member of a subclass, then class C is called an **abstract conceptual class**.

For example, assume that every *Payment* instance must more specifically be an instance of the subclass *CreditPayment*, *CashPayment,* or *CheckPayment*. This is illustrated in the Venn diagram of Figure 26.11 (b). Since every *Payment* member is also a member of a subclass, *Payment* is an abstract conceptual class by definition.

By contrast, if there can be *Payment* instances that are not members of a subclass, it is not an abstract class, as illustrated in Figure 26.11 (a).

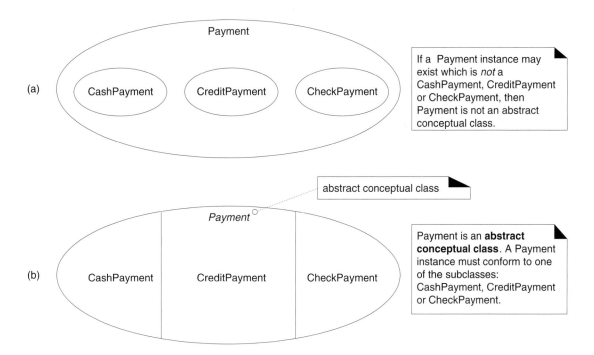

(a)

(b)

Figure 26.11 Abstract conceptual classes.

In the POS domain, every *Payment* is really a member of a subclass. Figure 26.11 (b) is the correct depiction of payments; therefore, *Payment* is an abstract conceptual class.

Abstract Class Notation in the UML

To review, the UML provides a notation to indicate abstract classes—the class name is italicized (see Figure 26.12).

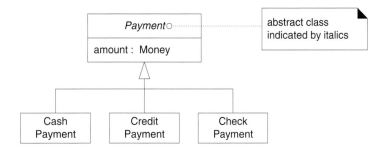

Figure 26.12 Abstract class notation.

Identify abstract classes and illustrate them with an italicized name in the Domain Model.

26.8   Modeling Changing States

Assume that a payment can either be in an unauthorized or authorized state, and it is meaningful to show this in the domain model (it may not really be, but assume so for the discussion). As shown in Figure 26.13, one modeling approach is to define subclasses of *Payment*: *UnauthorizedPayment* and *AuthorizedPayment*. However, note that a payment does not stay in one of these states; it typically transitions from unauthorized to authorized. This leads to the following guideline:

Do not model the states of a concept X as subclasses of X. Rather, either:

■ Define a state hierarchy and associate the states with X, or

■ Ignore showing the states of a concept in the domain model; show the states in state diagrams instead.

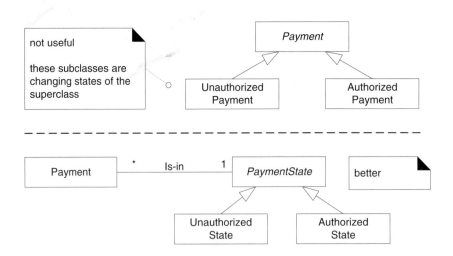

Figure 26.13 Modeling changing states.

26.9   Class Hierarchies and Inheritance in Software

This discussion of conceptual class hierarchies has not mentioned *inheritance*, because the discussion is focused on a domain model of things in the world, not software artifacts. In an object-oriented programming language, a software subclass **inherits** the attribute and operation definitions of its superclasses by the creation of **software class hierarchies**. **Inheritance** is a software mechanism to make superclass things applicable to subclasses. It supports refactoring code from subclasses and pushing it up class hierarchies. Therefore, inheritance has no real part to play in the discussion of the domain model, although it most definitely does when we transition to the design and implementation view.

The conceptual class hierarchies generated here may or may not be reflected in the Design Model. For example, the hierarchy of authorization service transaction classes may be collapsed or expanded into alternate software class hierarchies, depending on language features and other factors. For instance, C++ templatized classes can sometimes reduce the number of classes.

REFINING THE DOMAIN MODEL

> *PRESENT, n. That part of eternity dividing the domain*
> *of disappointment from the realm of hope.*
>
> —*Ambrose Bierce*

Objectives

- Add association classes to the Domain Model.
- Add aggregation relationships.
- Model the time intervals of applicable information.
- Choose how to model roles.
- Organize the Domain Model into packages.

Introduction

This chapter explores additional useful ideas and notation available for domain modeling and applies them to refine aspects of the NextGen POS Domain Model.

27.1 Association Classes

The following domain requirements set the stage for association classes:

- Authorization services assign a merchant ID to each store for identification during communications.
- A payment authorization request from the store to an authorization service needs the merchant ID that identifies the store to the service.

- Furthermore, a store has a different merchant ID for each service.

Where in the UP Domain Model should the merchant ID attribute reside?

Placing *merchantID* in *Store* is incorrect because a *Store* can have more than one value for *merchantID*. The same is true with placing it in *Authorization-Service* (see Figure 27.1).

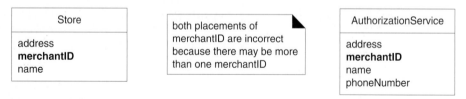

Figure 27.1 Inappropriate use of an attribute.

This leads to the following modeling principle:

> In a domain model, if a class C can simultaneously have many values for the same kind of attribute A, do not place attribute A in C. Place attribute A in another class that is associated with C.
>
> For example:
>
> - A *Person* may have many phone numbers. Place phone number in another class, such as *PhoneNumber* or *ContactInformation*, and associate many of these to *Person*.

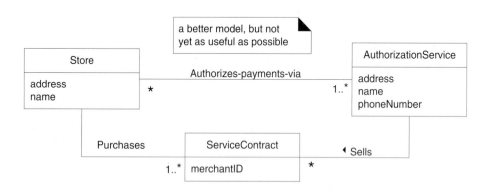

Figure 27.2 First attempt at modeling the merchantID problem.

The above principle suggests that something like the model in Figure 27.2 is more appropriate. In the business world, what concept formally records the information related to the services that a service provides to a customer?—a *Contract* or *Account*.

The fact that both *Store* and *AuthorizationService* are related to *ServiceContract* is a clue that it is dependent on the relationship between the two. The *merchantID* may be thought of as an attribute related to the association between *Store* and *AuthorizationService*.

This leads to the notion of an **association class**, in which we can add features to the association itself. *ServiceContract* may be modeled as an association class related to the association between *Store* and *AuthorizationService*.

In the UML, this is illustrated with a dashed line from the association to the association class. Figure 27.3 visually communicates the idea that a *Service-Contract* and its attributes are related to the association between a *Store* and *AuthorizationService*, and that the lifetime of the *ServiceContract* is dependent on the relationship.

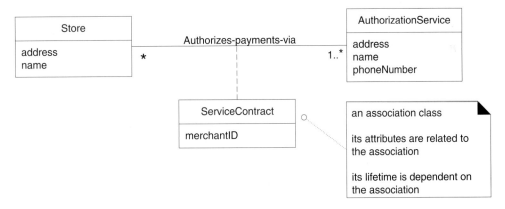

Figure 27.3 An association class.

Guidelines

Guidelines for adding association classes include the following:

Clues that an association class might be useful in a domain model:

- An attribute is related to an association.

- Instances of the association class have a life-time dependency on the association.

- There is a many-to-many association between two concepts, and information associated with the association itself.

The presence of a many-to-many association is a common clue that a useful association class is lurking in the background somewhere; when you see one, consider an association class.

Figure 27.4 illustrates some other examples of association classes.

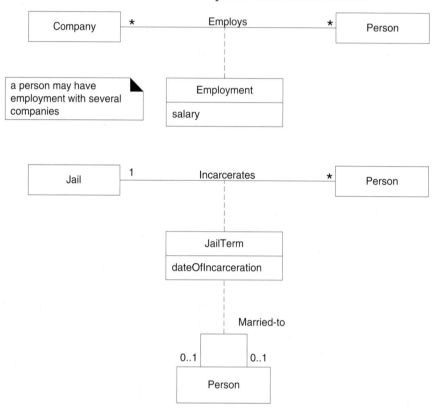

Figure 27.4 Association classes.

27.2   Aggregation and Composition

Aggregation is a kind of association used to model whole-part relationships between things. The whole is called the **composite**.

For instance, physical assemblies are organized in aggregation relationships, such as a *Hand* aggregates *Fingers*.

Aggregation in the UML

Aggregation is shown in the UML with a hollow or filled diamond symbol at the composite end of a whole-part association (see Figure 27.5).

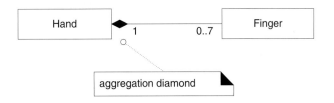

Figure 27.5 Aggregation notation.

Aggregation is a property of an association role.[1]

The association name is often excluded in aggregation relationships since it is typically thought of as *Has-part*. However, one may be used to provide more semantic detail.

Composite Aggregation—Filled Diamond

Composite aggregation, or **composition**, means that the part is a member of only one composite object, and that there is an existence and disposition dependency of the part on the composite. For example, a hand is in a composition relationship to a finger.

In the Design Model, composition and its existence dependency implication indicates that composite software objects create (or caused the creation of) the part software objects (for example, *Sale* creates *SalesLineItem*).

But in the Domain Model, since it does not represent software objects, the notion of the whole creating the part is seldom relevant (a real sale does not create a real sales line item). However, there is still an analogy. For example, in a "human body" domain model, one thinks of the hand as including the fingers, so if one says, "A hand has come into existence," we understand this to also mean that fingers have come into existence as well.

Composition is signified with a filled diamond. It implies that the composite solely owns the part, and that they are in a tree structure parts hierarchy; it is the most common form of aggregation shown in models.

For example, a finger is a part of at most one hand (we hope!), thus the aggregation diamond is filled to indicate composite aggregation (see Figure 27.6).

---

1. Recall that each end of an association is a role, and that a UML role has various properties, such as *multiplicity*, *name*, *navigability* and *isAggregate*.

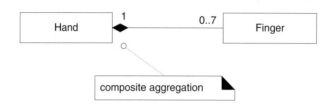

Figure 27.6 Composite aggregation.

If the multiplicity at the composite end is exactly one, the part may *not* exist separate from some composite. For example, if the finger is removed from one hand, it must be immediately attached to another composite object (another hand, a foot, ...); at least, that is what the model is declaring, regardless of the medical merits of this idea!

If the multiplicity at the composite end is 0..1, then the part may be removed from the composite, and still exist apart from membership in any composite. So, if you want fingers floating around by themselves, use 0..1.

Shared Aggregation—Hollow Diamond

Shared aggregation means that the multiplicity at the composite end may be more than one, and is signified with a hollow diamond. It implies that the part may be simultaneously in many composite instances. Shared aggregation seldom (if ever) exists in physical aggregates, but rather in nonphysical concepts.

For instance, a UML package may be considered to aggregate its elements. But an element may be referenced in more than one package (it is owned by one, and referenced in others), which is an example of shared aggregation (see Figure 27.7).

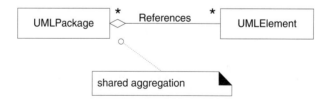

Figure 27.7 Shared aggregation.

How to Identify Aggregation

In some cases, the presence of aggregation is obvious—usually in physical assemblies. But sometimes, it is not clear.

> On aggregation: If in doubt, leave it out.

Here are some guidelines that suggest when to show aggregation:

> Consider showing aggregation when:
>
> - The lifetime of the part is bound within the lifetime of the composite—there is a create-delete dependency of the part on the whole.
>
> - There is an obvious whole-part physical or logical assembly.
>
> - Some properties of the composite propagate to the parts, such as the location.
>
> - Operations applied to the composite propagate to the parts, such as destruction, movement, recording.

Other than something being an obvious assembly of parts, the next most useful clue is the presence of a create-delete dependency of the part on the whole.

A Benefit of Showing Aggregation

Identifying and illustrating aggregation is *not* profoundly important; it is quite feasible to exclude it from a domain model. Most—if not all—experienced domain modelers have seen unproductive time wasted debating the fine points of these associations.

Discover and show aggregation because it has the following benefits, most of which relate to the design rather than the analysis, which is why its exclusion from the domain model is not very significant.

- It clarifies the domain constraints regarding the eligible existence of the part independent of the whole. In composite aggregation, the part may not exist outside of the lifetime of the whole.

  ○ During design work, this has an impact on the create-delete dependencies between the whole and part software classes and database elements (in terms of referential integrity and cascading delete paths).

- It assists in the identification of a creator (the composite) using the GRASP Creator pattern.

- Operations—such as copy and delete—applied to the whole often propagate to the parts.

Aggregation in the POS Domain Model

In the POS domain, the *SalesLineItems* may be considered a part of a composite *Sale*; in general, transaction line items are viewed as parts of an aggregate transaction (see Figure 27.8). In addition to conformance to that pattern, there is a create-delete dependency of the line items on the *Sale*—their lifetime is bound within the lifetime of the *Sale*.

By similar justification, *ProductCatalog* is an aggregate of *Product-Specifications*.

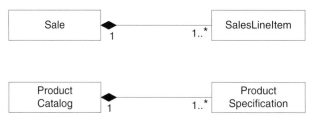

Figure 27.8 Aggregation in the point-of-sale application.

No other relationship is a compelling combination that suggests whole-part semantics, a create-delete dependency, and "If in doubt, leave it out."

27.3   Time Intervals and Product Prices—Fixing an Iteration 1 "Error"

In the first iteration, *SalesLineItems* were associated with *Product-Specifications*, that recorded the price of an item. This was a reasonable simplification for early iterations, but needs to be amended. It raises the interesting—and widely applicable—issue of **time intervals** associated with information, contracts, and the like.

If a *SalesLineItem* always retrieved the current price recorded in a *Product-Specification*, then when the price was changed in the object, old sales would refer to new prices, which is incorrect. What is needed is a distinction between the historical price when the sale was made, and the current price.

Depending on the information requirements, there are at least two ways to model this. One is to simply copy the product price into the *SalesLineItem*, and maintain the current price in the *ProductSpecification*.

The other approach, more robust, is to associate a collection of *ProductPrices* with a *ProductSpecification*, each with an associated applicable time interval. Thus, the organization can record all past prices (to resolve the sale price problem, and for trend analysis) and also record future planned prices (see Figure 27.9). See [CLD99] for a broader discussion of time intervals, under the category of **Moment-Interval** archetypes.

It is common that a collection of time interval related information needs to be maintained, rather than a simple value. Physical, medical, and scientific measurements, and many accounting and legal artifacts have this requirement.

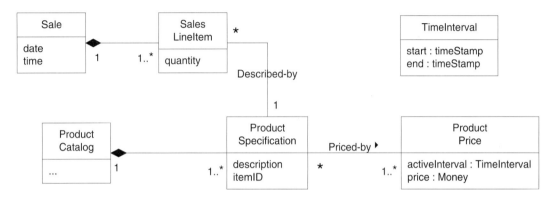

Figure 27.9 ProductPrices and time intervals.

27.4 Association Role Names

Each end of an association is a role, which has various properties, such as:

- name
- multiplicity

A role name identifies an end of an association and ideally describes the role played by objects in the association. Figure 27.10 shows role name examples.

An explicit role name is not required—it is useful when the role of the object is not clear. It usually starts with a lowercase letter. If not explicitly present, assume that the default role name is equal to the related class name, though starting with a lowercase letter.

As covered previously during a discussion of mapping designs to code, roles used in DCDs may be interpreted as the basis for attribute names during code generation.

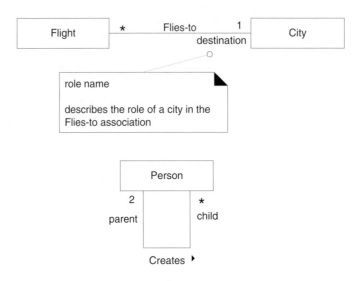

Figure 27.10 Role names.

27.5   Roles as Concepts vs. Roles in Associations

In a domain model, a real-world role—especially a human role—may be modeled in a number of ways, such as a discrete concept, or expressed as a role in an association.[2] For example, the role of cashier and manager may be expressed in at least the two ways illustrated in Figure 27.11.

The first approach may be called "roles in associations"; the second "roles as concepts." Both approaches have advantages.

Roles in associations are appealing because they are a relatively accurate way to express the notion that the same instance of a person takes on multiple (and dynamically changing) roles in various associations. I, a person, simultaneously or in sequence, may take on the role of writer, object designer, parent, and so on.

On the other hand, roles as concepts provides ease and flexibility in adding unique attributes, associations, and additional semantics. Furthermore, the implementation of roles as separate classes is easier because of limitations of current popular object-oriented programming languages—it is not convenient to dynamically mutate an instance of one class into another, or dynamically add behavior and attributes as the role of a person changes.

---

2. For simplicity, other excellent solutions such as those discussed in [Fowler96] are ignored.

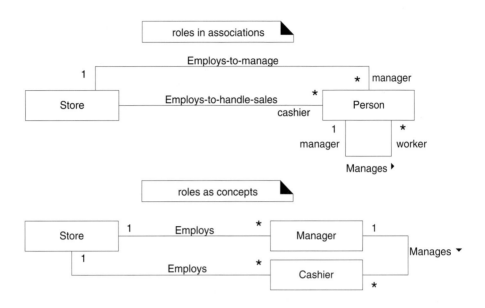

Figure 27.11 Two ways to model human roles.

27.6 Derived Elements

A derived element can be determined from others. Attributes and associations are the most common derived elements. When should derived elements be shown?

> Avoid showing derived elements in a diagram, since they add complexity without new information. However, add a derived element when it is prominent in the terminology, and excluding it impairs comprehension.

For example, a *Sale total* can be derived from *SalesLineItem* and *Product-Specification* information (see Figure 27.12). In the UML, it is shown with a "/" preceding the element name.

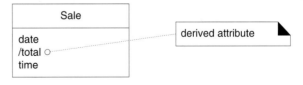

Figure 27.12 Derived attribute.

As another example, a *SalesLineItem quantity* is actually derivable from the number of instances of *Items* associated with the line item (see Figure 27.13).

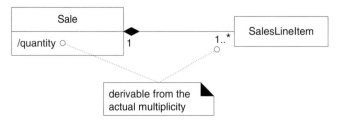

Figure 27.13 Derived attribute related to multiplicity.

27.7   Qualified Associations

A **qualifier** may be used in an association; it distinguishes the set of objects at the far end of the association based on the qualifier value. An association with a qualifier is a **qualified association**.

For example, *ProductSpecifications* may be distinguished in a *ProductCatalog* by their *itemID*, as illustrated in Figure 27.14 (b). As contrasted in Figure 27.14 (a) vs. (b), qualification reduces the multiplicity at the far end from the qualifier, usually down from many to one. Depicting a qualifier in a domain model communicates how, in the domain, things of one class are distinguished in relation to another class. They should not, in the domain model, be used to express design decisions about lookup keys, although that is suitable in other diagrams illustrating design decisions.

Qualifiers do not usually add compelling useful new information, and we can fall into the trap of "design-think." However, used judiciously, they can sharpen understanding about the domain. The qualified associations between *Product-Catalog* and *ProductSpecification* provide a reasonable example of a value-added qualifier.

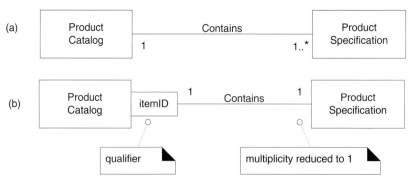

Figure 27.14 Qualified association.

27.8   Reflexive Associations

A concept may have an association to itself; this is known as a **reflexive associ-ation**[3] (see Figure 27.15).

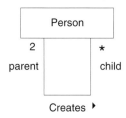

Figure 27.15 Reflexive association.

27.9   Ordered Elements

If associated objects are ordered, this can be shown as in Figure 27.16. For example, the *SalesLineItems* must be maintained in the order entered.

Figure 27.16 Ordered elements.

27.10 Using Packages to Organize the Domain Model

A domain model can easily grow large enough that it is desirable to factor it into packages of strongly related concepts, as an aid to comprehension and parallel analysis work in which different people do domain analysis within different sub-domains. The following sections illustrate a package structure for the UP Domain Model.

UML Package Notation

To review, a UML package is shown as a tabbed folder (see Figure 27.17). Subor-dinate packages may be shown within it. The package name is within the tab if

---

3. [MO95] constrains the definition of reflexive associations further.

the package depicts its elements; otherwise, it is centered within the folder itself.

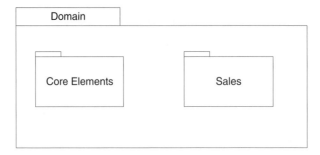

Figure 27.17 A UML package.

Ownership and References

An element is *owned* by the package within which it is defined, but may be *referenced* in other packages. In that case, the element name is qualified by the package name using the pathname format *PackageName::ElementName* (see Figure 27.18). A class shown in a foreign package may be modified with new associations, but must otherwise remain unchanged.

Figure 27.18 A referenced class in a package.

Package Dependencies

If a model element is in some way dependent on another, the dependency may be shown with a dependency relationship, depicted with an arrowed line. A package dependency indicates that elements of the dependent package in some way know about or are coupled to elements in the target package.

For example, if a package references an element owned by another, a dependency exists. Thus, the *Sales* package has a dependency on the *Core Elements* package (see Figure 27.19).

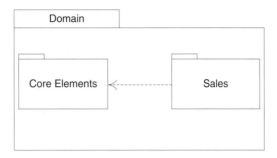

Figure 27.19 A package dependency.

Package Indication without Package Diagram

At times, it is inconvenient to draw a package diagram, but still desirable to indicate the package that the elements are a member of.

In this situation, include a note (dog-eared note) on the diagram, as illustrated in Figure 27.20.

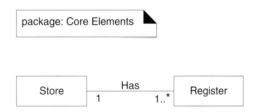

Figure 27.20 Illustrating package ownership with a note.

How to Partition the Domain Model

How should the classes in a domain model be organized within packages? Apply the following general guidelines:

> To partition the domain model into packages, place elements together that:
>
> - are in the same subject area—closely related by concept or purpose
> - are in a class hierarchy together
> - participate in the same use cases
> - are strongly associated

It is useful if all elements related to the domain model are rooted in a package called *Domain*, and all widely shared, common, core concepts are defined in a packaged named something like *Core Elements* or *Common Concepts*, in the absence of any other meaningful package within which to place them.

POS Domain Model Packages

Based on the above criteria, the package organization for the POS Domain Model is shown in Figure 27.21.

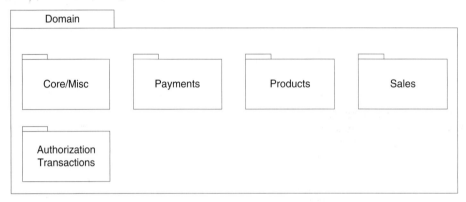

Figure 27.21 Domain concept packages.

Core/Misc Package

A Core/Misc package (see Figure 27.22) is useful to own widely shared concepts or those without an obvious home. In later references, the package name will be abbreviated to *Core*.

There are no new concepts or associations particular to this iteration in this package.

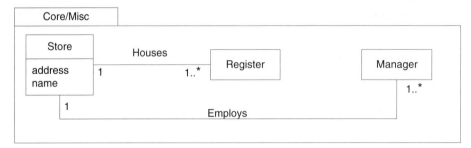

Figure 27.22 Core package.

Payments

As in iteration 1, new associations are primarily motivated by a need-to-know criterion. For example, there is a need to remember the relationship between *CreditPayment* and *CreditCard*. In contrast, some associations are added more for comprehension, such as *DriversLicense Identifies Customer* (see Figure 27.23).

Note that *PaymentAuthorizationReply* is expressed as an association class. A reply arises out of association between a payment and its authorization service.

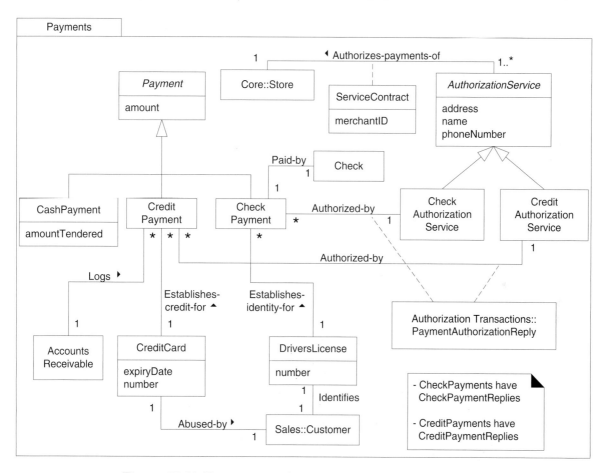

Figure 27.23 Payments package.

Products

With the exception of composite aggregation, there are no new concepts or associations particular to this iteration (see Figure 27.24).

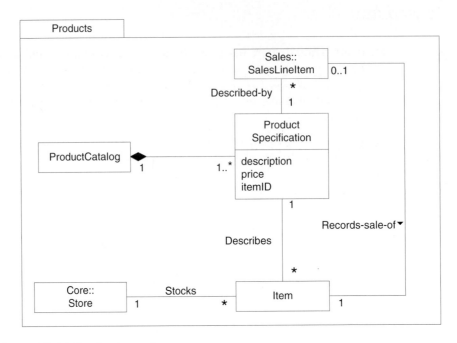

Figure 27.24 Products package.

Sales

With the exception of composite aggregation and derived attributes, there are no
new concepts or associations particular to this iteration (see Figure 27.25).

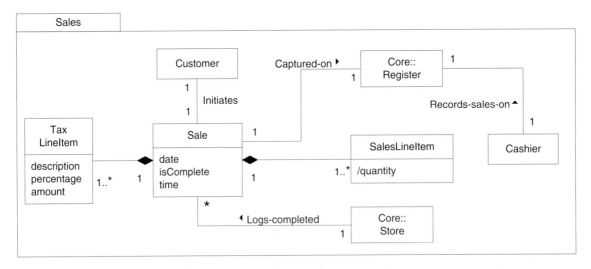

Figure 27.25 Sales package.

Authorization Transactions

Although providing meaningful names for associations is recommended, in some circumstances it may not be compelling, especially if the purpose of the association is considered obvious to the audience. A case in point is the associations between payments and their transactions. Their names have been left unspecified because we can assume the audience reading the class diagram in Figure 27.26 will understand that the transactions are for the payment; adding the names merely makes the diagram more busy.

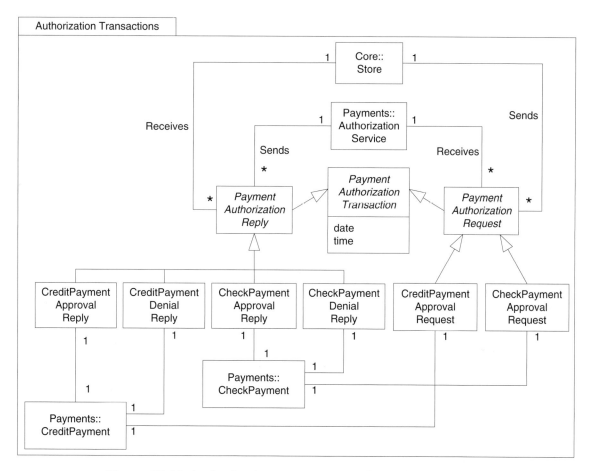

Figure 27.26 Authorization transaction package.

Is this diagram too detailed, showing too many specializations? It depends. The real criteria is usefulness. Although it is not incorrect, does it add any value in improving understanding of the domain? The answer should influence how many specializations to illustrate in a domain model.

ADDING NEW SSDs AND CONTRACTS

Virtue is insufficient temptation.

—*George Bernard Shaw*

Objectives

■ Define SSDs and system operation contracts for the current iteration.

28.1 New System Sequence Diagrams

In the current iteration, the new payment handling requirements involve new collaborations with external systems. To review, SSDs use sequence diagram notation to illustrate inter-system collaborations, treating each system as a black-box. It is useful to illustrate the new system events in SSDs in order to clarify:

■ new system operations that the NextGen POS system will need to support

■ calls to other systems, and the responses to expect from these calls

Common Beginning of Process Sale Scenario

The SSD for the beginning portion of a basic scenario includes *makeNewSale, enterItem* and *endSale* system events; it is common regardless of the payment method (see Figure 28.1).

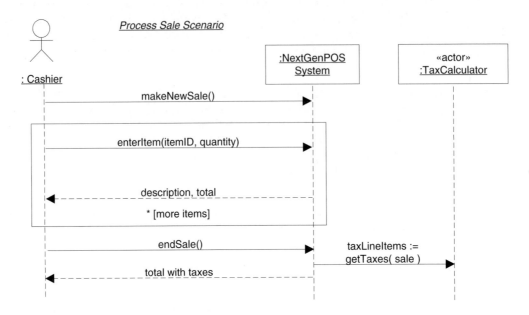

Figure 28.1 SSD common beginning.

Credit Payment

This credit payment scenario SSD starts after the common beginning (see Figure 28.2).

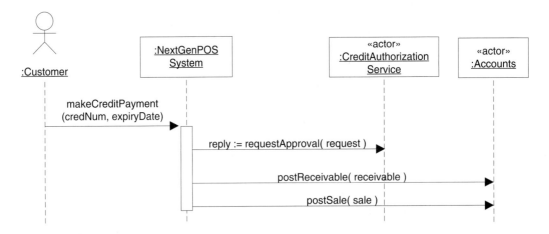

Figure 28.2 Credit payment SSD.

In both cases of credit and check payments, a simplifying assumption is made (for this iteration) that the payment is exactly equal to the sale total, and thus a different "tendered" amount does not have be an input parameter.

Note that the call to the external *CreditAuthorizationService* is modeled as a regular synchronous message with a return value. This is an abstraction; it could be implemented with a SOAP request over secure HTTPS, or any remote communication mechanism. The resource adapters defined in the prior iteration will hide the specific protocol.

The *makeCreditPayment* system operation—and the use case—assume that the credit information of the customer is coming from a credit card, and thus a credit account number and expiry date enter the system (probably via a card reader). Although it is recognized that in the future, alternative mechanisms for communicating credit information will arise, the assumption that credit cards will be supported is very stable.

Recall that when a credit authorization service approves a credit payment, it owes the store for the payment; thus, a receivables entry needs to be added to the accounts receivable system.

Check Payment

The SSD for the check payment scenario is shown in Figure 28.3.

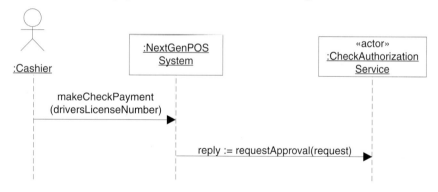

Figure 28.3 Check payment SSD.

According to the use case, the cashier must enter the driver's license number for validation.

28.2 New System Operations

In this iteration, the new system operations that our system must handle are:

- *makeCreditPayment*
- *makeCheckPayment*

In the first iteration, the system event and operation for the cash payment was simply *makePayment*. Now that the payments are of different types, it is renamed to *makeCashPayment*.

28.3 New System Operation Contracts

To review, system operation contracts are an optional requirements artifact (part of the Use-Case Model) that adds fine detail regarding the results of a system operation. Sometimes, the use case text is itself sufficient, and these contracts are not necessary. But on occasion, they bring value by their precise and detailed approach to identifying what happens when a complex operation is invoked on the system, in terms of state changes to objects defined in the Domain Model.

Here are contracts for the new system operations:

Contract CO5: makeCreditPayment

Operation:	makeCreditPayment(creditAccountNumber, expiryDate)
Cross References:	Use Cases: Process Sale
Preconditions:	An underway sale exists and all items have been entered.
Postconditions:	– a CreditPayment pmt was created
	– pmt was associated with the current Sale sale
	– a CreditCard cc was created; cc.number = creditAccountNumber, cc.expiryDate = expiryDate
	– cc was associated with pmt
	– a CreditPaymentRequest cpr was created
	– pmt was associated with cpr
	– a ReceivableEntry re was created
	– re was associated with the external AccountsReceivable
	– sale was associated with the Store as a completed sale

Note the postcondition indicating the association of a new receivable entry in accounts receivable. Although this responsibility is outside the bounds of the NextGen system, the accounts receivable system is within the control of the business, and so the statement has been added as a correctness check.

For example, during testing, it is clear from this post-condition that the accounts receivable system should be tested for the presence of a new receivable entry.

Contract CO6: makeCheckPayment

Operation:	makeCheckPayment(driversLicenceNumber)
Cross References:	Use Cases: Process Sale
Preconditions:	An underway sale exists and all items have been entered.
Postconditions:	– a CheckPayment pmt was created
	– pmt was associated with the current Sale sale
	– a DriversLicense dl was created; dl.number = driversLicenseNumber
	– dl was associated with pmt
	– a CheckPaymentRequest cpr was created.
	– pmt was associated with cpr
	– sale was associated with the Store as a completed sale

MODELING BEHAVIOR IN STATECHART DIAGRAMS

Usability is like oxygen—you never notice it until it is missing.

—anonymous

Objectives

- Create statechart diagrams for classes and use cases.

Introduction

The UML includes statechart diagram notation to illustrate the events and states of things—transactions, use cases, people, and so forth. The most important notational features are shown, but there are others not covered in this introduction.

The use of statechart diagrams is emphasized for showing system events in use cases, but they may additionally be applied to any class.

29.1 Events, States, and Transitions

An **event** is a significant or noteworthy occurrence. For example:

- A telephone receiver is taken off the hook.

A **state** is the condition of an object at a moment in time—the time between events. For example:

- A telephone is in the state of being "idle" after the receiver is placed on the hook and until it is taken off the hook.

A **transition** is a relationship between two states that indicates that when an event occurs, the object moves from the prior state to the subsequent state. For example:

- When the event "off hook" occurs, transition the telephone from the "idle" to "active" state.

29.2   Statechart Diagrams

A UML statechart diagram, as shown in Figure 29.1, illustrates the interesting events and states of an object, and the behavior of an object in reaction to an event. Transitions are shown as arrows, labeled with their event. States are shown in rounded rectangles. It is common to include an initial pseudo-state, which automatically transitions to another state when the instance is created.

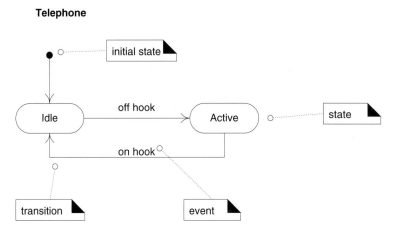

Figure 29.1 Statechart diagram for a telephone.

A statechart diagram shows the lifecycle of an object: what events it experiences, its transitions, and the states it is in between these events. It need not illustrate every possible event; if an event arises that is not represented in the diagram, the event is ignored as far as the statechart diagram is concerned. Therefore, we can create a statechart diagram that describes the lifecycle of an object at arbitrarily simple or complex levels of detail, depending on our needs.

Subject of a Statechart Diagram

A statechart diagram may be applied to a variety of UML elements, including:

- classes (conceptual or software)
- use cases

Since an entire "system" may be represented by a class, it too may have its own statechart diagram.

29.3 Statechart Diagrams in the UP?

There is not one model in the UP called the "state model." Rather, any element in any model (Design Model, Domain Model, and so forth) may have a statechart to better understand or communicate its dynamic behavior in response to events. For example, a statechart associated with the *Sale* design class of the Design Model is itself part of the Design Model.

29.4 Use Case Statechart Diagrams

A useful application of statechart diagrams is to describe the legal sequence of external system events that are recognized and handled by a system in the context of a use case. For example:

- During the *Process Sale* use case in the NextGen POS application, it is not legal to perform the *makeCreditPayment* operation until the *endSale* event has happened.
- During the *Process Document* use case in a word processor, it is not legal to perform the File-Save operation until the File-New or File-Open event has happened.

A statechart diagram that depicts the overall system events and their sequence within a use case is a kind of **use case statechart diagram**. The use case statechart diagram in Figure 29.2 shows a simplified version of the system events for the *Process Sale* use case in the POS application. It illustrates that it is not legal to generate a *makePayment* event if an *endSale* event has not previously caused the system to transition to the *WaitingForPayment* state.

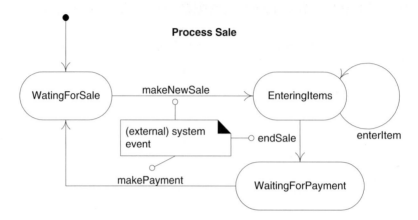

Figure 29.2 Use case statechart diagram for *Process Sale*.

Utility of Use Case Statechart Diagrams

The number of system events and their legal order for the *Process Sale* use case are (so far) relatively trivial, thus the use of a statechart diagram to show legal sequence may not seem compelling. But for a complex use case with myriad system events—such as when using a word processor—a statechart diagram that illustrates the legal order of external events is helpful.

Here's how: During design and implementation work, it is necessary to create and implement a design that ensures no out-of-sequence events occur, otherwise an error condition is possible. For example, the system should not be allowed to receive a payment unless a sale is complete; code must be written to guarantee that.

Given a set of use case statechart diagrams, a designer can methodically develop a design that ensures correct system event order. Possible design solutions include:

- hard-coded conditional tests for out-of-order events

- use of the *State* pattern (discussed in a subsequent chapter)

- disabling widgets in active windows to disallow illegal events (a desirable approach)

- a state machine interpreter that runs a state table representing a use case statechart diagram

In a domain with many system events, the conciseness and thoroughness of use case statechart diagrams help a designer ensure that nothing is missed.

29.5   Use Case Statechart Diagrams for the POS Application

Process Sale

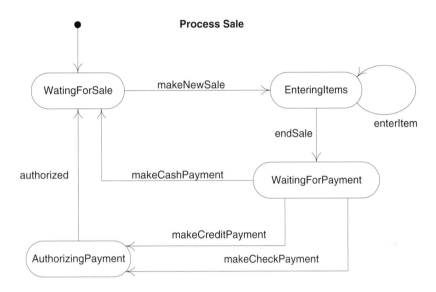

Figure 29.3 A sample statechart.

29.6   Classes that Benefit from Statechart Diagrams

In addition to statechart diagrams for use cases or the overall system, they may be created for virtually any type or class.

State-Independent and State-Dependent Objects

If an object always responds the same way to an event, then it is considered **state-independent** (or modeless) with respect to that event. For example, if an object receives a message, and the responding method always does the same thing—the method will typically have no conditional logic. The object is state-independent with respect to that message. If, for all events of interest, an object always reacts the same way, it is a **state-independent object**. By contrast, **state-dependent objects** react differently to events depending on their state.

Create statecharts for state-dependent objects with complex behavior.

In general, business information systems have a minority of interesting state-dependent classes. By contrast, process control and telecommunication domains often have many state-dependent objects.

Common State-dependent Classes

Following is a list of common objects which are usually state-dependent, and for which it may be useful to create a statechart diagram:

- **Use cases**

  o Viewed as a class, the *Process Sale* use case reacts differently to the *endSale* event dependent of if a sale is underway or not.

- **Stateful sessions**—These are server-side software objects representing ongoing sessions or conversations with a client; for example, EJB stateful session objects.

  o Another very common example is server-side handling of web client application and presentation flow logic; for example, a Java technology servlet helper or "controller" that remembers the state of the session with a Web client, and controls the transitions to new web pages, or the modified display of the current web page, based upon the state of the session or conversation.

  o A stateful session can usually be viewed as a software class representing a use case. Recall that one of the GRASP Controller pattern variants is a use case controller, which is a use case stateful session object.

- **Systems**—This is a class representing the overall application or system.

  o The *"POS system."*

- Windows

  o The Edit-Paste action is only valid if there is something in the "clipboard" to paste.

- **Controllers**—These are GRASP controller objects.

  o The *Register* class, which handles the *enterItem* and *endSale* system events.

- **Transactions**—These are ways a transaction (a sale, order, payment) reacts to an event is often dependent on its current state within its overall lifecycle.

  o If a *Sale* received a *makeLineItem* message after the *endSale* event, it should either raise an error condition or be ignored.

- **Devices**
  - TV, microwave oven: they react differently to a particular event depending upon their current state.
- **Role Mutators**—These are classes that change their role.
  - A *Person* changing roles from being a civilian to a veteran.

29.7   Illustrating External and Interval Events

Event Types

It is useful to categorize events as follows:

- **External event**—Also known as a system event, is caused by something (for example, an actor) outside our system boundary. SSDs illustrate external events. Noteworthy external events precipitate the invocation of system operations to respond to them.
  - When a cashier presses the "enter item" button on a POS terminal, an external event has occurred.
- **Internal event**—Caused by something inside our system boundary. In terms of software, an internal event arises when a method is invoked via a message or signal that was sent from another internal object. Messages in interaction diagrams suggest internal events.
  - When a *Sale* receives a *makeLineItem* message, an internal event has occurred.
- **Temporal event**—Caused by the occurrence of a specific date and time or passage of time. In terms of software, a temporal event is driven by a real-time or simulated-time clock.
  - Suppose that after an *endSale* operation occurs, a *makePayment* operation must occur within five minutes, otherwise the current sale is automatically purged.

Statechart Diagrams for Internal Events

A statechart diagram can show *internal* events that typically represent messages received from other objects. Since interaction diagrams also show messages and their reactions (in terms of other messages), why use a statechart diagram to illustrate internal events and object design? The object design paradigm is that of objects that collaborate via messages to fulfill tasks; the UML interaction diagrams directly illustrates that paradigm. It is somewhat incongruous to use a statechart diagram to show a design of object messaging and interaction.[1]

Consequently, I have reservations about recommending the use of statechart diagrams that show internal events for the purpose of creative object design.[2] However, they may be useful to summarize the results of a design, after it is complete.

By contrast, as the previous discussion on use case statechart diagrams explained, a statechart diagram for *external* events can be a helpful and succinct tool.

> Prefer using statechart diagrams to illustrate external and temporal events, and the reaction to them, rather than using them to design object behavior based on internal events.

29.8 Additional Statechart Diagram Notation

The UML notation for statechart diagrams contains a rich set of features that are not exploited in this introduction. Three significant features are:

- transition actions
- transition guard conditions
- nested states

Transition Actions and Guards

A transition can cause an action to fire. In a software implementation, this may represent the invocation of a method of the class of the statechart diagram.

A transition may also have a conditional guard—or boolean test. The transition only occurs if the test passes.

---

1. A reader of OOA/D literature will encounter periodical and textbook examples of complex statechart diagrams that are devoted to *internal* events and the object's reaction to them. Essentially, their creators have replaced the paradigm of object interaction and collaboration via messages with the paradigm of objects as state machines, and have used statechart diagrams to design the behavior of objects, rather than using collaboration diagrams. Abstractly, the two views are equivalent.

2. One reasonable use of statechart diagrams to show object design based on internal events is when code is to be produced with a code generator that is driven by the statechart diagrams, or when a state machine interpreter will be used to run the software system.

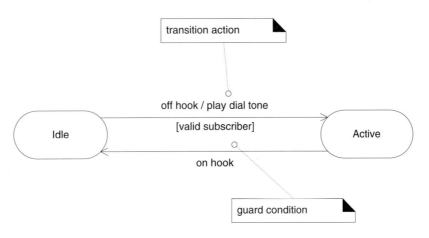

Figure 29.4 Transition action and guard notation.

Nested States

A state allows nesting to contain substates; a substate inherits the transitions of its superstate (the enclosing state). This is a key contribution of the Harel statechart diagram notation that UML is based on, as it leads to succinct statechart diagrams. Substates may be graphically shown by nesting them in a superstate box.

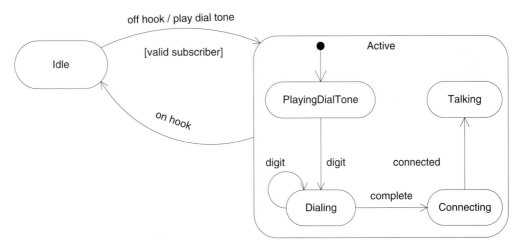

Figure 29.5 Nested states.

For example, when a transition to the *Active* state occurs, creation and transition into the *PlayingDialTone* substate occurs. No matter what substate the object is in, if the *on hook* event related to the *Active* superstate occurs, a transition to the *Idle* state occurs.

29.9   Further Readings

The application of state models to OOA/D is well-covered in *Designing Object Systems* by Cook and Daniels. *Doing Hard Time* by Douglass also provides an excellent discussion of state modeling; the content emphasizes real-time systems, but is broadly applicable.

DESIGNING THE LOGICAL ARCHITECTURE WITH PATTERNS

0x2B | ~0x2B

—Hamlet

Objectives

■ Design a logical architecture in terms of layers and partitions with the Layers pattern.

■ Illustrate the logical architecture using UML package diagrams.

■ Apply the Facade, Observer and Controller patterns.

Introduction

First, to set the expectation level, this is an *introduction* to the topic of logical architecture, a fairly large topic.

The prior iterations emphasized a strongly related group of "domain" software objects in the Design Model (such as *Sale* and *Payment*). No attention was paid to the user interface or access to resources such as a database. The motivation was to keep things simple and focus on core object design skills.

However, a typical system is composed of many logical packages, such as a user interface package, a database access package, and so forth. Each package groups a set of cohesive responsibilities (e.g., database access). This is the basic practice of modularization to support a separation of concerns.

This chapter briefly explores logical architectures, and communication and coupling between packages.

30.1   Software Architecture

One definition of **software architecture** is:

> An architecture is the set of significant decisions about the orga-
> nization of a software system, the selection of the structural ele-
> ments and their interfaces by which the system is composed,
> together with their behavior as specified in the collaborations
> among those elements, the composition of these structural and
> behavioral elements into progressively larger subsystems, and
> the architectural style that guides this organization---these ele-
> ments and their interfaces, their collaborations, and their com-
> position. [BRJ99]

Regardless of the definition (and there are many) the common theme in all software architecture definitions is that it has to do with the large scale—the Big
Ideas in the forces, organization, styles, patterns, responsibilities, collaborations, connections, and motivations of a system (or a system of systems), and
major subsystems.

In software development, architecture is thought of as both a noun and a verb.

As a noun, the architecture includes—as the prior definition indicates—the
organization and structure of the major elements of the system. Beyond this
static definition, it includes the system behavior, especially in terms of large
scale responsibilities of systems and subsystems, and their collaborations. In
terms of a description, the architecture includes the *motivations* or rationale for
why the system is designed the way it is.

As a verb, architecture is part investigation and part design work; for clarity,
the term is best qualified, as in architectural investigation or architectural
design.

Architectural investigation involves identifying those functional and (especially) non-functional requirements that have (or should have) a significant
impact on the system design, such as market trends, performance, cost, maintainability, and points of evolution. Broadly, it is requirements analysis with a
focus on those requirements that have special influence on the major system
design decisions.

Architectural design is the resolution of these forces and requirements in the
design of the software, the hardware and networking, operations, policies, and
so forth.

In the UP, architectural investigation and design are together called **architectural analysis**, the process of which is briefly introduced in Chapter 32.

Architectural Dimensions and Views in the Unified Process

The architecture of a system encompasses several dimensions. For example:

- The **logical architecture**, which describes the system in terms of its conceptual organization in layers, packages, major frameworks, classes, interfaces, and subsystems.

- The **deployment architecture**, which describes the system in terms of the allocation of processes to processing units, and the network configuration.

The Unified Process suggests six views of the architecture (logical, deployment, and so on), all of which are defined in Chapter 32.

> This chapter focuses on a logical view of the architecture.

Architectural Patterns and Pattern Categories

There are well-known best practices in architectural design, especially regarding large-scale logical architecture, and these have been written as patterns, such as Layers. The first book dedicated to the subject of architectural patterns was *Pattern-Oriented Software Architecture* (POSA) [BMRSS96].

The POSA book also offered a simple, useful categorization of patterns at different levels:

1. **Architectural patterns**—related to the large-scale and coarse-grained design, and typically applied during the early iterations (the elaboration phase) when the major structures and connections are established.

   o The Layers patterns, which structures a system into major layers.

2. **Design patterns**—related to the small and medium-scale design of objects and frameworks. Applicable to designing a solution for connecting the large scale elements defined via architectural patterns, and during detailed design work for any local design aspect. Also known as micro-architectural patterns.

   o The Facade pattern, which can be used to provide the interface from one layer to the next.

   o The Strategy pattern, to allow pluggable algorithms.

3. **Idioms**—language or implementation-oriented low-level design solutions.

   o The Singleton pattern, to ensure global access to a single instance of a class.

> This chapter focuses on architectural patterns and the application of design patterns to make connections between the large-scale structures.

There are other pattern categories. The POSA categories form a neat triad, and are useful for many patterns, but do not cover the entire gamut of published patterns. As the risk of oversimplification, a pattern is the repeating best practice of what works—in any domain. Other published categories of patterns include:

- organizational and software development process patterns

- user interface patterns

- testing patterns

30.2   Architectural Pattern: Layers

Solution   The essential ideas of the Layers pattern [BMRSS96] are simple:

- Organize the large-scale logical structure of a system into discrete layers of distinct, related responsibilities, with a clean, cohesive separation of concerns such that the "lower" layers are low-level and general services, and the higher layers are more application specific.

- Collaboration and coupling is from higher to lower layers; lower-to-higher layer coupling is avoided.

A layer is a large-scale element, often composed of several packages or subsystems.

The Layers pattern relates to the logical architecture; that is, it describes the conceptual organization of the design elements into groups, independent of their physical packaging or deployment.

Layers defines a general N-tier model for the logical architecture; it produces a **layered architecture**. It has been applied and written about so often as a pattern that the *Pattern Almanac 2000* [Rising00] lists over 100 patterns that are variants of or related to the Layers pattern.

Problems
- Source code changes are rippling throughout the system—many parts of the systems are highly coupled.

- Application logic is intertwined with the user interface, and so can not be reused with a different interface, nor distributed to another processing node.

- Potentially general technical services or business logic is intertwined with more application-specific logic, and so can not be reused, distributed to another node, or easily replaced with a different implementation.

■ There is high coupling across different areas of concern. It is thus difficult to divide the work along clear boundaries for different developers.

■ Due to the high coupling and mixing of concerns, it is hard to evolve the functionality, scale up the system, or update it to use new technologies.

Example The purpose and number of layers varies across applications and application domains (information systems, operating systems, and so forth. Applied to information systems, typical layers are illustrated and explained in Figure 30.1.

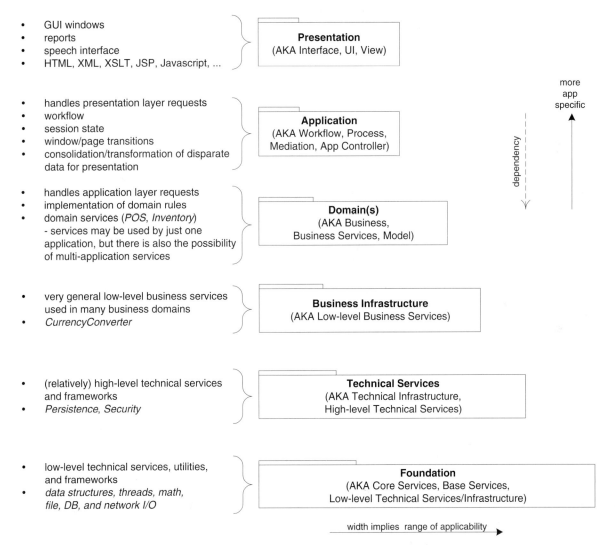

Figure 30.1 Common layers in an information system logical architecture.[1]

Figure 30.1 Common layers in an information system logical architecture.[1]

Based on these archetypes, Figure 30.2 illustrates a partial logical layered architecture for the NextGen application.

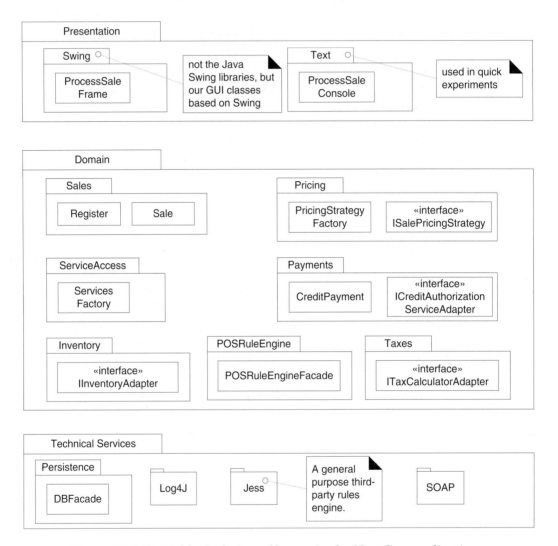

Figure 30.2 Partial logical view of layers in the NextGen application.

UML notation—Package diagrams are used to illustrate the layers. In the UML, a layer is simply a package.

---

1. The width of the package is used to communicate range of applicability in this diagram, but this is not a general UML practice. AKA means also known as.

Note the absence of an Application layer for this iteration of the design; as discussed later, it is not always necessary.

Since this is iterative development, it is normal to create a design of layers that starts simple, and evolves over the iterations of the elaboration phase. One goal of this phase is to have the core architecture established (designed and implemented) by the end of the iterations in elaboration, but this does not mean doing a large up-front speculative architectural design before starting to program. Rather, a tentative logical architecture is designed in the early iterations, and it evolves incrementally through the elaboration phase.

Observe that just a few sample types are present in this package diagram; this is not only motivated by limited page space in formatting this book, but is a signature quality of an **architectural view** diagram—it only shows a few noteworthy elements in order to concisely convey the major ideas of the architecturally significant aspects. The idea in a UP architectural view document is to say to the reader, "I've chosen this small set of instructive elements to convey the big ideas."

Diagram Comments:

■ There are other types in these packages; only a few are shown to indicate noteworthy aspects.

■ The Foundation layer was not shown in this view; the architect (me) decided it did not add interesting information, even though the development team will certainly be adding some Foundation classes, such as more advanced *String* manipulation utilities.

■ For now, a separate Application layer is not used. The responsibilities of control or session objects in the Application layer are handled by the *Register* object. The architect will add an Application layer in a later iteration as the behavior grows in complexity, and alternative client interfaces are introduced (such as a web browser and wireless networked handheld PDA).

Inter-Layer and Inter-Package Coupling

It is also informative to include a diagram in the logical view that illustrates noteworthy coupling between the layers and packages. A partial example is illustrated in Figure 30.3.

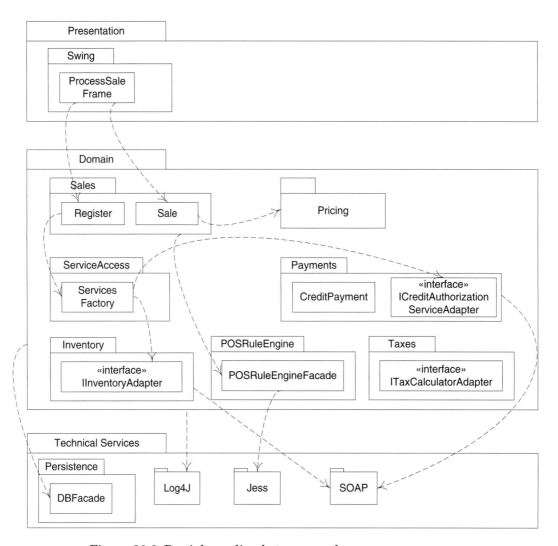

Figure 30.3 Partial coupling between packages.

UML notation:

■ Observe that dependency lines can be used to communicate coupling between packages or types in packages. Plain dependency lines are excellent when the communicator does not care to be more specific on the exact dependency (attribute visibility, subclassing, ...), but just wants to highlight general dependencies.

■ Note also the use of a dependency line emitting from a package rather than a particular type, such as from the *Sales* package to *POSRuleEngineFacade* class, and the *Domain* package to the *Log4J* package. This is useful when either the specific dependent type is not interesting, or the communicator

wants to suggest that many elements of the package may share that
dependency.

Another common use of a package diagram is to hide the specific types, and
focus on illustrating the package-package coupling, as in the partial diagram of
Figure 30.4.

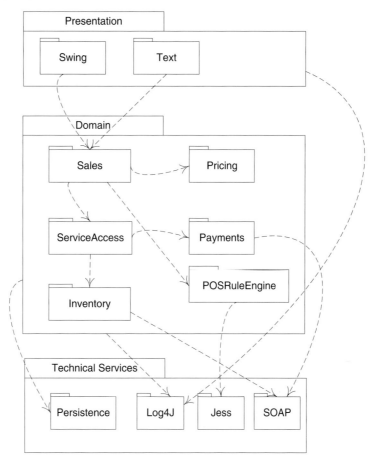

Figure 30.4 Partial package coupling.

In fact, Figure 30.4 illustrates probably the most common style of logical architecture diagram in the UML—a package diagram that shows between perhaps 5
to 20 major packages, and their dependencies.

Inter-Layer and Inter-Package Interaction Scenarios

Package diagrams show static information. To understand the dynamics of how
objects across the layers connect and communicate, an interaction diagram is
informative. In the spirit of an "architectural view" which hides uninteresting
details, and emphasizes what the architect wants to convey, an interaction dia-

gram in the logical view of the architecture focuses on the collaborations as they cross layer and package boundaries. A set of interaction diagrams that illustrate **architecturally significant scenarios** (in the sense that they illustrate many aspects of the large-scale or big ideas in the design) is thus useful.

For example, Figure 30.5 illustrates part of a *Process Sale* scenario that emphasizes the connection points across the layers and packages.

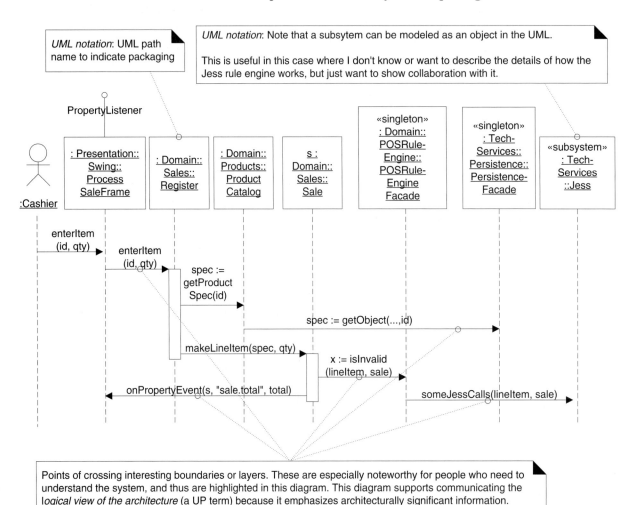

Figure 30.5 An architecturally significant interaction diagram that emphasizes cross-boundary connections.

UML notation:

- The package of a type can optionally be shown by qualifying the type with the UML **path name** expression *<PackageName>::<TypeName>*. For example, *Domain::Sales::Register*. This can be exploited to highlight to the reader the inter-package and inter-layer connections in the interaction diagram.

- Note also the use of the «subsystem» stereotype. In the UML, a subsystem is a discrete entity that has behavior and interfaces. A subsystem can be modeled as a special kind of package, or—as shown here—as an object, which is useful when one wants to show inter-subsystem (or system) collaborations. In the UML, the entire system is also a "subsystem" (the root one), and thus can also be shown as an object in interaction diagrams (such as an SSD).

Observe that the diagram ignores showing some messages, such as certain *Sale* collaborations, in order to highlight architecturally significant interactions.

Collaborations Two design decisions at an architectural level are:

1. What are the big parts?

2. How are they connected?

Whereas the architectural Layers pattern guides defining the big parts, micro-architectural design patterns such as Facade, Controller, and Observer are commonly used for the design of the connections between layers and packages. This section examines patterns in connection and communication between layers and packages.

Simple Packages vs. Subsystems

Some packages or layers are not just conceptual groups of things, but are true subsystems with behavior and interfaces. To contrast:

- The *Pricing* package is not a subsystem; it simply groups the factory and strategies used in pricing. Likewise with Foundation packages such as *java.util*.

- On the other hand, the *Persistence*, *POSRuleEngine,* and *Jess* packages are subsystems. They are discrete engines with cohesive responsibilities that do work.

In the UML, a subsystem can be identified with a stereotype, as in Figure 30.6.

Facade

For packages that represent subsystems, the most common pattern of access is Facade, a GoF design pattern. That is, a public facade object defines the services for the subsystem, and clients collaborate with the facade, not internal subsystem components. This is true of the *POSRuleEngineFacade* and the *PersistenceFacade* for access to the rules engine and persistence subsystem.

The facade should not normally expose many low-level operations. Rather, it is desirable for the facade to expose a small number of high-level operations—the coarse-grained services. When a facade does expose many low-level operations, it tends to become incohesive. Furthermore, if the facade will be, or might become, a distributed or remote object (such as an EJB session bean, or RMI server object), fine-grained services lead to remote communication performance problems—lots of little remote calls are a performance bottleneck in distributed systems.

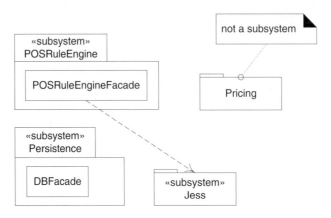

Figure 30.6 Subsystem stereotypes.

Also, a facade does not normally do its own work. Rather, it is consolidator or mediator to the underlying subsystem objects, which do the work.

For example, the *POSRuleEngineFacade* is the wrapper and single point of access into the rules engine for the POS application. Other packages do not see the implementation of this subsystem, as it is hidden behind the facade. Suppose (this is just one of many implementations) that the POS rules engine subsystem is implemented by collaborating with the Jess rules engine. Jess is a subsystem which exposes many fine-grained operations (this is common for very general, third-party subsystems). But the *POSRuleEngineFacade* does not expose the low level Jess operations in its interface. Rather, it provides only a few high-level operation such as *isInvalid(lineItem, sale)*.

If the application has only a "small" number of system operations, then it is common for the Application or Domain layer to expose only one object to an upper layer. On the other hand, the Technical Services layer, which contains several subsystems, exposes at least one facade (or several public objects, if facades aren't used) for each subsystem to upper layers. See Figure 30.7.

Session Facades and the Application Layer

In contrast to Figure 30.7, when an application has many system operations and supports many use cases, it is common to have more than one object mediating between the Presentation and Domain layers.

In the current version of the NextGen system, there is a simple design of a single *Register* object acting as the facade onto the Domain layer (by virtue of the GRASP controller pattern).

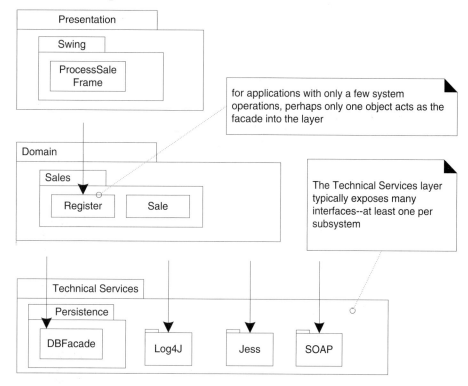

Figure 30.7 Number of interfaces exposed to upper layers.

However, as the system grows to handle many use cases and system operations, it is not uncommon to introduce an Application layer of objects that maintain session state for the operations of a use case, where each session instance represents a session with one client. These are called Session Facades, and their use is another recommendation of the GRASP Controller pattern, such as in the use-case session facade controller variant of the pattern. See Figure 30.8 for an example of how the NextGen architecture may evolve with an Application layer and session facades.

Controller

The GRASP Controller pattern describes common choices in client-side handlers (or controllers, as they've been called) for system operation requests emitting from the Presentation layer. Figure 30.9 illustrates.

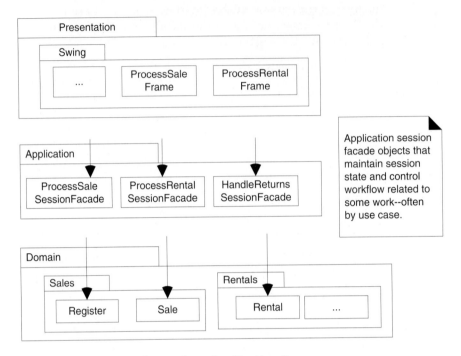

Figure 30.8 Session facades and an Application Layer.

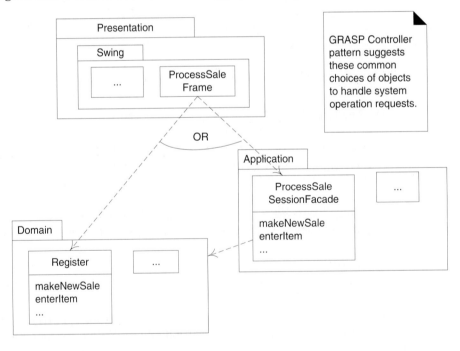

Figure 30.9 The Controller choices.

System Operations and Layers

The SSDs illustrate the system operations, hiding presentation objects from the diagram. The system operations being invoked on the system in Figure 30.10 are requests being generated by an actor via the Presentation layer, onto the Application or Domain layer.

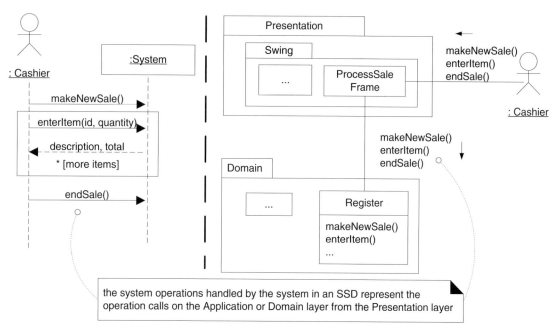

Figure 30.10 System operations in the SSDs and in terms of layers.

Upward Collaboration with Observer

The Facade pattern is commonly used for "downward" collaboration from a higher to a lower layer, or for access to services in another subsystem of the same layer. When the lower Application or Domain layer needs to communicate upward with the Presentation layer, it is usually via the Observer pattern. That is, UI objects in the higher Presentation layer implement an interface such as *PropertyListener* or *AlarmListener*, and are subscribers or listeners to events (such as property or alarm events) coming from objects in the lower layers. The lower layer objects are directly sending messages to the upper layer UI objects, but the coupling is only to the objects viewed as things that implement an interface such as *PropertyListener*, not viewed as specific GUI windows.

This was examined when the Observer pattern was introduced. Figure 30.11 summarizes the idea in relation to layers.

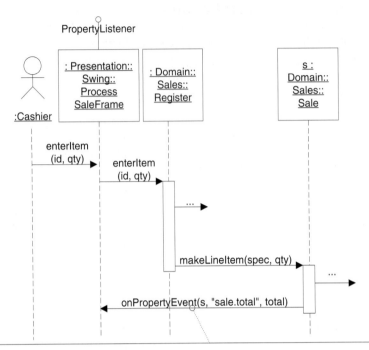

Figure 30.11 Observer for "upward" communication to the Presentation layer.

Relaxed Layered Coupling

The layers in most layered architectures are *not* coupled in the same limited sense as a network protocol based on the OSI 7-Layer Model. In the protocol model, there is strict restriction that elements of layer N only access the services of the immediate lower layer N-1.

This is rarely followed in information system architectures. Rather, the standard is a "relaxed layered" or "transparent layered" architecture [BMRSS96], in which elements of a layer collaborate with or are coupled to several other layers.

Comments on typical coupling between layers:

■ All higher layers have dependencies on the Technical Services and Foundations layer.

　○ For example, in Java all layers depend on *java.util* package elements.

■ It is primarily the Domain layer that has dependency on the Business Infrastructure layer.

- The Presentation layer makes calls on the Application layer, which makes service calls on the Domain layer; the Presentation layer does not call on the Domain, unless there is no Application layer.

- If it is a single-process "desktop" application, software objects in the Domain layer are directly visible to, or passed between, Presentation, Application, and to a lesser extent, Technical Services.

   ○ For example, assuming the NextGen POS system is of this type, a *Sale* and a *Payment* object could be directly visible to the GUI Presentation Layer, and also passed into the Persistence subsystem in the Technical Services layer.

- On the other hand, if it is a distributed system, then serializable **replicates** (also known as **data holder** or **value objects**) of objects in the Domain layer are usually passed to a Presentation layer. In this case, the Domain layer is deployed on a server computer, and client nodes get copies of server data.

Isn't Coupling to Technical Service and Foundation Layers Dangerous?

As the GRASP Protected Variations and Low Coupling discussions explored, it is not coupling per se that is a problem, but unnecessary coupling to variation and evolution points that are unstable and expensive to fix. There is very little justification in spending time and money attempting to abstract or hide something that is unlikely to change, or if it did, the change impact cost would be negligible. For example, if building a Java technologies application, what value is there in hiding the application from access to the Java libraries? High coupling into many points of the libraries is an unlikely problem, as they are (relatively) stable and ubiquitous.

Discussion   In addition to the structural and collaboration issues discussed above for this pattern, other issues include the following.

External Resources or External Database Layer at the Bottom?

Most systems rely on external resources or services, such as an Oracle database and a Novell LDAP naming and directory service. These are *physical* implementation components, not a layer in the *logical* view of the architecture.

Showing external resources such as a particular database in a layer "below" the Foundation layer (for example) mixes up the logical view and the deployment or implementation views of the architecture.

Rather, in terms of the logical view of the architecture and its layers, access to a particular set of persistent data (such as inventory data) can be viewed as a subdomain of the Domain Layer—the Inventory subdomain. And the general services that provide access to databases may be viewed as a Technical Service partition—the Persistence service. See Figure 30.12.

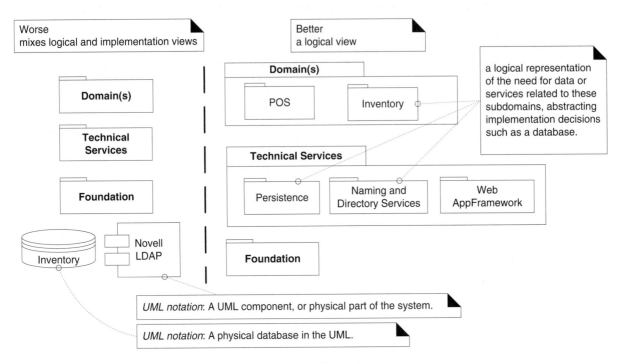

Figure 30.12 Mixing views of the architecture.

Logical vs. Process and Deployment Views of the Architecture

The architectural layers are a logical view of the architecture, not a deployment view of elements to processes and processing nodes. Depending on the platform, *all* layers could be deployed within the same process on the same node, such as an application within a handheld PDA, or spread across many computers and processes for a large-scale web application.

The UP Deployment Model that maps this logical architecture to processes and nodes is strongly influenced by the choice of software and hardware platform and associated application frameworks. For example, J2EE versus .NET influence the deployment architecture.

There are many ways to slice and dice these logical layers for deployment, and in general the subject of deployment architecture will only be lightly introduced, as it is non-trivial, largely outside the scope of the book, and dependent on detailed discussion of the chosen software platform, such as J2EE.

Optional Application Layer?

If present, the Application layer contains objects responsible for knowing the session state of clients, mediating between the Presentation and Domain layers, and controlling the flow of work.

The flow may be organized by controlling the order of windows or web pages, for example.

In terms of the GRASP patterns, GRASP Controller objects such as a use case facade controller are part of this layer. In distributed systems, components such as EJB session beans (and stateful session objects in general) are part of this layer.

In some applications, this layer is not required. It is useful (this is not an exhaustive list) when one or more of the following is true:

- Multiple user interfaces (for example, web pages and a Swing GUI) will be used for the system. The Application layer objects can act as Adapters that collect and consolidate the data as needed for different UIs, and as Facades that wrap and hide access to the Domain layer.

- It is a distributed system and the Domain layer is on a different node than the Presentation layer, and shared by multiple clients. It is usually necessary to keep track of session state, and Application layer objects are a useful choice for this responsibility.

- The Domain Layer can not or should not maintain session state.

- There is a defined workflow in terms of the controlled order of windows or web pages that must be presented.

Fuzzy Set Membership in Different Layers

Some elements are strongly a member of one layer; a *Math* class is part of the Foundation layer. However, especially between the Technical Services and Foundation layers, and Domain and Business Infrastructure, some elements are harder to classify, because the differentiation between these layers is, roughly, "high" versus "low," or "specific" versus "general." which are fuzzy set terms. This is normal, and it is seldom necessary to decide upon a definitive categorization—the development team may consider an element roughly part of the Technical Services and/or Foundations layer considered as a group, broadly called the Infrastructure layer.[2]

For example:

- Suppose this is a Java technologies project, and the open source logging framework *Log4J* (part of the Jakarta project) has been chosen. Is logging part of the Technical Service or Foundation layer? Log4J is a low-level, small, general framework. It is moderately a member of both the Technical Services and the Foundations fuzzy sets.

---

2. Note that there are not well-established naming conventions for layers, and name overloading and contradiction in the architecture literature is common.

- Suppose this is a web application, and the Jakarta *Struts* framework for web applications has been chosen. Struts is a relatively high-level, large, specific technical framework. It is arguably strongly a member of the Technical Services set, and weakly a member of the Foundation set.

But, one person's High-level Technical Service is another's Foundation...

Finally, it is not the case that the libraries provided by a software platform only represent low-level Foundation services. For example, in both .NET and J2SE+J2EE, services include relatively high-level functions such as naming and directory services.

Terminology: Tiers, Layers, and Partitions

The original notion of a **tier** in architecture was a logical layer, not a physical node, but the word has become widely used to mean a physical processing node (or cluster of nodes), such as the "client tier" (the client computer). This presentation will avoid the term for clarity, but bear this in mind when reading architecture literature.

The **layers** of an architecture are said to represent the vertical slices, while **partitions** represent a horizontal division of relatively parallel subsystems of a layer. For example, the *Services* layer may be divided into partitions such as *Security* and *Reporting* (Figure 30.13).

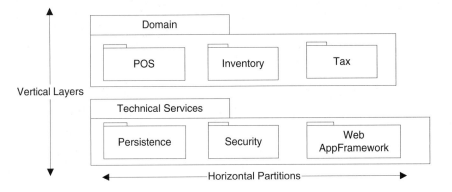

Figure 30.13 Layers and partitions.

Contraindications and Liabilities

- In some contexts, adding layers introduces performance problems. For example, in a high-performance graphics-intensive game adding layers of abstraction and indirection on top of direct access to graphics card components may introduce performance problems.

- The Layers pattern is one of several core architectural patterns; it is not applicable to every problem. For example, an alternate is Pipes and Filters [BMRSS96]. This is useful when the main theme of the application involves processing something through a series transformations, such as image transformations, and the ordering of the transformations is changeable. Yet even in the case when the highest level architectural pattern is Pipes and Filters, individual pipes or filters can be design with Layers.

Benefits
- In general, there is a separation of concerns, a separation of high from low-level services, and of application-specific from general services. This reduces coupling and dependencies, improves cohesion, increases reuse potential, and increases clarity.

- Related complexity is encapsulated and decomposable.

- Some layers can be replaced with new implementations. This is generally not possible for lower-level Technical Service or Foundation layers (e.g., *java.util*), but may be possible for Presentation, Application, and Domain layers.

- Lower layers contain reusable functions.

- Some layers (primarily the Domain and Technical Services) can be distributed.

- Development by teams is aided because of the logical segmentation.

Implementation

Implementing the Layers: People and Process

It is common and recommended, within an iteration, to have a developer specialize within one layer or one service.

Yet, it is not the case that the entire project team focuses on one layer or service in an iteration. Rather, it is more common to implement vertical slices across the layers. This is the UP approach in the elaboration phase: Choose scenarios and requirements that force, in each iteration, a broad coverage across many architecturally significant packages/layers/subsystems, in order to reveal and stabilize the major architectural elements in the early iterations.

However, in this book, this approach was not illustrated in the NextGen case study, because to do so would require early discussion across many and vast topics—from GUI programming to object-relational mapping and optimizing SQL statements. The book case study has focused on the design of Domain layer objects, while recognizing that in reality there would be parallel work going on to develop other layers and subsystems.

The design principles illustrated for the case study are applicable in virtually all layers of the design.

Implementation View: Mapping Source Code Organization to Layers and Packages

Part of the UP Implementation Model is the organization of the source code. For languages such as Java or C#, which provide easy package (namespace) support, the mapping from the logical packaging to the implementation packaging is similar, with notable exceptions when third-party libraries are used.[3] In fact, it is only in the early stages of development, when packages have been speculatively drawn, but not implemented, that there are meaningful differences.

Over time, as the code base grows, it is common to abandon the early speculative drawings (such as the ones we have just seen), and instead use a reverse-engineering UML CASE tool that reads the source code and generates a package diagram. Then, these automatically generated package diagrams, which accurately reflect the code (the real design) become the basis for the logical view of the architecture.

To use Java as an example for mapping to implementation packages, the layers and packages illustrated in Figure 30.4 might map to Java package names as follows:

```
// --- PRESENTATION

com.foo.nextgen.ui.swing
com.foo.nextgen.ui.text


// --- DOMAIN

    // packages relatively specific to the NextGen project
com.foo.nextgen.domain.sales
com.foo.nextgen.domain.pricing
com.foo.nextgen.domain.serviceaccess
com.foo.nextgen.domain.posruleengine

    // packages that can easily be designed as
    // multi-application common business services
com.foo.domain.inventory
com.foo.domain.creditpayment


// --- TECHNICAL SERVICES

    // our team creates
com.foo.service.persistencelite

    // third party
org.apache.log4j
org.apache.soap.rpc
jess


// --- FOUNDATION

    // our team creates
com.foo.util
com.foo.stringutil
```

Notice that an effort has been made to avoid using a specific application qualifier ("nextgen") in the package names unless necessary. For example, the UI

---

3. C++ also supports namespaces, but it is awkward to use the language with dozens or hundreds of fine-grained namespaces; not so for Java or C#.

packages are related to the NextGen application, and so are qualified with the application name *com.foo.nextgen.ui.**.

To support reuse, one practice is to name elements in an application-independent manner, when appropriate. As a straightforward example, general purpose *String* utilities created by the NextGen team, are placed in *com.foo.stringutils*, not *com.foo.nextgen.stringutils*. Furthermore, *com.foo.stringutils* should be placed in the company's source code repository at a company level, rather than buried within the NextGen project's source code folders. You can't reuse it if you can't see it.

As another example, consider the services to access external third-party inventory and credit payment authorization systems. Although they were created by the NextGen team in the service of the NextGen POS project, they are general business services—one could imagine accessing inventory systems from within other applications; so too for credit payment authorization. Hence, *com.foo.domain.inventory* rather than *com.foo.nextgen.domain.inventory*.

On the other hand, the POSRuleEngine package is completely related to the NextGen POS project. Thus, *com.foo.nextgen.domain.posruleengine*.

If in doubt, qualify the package with the project name. It can always be refactored at a later date.

Known Uses   A vast number of modern object-oriented systems (from desktop applications to distributed J2EE web systems) are developed with Layers; it might be harder to find one that is not, than is. Going farther back in history:

Virtual Machines and Operating Systems

Starting in the 1960s, operating system architects advocated the design of operating systems in terms of clearly defined layers, where the "lower" layers encapsulated access to the physical resources and provided process and I/O services, and higher layers called on these services. These included Multics [CV65] and the THE system [Dijkstra68].

Earlier still—in the 1950s—researchers suggested the idea of a virtual machine (VM) with a bytecode universal machine language (for example, UNCOL [Conway1958]), so that applications could be written at higher layers in the architecture (and executed without recompilation across different platforms), on top of the virtual machine layer, which in turn would sit on top of the operating system and machine resources. A VM layered architecture was applied by Alan Kay in his landmark Flex object-oriented based personal computer system [Kay68] and later (1972) by Kay and Dan Ingalls in the influential Smalltalk virtual machine [GK76]—the progenitor of more recent VMs such as the Java Virtual Machine.

Information Systems: The Classic Three-Tier Architecture

An early influential description of a layered architecture for information systems that included a user interface and persistent storage of data was known as a **three-tier architecture** (Figure 30.14), described in the 1970s in [TK78]. The phrase did not achieve popularity until the mid 1990s, in part due to its promotion in [Gartner95] as a solution to problems associated with the widespread use of two-tier architectures.

The original term is now less common, but its motivation is still relevant.

A classic description of the vertical tiers in a three-tier architecture is:

1. **Interface**—windows, reports, and so on.

2. **Application Logic**—tasks and rules that govern the process.

3. **Storage**—persistent storage mechanism.

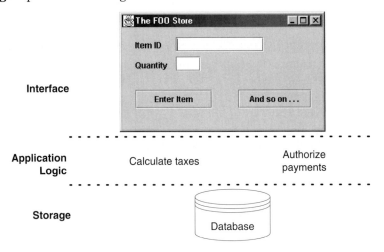

Figure 30.14 Classic view of a three-tier architecture.

The singular quality of a three-tier architecture is the separation of the application logic into a distinct logical middle tier of software. The interface tier is relatively free of application processing; windows or web pages forward task requests to the middle tier. The middle tier communicates with the back-end storage layer.

There was some misunderstanding that the original description implied or required a physical deployment on three computers, but the intended description was purely logical; the allocation of the tiers to compute nodes could vary from one to three. See Figure 30.15.

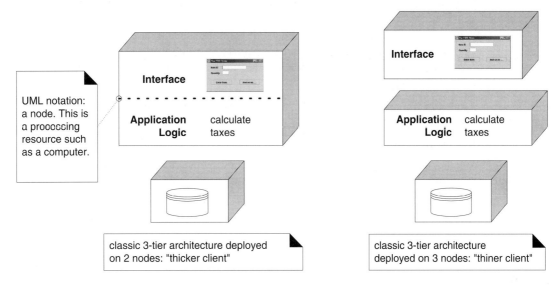

Figure 30.15 A three-tier logical division deployed in two physical architectures.

The three-tier architecture was contrasted by the Gartner Group with a **two-tier** design, in which, for example, application logic is placed within window definitions, which read and write directly to a database; there is no middle tier that separates out the application logic. Two-tier client-server architectures became especially popular with the rise of tools such as Visual Basic and PowerBuilder.

Two-tier designs have (in some cases) the advantage of initial quick development, but can suffer the complaints covered in the *Problems* section. Nevertheless, there are applications that are primarily simple CRUD (create, retrieve, update, delete) data intensive systems, for which this is a suitable choice.

Related Patterns
- Indirection—layers can add a level indirection to lower-level services.
- Protected Variation—layers can protect against the impact of varying implementations.
- Low Coupling and High Cohesion—layers strongly support these goals.
- Its application specifically to object-oriented information systems is described in [Fowler96].

Also Known As Layered Architecture [Shaw96, Gemstone00]

30.3   The Model-View Separation Principle

This principle has been discussed several times; this section summarizes it.

What kind of visibility should other packages have to the Presentation layer?

How should non-window classes communicate with windows? It is desirable that there is no direct coupling from other components to window objects because the windows are related to a particular application, while (ideally) the non-windowing components may be reused in new applications or attached to a new interface. The is the Model-View Separation principle.

In this context, **model** is a synonym for the Domain layer of objects. **View** is a synonym for presentation objects, such as windows, applets and reports.

The **Model-View Separation** principle[4] states that model (domain) objects should not have *direct* knowledge of view (presentation) objects, at least as view objects. So, for example, a *Register* or *Sale* object should not directly send a message to a GUI window object *ProcessSaleFrame*, asking it to display something, change color, close, and so forth.

As previously discussed, a legitimate relaxation of this principle is the Observer pattern, where the domain objects send messages to UI objects viewed only in terms of an interface such as *PropertyListener* or *AlarmListener*.

A further part of this principle is that the domain classes encapsulate the information and behavior related to application logic. The window classes are relatively thin; they are responsible for input and output, and catching GUI events, but do not maintain data or directly provide application functionality.

The motivation for Model-View Separation includes:

■ To support cohesive model definitions that focus on the domain processes, rather than on user interfaces.

■ To allow separate development of the model and user interface layers.

■ To minimize the impact of requirements changes in the interface upon the domain layer.

■ To allow new views to be easily connected to an existing domain layer, without affecting the domain layer.

■ To allow multiple simultaneous views on the same model object, such as both a tabular and business chart view of sales information.

■ To allow execution of the model layer independent of the user interface layer, such as in a message-processing or batch-mode system.

■ To allow easy porting of the model layer to another user interface framework.

---

4. This is a key principle in the pattern *Model-View-Controller* (MVC). MVC was originally a small-scale Smalltalk-80 pattern, and related data objects (models), GUI widgets (views), and mouse and keyboard event handlers (controllers). More recently, the term "MVC" has been coopted by the distributed design community to also apply on a large-scale architectural level. The Model is the Domain Layer, the View is the Presentation Layer, and the Controllers are the workflow objects in the Application layer.

Model-View Separation and "Upward" Communication

How can windows obtain information to display? Usually, it is sufficient for them to send messages to domain objects, querying for information which they then display in widgets—a **polling** or **pull-from-above** model of display updates.

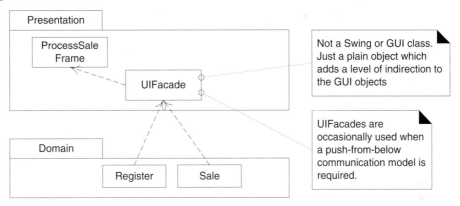

Figure 30.16 A Presentation layer UIFacade is occasionally used for push-from-below designs.

However, a polling model is sometimes insufficient. For example, polling every second across thousands of objects to discover only one or two changes, which are then used to refresh a GUI display, is not efficient. In this case it is more efficient for the few changing domain objects to communicate with windows to cause a display update as the state of domain objects changes. Typical situations of this case include:

■ Monitoring applications, such as telecommunications network management.

■ Simulation applications which require visualization, such as aerodynamics modeling.

In these situations, a **push-from-below** model of display update is required. Because of the restriction of the Model-View Separation pattern, this leads to the need for "indirect" communication from lower objects up to windows—pushing up notification to update from below.

There are two common solutions:

1. The Observer pattern, via making the GUI object simply appear as an object that implements an interface such as *PropertyListener*.

2. A Presentation facade object. That is, adding a facade within the Presentation layer that receives requests from below. This is an example of adding Indirection to provide Protected Variation if the GUI changes. For example, see Figure 30.16.

30.4   Further Readings

There's a wealth of literature on layered architectures, both in print and on the Web. A series of patterns in *Pattern Languages of Program Design*, volume 1, [CS95] first address the topic in pattern form, although layered architectures have been used and written about since at least the 1960s; volume 2 continues with further layers-related patterns. *Pattern-Oriented Software Architecture* volume 1 [BMRSS96] provides a good treatment of the Layers pattern.

Organizing the Design and Implementation Model Packages

If you were plowing a field, which would you rather use? Two strong oxen or 1024 chickens?

—*Seymour Cray*

Objectives

- Organize packages to reduce the impact of changes.
- Know alternative UML package structure notation.

Introduction

If some package X is widely depended upon by the development team, it is undesirable for X to be very unstable (going through many new versions), since it increases the impact on the team in terms of constant version re-synchronization and fixing dependent software that breaks in response to changes in X (**version thrashing**).

This sounds and is obvious, but sometimes a team does not pay attention to identifying and stabilizing the most depended-upon packages, and ends up experiencing more version thrashing than necessary.

This chapter builds on the previous chapter's introduction to layers and packages, by suggesting more fine-grained heuristics for the organization of packages, to reduce these kinds of change impact. The goal is to create a robust physical package design.

One feels the pain of fragile dependency-sensitive package organization much more quickly in C++ than in Java because of the hyper-sensitive compile and link dependencies in C++; a change in one class can have a strong transitive dependency impact leading to recompilation of many classes, and re-linking.[1] Therefore, these suggestions are especially helpful for C++ projects, and moderately so for Java, Smalltalk, or C# (as examples) projects.

The useful work of Robert Martin [Martin95], who has grappled with physical design and packaging of C++ applications, influenced some of the following guidelines.

Source Code Physical Design in the Implementation Model

This issue is an aspect of **physical design**—the UP Implementation Model for source code packaging.

While simply diagramming a package design on a whiteboard or CASE tool, we can arbitrarily place types in any functionally cohesive package without impact. But during source code physical design—the organization of types into physical units of release as Java or C++ "packages"—our choices will influence the degree of developer impact when changes in those packages occur, if there are many developers sharing a common code base.

31.1   Package Organization Guidelines

Guideline: Package Functionally Cohesive Vertical and Horizontal Slices

The basic "intuitive" principle is modularization based on functional cohesion—types are grouped together that are strongly related in terms of their participation in a common purpose, service, collaborations, policy, and function. For example, all the types in the NextGen *Pricing* package are related to product pricing. The layers and packages in the NextGen design are organized by functional groups.

In addition to the usually sufficient informal guesswork on grouping by function ("I think class *SalesLineItem* belongs in *Sales*") another clue to functional grouping is a cluster of types with strong internal coupling and weaker extra-cluster coupling. For example, *Register* has a strong coupling to *Sale*, which has a strong coupling to *SalesLineItem*.

---

1. In C++ the packages may be realized as namespaces, but more likely it means the organization of the source code into separate physical directories—one for each "package."

Internal package coupling, or **relational cohesion**, can be quantified, although such formal analysis is rarely of practical necessity. For the curious, one measure is:

$$RC = \frac{NumberOfInternalRelations}{NumberOfTypes}$$

Where *NumberOfInternalRelations* includes attribute and parameter relations, inheritance, and interface implementations between types in the package.

A package of 6 types with 12 internal relations has RC=2. A package of 6 types with 3 intra-type relations has RC=0.5. Higher numbers suggest more cohesion or relatedness for the package.

Note that this measure is less applicable to packages of mostly interfaces; it is most useful for packages that contain some implementation classes.

A very low RC value suggests either:

■ The package contains unrelated things and is not factored well.

■ The package contains unrelated things and the designer deliberately does not care. This is common with utility packages of disparate services (e.g., *java.util*), where high or low RC is not important.

■ It contains one or more subset clusters with high RC, but overall does not.

Guideline: Package a Family of Interfaces

Place a family of functionally related *interfaces* in a separate package—separate from implementation classes. This is not primarily for the case of one or two related interfaces, but rather when there is a family of perhaps three or more interfaces. The Java technologies EJB package *javax.ejb* is an example: It is a package of at least twelve interfaces; implementations are in separate packages.

Guideline: Package by Work and by Clusters of Unstable Classes

The context for this discussion is that packages are usually the basic unit of development work and of release. It is less common to work on and release just one class.

Suppose 1) there is an existing large package P1 with thirty classes, and 2) there is a work trend that a particular subset of ten classes (C1 through C10) is regularly modified and re-released.

In this case, refactor P1 into P1-a and P1-b, where P1-b contains the ten frequently worked on classes.

Thus, the package has been refactored into more stable and less stable subsets, or more generally, into groups related to work. That is, if most types in a package are worked on together, then it is a useful grouping.

Ideally, fewer developers have a dependency on P1-b than on P1-a, and by factoring out this unstable part to a separate package, not as many developers are affected by new releases of P1-b as by re-releasing the larger original package P1.

Note that this refactoring is in reaction to an emerging work trend. It is difficult to speculatively identify a good package structure in very early iterations. It incrementally evolves over the elaboration iterations, and it should be a goal of the elaboration phase (because it is architecturally significant) to have the majority of the package structure stabilized by elaboration completion.

This guideline illustrates the basic strategy: **Reduce widespread dependency on unstable packages**.

Guideline: Most Responsible Are Most Stable

If the most responsible (depended-on) packages are unstable, there is a greater chance of widespread change dependency impact. As an extreme case, if a widely used utility package such as *com.foo.util* changed frequently, many things could break. Therefore, Figure 31.1 illustrates an appropriate dependency structure.

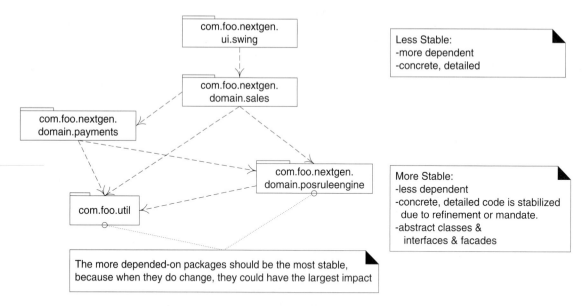

Figure 31.1 More responsible packages should be more stable.

Visually, the lower packages in this diagram should be the most stable. There are different ways to increase stability in a package:

- It contains only or mostly interfaces and abstract classes.

  ○ For example, *java.sql* contains eight interfaces and six classes, and the classes are mostly simple, stable types such as *Time* and *Date*.

- It has no dependencies on other packages (it is independent), or it depends on other very stable packages, or it encapsulates its dependencies such that dependents are not affected.

  ○ For example, *com.foo.ncxtgen.domain.posruleengine* hides its rule engine implementation behind a single facade object. Even if the implementation changes, dependent packages are not affected.

- It contains relatively stable code because it was well-exercised and refined before release.

  ○ For example, *java.util*.

- It is mandated to have a slow change schedule.

  ○ For example, *java.lang*, the core package in the Java libraries, is simply not allowed to change frequently.

Guideline: Factor out Independent Types

Organize types that can be used independently or in different contexts into separate packages. Without careful consideration, grouping by common functionality may not provide the right level of granularity in the factoring of packages.

For example, suppose that a subsystem for persistence services has been defined in one package *com.foo.service.persistence*. In this package are two very general utility/helper classes *JDBCUtililities* and *SQLCommand*. If these are general utilities for working with JDBC (Java's services for relational database access), then they can be used independently of the persistence subsystem, for any occasion when the developer is using JDBC. Therefore, it is better to migrate these types into a separate package, such as *com.foo.util.jdbc*. Figure 31.2 illustrates.

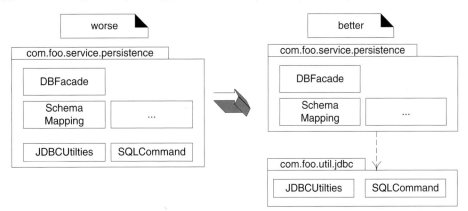

Figure 31.2 Factoring out independent types.

Guideline: Use Factories to Reduce Dependency on Concrete Packages

One way to increase package stability is to reduce its dependency on concrete classes in other packages. Figure 31.3 illustrates the "before" situation.

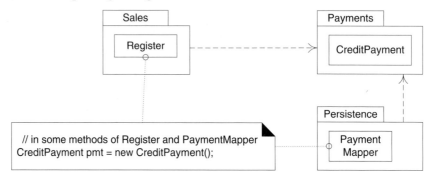

Figure 31.3 Direct coupling to concrete package due to creation.

Suppose that both *Register* and *PaymentMapper* (a class that maps payment objects to/from a relational database) create instances of *CreditPayment* from package *Payments*. One mechanism to increase the long-term stability of the *Sales* and *Persistence* packages is to stop explicitly creating concrete classes defined in other packages (*CreditPayment* in *Payments*).

We can reduce the coupling to this concrete package by using a factory object that creates the instances, but whose create methods return objects declared in terms of interfaces rather than classes. See Figure 31.4.

Domain Object Factory Pattern

The use of domain object factories with interfaces for the creation of *all* domain objects is a common design idiom. I have seen it mentioned informally in design literature as the Domain Object Factory pattern, but do not know of a reference to it formally written as a pattern.

Guideline: No Cycles in Packages

If a group of packages have cyclic dependency then they may need to be treated as one larger package in terms of a release unit. This is undesirable because releasing larger packages (or package aggregates) increases the likelihood of affecting something.

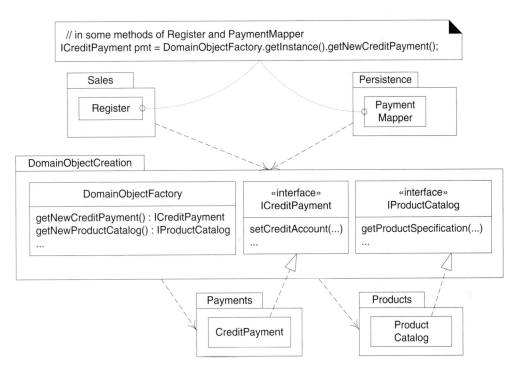

Figure 31.4 Reduced coupling to a concrete package by using a factory object.

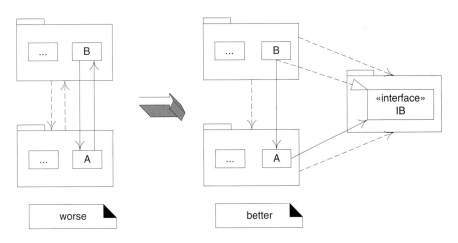

Figure 31.5 Breaking a cyclic dependency.

There are two solutions:

1. Factor out the types participating in the cycle into a new smaller package.

2. Break the cycle with an interface.

The steps to break the cycle with an interface are:

1. Redefine the depended-on classes in one of the packages to implement new interfaces.

2. Define the new interfaces in a new package.

3. Redefine the dependent types to depend on the interfaces in the new package, rather than the original classes.

Figure 31.5 illustrates this strategy.

31.2   More UML Package Notation

Finally, while on the subject of packages, the UML provides alternate notation to illustrate outer and inner packages. Sometimes it is awkward to draw an outer package box around inner packages. Alternatives are shown in Figure 31.6.

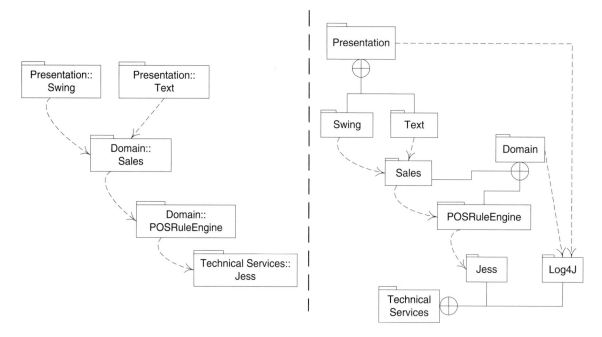

Figure 31.6 Alternate UML approaches to showing packages structure, using UML path names, or the circle-cross symbol.

31.3 Further Readings

Most of the detailed work—not surprisingly—on improving package design to reduce dependency impact comes from the C++ community, although the principles apply to other languages. Martin's *Designing Object-Oriented C++ Applications Using the Booch Method* [Martin95] provides good coverage, as does *Large-Scale C++ Software Design* [Lakos96]. The subject is also introduced in *Java 2 Performance and Idiom Guide* [GL99].

INTRODUCTION TO ARCHITECTURAL ANALYSIS AND THE SAD

Error, no keyboard - press F1 to continue.

—early PC BIOS message

Objectives

- Create architectural factor tables.

- Create technical memos that record architectural decisions.

- Know basic principles of architectural design.

- Know resources for learning architectural patterns.

Introduction

The essence of architectural analysis is to identify factors which should influence the architecture, understand their variability and priority, and resolve them. The difficult part is knowing what questions to ask, weighing the trade-offs, and knowing the many ways to resolve an architecturally significant factor, ranging from benign neglect, to fancy designs, to third-party products.

In the UP, the architectural factors are recorded in the Supplementary Specification, and the architectural decisions that resolve them are recorded in the **Software Architecture Document** (SAD, described in more detail near the end of this chapter).

Architectural analysis starts early, during the inception phase, and is a focus of the elaboration phase; it is a high-priority and very influential activity in software development. The topic was deferred until this point of the book so that fundamentals of OOA/D could be first presented. It is a useful activity to:

- reduce the risk of missing something centrally important in the design of the systems

- avoid applying excessive effort to low priority issues

- help align the product with business goals

This chapter is an introduction to basic steps and ideas in architectural analysis from a UP perspective; that is, to the method, rather than to tips and tricks of master architects. Thus, it is not a cookbook of architectural solutions—a large and context-dependent subject that is beyond the scope of this introductory book. Nevertheless, the NextGen POS case study comments in the chapter do provide concrete examples of architectural solutions.

32.1   Architectural Analysis

Architectural analysis is concerned with the identification and resolution of the system's non-functional (for example, quality) requirements, in the context of the functional requirements.

In the UP, the term encompasses both architectural investigation (identification) and architectural design (resolution). Here are some examples of the many issues to be identified and resolved at an architectural level:

- How do reliability and fault-tolerance requirements affect the design?

  - For example, in the NextGen POS, for what remote services (e.g., tax calculator) will fail-over to local services be allowed? Why? Do they provide exactly the same services locally as remotely, or are there differences?

- How do the licensing costs of purchased subcomponents affect profitability?

  - For example, the producer of the excellent database server, *Clueless,* wants 2% of each NextGen POS sale, if their product is used as a subcomponent. Using their product will speed development (and time to market) because it is robust and provides many services, and many developers know it, but at a price. Should the team instead use the less robust, open source *YourSQL* database server? At what risk? How does it restrict the ability to charge for the NextGen product?

- How does distribution of services affect the quality requirements and functional requirements?

  - For example, using a remote (single, centralized) tax calculator reduces the footprint of each NextGen client, reduces licensing fees (only one copy is needed), and minimizes the custom configuration effort (each installation requires weekly adjustment due to changing government and business policies). However, the remote service reduces response time sufficiently that taxes can only be calculated once, after all line items have been entered; one cannot see a running total with taxes after each line item entry; and the remote call takes too long. It also creates a single point of failure.

- How do the adaptability and configurability requirements affect the design?

  ○ For example, most retailers have variations in business rules they want represented in their POS applications. What are the variations? What is the "best" way to design for them? What is the criteria for best? Can NextGen make more money by requiring customized programming for each customer (and how much effort will that be?), or with a solution that allows the customer to add the customization easily themselves? Should "more money" be the goal in the short-run?

Common Steps in Architectural Analysis

There are several methods of architectural analysis. Common to most of these is some variation of the following steps:

1. Identify and analyze the non-functional requirements that have an impact on the architecture. Functional requirements are also relevant (especially in terms of variability or change), but the non-functional are given thorough attention. In general, all these may be called **architectural factors** (also known as the **architectural drivers**).

   ○ This step could be characterized as regular requirements analysis, but since it is done in the context of identifying architectural impact and deciding high-level architectural solutions, it is considered a part of architectural analysis in the UP.

   ○ In terms of the UP, some of these requirements will be roughly identified and recorded in the Supplementary Specification or use cases during inception. During architectural analysis, which occurs in early elaboration, the team investigates these requirements more closely.

2. For those requirements with a significant architectural impact, analyze alternatives and create solutions that resolve the impact. These are **architectural decisions**.

   ○ Decisions range from "remove the requirement," to a custom solution, to "stop the project," to "hire an expert."

This presentation introduces these basic steps in the context of the NextGen POS case study. For simplicity, it avoids architectural deployment issues such as the hardware and operating system configuration, which are very context and time sensitive.

32.2   Types and Views of Architecture

Some descriptions of architecture define different types, such as the "application architecture" (allocation of features to components) or "system architecture" (hardware and operating system configuration).

In the UP, there is a similar specialization of information, but these are described in "views" of the architecture, which summarize and emphasize a particular perspective. For example, the **logical view** of the architecture, which was introduced in Chapter 30, summarizes the organization and functionality of the major software elements (such as the layers)—it is similar to the term application architecture. The **deployment view** summarizes the system topology, communications, and mapping of executable elements to processing nodes—it is similar to the term system architecture.

The UP defines six views of the architecture, which are described in detail near the end of this chapter. Concretely, the views combine text and diagrams, and—if described at all—are recorded in the SAD.

Architectural analysis is related to the architectural views because the architectural decisions are reflected in, and described in, one or more architectural views.

32.3   The Science: Identification and Analysis of Architectural Factors

Architectural Factors

Any and all of the FURPS+ requirements may have a significant influence on the architecture of a system, ranging from reliability, to schedule, to skills, and to cost constraints. For example, a case of tight schedule with limited skills and sufficient money probably favors buying or outsourcing to specialists, rather than building all components in-house.

However, the factors with the strongest architectural influence tend to be within the high-level FURPS+ categories of functionality, reliability, performance, supportability, implementation, and interface (see Chapter 5 for a detailed breakdown). Interestingly, it is usually the non-functional quality attributes (such as reliability or performance) that give a particular architecture its unique flavor, rather than its functional requirements. For example, the design in the Next-Gen system to support different third-party components with unique interfaces, and the design to support easily plugging in different sets of business rules.

In the UP, these factors with architectural implications are called **architecturally significant requirements**. "Factors" is used here for brevity.

Many technical and organizational factors can be characterized as *constraints* that restrict the solution in some way (such as, must run on Linux, or, the budget for purchasing third-party components is X).

Quality Scenarios

When defining quality requirements during architectural factor analysis, **quality scenarios**[1] are recommended, as they define measurable (or at least observable) responses, and thus can be verified. It is not much use to vaguely state "the system will be easy to modify" without some measure of what that means.

Quantifying some things, such as performance goals and mean time between failure, are well known practices, but quality scenarios extend this idea and encourages recording all (or at least, most) factors as measurable statements.

Quality scenarios are short statements of the form <stimulus> <measurable response>; for example:

- When the completed sale is sent to the remote tax calculator to add the taxes, the result is returned within 2 seconds "most" of the time, measured in a production environment under "average" load conditions.

- When a bug report arrives from a NextGen beta test volunteer, reply with a phone call within 1 working day.

Note that "most" and "average" will need further investigation and definition by the NextGen architect; a quality scenario is not really valid until it is testable, which implies fully specified. Also, observe the qualification in the first quality scenario in terms of the environment to which it applies. It does little good to specify a quality scenario, verify that it passes in a lightly loaded development environment, but fail to evaluate it in a realistic production environment.

Pick Your Battles

A caution: Writing these quality scenarios can be a mirage of usefulness. It's easy to *write* these detailed specifications, but not to realize them. Will anyone ever really test them? How and by whom? A strong dose of realism is required when writing these; there's no point in listing many sophisticated goals if no one will ever really follow through on testing them.

There is a relationship here to the "pick your battles" discussion that was presented in an earlier chapter on the Protected Variations pattern. What are the really critical make-or-break quality scenarios? For example, in an airline reservation system, consistently fast transaction completion under very high load conditions is truly critical to the success of the system—it must definitely be

---

1. A term used in various architectural methods promoted by the Software Engineering Institute (SEI); for example, in the *Architecture Based Design* method.

tested. In the NextGen system, the application really must be fault-tolerant and fail over to local replicated services when the remote ones fail—it must definitely be properly tested and validated. Therefore, focus on writing quality scenarios for the important battles, and follow through with a plan for their evaluation.

Describing Factors

One important goal of architectural analysis is to understand the influence of the factors, their priorities, and their variability (immediate need for flexibility and future evolution). Therefore, most architectural methods (for example, see [HNS00]) advocate creating a table or tree with variations of the following information (the format varies depending on the method). The following style shown in Table 32.1 is called a **factor table**, which in the UP is part of the Supplementary Specification.

Factor	Measures and quality scenarios	Variability (current flexibility and future evolution)	Impact of factor (and its variability) on stakeholders, architecture and other factors	Priority for Success	Difficulty or Risk
Reliability—Recoverability					
Recovery from remote service failure	When a remote service fails, reestablish connectivity with it within 1 minute of its detected re-availability, under normal store load in a production environment.	current flexibility - our SME says local client-side simplified services are acceptable (and desirable) until reconnection is possible. evolution - within 2 years, some retailers may be willing to pay for full local replication of remote services (such as the tax calculator). Probability? High.	High impact on the large-scale design. Retailers really dislike it when remote services fail, as it prevents or restricts them from using a POS to make sales.	H	M
...	...	...	...		

Table 32.1 Sample factor table. Legend: H-high. M-medium. SME-subject matter expert.

Notice the categorization scheme: *Reliability—Recoverability* (from the FURPS+ categories). This isn't presented as the best or only scheme, but it is useful to group architectural factors into categories. For example, certain categories (such as reliability and performance) strongly relate to identifying and defining test plans, and thus it is useful to group them.

The basic priority and risk code values of H/M/L are simply suggestive of using some codes the team finds useful; there are a variety of coding schemes (numeric and qualitative) from different architectural methods and standards (such as ISO 9126). A caution: If the extra effort of using a more complex scheme does not lead to any practical action, it isn't worthwhile.

Factors and UP Artifacts

The central functional requirements repository in the UP are the use cases, and they, along with the Vision and Supplementary Specification, are an important source of inspiration when creating a factor table. In the use cases, the *Special Requirements*, *Technology Variations*, and *Open Issues* should be reviewed, and their implied or explicit architectural factors consolidated in the Supplementary Specification.

It is reasonable to at first record use-case related factors with the use case during its creation, because of the obvious relationship, but it is ultimately more convenient (in terms of content management, tracking, and readability) to consolidate all the architectural factors in one location—in the factor table in the Supplementary Specification.

Use Case UC1: Process Sale

Main Success Scenario:
1. ...
Special Requirements:
– Credit authorization response within 30 seconds 90% of the time.
– Somehow, we want robust recovery when access to remote services such the inventory system is failing.
– . . .
Technology and Data Variations List:
2a. Item identifier entered by bar code laser scanner (if bar code is present) or keyboard.
....
Open Issues:
– What are the tax law variations?
– Explore the remote service recovery issue.

32.4   Example: Partial NextGen POS Architectural Factor Table

The partial factor table in Table 32.2 shows some factors related to later discussion.

Factor	Measures and quality scenarios	Variability (current flexibility and future evolution)	Impact of factor (and its variability) on stakeholders, architecture and other factors	Priority for Success	Difficulty or Risk
Reliability—Recoverability					
Recovery from remote service failure	When a remote service fails, reestablish connectivity with it within 1 minute of its detected re-availability, under normal store load in a production environment.	current flexibility - our SME says local client-side simplified services are acceptable (and desirable) until reconnection is possible. evolution - within 2 years, some retailers may be willing to pay for full local replication of remote services (such as the tax calculator). Probability? High.	High impact on the large-scale design. Retailers really dislike it when remote services fail, as it prevents them from using a POS to make sales.	H	M
Recovery from remote product database failure	as above	current flexibility - our SME says local client-side use of cached "most common" product info is acceptable (and desirable) until reconnection is possible. evolution - within 3 years, client-side mass storage and replication solutions will be cheap and effective, allowing permanent complete replication and thus local usage. Probability? High.	as above	H	M
Supportability - Adaptability					
Support many third-party services (tax calculator, inventory, HR, accounting). They will vary at each installation.	When a new third-party system must be integrated, it can be, and within 10 person days of effort.	current flexibility - as described by factor evolution - none	Required for product acceptance. Small impact on design.	H	L
Support wireless PDA terminals for the POS client?	When support is added, it does not require a change to the design of the non-UI layers of the architecture.	current flexibility - not required at present evolution - within 3 years, we think the probability is very high that wireless "PDA" POS clients will be desired by the market.	High design impact in terms of protected variation from many elements. For example, the operating systems and UIs are different on small devices.	L	H
Other - Legal					
Current tax rules must be applied.	When the auditor evaluates conformance, 100% conformance will be found. When tax rules change, they will be operational within the period allowed by government.	current flexibility - conformance is inflexible, but tax rules can change almost weekly because of the many rules and levels of government taxation (national, state, ...) evolution - none	Failure to comply is a criminal offense. Impacts tax calculation services. Difficult to write our own service--complex rules, constant change, need to track all levels of government. But, easy/low risk if buy a package.	H	L

Table 32.2 Partial factor table for the NextGen architectural analysis.

32.5   The Art: Resolution of Architectural Factors

One could say the *science* of architecture is the collection and organization of information about the architectural factors, as in the factor table. The *art* of architecture is making skillful choices to resolve these factors, in light of trade-offs, interdependencies, and priorities.

Adept architects have knowledge in a variety of areas (for example, architectural styles and patterns, technologies, products, pitfalls, and trends) and apply this to their decisions.

Recording Architectural Alternatives, Decisions, and Motivation

Ignoring for now principles of architectural decision-making, virtually all architectural methods recommend keeping a record of alternative solutions, decisions, influential factors, and motivations for the noteworthy issues and decisions.

Such records have been called **technical memos** [Cunningham96], **issue cards** [HNS00], and **architectural approach documents** (SEI architectural proposals), with varying degrees of formality and sophistication. In some methods, these memos are the basis for yet another step of review and refinement.

In the UP, the memos should be recorded in the SAD.

An important aspect of the technical memo is the *motivation* or rationale. When a future developer or architect needs to modify the system,[2] it is immensely helpful to understand the motivations behind the design, such as *why* a particular approach to recovery from remote service failure in the NextGen POS was chosen and others rejected, in order to make informed decisions about changing the system.

Explaining the rationale of rejecting the alternatives is important, as during future product evolution, an architect may reconsider these alternatives, or at least want to know what alternatives were considered, and why one was chosen.

A sample technical memo follows that records an architectural decision for the NextGen POS. The exact format is, of course, not important. Keep it simple and just record information that will help the future reader make an informed decision when changing the system.

---

2. Or when four weeks have passed and the original architect has forgotten their own rationale!

Technical Memo
Issue: Reliability—Recovery from Remote Service Failure

Solution Summary: Location transparency using service lookup, failover from remote to local, and local service partial replication.

Factors

- Robust recovery from remote service failure (e.g., tax calculator, inventory)
- Robust recovery from remote product (e.g., descriptions and prices) database failure

Solution

Achieve protected variation with respect to location of services using an Adapter created in a Services-Factory. Where possible, offer local implementations of remote services, usually with simplified or constrained behavior. For example, the local tax calculator will use constant tax rates. The local product information database will be a small cache of the most common products. Inventory updates will be stored and forwarded at reconnection.

See also the *Adaptability—Third-Party Services* technical memo for the adaptability aspects of this solutions, because remote service implementations will vary at each installation.

To satisfy the quality scenarios of reconnection with the remote services ASAP, use smart Proxy objects for the services, that on each service call test for remote service reactivation, and redirect to them when possible.

Motivation

Retailers really don't want to stop making sales! Therefore, if the NextGen POS offers this level of reliability and recovery, it will be a very attractive product, as none of our competitors provide this capability. The small product cache is motivated by very limited client-side resources. The real third-party tax calculator is not replicated on the client primarily because of the higher licensing costs, and configuration efforts (as each calculator installation requires almost weekly adjustments). This design also supports the evolution point of future customers willing and able to permanently replicate services such as the tax calculator to each client terminal.

Unresolved Issues

Alternatives Considered

A "gold level" quality of service agreement with remote credit authorization services to improve reliability. It was available, but much too expensive.

Note as illustrated in this example—and this is a key point—that an architectural decision described in one technical memo may resolve a group of factors, not only one.

Priorities

There is a hierarchy of goals that guides architectural decisions:

1. Inflexible constraints, including safety and legal compliance.
   o The NextGen POS must correctly apply tax policies.

2. Business goals.

   ○ Demo of noteworthy features ready for the POSWorld trade show in Hamburg in 18 months.

   ○ Has qualities and features attractive to department stores in Europe (for example, multi-currency support and customizable business rules).

3. All other goals

   ○ These can often be traced back to directly stated business goals, but are indirect. For example, "easily extendible: can add <some unit of functionality> in 10 person weeks" could trace to a business goal of "new release every six months."

In the UP, many of these goals are recorded in the Vision artifact. Mind that the *Priority for Success* scores in the factor table should reflect the priority of these goals.

There is a distinguishing aspect of decision-making at this level vs. small-scale object design: one has to simultaneously consider more (and often globally influential) goals and their trade-offs. Furthermore, the business goals become central to the technical decisions (or at least they should). For example:

Technical Memo
Issue: Legal—Tax Rule Compliance

Solution Summary: Purchase a tax calculator component.

Factors

■ Current tax rules must be applied, by law.

Solution

Purchase a tax calculator with a licensing agreement to receive ongoing tax rule updates. Note that different calculators may be used at different installations.

Motivation

Time-to-market, correctness, low maintenance requirements, and happy developers (see alternatives). These products are costly, which affects our cost-containment and product pricing business goals, but the alternative is considered unacceptable.

Unresolved Issues

What are the leading products and their qualities?

Alternatives Considered

Build one by the NextGen team? It is estimated to take too long, be error prone, and create an ongoing costly and uninteresting (to the company's developers) maintenance responsibility, which affects the goal of "happy developers" (surely, the most important goal of all).

Priorities and Evolution Points: Under- and Over-engineering

Another distinguishing feature of architectural decision-making is prioritization by probability of **evolution points**—points of variability or change that *may* arise in the future. For example, in NextGen, there is a chance that wireless handheld client terminals will become desirable. Designing for this has a significant impact because of differences in operating systems, user interface, hardware resources, and so forth.

The company could spend a huge amount of money (and increase a variety of risks) to achieve this "future proofing." If it turns out in the future that this was not relevant, doing it would be a very expensive exercise in over-engineering. Note also that future proofing is arguably rarely perfect, since it is speculation; even if the predicted change occurs, some change in the speculated design is likely.

On the other hand, future proofing against the Y2K date problem would have been money very well spent; instead, there was under-engineering with a wickedly expensive result.

> The art of the architect is knowing what battles are worth fighting—where it's worth investing in designs that provide protection against evolutionary change.

To decide if early "future-proofing" should be avoided, realistically consider the scenario of deferring the change to the future, when it is called for. How much of the design and code will actually have to change? What will be the effort? Perhaps a close look at the potential change will reveal that what was at first considered a gigantic issue to protect against, is estimated to consume only a few person-weeks of effort.

This is just a hard problem; "Prediction is very difficult, especially if it's about the future" (unverifiably attributed to Niels Bohr).

Basic Architectural Design Principles

The core design principles explored in much of this book that were applicable to small-scale object design are still dominant principles at the large-scale architectural level:

- low coupling
- high cohesion
- protected variation (interfaces, indirection, service lookup, and so forth)

However, the granularity of the components is larger—it is low coupling between applications, subsystems, or process rather than between small objects.

Furthermore, at this larger scale, there are more or different mechanisms to achieve qualities such as low coupling and protected variation. For example, consider this technical memo:

Technical Memo
Issue: Adaptability—Third-Party Services

Solution Summary: Protected Variation using interfaces and Adapters

Factors

■ Support many and changeable third-party services (tax calculators, credit authorization, inventory, ...)

Solution

Achieve protected variation as follows: Analyze several commercial tax calculator products (and so forth for the other product categories) and construct common interfaces for the lowest common denominators of functionality. Then use Indirection via the Adapter pattern. That is, create a resource Adapter object that implements the interface and acts as connection and translator to a particular back-end tax calculator.

See also the *Reliability—Recovery from Remote Service Failure* technical memo for the location transparency aspects of this solution.

Motivation

Simple. Cheaper, and faster communication than using a messaging service (see alternatives), and in any event a messaging service can't be used to directly connect to the external credit authorization service.

Unresolved Issues

Will the lowest common denominator interfaces create an unforeseen problem, such as too limited?

Alternatives Considered

Apply indirection by using a messaging or publish-subscribe service (e.g., a JMS implementation) between the client and tax calculator, with adapters. But not directly usable with a credit authorizer, costly (for reliable ones), and more reliability in message delivery than is practically needed.

The point is that at the architectural level, there are usually new mechanisms to achieve protected variation (and other goals), often in collaboration with third-party components, such as using a Java Messaging Service (JMS) or EBJ server.

Separation of Concerns and Localization of Impact

Another basic principle applied during architectural analysis is to achieve a **separation of concerns**. It is also applicable at the scale of small objects, but achieves prominence during architectural analysis.

Cross-cutting concerns are those with a wide application or influence in the system, such as data persistence or security. One *could* design persistence support in the NextGen application such that each object (that contained application logic code) itself also communicated with a database to save its data. This would weave the concern of persistence in with the concern of application logic, in the source code of the classes—so too with security. Cohesion drops and coupling rises.

In contrast, designing for a separation of concerns factors out persistence support and security support into separate "things" (there are very different mechanisms for this separation). An object with application logic just has application logic, not persistence or security logic. Similarly, a persistence subsystem focuses on the concern of persistence, not security. A security subsystem doesn't do persistence.

Separation of concerns is a large-scale way of thinking about low coupling and high cohesion at an architectural level. It also applies to small-scale objects, because its absence results in incohesive objects that have multiple areas of responsibility. But it is especially an architectural issue because the concerns are broad, and the solutions involve major, fundamental design choices.

There are at least three large-scale techniques to achieve a separation of concerns:

1. Modularize the concern into a separate component (for example, subsystem) and invoke its services.

   ○ This is the most common approach. For example, in the NextGen system, the persistence support could be factored into a subsystem called the *persistence service*. Via a facade, it can offer a public interface of services to other components. Layered architectures also illustrate this separation of concerns.

2. Use decorators.

   ○ This is the second most common approach; first popularized in the Microsoft Transaction Service, and afterwards with EJB servers. In this approach, the concern (such as security) is decorated onto other objects with a Decorator object that wraps the inner object and interposes the service. The Decorator is called a **container** in EJB terminology. For example, in the NextGen POS system, security control to remote services such as the HR system can be achieved with an EJB container that adds security checks in the outer Decorator, around the application logic of the inner object.

3. Use post-compilers and aspect-oriented technologies.

   ○ For example, with EJB entity beans one can add persistence support to classes such as *Sale*. One specifies in a property descriptor file the persistence characteristics of the *Sale* class. Then, a post-compiler (by which I mean another compiler that executes after the "regular" compiler) will add the necessary persistence support in a modified *Sale* class (modifying just the bytecode) or subclass. The developer continues to see the original class as a "clean" application-logic-only class. Another variation is **aspect-oriented** technologies such as AspectJ (www.aspectj.org), which similarly support post-compilation weaving in of cross-cutting concerns into the code, in a manner that is transparent to the developer. These approaches maintain the illusion of separation during development work, and weave in the concern before execution.

Promotion of Architectural Patterns

An exploration of architectural patterns and how they could apply (or misapply) to the NextGen case study is out of scope in this introductory text. However, a few pointers:

Probably the most common mechanism to achieve low coupling, protected variation, and a separation of concerns at the architectural level is the Layers pattern, which has been introduced a previous chapter. This is an example of the most common separation technique—modularizing concerns into separate components or layers.

There is a large and growing body of written architectural patterns. Studying these is the fastest way I know of to learn architectural solutions. Please see the recommended readings.

32.6   Summary of Themes in Architectural Analysis

One theme to note is that "architectural" concerns are especially related to non-functional requirements, and include an awareness of the business or market context of the application. At the same time, the functional requirements (for example, processing sales) cannot be ignored; they provide the context within which these concerns must be resolved. Further, identification of their variability is architecturally significant.

A second theme is that architectural concerns involve system-level, large-scale, and broad problems whose resolution usually involves large-scale or fundamental design decisions; for example, the choice of—or even use of—an application server.

A third theme in architectural analysis is interdependencies and trade-offs. For example, improved security may affect performance or usability, and most choices affect cost.

A fourth theme in architecture analysis is the generation and evaluation of alternative solutions. A skilled architect can offer design solutions that involve building new software, and also suggest solutions (or partial solutions) using commercial or publicly available software and hardware. For example, recovery in a remote server of the NextGen POS can be achieved through designing and programming "watchdog" processes, or perhaps through clustering, replication, and failover services offered by some operating system and hardware components. Good architects know third-party hardware and software products.

The opening definition of architectural concerns provides the framework for how to think about the subject of architecture: identifying the issues with large-scale or system-level implications, and resolving them.

> Architectural analysis is concerned with the identification and resolution of the system's non-functional (e.g., quality) requirements, in the context of the functional requirements.

32.7   Architectural Analysis within the UP

Caution: Waterfall Architectural Analysis

Architectural analysis methods and books often implicitly encourage waterfall-style extensive architectural design decisions before implementation. In iterative development and UP, apply these ideas in the context of small steps, feedback, and adaptation, rather than attempting to fully resolve the architecture before programming. Tackle implementation of the riskiest or most difficult solutions in early iterations, and adjust the architectural solutions based on feedback and growing insight.

Architectural Information in the UP Artifacts

- The architectural factors (for example, in a factor table) are recorded in the Supplementary Specification.
- The architectural decisions are recorded in the SAD. This includes the technical memos and descriptions of the architectural views.

The SAD and Its Architectural Views

In addition to the UML package, class, and interaction diagrams, another key artifact in the UP Design Model is the SAD. It describes the big ideas in the architecture, including the decisions of architectural analysis. Practically, it is a *learning aid* for developers who need to understand the essential ideas of the system.

When someone joins the team, a project coach can say, "Welcome to the NextGen project! Please go to the project website and read the ten page SAD in order to get an introduction to the major ideas." During a later release, when new people work on the system, the SAD is a key learning aid.

Therefore, it should be written with this audience and goal in mind: What do I need to say (and draw in the UML) that will quickly help someone understand the major ideas in this system?

The essence of the SAD is a summary of the architectural decisions (such as with technical memos) and the UP architectural views.

Architectural Views in the SAD

Having an architecture is one thing; describing it is something else.

In [Kruchten95], the influential idea of describing an architecture with multiple views was promoted. The essential idea of an **architectural view** is this:

Architectural View

A view of the system architecture from a given perspective; focuses primarily on structure, modularity, essential components, and the main control flows. [RUP].

An important aspect of the view missing from this RUP definition is the *motivation*. That is, an architectural view should explain why the architecture is the way it is.

An architectural view is a window onto the system from a particular perspective that emphasizes the key noteworthy information or ideas, and ignores the rest.

An architectural view is a tool of communication, education, or thought; it is expressed in text and UML diagrams.

In the UP, six views of the architecture are suggested (more are allowed, such as a security view).[3] All are optional, but documenting at least the logical, process, use case, and deployment views is recommended. The six views are:

1. **Logical**

   ○ Conceptual organization of the software in terms of the most important layers, subsystems, packages, frameworks, classes, and interfaces. Also summarizes the functionality of the major software elements, such as each subsystem.

   ○ Shows outstanding use-case realization scenarios (as interaction diagrams) that illustrate key aspects of the system.

   ○ A view onto the UP Design Model, visualized with UML package, class, and interaction diagrams.

---

3. Early versions of the UP described the "4+1" views as defined in [Kruchten95], which evolved into the six views.

2. **Process**

   ○ Processes and threads. Their responsibilities, collaborations, and the allocation of logical elements (layers, subsystems, classes, ...) to them.

   ○ A view onto the UP Design Model, visualized with UML class and interaction diagrams, using the UML process and thread notation.

3. **Deployment**

   ○ Physical deployment of processes and components to processing nodes, and the physical network configuration between nodes.

   ○ A view onto the UP Deployment Model, visualized with UML deployment diagrams. Normally, the "view" is simply the entire model rather than a subset, as all of it is noteworthy. See Chapter 38 for the UML deployment diagram notation.

4. **Data**

   ○ Overview of the persistent data schema, the schema mapping from objects to persistent data (usually in a relational database), the mechanism of mapping from objects to a database, database stored procedures and triggers.

   ○ A view onto the UP Data Model, visualized with UML class diagrams used to describe a data model.

5. **Use case**

   ○ Summary of the most architecturally significant use cases and their non-functional requirements. That is, those use cases that, by their implementation, illustrate significant architectural coverage or that exercise many architectural elements. For example, the *Process Sale* use case, when fully implemented, has these qualities.

   ○ A view onto the UP Use-Case Model, expressed in text and visualized with UML use case diagrams.

6. **Implementation**

   ○ First, a definition of the Implementation Model: In contrast to the other UP models, which are text and diagrams, this "model" *is* the actual source code, executables, and so forth. It has two parts: 1) deliverables, and 2) things that create deliverables (such as source code and graphics). The Implementation Model is all of this stuff, including web pages, DLLs, executables, source code, and so forth, and their organization—such as source code in Java packages, and bytecode organized into JAR files.

   ○ The implementation view is a summary description of the noteworthy organization of deliverables and the things that create deliverables (such as the source code).

○ A view onto the UP Implementation Model, expressed in text and visualized with UML package and component diagrams.

For example, the NextGen package and interaction diagrams shown in Chapter 30 on layering and logical architecture show the big ideas of the logical structure of the software architecture. In the SAD, the architect will create a section called *Logical View*, insert those UML diagrams, and add some written commentary on what each package and layer is for, and the motivation behind the logical design. Likewise with the process and deployment views.

A key idea of the architectural views—which concretely are text and diagrams—is that they do *not* describe *all* of the system from some perspective, but only outstanding ideas from that perspective. A view is, if you will, the "one minute elevator" description: What are the most important things you would say in one minute in an elevator to a colleague on this perspective?

Architectural views may be created:

- after the system is built, as a summary and learning aid for future developers

- at the end of certain iteration milestones (such as the end of elaboration) to serve as a learning aid for the current development team, and new members

- speculatively, during early iterations, as an aid in creative design work, recognizing that the original view will change as design and implementation proceeds

Sample Structure of a SAD

Software Architecture Document

Architectural Representation

(Summary of how the architecture will be described in this document, such as using by technical memos and the architectural views. This is useful for someone unfamiliar with the idea of technical memos or views. Note that not all views are necessary.)

Architectural Factors and Decisions

(Reference to the Supplementary Specification to view the Factor Table. Also, the set of technical memos the summarize the decisions.)

Logical View

(UML package diagrams, and class diagrams of major elements. Commentary on the large scale structure and functionality of major components.)

Process View

(UML class and interaction diagrams illustrating the processes and threads of the system. Group this by threads and processes that interact. Comment on how the interprocess communication works (e.g., by Java RMI).

Use-Case View

(Brief summary of the most architecturally significant use cases. UML interaction diagrams for some architectural significant use-case realizations, or scenarios, with commentary on the diagrams explaining how they illustrate the major architectural elements.)

Deployment View

(UML deployment diagrams showing the nodes and allocation of processes and components. Commentary on the networking.)

Phases

Inception—If it is unclear if it is technically possible to satisfy the architecturally significant requirements, the team may implement an **architectural proof-of-concept** (POC) to determine feasibility. In the UP, its creation and assessment is called **Architectural Synthesis**. This is distinct from plain old small POC programming experiments for isolated technical questions. An architectural POC lightly covers *many* of the architecturally significant requirements to assess their *combined* feasibility.

Elaboration—A major goal of this phase is to implement the core risky architectural elements, thus most architectural analysis is completed during elaboration. It is normally expected that the majority of factor table, technical memo, and SAD content can be completed by the end of elaboration.

Transition—Although ideally the architecturally significant factors and decisions were resolved long before transition, the SAD will need a review and possible revision at the end of this phase to ensure it accurately describes the final deployed system.

Subsequent evolution cycles—Before the design of new versions, it is common to revisit architectural factors and decisions. For example, the decision in version 1.0 to create a single remote tax calculator service, rather than one duplicated on each POS node, could have been motivated by cost (to avoid multiple licenses). But perhaps in the future the cost of tax calculators is reduced, and thus, for fault tolerance or performance reasons, the architecture is changed to use multiple local tax calculators.

32.8   Further Readings

There is a growing body of architecture-related patterns, and general software architecture advice. Suggestions:

- *Pattern-Oriented Software Architecture*, both volumes.

- *Software Architecture in Practice* [BCK98].

- *Pattern Languages of Program Design*, all volumes. Each volume has a section on architecture-related patterns.

- Online Web articles on architectural patterns (such as J2EE architectures), available at Sun, IBM, and other websites.

- Online Web articles on architecture available at the Carnegie Mellon University Software Engineering Institute (SEI), which has long been a center of architecture investigation (www.sei.cmu.edu).

DESIGNING MORE USE-CASE REALIZATIONS WITH OBJECTS AND PATTERNS

*On two occasions I have been asked (by members of Parliament),
"Pray, Mr. Babbage, if you put into the machine wrong figures, will
the right answers come out?" I am not able rightly to apprehend the
kind of confusion of ideas that could provoke such a question.*

—*Charles Babbage*

Objectives

- Apply GRASP and GoF patterns in the design.

Introduction

This chapter explores some partial designs for the current iteration, handling
requirements such as failover to local services, POS device handling, and payment authorization.

33.1 Failover to Local Services; Performance with Local Caching

One of the NextGen requirements is some degree of recovery from remote service failure, such as a (temporarily) unavailable product database.

Access to product information is the first case used to explore the recovery and failover design strategy. Afterwards, access to the accounting service is explored, which has a slightly different solution.

To review part of the technical memo:

Technical Memo
Issue: Reliability—Recovery from Remote Service Failure

Solution Summary: Location transparency using service lookup, failover from remote to local, and local service partial replication.

Factors

- Robust recovery from remote service failure (e.g., tax calculator, inventory)
- Robust recovery from remote product (e.g., descriptions and prices) database failure

Solution

Achieve protected variation with respect to location of services using the Adapter served up from a ServicesFactory. Where possible, offer local implementations of remote services, usually with simplified or constrained behavior. For example, the local tax calculator will use constant tax rates. The local product information database will be a small cache of the most common products. Inventory updates will be stored and forwarded at reconnection.

See also the *Adaptability—Third-Party Services* technical memo for the adaptability aspects of this solutions, because remote service implementations will vary at each installation.

To satisfy the quality scenarios of reconnection with the remote services, use smart Proxy objects for the services, that on each service call test for remote service reactivation, and redirect to them when possible.

Motivation

Retailers really don't want to stop making sales! Therefore, if the NextGen POS offers this level of reliability and recovery, it will be a very attractive product, as none of our competitors provide this capability.

Before solving the failover and recovery aspects, note that for both performance reasons and to improve recoverability when access to the remote database fails, the architect (me) has recommended a local cache (reliably persisted on the local hard disk in a simple file) of *ProductSpecification* objects. Therefore, the local cache should always be searched for a "cache hit" before attempting a remote access.

This can be neatly achieved with our existing adapter and factory design:

1. The *ServicesFactory* will always return an adapter to a local product information service.

2. The local products "adapter" is not really an adapter to another component. It will itself implement the responsibilities of the local service.

3. The local service is initialized to a reference to a second adapter to the true remote product service.

4. If the local service finds the data in its cache, it returns it; otherwise, it forwards the request to the adapter for the external service.

Note that there are two levels of client-side cache:

1. The in-memory *ProductCatalog* object will maintain an in-memory collection (such as a Java *HashMap*) of some (for example, 1,000) *ProductSpecification* objects that have been retrieved from the product information service. The size of this collection can be adjusted depending on local memory availability.

2. The local products service will maintain a larger persistent (hard disk based) cache that maintains some quantity of product information (such as 1 or 100MB of file space). Again, it can be adjusted depending on the local configuration. This persistent cache is important for fault tolerance, so that even if the POS application crashes and the in-memory cache of the *ProductCatalog* object is lost, the persistent cache remains.

This design does not break existing code—the new local service object is inserted without affecting the design of the *ProductCatalog* object (which collaborates with the product service).

So far, no new patterns have been introduced; Adapter and Factory are used.

Figure 33.1 illustrates the types in the design, and Figure 33.2 illustrates the initialization..

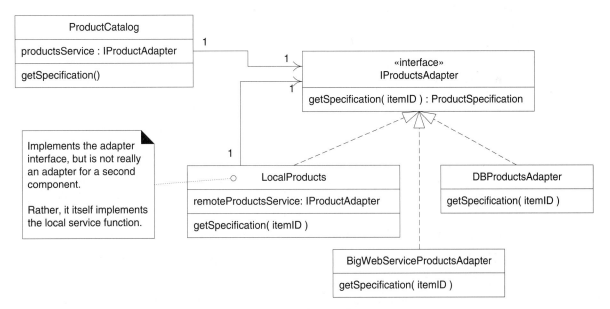

Figure 33.1 Adapters for product information.

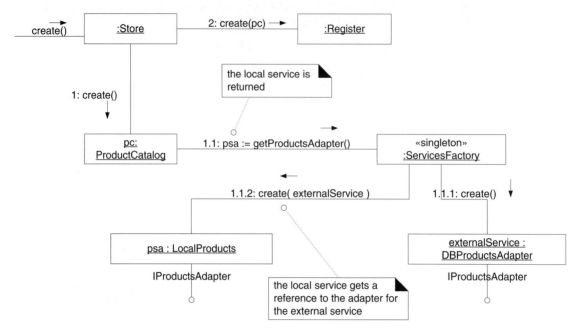

Figure 33.2 Initialization of the product information service.

Figure 33.3 shows the initial collaboration from the catalog to the products service.

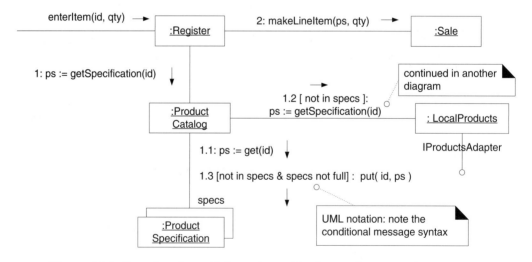

Figure 33.3 Starting the collaboration with the products service.

If the local product service does not have the product in its cache, it collaborates with the adapter to the external service, as shown in Figure 33.4. Note that the local product service caches the *ProductSpecification* objects as true serialized objects.

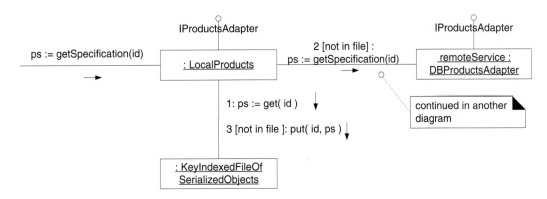

Figure 33.4 Continuing the collaboration for product information.

If the true external service was changed from a database to a new Web service, only the factory's configuration of the remote service needs to change. See Figure 33.5.

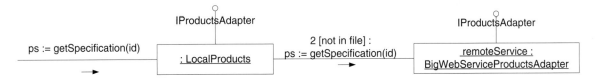

Figure 33.5 New external services do not affect the design.

To continue with the case of collaborating with the *DBProductsAdapter*, it will interact with an object-relational (O-R) mapping persistence subsystem (see Figure 33.6).

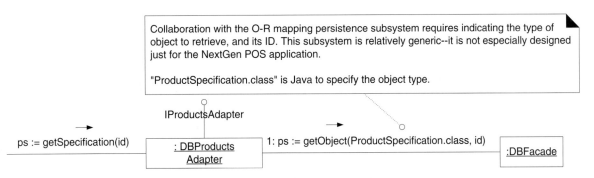

Figure 33.6 Collaboration with the persistence subsystem.

Caching Strategies

Consider the alternatives for loading the in-memory *ProductCatalog* cache and the *LocalProducts* file-based cache: One approach is lazy initialization, in which the caches fill slowly as external product information is retrieved; another approach is eager initialization, in which the caches are loaded during the *StartUp* use case. If the designer is unsure which approach to use and wants to experiment with alternatives, a family of different *CacheStrategy* objects based on the Strategy pattern can neatly solve the problem.

Stale Cache

Since product prices change quickly, and perhaps at the whim of the store manager, caching the product price creates a problem—the cache contains stale data; this is always a concern when data is replicated. One solution is to add a remote service operation that answers today's current changes; the *LocalProducts* object queries it every n minutes and updates its cache.

Threads in the UML

If the *LocalProducts* object is going to solve the stale cache problem with a query for updates every n minutes, one approach to the design is to make it an **active object** that owns a thread of control. The thread will sleep for n minutes, wake up, the object will get the data, and the thread will go back to sleep. The UML provides notation to illustrate threads and asynchronous calls, as shown in Figure 33.7.

In an interaction diagram, an instance of an active object may be tagged with the property *{active}*. In a class diagram, a class of active objects (an **active class**) which owns its own thread can be stereotyped with «thread». See Figure 33.8.

33.2 Handling Failure

The preceding design provides a solution for client-side caching of *Product-Specification* objects in a persistent file, to improve performance, and also to provide at least a partial fall-back solution if the external products service can't be accessed. Perhaps 10,000 products are cached in the local file, which may satisfy most requests for product information even when the external service fails.

What to do in the case where there isn't a local cache hit and access to the external products service fails? Suppose that the stakeholders asked us create a solution that signals the cashier to manually enter the price and description, or cancel the line item entry.

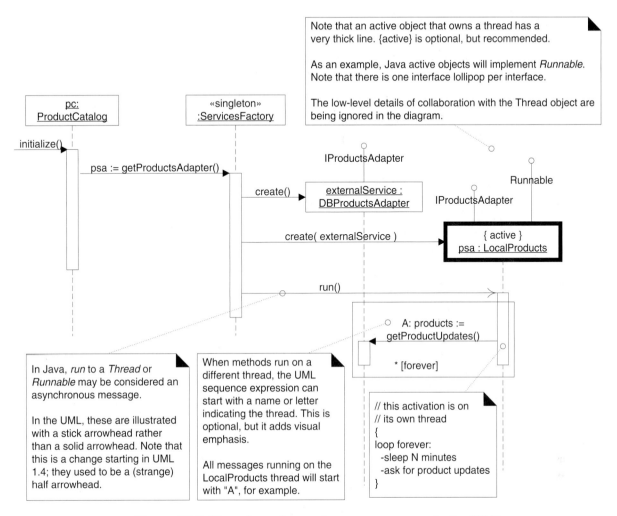

Note that an active object that owns a thread has a very thick line. {active} is optional, but recommended.

As an example, Java active objects will implement *Runnable*. Note that there is one interface lollipop per interface.

The low-level details of collaboration with the Thread object are being ignored in the diagram.

IProductsAdapter

Runnable

IProductsAdapter

pc:
ProductCatalog

«singleton»
:ServicesFactory

initialize()

psa := getProductsAdapter()

create()

externalService :
DBProductsAdapter

create(externalService)

{ active }
psa : LocalProducts

run()

A: products :=
getProductUpdates()

* [forever]

In Java, *run* to a *Thread* or *Runnable* may be considered an asynchronous message.

In the UML, these are illustrated with a stick arrowhead rather than a solid arrowhead. Note that this is a change starting in UML 1.4; they used to be a (strange) half arrowhead.

When methods run on a different thread, the UML sequence expression can start with a name or letter indicating the thread. This is optional, but it adds visual emphasis.

All messages running on the LocalProducts thread will start with "A", for example.

// this activation is on
// its own thread
{
loop forever:
  -sleep N minutes
  -ask for product updates
}

Figure 33.7 Threads and asynchronous messages in the UML.

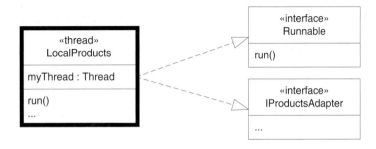

«thread»
LocalProducts

myThread : Thread

run()
...

«interface»
Runnable

run()

«interface»
IProductsAdapter

...

Figure 33.8 Active class notation.

This is an example of an error or failure condition, and it will be used as a context to describe some general patterns in dealing with failures and exception handling. Exception and error handling is a large topic, and this introduction will just focus on some patterns specific to the context of the case study. First, some terminology:

- **Fault**—the ultimate origin or cause of misbehavior.

  ○ Programmer misspelled the name of a database.

- **Error**—a manifestation of the fault in the running system. Errors are detected (or not).

  ○ When calling the naming service to obtain a reference to the database (with the misspelled name), it signals an error.

- **Failure**—a denial of service caused by an error.

  ○ The Products subsystem (and the NextGen POS) fails to provide a product information service.

Throwing Exceptions

A straightforward approach to signaling the failure under consideration is to throw an exception.

> Exceptions are especially appropriate when dealing with resource failures (disk, memory, network or database access, and other external services).

An exception will be thrown from within the persistence subsystem (actually, probably starting from within something like a Java JDBC implementation), where a failure to use the external products database is first detected. The exception will unwind the call stack back up to an appropriate point for its handling.[1]

Suppose that the original exception (using Java as an example) is a *java.sql.SQLException*. Should a *SQLException* per se be thrown all the way up to the presentation layer? No. It is at the wrong level of abstraction. This leads to a common exception handling pattern:

---

1. Checked vs. unchecked exception handling is not covered, as it is not supported in all popular OO languages—C++, C#, and Smalltalk, for example.

> ### Pattern: Convert Exceptions [Brown01]
>
> Within a subsystem, avoid emitting lower level exceptions coming from lower subsystems or services. Rather, convert the lower level exception into one that is meaningful at the level of the subsystem. The higher level exception usually wraps the lower-level exception, and adds information, to make the exception more contextually meaningful to the higher level.
>
> This is a guideline, not an absolute rule.
>
> "Exception" is used here in the vernacular sense of something that can be thrown; in Java, the equivalent is a *Throwable*.
>
> Also known as Exception Abstraction [Renzel97].

For example, the persistence subsystem catches a particular *SQLException*, and (assuming it can't handle it[2]) throws a new *DBUnavailableException*, which contains the *SQLException*. Note that the *DBProductAdapter* is like a facade onto a logical subsystem for product information. Thus, the higher level *DBProductAdapter* (as the representative for a logical subsystem) catches the lower level *DBUnavailableException* and (assuming it can't handle it) throws a new *ProductInfoUnavailableException*, which wraps the *DBUnavailableException*.

Consider the names of these exceptions: Why *DBUnavailableException* rather than, say, *PersistenceSubsystemException*? There is a pattern for this:

> ### Pattern: Name The Problem Not The Thrower [Grosso00]
>
> What to call an exception? Assign a name that describes why the exception is being thrown, not the thrower. The benefit is that it makes it easier for the programmer to understand the problem, and it the highlights the essential similarity of many classes of exceptions (in a way that naming the thrower does not).

Exceptions in the UML

This is an appropriate time to introduce the UML notation for throwing[3] and catching exceptions.

---

2. Resolving an exception near the level at which it was raised is a laudable but difficult goal, because the requirement for how to handle an error is often application-specific.

3. Officially in the UML, one *sends* an exception, but *throws* is a sufficient and more familiar usage.

Two common notation questions in the UML are:

1. In a class diagram, how to show what exceptions a class catches and throws?
2. In an interaction diagram, how to show throwing an exception?

For a class diagram, Figure 33.9 presents the notation:

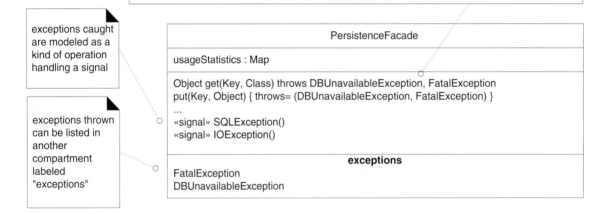

UML notation: The UML has a "default" syntax for operations. But it does not include an official solution to show exceptions thrown by an operation. There are at least three solutions:

1. The UML allows the operation syntax to be any other language, such as Java. In addition, some UML CASE tools allow display of operations explicitly in Java syntax.Thus,

    Object get(Key, Class) throws DBUnavailableException, FatalException

2. The default syntax allows the last element to be a "property string." This is a list of arbitrary property+value pairs, such as { author=Craig, kids=(Hannah, Haley), ...}. Thus,

    put(Object, id) { throws= (DBUnavailableException, FatalException) }

3. Some UML CASE tools allow one to specify (in a special dialog box) the exceptions that an operation throws.

exceptions caught
are modeled as a
kind of operation
handling a signal

exceptions thrown
can be listed in
another
compartment
labeled
"exceptions"

PersistenceFacade
usageStatistics : Map
Object get(Key, Class) throws DBUnavailableException, FatalException put(Key, Object) { throws= (DBUnavailableException, FatalException) } ... «signal» SQLException() «signal» IOException()
exceptions
FatalException DBUnavailableException

Figure 33.9 Exceptions caught and thrown by a class.

In the UML, an *Exception* is a specialization of a *Signal*, which is the specification of an asynchronous communication between objects. This means that in interaction diagrams, exceptions are illustrated as **asynchronous messages**.[4]

---

4. Note that starting in UML 1.4, the notation for an asynchronous message changed from a half arrowhead to a stick arrowhead.

Figure 33.10 shows the notation, using the prior description of *SQLException* translated to *DBUnavailableException* as an example.

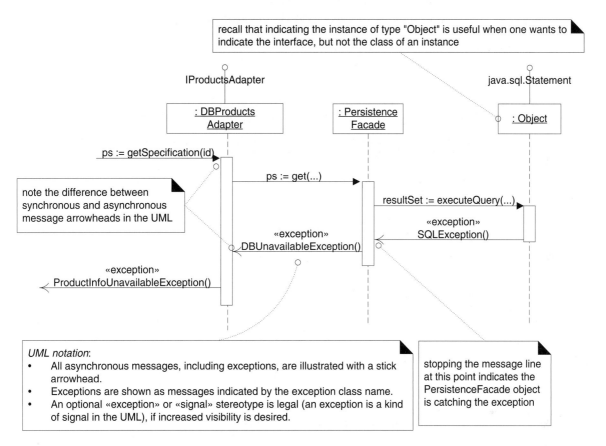

Figure 33.10 Exceptions in an interaction diagram.

In summary, UML notation exists to show exceptions. However, it is rarely used.

This is not a recommendation to avoid early consideration of exception handling. Quite the opposite: At an architectural level, the basic patterns, policies, and collaborations for exception handling need to be established early, because it is awkward to insert exception handling as an afterthought. However, the low-level design of handling particular exceptions is felt by many developers to be most appropriately decided during programming or via less detailed design descriptions, rather than via detailed UML diagrams.

Handling Errors

One side of the design has been considered: throwing exceptions, in terms of converting, naming, and illustrating them. The other side is the handling of an exception.

Two patterns to apply in this and most cases are:

Pattern: Centralized Error Logging [Renzel97]

Use a Singleton-accessed central error logging object and report all exceptions to it. If it is a distributed system, each local singleton will collaborate with a central error logger. Benefits:

- Consistency in reporting.

- Flexible definition of output streams and format.

Also known as Diagnostic Logger [Harrison98].

It is a simple pattern. The second is:

Pattern: Error Dialog [Renzel97]

Use a standard Singleton-accessed, application-independent, non-UI object to notify users of errors. It wraps one or more UI "dialog" objects (such as a GUI modal dialog, text console, sound beeper, or speech generator) and delegates the notification of the error to the UI objects. Thus, output could go to both a GUI dialog and to a speech generator. It will also report the exception to the centralized error logger. A Factory reading from system parameters will create the appropriate UI objects. Benefits:

- Protected Variations with respect to changes in the output mechanism.

- Consistent style of error reporting; for example, all GUI windows can call on this singleton to display the error dialog.

- Centralized control of the common strategy for error notification.

- Minor performance gain; if an "expensive" resource such as a GUI dialog is used, it is easy to hide and cache it for recycled use, rather than recreate a dialog for each error.

Should a UI object (for example, *ProcessSaleFrame*) handle an error by catching the exception and notifying the user? For applications with only a few windows, and simple, stable navigation paths between windows, this straightforward design is fine. This is currently true for the NextGen application.

Keep in mind however, that this places some "application logic" related to error handling in the presentation (GUI) layer. The error handling relates to user notification, so this is logical, but it is a trend to watch. It is not inherently a problem for simple UIs with a low chance of UI replacement, but it is a point of fragility. For example, suppose a team wants to replace a Java Swing UI with the IBM Java MicroView GUI framework for handheld computers. There is now some application logic in the Swing version that has to be identified and replicated in the MicroView version. To some degree, this is inevitable with UI replacements; but it will be aggravated as more application logic migrates upwards. In general, as more non-UI application logic responsibilities migrate to the presentation layer, the probability of design or maintenance headaches increases.

For systems with many windows and complex (perhaps even changing) navigation paths, there are other solutions. For example, an application layer of one or more controllers can be inserted between the presentation and domain layers.

Furthermore, a "view manager mediator" object [GHJV95, BMRSS96] that is responsible for having a reference to all open windows, and knowing the transitions between windows, given some event E1 (such as an error), can be inserted.

This mediator is abstractly a state machine that encapsulates the states (displayed window) and transitions between states, based on events. It may read the state (window) transition model from an external file, so that the navigation paths can be data-driven (source code changes are not necessary). It can also close all the application windows, or tile or minimize them, since it has a reference to all windows.

In this design, an application layer controller may be designed with a reference to this view manager mediator (hence, the application controller is coupled "upwards" to the presentation layer). The application controller may catch the exception and collaborate with the view manager mediator to cause notification (based on the Error Dialog pattern). In this way, the application controller is involved with workflow for the application, and some error logic handling is kept out of the windows.

Detailed UI control and navigation design is outside the scope of this introduction, and the simple design of the window catching the exception will suffice. A design using an Error Dialog is shown in Figure 33.11.

33.3   Failover to Local Services with a Proxy (GoF)

Failover to a local service for the product information was achieved by inserting the local service in front of the external service; the local service is always tried first. However, this design is not appropriate for all services; sometimes the external service should be tried first, and a local version second. For example, consider the posting of sales to the accounting service. Business wants them posted as soon as possible, for real-time tracking of store and register activity.

In this case, another GoF pattern can solve the problem: Proxy. Proxy is a simple pattern, and widely used in its **Remote Proxy** variant. For example, in Java's RMI and in CORBA, a local client-side object (called a "stub") is called upon to access a remote object's services. The client-side stub is a local proxy, or a representative for a remote object.

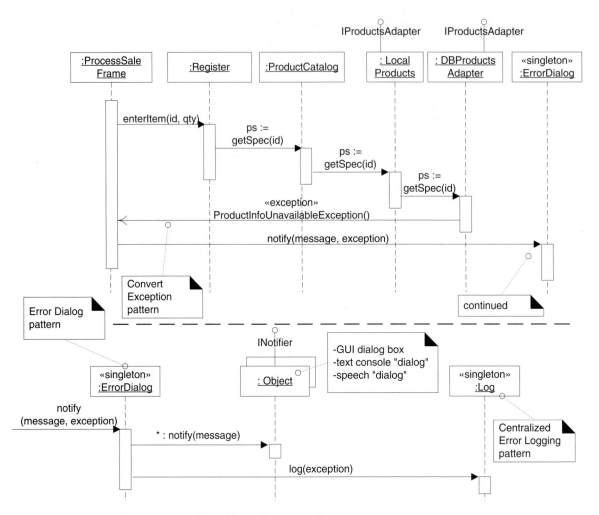

Figure 33.11 Handling the exception.

This NextGen example use of Proxy is not the Remote Proxy variant, but rather the **Redirection Proxy** (also known as a **Failover Proxy**) variant.

Regardless of the variant, the structure of Proxy is always the same; the variations are related to what the proxy does once called.

A proxy is simply an object that implements the same interface as the subject object, holds a reference to the real subject, and is used to control access to it. For the general structure, see Figure 33.12.

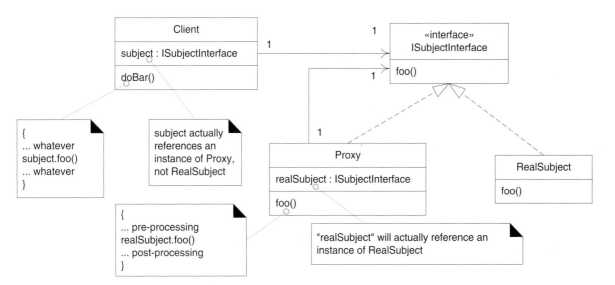

Figure 33.12 General structure of the Proxy pattern.

Applied to the NextGen case study for external accounting service access, a redirection proxy is used as follows:

1. Send a *postSale* message to the redirection proxy, treating it as though it was the actual external accounting service.

2. If the redirection proxy fails to make contact with the external service (via its adapter), then it redirects the *postSale* message to a local service, which locally stores the sales for forwarding to the accounting service, when it is active.

Figure 33.13 illustrates a class diagram of the interesting elements.

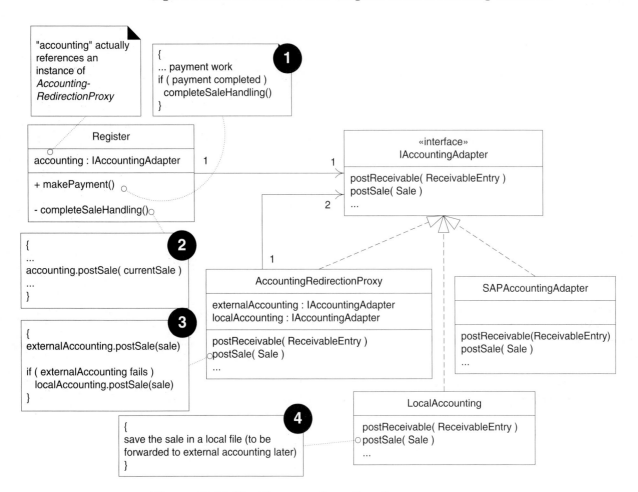

Figure 33.13 NextGen use of a redirection proxy.

UML notation:

- To avoid creating an interaction diagram to show the dynamic behavior, observe how this static diagram uses numbering to convey the sequence of interaction. An interaction diagram is usually preferred, but this style is presented to illustrate an alternative style.

- Observe the public and private (+, -) visibility markers beside *Register* methods. If absent, they are unspecified, rather than defaulting to public or private. However, by common convention, unspecified visibility is interpreted by most readers (and code generating CASE tools) as meaning private attributes and public methods. However, in this diagram, I especially want to convey the fact that *makePayment* is public, and by contrast, *completeSaleHandling* is private. Visual noise and information overload are always concerns in communication, so it is desirable to exploit conventional interpretation to keep the diagrams simple.

To summarize, a proxy is an outer object that wraps an inner object, and both implement the same interface. A client object (such as a *Register*) does not know that it references a proxy—it is designed as though it is collaborating with the real subject (for example, the *SAPAccountingAdapter*). The Proxy intercepts calls in order to enhance access to the real subject, in this case by redirecting the operation to a local service (*LocalAccounting*) if the external service is not accessible.

33.4 Designing for Non-Functional or Quality Requirements

Before moving on to the next section, notice that the design work up to this point in the chapter did not relate to business logic, but to non-functional or quality requirements related to reliability and recovery.

Interestingly—and this a key point in software architecture—it is common that the large-scale themes, patterns, and structures of the software architecture are shaped by the designs to resolve the non-functional or quality requirements, rather than the basic business logic.

33.5 Accessing External Physical Devices with Adapters; Buy vs. Build

Another requirement in this iteration is to interact with physical devices that comprise a POS terminal, such as opening a cash drawer, dispensing change from the coin dispenser, and capturing a signature from the digital signature device.

The NextGen POS must work with a variety of POS equipment, including that sold by IBM, Epson, NCR, Fujitsu, and so forth.

Fortunately, the software architect has done some investigation, and has discovered that there is now an industry standard, UnifiedPOS (www.nrf-arts.org), that defines standard object-oriented interfaces (in the UML sense) for all common POS devices. Furthermore, there is the JavaPOS (www.javapos.com)—a Java mapping of the UnifiedPOS.

Therefore, in the Software Architecture Document, the architect adds a technical memo to communicate this significant architectural choice:

Technical Memo

Issue: POS Hardware Device Control

Solution Summary: Use Java software from the device manufacturers that conforms to the JavaPOS standard interfaces.

Factors

■   Correctly controls the devices

■   Cost to buy vs. build and maintain

Solution

The UnifiedPOS (www.nrf-arts.org) defines an industry standard UML model of interfaces for POS devices. The JavaPOS (www.javapos.com) is an industry standard mapping of UnifiedPOS to Java. POS device manufactures (e.g., IBM, NCR) sell Java implementations of these interfaces that control their devices.

Buy these, rather than build them.

Use a Factory that reads from a system property to load IBM or NCR (etc.) set of classes, and return instances based on their interface.

Motivation

Based on an informal survey, we believe they work well, and the manufacturers have a regular update process for their improvement. It is difficult to get the expertise and other resources to write these ourselves.

Alternatives Considered

Writing them ourselves--difficult and risky.

Figure 33.14 shows some of the interfaces, which have been added as another package of the domain layer in our Design Model.

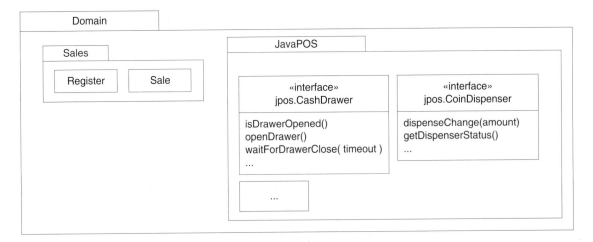

Figure 33.14 Standard JavaPOS interfaces.

Assume that the major manufacturers of POS equipment now provide JavaPOS implementations. For example, if we buy an IBM POS terminal with a cash drawer, coin dispenser, and so forth, we can also get Java classes from IBM that implement the JavaPOS interfaces, and that control the physical devices.

> Consequently, this part of the architecture is resolved by buying software components, rather than building them. Encouraging the use of existing components is one of the UP best practices.

How do they work? At a low level, a physical device has a device driver for the underlying operating system. A Java class (for example, one that implements *jpos.CashDrawer*) uses JNI (Java Native Interface) to make calls out to these device drivers.

> These Java classes adapt the low-level device driver to the JavaPOS interfaces, and thus can be characterized as Adapter objects in the GoF pattern sense. They can also be called Proxy objects—local proxies that control or enhance access to the physical devices.
>
> It is not uncommon to be able to classify a design in terms of multiple patterns.

33.6   Abstract Factory (GoF) for Families of Related Objects

The JavaPOS implementations will be purchased from manufacturers. For example[5]:

```
// IBM's drivers
com.ibm.pos.jpos.CashDrawer (implements jpos.CashDrawer)
com.ibm.pos.jpos.CoinDispenser (implements jpos.CoinDispenser)
...
// NCR's drivers
com.ncr.posdrivers.CashDrawer (implements jpos.CashDrawer)
com.ncr.posdrivers.CoinDispenser (implements jpos.CoinDispenser)
...
```

Now, how to design the NextGen POS application to use the IBM Java drivers if IBM hardware is used, NCR drivers if appropriate, and so forth?

Note that there are families of classes (*CashDrawer+CoinDispenser+...*) that need to be created, and each family implements the same interfaces.

---

5. These are fictitious package names.

For this situation, a commonly used GoF pattern exists: Abstract Factory.

Abstract Factory

Context / Problem

How to create families of related classes that implement a common interface?

Solution

Define a factory interface (the abstract factory). Define a concrete factory class for each family of things to create. Optionally, define a true abstract class that implements the factory interface and provides common services to the concrete factories that extend it.

Figure 33.15 illustrates the basic idea; it is improved upon in the next section.

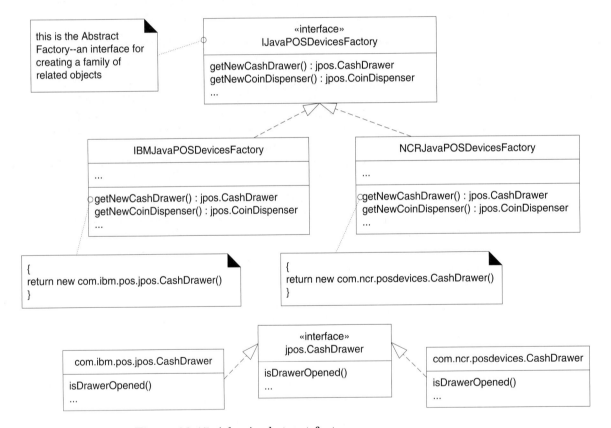

Figure 33.15 A basic abstract factory.

An Abstract Class Abstract Factory

A common variation on Abstract Factory is to create an abstract class factory that is accessed using the Singleton pattern, reads from a system property to decide which of its subclass factories to create, and then returns the appropriate subclass instance. This is used, for example, in the Java libraries with the *java.awt.Toolkit* class, which is an abstract class abstract factory for creating families of GUI widgets for different operating system and GUI subsystems.

The advantage of this approach is that it solves this problem: How does the application know which abstract factory to use? *IBMJavaPOSDevicesFactory*? *NCRJavaPOSDevicesFactory*?

The following refinement solves this problem. Figure 33.16 illustrates the solution.

With this abstract class factory and Singleton pattern *getInstance* method, objects can collaborate with the abstract superclass, and obtain a reference to one of its subclass instances. For example, consider the statement:

```
cashDrawer = JavaPOSDevicesFactory.getInstance().getNewCashDrawer();
```

The expression *JavaPOSDevicesFactory.getInstance()* will return an instance of *IBMJavaPOSDevicesFactory* or *NCRJavaPOSDevicesFactory,* depending on the system property that is read in. Notice that by changing the external system property *"jposfactory.classname"* (which is the class name as a String) in a properties file, the NextGen system will use a different family of JavaPOS drivers. Protected Variations with respect to a changing factory has been achieved with a data-driven (reading a properties file) and reflective programming design, using the *c.newInstance()* expression.

Interaction with the factory will occur in a *Register.* By the goal of low representational gap, it is reasonable for the software *Register* (whose name is suggestive of the overall POS terminal) to hold a reference to devices such as *CashDrawer.* For example:

```
class Register
{
private jpos.CashDrawer cashDrawer;
private jpos.CoinDispenser coinDispenser;

public Register()
{
    cashDrawer =
       JavaPOSDevicesFactory.getInstance().getNewCashDrawer();
    //...
}
//...
}
```

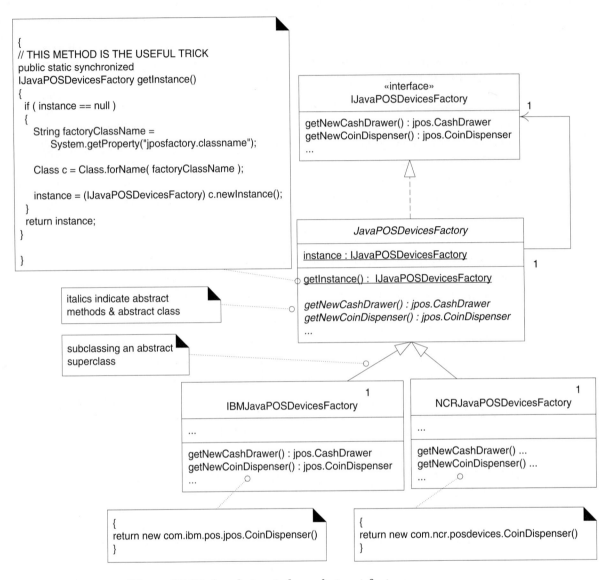

Figure 33.16 An abstract class abstract factory.

33.7   Handling Payments with Polymorphism and Do It Myself

One of the common ways to apply polymorphism (and Information Expert) is in the context of what Peter Coad calls the "Do It Myself" strategy or pattern [Coad95]. That is:

Do It Myself

"I (a software object) do those things that are normally done to the actual object that I'm an abstraction of." [Coad95]

This is the classic object-oriented design style: *Circle* objects draw themselves, *Square* objects draw themselves, *Text* objects spell-check themselves, and so forth.

Notice that a *Text* object spell-checking itself is an example of Information Expert: *The object that has the information related to the work does it* (a *Dictionary* is also a candidate, by Expert).

Do It Myself and Information Expert usually lead to the same choice.

Similarly, notice that *Circle* and *Square* objects drawing themselves are examples of Polymorphism: *When related alternatives vary by type, assign responsibility using polymorphic operations to the types for which the behavior varies.*

Do It Myself and Polymorphism usually lead to the same choice.

Yet, as was explored in the Pure Fabrication discussion, it is often contraindicated due to problems in coupling and cohesion, and instead, a designer uses pure fabrications such as strategies, factories, and the like.

Nevertheless, when appropriate, Do It Myself is attractive in part because of its support for low representational gap. The design for handling payments will be accomplished with Do It Myself and Polymorphism.

One of the requirements for this iteration is to handle multiple payment types, which essentially means to handle the authorization and accounting steps. Different kinds of payments are authorized in different ways:

- Credit and debit payments are authorized with an external authorization service. Both require recording a receivable entry in accounts receivable—money owing from the financial institution that does the authorization.

- Cash payments are authorized in some stores (it is a trend in some countries) using a special paper bill analyzer attached to the POS terminal that checks for counterfeit money. Other stores do not do this.

- Check payments are authorized in some stores using a computerized authorization service. Other stores do not do authorize checks.

CreditPayments are authorized in one way; *CheckPayments* are authorized in another. This is a classic case for Polymorphism.

Thus, as shown in Figure 33.17, each *Payment* subclass has its own *authorize* method.

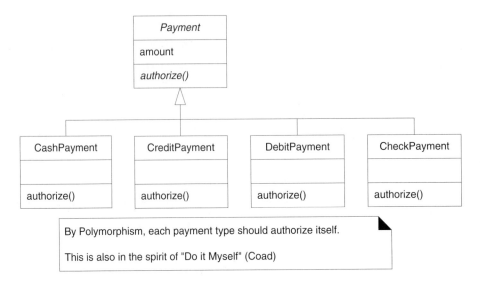

Figure 33.17 Classic polymorphism with multiple *authorize* methods.

For example, as illustrated in Figure 33.18 and Figure 33.19, a *Sale* instantiates a *CreditPayment* or *CheckPayment* and asks it to authorize itself. .

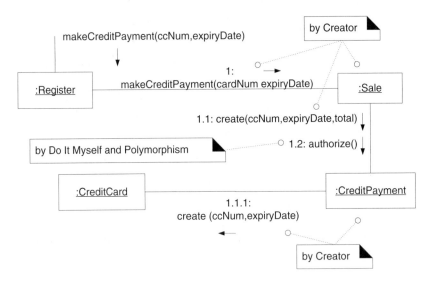

Figure 33.18 Creating a CreditPayment.

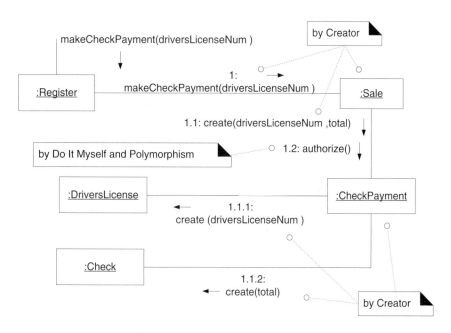

Figure 33.19 Creating a CheckPayment.

Fine-Grained Classes?

Consider the creation of the *CreditCard*, *DriversLicense,* and *Check* software objects. Our first impulse might be to record the data they hold simply in their related payment classes, and eliminate such fine-grained classes. However, it is usually a more profitable strategy to use them; they often end up providing useful behavior and being reusable. For example, the *CreditCard* is a natural Expert on telling you its credit company type (Visa, MasterCard, and so on). This behavior will turn out to be necessary for our application.

Credit Payment Authorization

The system must communicate with an external credit authorization service, and we have already created the basis of the design based on adapters to support this.

Relevant Credit Payment Domain Information

Some context for the upcoming design:

- POS systems are physically connected with external authorization services in several ways, including phone lines (which must be dialed) and always-on broadband Internet connections.

- Different application-level protocols and associated data formats are used, such as Secure Electronic Transaction (SET). New ones may become popular, such as XMLPay.

- Payment authorization can be viewed as a regular synchronous operation: a POS thread blocks, waiting for a reply from the remote service (within the limits of a time-out period).

- All payment authorization protocols involve sending identifiers uniquely identifying the store (with a "merchant ID"), and the POS terminal (with a "terminal ID"). A reply includes an approval or denial code, and a unique transaction ID.

- A store may use different external authorization services for different credit card types (one for Visa, one for MasterCard). For each service, the store has a different merchant ID.

- The credit company type can be deduced from the card number. For example, numbers starting with 5 are MasterCard; numbers starting with 4 are Visa.

- The adapter implementations will protect the upper layers of the system against all these variations in payment authorization. Each adapter is responsible for ensuring the authorization request transaction is in the appropriate format, and for collaborating with the external service. As discussed in a prior iteration, the *ServicesFactory* is responsible for delivering the appropriate *ICreditAuthorizationServiceAdapter* implementation.

A Design Scenario

Figure 33.20 starts the presentation of an annotated design that satisfies these details and requirements. Messages are annotated to illustrate the reasoning.

Once the correct *ICreditAuthorizationServiceAdapter* is found, it is given the responsibility for completing the authorization, as shown in Figure 33.21.

Once a reply is obtained by *CreditPayment* (which has been given the responsibility for handling its completion by Polymorphism and Do It Myself), assuming it is approved, it completes its tasks, as shown in Figure 33.22.

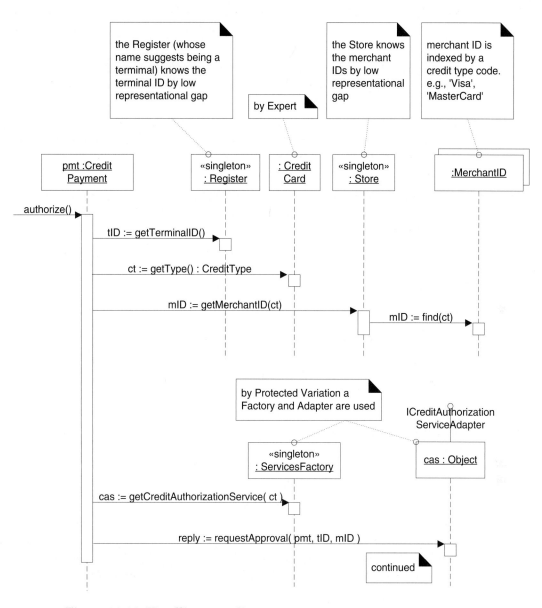

Figure 33.20 Handling a credit payment.

UML notation—Observe in this sequence diagram that some objects were stacked. This is legal, although few CASE tools support it. It is helpful in publishing, where width is constrained.

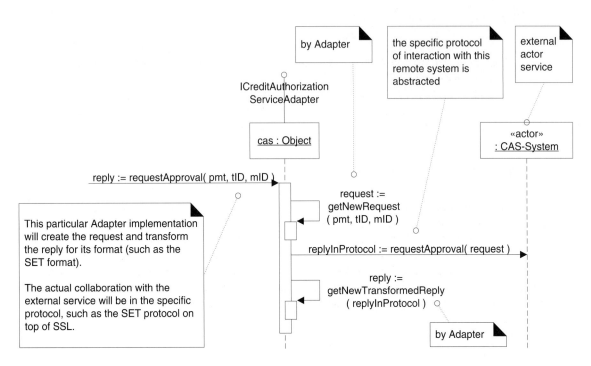

Figure 33.21 Completing the authorization.

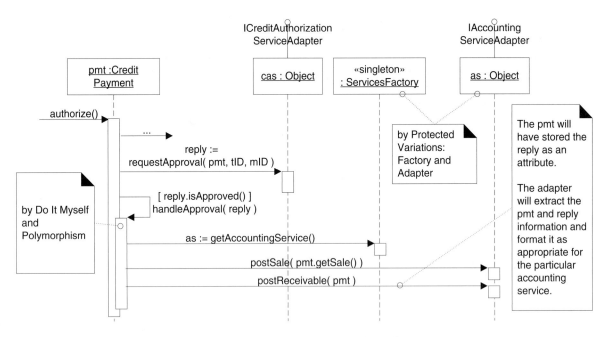

Figure 33.22 Completion of an approved credit payment.

33.8   Conclusion

The point of this case study was not to show the correct solution—there isn't a single best solution, and I'm sure readers can improve on what I've suggested. My sincere hope has been to demonstrate that doing object design can be reasoned through by core principles such as low coupling and the application of patterns, rather than being a mysterious process.

Caution: Pattern-itis

This presentation has used GoF design patterns at many points, which is one point of the case study as a learning aid. But, there have been reports of designers excessively force-fitting patterns in a creative frenzy of pattern-itis. I think a conclusion to draw from this is that patterns require study in multiple examples to be well-digested. A popular learning vehicle is a lunchtime or after-work study group in which participants shares ways they have seen or could see the application of patterns, and discuss a section of a patterns book.

Designing a Persistence Framework with Patterns

Le temps est un grand professeur, mais
malheureusement il tue tous ses élèves
(Time is a great teacher, but unfortunately it kills all its pupils).

—Hector Berlioz

Objectives

- Design part of a framework with the Template Method, State, and Command patterns.
- Introduce issues in object-relational (O-R) mapping.
- Implement lazy materialization with Virtual Proxies.

Introduction

The NextGen application—like most—requires storing and retrieving information in a persistent storage mechanism, such as a relational database (RDB). This chapter explores the design of a framework for storing persistent objects.

It is usually better to get or buy than build one of these, either as a standalone product or as part of container-managed persistence for entity beans if using EJBs and other Java technologies. Building an industrial-strength O-R persistence service can consume person-years of effort, and there are subtle issues requiring specialized expertise. Furthermore, technologies such as those based on the Java Data Objects (JDO) specification offer partial solutions.

Therefore, the intention is not to show an industrial-strength framework or suggest ignoring technologies like JDO, but rather to use a persistence framework as a vehicle for explaining general framework design with patterns, because it makes an especially good case study. It is also another demonstration of using the UML to communicate a software design.

> This framework is presented to introduce framework design, not as a recommended approach to design an industrial persistence service.

34.1 The Problem: Persistent Objects

Assume that in the NextGen application, *ProductSpecification* data resides in a relational database. It must be brought into local memory during application use. **Persistent objects** are those that require persistent storage, such as *ProductSpecification* instances.

Storage Mechanisms and Persistent Objects

Object databases—If an object database is used to store and retrieve objects, no additional custom or third-party persistence services are required. This is one of several attractions for its use.

Relational databases—Because of the prevalence of RDBs, their use is often required, rather than the more convenient object databases. If this is the case, a number of problems arise due to the mismatch between record-oriented and object-oriented representations of data; these problems are explored later. A special O-R mapping service is required.

Other—In addition to RDBs, it is sometimes desirable to store objects in other storage mechanisms or formats, such as flat files, XML structures, Palm OS PDB files, hierarchical databases, and so on. As with relational databases, a representation mismatch exists between objects and these non-object-oriented formats. And as with RDBs, special services are required to make them work with objects.

34.2 The Solution: A Persistence Service from a Persistence Framework

A **persistence framework** is a general-purpose, reusable, and extendable set of types that provides functionality to support persistent objects. A **persistence service** (or subsystem) actually provides the service, and will be created with a persistence framework. A persistence service is usually written to work with RDBs, in which case it is also called an **O-R mapping service**. Typically, a persistence service must translate objects into records (or some other form of structured data such as XML) and save them in a database, and translate records into objects when retrieving from a database.

In terms of the layered architecture of the NextGen application, a persistence service is a subsystem within the technical services layer.

34.3 Frameworks

At the risk of oversimplification, a framework is an *extendable* set of objects for related functions. The quintessential example is a GUI framework, such as Java's AWT or Swing.

The signature quality of a framework is that it provides an implementation for the core and unvarying functions, and includes a mechanism to allow a developer to plug in the varying functions, or to extend the functions.

For example, Java's Swing GUI framework provides many classes and interfaces for core GUI functions. Developers can add specialized widgets by subclassing from the Swing classes and overriding certain methods. Developers can also plug in varying event response behavior to predefined widget classes (such as *JButton*) by registering listeners or subscribers based on the Observer pattern. That's a framework.

In general, a **framework**:

- Is a cohesive set of interfaces and classes that collaborate to provide services for the core, unvarying part of a logical subsystem.

- Contains concrete (and especially) abstract classes that define interfaces to conform to, object interactions to participate in, and other invariants.

- Usually (but not necessarily) requires the framework user to define subclasses of existing framework classes to make use of, customize, and extend the framework services.

- Has abstract classes that may contain both abstract and concrete methods.

- Relies on the **Hollywood Principle**— *"Don't call us, we'll call you."* This means that the user-defined classes (for example, new subclasses) will receive messages from the predefined framework classes. These are usually handled by implementing superclass abstract methods.

The following persistence framework example will demonstrate these principles.

Frameworks Are Reusable

Frameworks offer a high degree of reuse—much more so than individual classes. Consequently, if an organization is interested (and who isn't?) in increasing its degree of software reuse, then it should emphasize the creation of frameworks.

34.4   Requirements for the Persistence Service and Framework

For the NextGen POS application, we need a persistence service to be built with a persistence framework (which could be used to also create other persistence services). Let's call the framework PFW (Persistence Framework). PFW is a simplified framework—a full-blown, industrial-strength persistence framework is outside the scope of this introduction.

The framework should provide functions such as:

■   store and retrieve objects in a persistent storage mechanism

■   *commit* and *rollback* transactions

The design should be extendable to support different storage mechanisms and formats, such as RDBs, records in flat files, or XML in files.

34.5   Key Ideas

The following key ideas will be explored in subsequent sections:

■   **Mapping**—There must be some mapping between a class and its persistent store (for example, a table in a database), and between object attributes and the fields (columns) in a record. That is, there must be a **schema mapping** between the two schemas.

■   **Object identity**—To easily relate records to objects, and to ensure there are no inappropriate duplicates, records and objects have a unique object identifier.

■   **Database mapper**—A Pure Fabrication database mapper is responsible for materialization and dematerialization.

■   **Materialization and dematerialization**—Materialization is the act of transforming a non-object representation of data (for example, records) from a persistent store into objects. Dematerialization is the opposite activity (also known as passivation).

■   **Caches**—Persistence services cache materialized objects for performance.

■   **Transaction state of object**—It is useful to know the state of objects in terms of their relationship to the current transaction. For example, it is useful to know which objects have been modified (are *dirty*) so that it is possible to determine if they need to be saved back to their persistent store.

■   **Transaction operations**—Commit and rollback operations.

■   **Lazy materialization**—Not all objects are materialized at once; a particular instance is only materialized on-demand, when needed.

■ **Virtual proxies**—Lazy materialization can be implemented using a smart reference known as a virtual proxy.

34.6   Pattern: Representing Objects as Tables

How do you map an object to a record or relational database schema?

The **Representing Objects as Tables** pattern [BW96] proposes defining a table in an RDB for each persistent object class. Object attributes containing primitive data types (number, string, boolean, and so on) map to columns.

If an object has only attributes of primitive data types, the mapping is straight-forward. But as we will see, matters are not that simple, since objects may have attributes that refer to other complex objects, while the relational model requires that values be atomic (that is, First Normal Form) (see Figure 34.1).

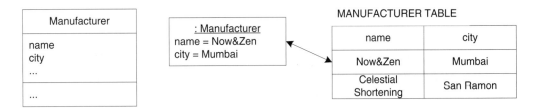

Figure 34.1 Mapping objects and tables.

34.7   UML Data Modeling Profile

While on the subject of RDBs, not surprisingly, the UML has become a popular notation for **data models**. Note that one of the official UP artifacts is the Data Model, which is part of the Design discipline. Figure 34.2 illustrates some notation in the UML for data modeling.

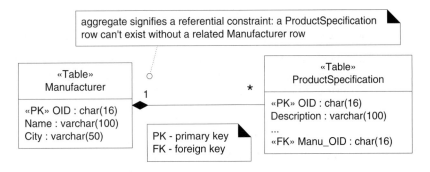

Figure 34.2 UML Data Modeling Profile example.

These stereotypes are not part of the core UML—they are an extension. To generalize, the UML has the concept of a **UML profile**: a coherent set of UML stereotypes, tagged values, and constraints for a particular purpose. Figure 34.2 illustrates part of the proposed (to the OMG) UML Data Modeling Profile; at the time of this writing it had not been approved. A profile does not have to be OMG-approved to be a profile, but some common cases—such as data modeling—are being submitted.

34.8   Pattern: Object Identifier

It is desirable to have a consistent way to relate objects to records, and to be able to ensure that repeated materialization of a record does not result in duplicate objects.

The **Object Identifier** pattern [BW96] proposes assigning an **object identifier** (OID) to each record and object (or proxy of an object).

An OID is usually an alphanumeric value; each is unique to a specific object. There are various approaches to generating unique IDs for OIDs, ranging from unique to one database, to globally unique: database sequence generators, the High-Low key generation strategy [Ambler00], and others.

Within object land, an OID is represented by an OID interface or class that encapsulates the actual value and its representation. In an RDB, it is usually stored as a fixed length character value.

Every table will have an OID as primary key, and each object will (directly or indirectly) also have an OID. If every object is associated with an OID, and every table has an OID primary key, every object can be uniquely mapped to some row in some table (see Figure 34.3).

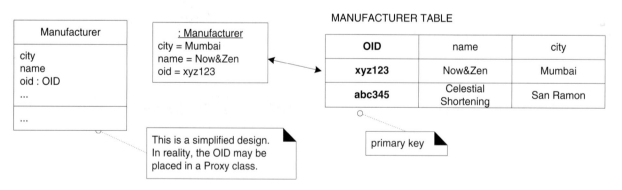

Figure 34.3 Object identifiers link objects and records.

This is a simplified view of the design. In reality, the OID may not actually be placed in the persistent object—although that is possible. Instead, it may be placed in a Proxy object wrapping the persistent object. The design is influenced by the choice of language.

An OID also provides a consistent key type to use in the interface to the persistence service.

34.9   Accessing a Persistence Service with a Facade

Step one in the design of this subsystem is to define a facade for its services; recall that Facade is a common pattern to provide a unified interface to a subsystem. To begin, an operation is needed to retrieve an object given an OID. But in addition to an OID, the subsystem needs to know what type of object to materialize; therefore, the class type will also be provided. Figure 34.4 illustrates some operations of the facade and its use in collaboration with one of the Next-Gen service adapters.

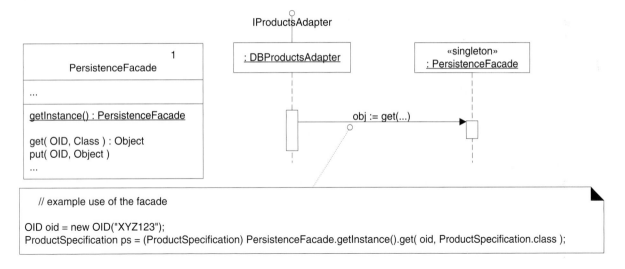

Figure 34.4 The PersistenceFacade.

34.10   Mapping Objects: Database Mapper or Database Broker Pattern

The *PersistenceFacade*—as true of all facades—does not do the work itself, but delegates requests to subsystem objects.

Who should be responsible for materialization and dematerialization of objects (for example, a *ProductSpecification*) from a persistent store?

The Information Expert pattern suggests that the persistent object class itself (*ProductSpecification*) is a candidate, because it has some of the data (the data to be saved) required by the responsibility.

If a persistent object class defines the code to save itself in a database, it is called a **direct mapping** design. Direct mapping is workable *if* the database related code is automatically generated and injected into the class by a post-processing compiler, and the developer never has to see or maintain this complex database code cluttering his or her class.

But if direct mapping is manually added and maintained, it has a number of defects and does not tend to scale well in terms of programming and maintenance. Problems include:

- Strong coupling of the persistent object class to persistent storage knowledge—violation of Low Coupling.

- Complex responsibilities in a new and unrelated area to what the object was previously responsible for—violation of High Cohesion and maintaining a separation of concerns. Technical service concerns are mixing with application logic concerns.

We will explore a classic **indirect mapping** approach, that uses other objects to do the mapping for persistent objects.

Part of this approach is to use the **Database Broker** pattern [BW95]. It proposes making a class that is responsible for materialization, dematerialization, and object caching. This has also been called the **Database Mapper** pattern in [Fowler01], which is a better name than Database Broker, as it describes its responsibility, and the term "broker" in distributed systems [BMRSS96] design has a long-standing and different meaning.[1]

A different mapper class is defined for each persistent object class. Figure 34.5 illustrates that each persistent object may have its own mapper class, and that there may be different kinds of mappers for different storage mechanisms. A snippet of code:

```
class PersistenceFacade
{
//...
public Object get( OID oid, Class persistenceClass )
{
    // an IMapper is keyed by the Class of the persistent object
    IMapper mapper = (IMapper) mappers.get( persistenceClass );

    // delegate
    return mapper.get( oid );
}
//...
}
```

---

1. In distributed systems, a **broker** is a front-end server process that delegates tasks to back-end server processes.

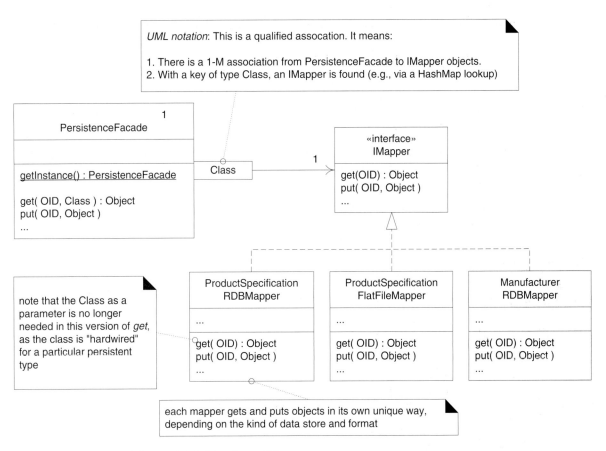

Figure 34.5 Database Mappers.

Although this diagram indicates two *ProductSpecification* mappers, only one will be active within a running persistence service.

Metadata-Based Mappers

More flexible, but more involved, is a mapper design based on **metadata** (data about data). In contrast to hand-crafting individual mapper classes for different persistent types, metadata-based mappers dynamically generate the mapping from an object schema to another schema (such as relational) based on reading in metadata that describes the mapping, such as "TableX maps to Class Y; column Z maps to object property P" (it gets much more complex). This approach is feasible for languages with reflective programming capabilities, such as Java, C#, or Smalltalk, and awkward for those that don't, such as C++.

With metadata-based mappers, we can change the schema mapping in an external store and it will be realized in the running system, without changing source code—Protected Variations with respect to schema variations.

Nevertheless, a useful quality of the framework presented here is that hand-coded or metadata mappers can be used without affecting clients—encapsulation of the implementation.

34.11   Framework Design with the Template Method Pattern

The next section describes some of the essential design features of the Database Mappers, which are a central part of the PFW. These design features are based on the **Template Method** GoF design pattern [GHJV95].[2] This pattern is at the heart of framework design,[3] and is familiar to most OO programmers by practice if not by name.

The idea is to define a method (the Template Method) in a superclass that defines the skeleton of an algorithm, with its varying and unvarying parts. The Template Method invokes other methods, some of which are methods that may be overridden in a subclass. Thus, subclasses can override the varying methods in order to add their own unique behavior at points of variability (see Figure 34.6).

34.12   Materialization with the Template Method Pattern

If we were to program two or three mapper classes, some commonality in the code would become apparent. The basic repeating algorithm structure for materializing an object is:

```
if (object in cache)
    return it
else
    create the object from its representation in storage
    save object in cache
    return it
```

The point of variation is how the object is created from storage.

We will create the *get* method to be the template method in an abstract superclass *AbstractPersistenceMapper* that defines the template, and use a hook method in subclasses for the varying part. Figure 34.7 shows the essential design.

---

2. This pattern is unrelated to C++ templates. It describes the *template* of an algorithm.

3. More specifically, of **whitebox frameworks**. These are usually class hierarchy and subclassing-oriented frameworks that require the user to know something about their design and structure; hence, whitebox.

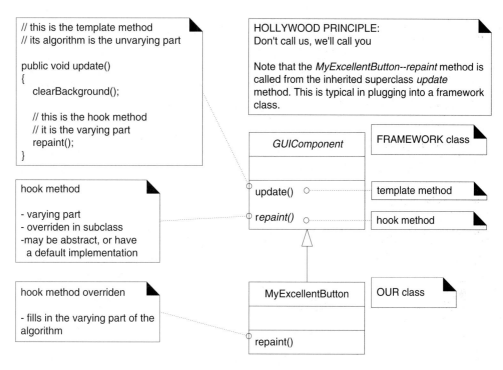

Figure 34.6 Template Method pattern in a GUI framework.

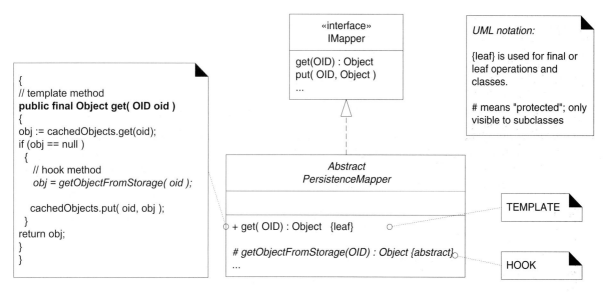

Figure 34.7 Template Method for mapper objects.

As shown in this example, it is common for the template method to be *public*, and the hook method to be *protected*. *AbstractPersistenceMapper* and *IMapper* are part of the PFW. Now, an application programmer can plug into this framework by adding a subclass, and overriding or implementing the *getObjectFromStorage* hook method. Figure 34.8 shows an example.

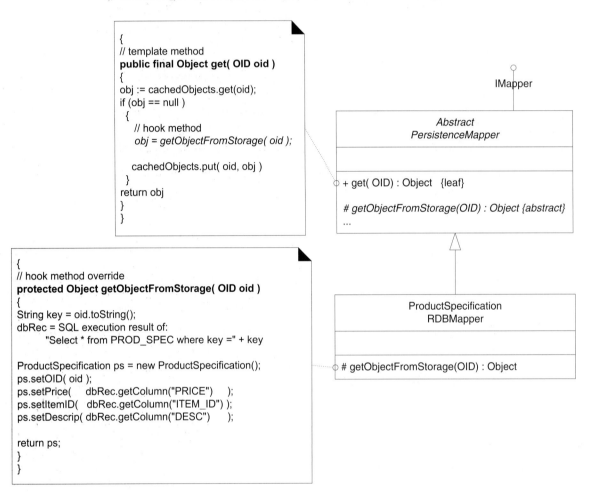

Figure 34.8 Overriding the hook method.[4]

Assume in the hook method implementation of Figure 34.8 that the beginning part of the algorithm—doing a SQL SELECT—is the same for all objects, only the database table name varies.[5] If that assumption held, then once again, the

---

4. In Java as an example, the *dbRec* that is returned from executing a SQL query will be a JDBC *ResultSet*.
5. In many cases, the situation is not so simple. An object may be derived from data from two or more tables or from multiple databases, in which case, the first version of the Template Method design offers more flexibility.

Template Method pattern could be applied to factor out the varying and unvarying parts of the algorithm. In Figure 34.9, the tricky part is that *AbstractRDB-Mapper--getObjectFromStorage* is a hook method with respect to *AbstractPersistenceMapper--get*, but a template method with respect to the new hook method *getObjectFromRecord*.

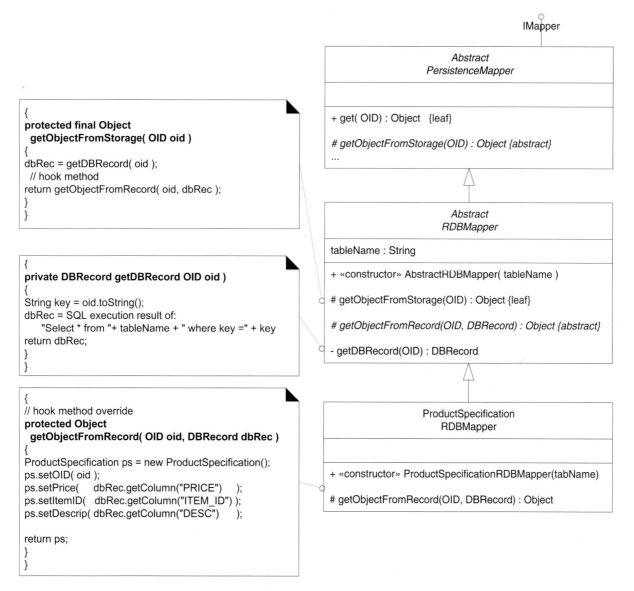

Figure 34.9 Tightening up the code with the Template Method again.

UML notation—Observe how constructors can be declared in the UML. The stereotype is optional, and if the naming convention of constructor name equal to class name is used, probably unnecessary.

Now, *IMapper*, *AbstractPersistenceMapper*, and *AbstractRDBMapper* are part of the framework. The application programmer needs only to add his or her subclass, such as *ProductSpecificationRDBMapper*, and ensure it is created with the table name (to pass via constructor chaining up to the *AbstractRDBMapper*).

The Database Mapper class hierarchy is an essential part of the framework; new subclasses may be added by the application programmer to customize it for new kinds of persistent storage mechanisms or for new particular tables or files within an existing storage mechanism. Figure 34.10 shows some of the package and class structure. Notice that the NextGen-specific classes do not belong in the general technical services *Persistence* package. I think this diagram, combined with Figure 34.9, illustrates the value of a visual language like the UML to describe parts of software; this succinctly conveys much information.

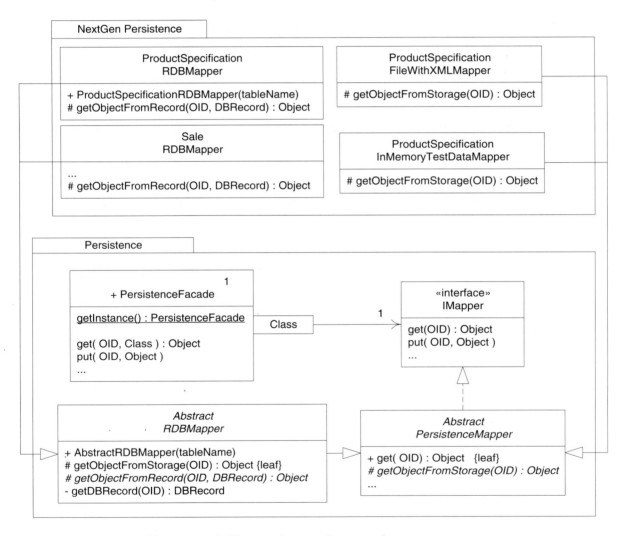

Figure 34.10 The persistence framework.

Notice the class *ProductSpecificationInMemoryTestDataMapper*. Such classes can be used to serve up hard-coded objects for testing, without accessing any external persistent store.

The UP and the Software Architecture Document

In terms of the UP and documentation, recall that the SAD is a learning aid for future developers, which contains architectural views of key noteworthy ideas. Including diagrams such as Figure 34.9 and Figure 34.10 in the SAD for the NextGen project is very much in the spirit of the kind of information an SAD should contain.

Synchronized or Guarded Methods in the UML

The *AbstractPersistenceMapper--get* method contains critical section code that is not thread safe—the same object could be being materialized concurrently on different threads. As a technical service subsystem, the persistence service needs to be designed with thread safety in mind. Indeed, the entire subsystem may be distributed to a separate process on another computer, with the *PersistenceFacade* transformed into a remote server object, and with many threads simultaneously running in the subsystem, serving multiple clients.

The method should therefore have thread concurrency control—if using Java, add the *synchronized* keyword. Figure 34.11 illustrates a synchronized method in a class diagram.

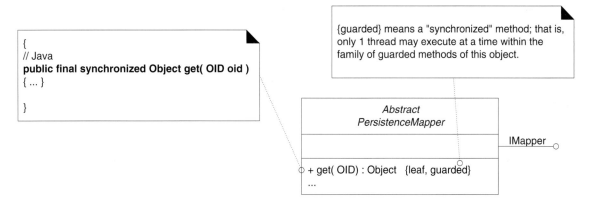

Figure 34.11 Guarded methods in the UML.

34.13 Configuring Mappers with a MapperFactory

Similar to previous examples of factories in the case study, the configuration of the *PersistenceFacade* with a set of *IMapper* objects can be achieved with a factory object, *MapperFactory*. However, as a slight twist, it is desirable to not name each mapper with a different operation. For example, this is not desirable:

```
class MapperFactory
{
public IMapper getProductSpecificationMapper() {...}
public IMapper getSaleMapper() {...}
...
}
```

This does not support Protected Variations with respect to a growing list of mappers—and it will grow. Consequently, the following is preferred:

```
class MapperFactory
{
public Map getAllMappers() {...}
...
}
```

where the *java.util.Map* (probably implemented with a *HashMap*) keys are the *Class* objects (the persistent types), and the *IMappers* are the values.

Then, the facade can initialize its collection of *IMappers* as follows:

```
class PersistenceFacade
{
private java.util.Map mappers =
    MapperFactory.getInstance().getAllMappers();
...
}
```

The factory can assign a set of *IMappers* using a data-driven design. That is, the factory can read system properties to discover which *IMapper* classes to instantiate. If a language with reflective programming capabilities is used, such as Java, then the instantiation can be based on reading in the class names as strings, and using something like a *Class.newInstance* operation for instantiation. Thus, the mapper set can be reconfigured without changing the source code.

34.14 Pattern: Cache Management

It is desirable to maintain materialized objects in a local cache to improve performance (materialization is relatively slow) and support transaction management operations such as a commit.

The **Cache Management** pattern [BW96] proposes making the Database Mappers responsible for maintaining its cache. If a different mapper is used for each class of persistent object, each mapper can maintain its own cache.

When objects are materialized, they are placed in the cache, with their OID as the key. Subsequent requests to the mapper for an object will cause the mapper to first search the cache, thus avoiding unnecessary materialization.

34.15 Consolidating and Hiding SQL Statements in One Class

Hard-coding SQL statements into different RDB mapper classes is not a terrible sin, but it can be improved upon. Suppose instead:

- There is a single Pure Fabrication class (and it's a singleton) *RDBOperations* where all SQL operations (SELECT, INSERT, ...) are consolidated.

- The RDB mapper classes collaborate with it to obtain a DB record or record set (for example, *ResultSet*).

- Its interface looks something like this:

```
class RDBOperations
{
public ResultSet getProductSpecificationData( OID oid ) {...}
public ResultSet getSaleData( OID oid ) {...}
...
}
```

So that, for example, a mapper has code like this:

```
class ProductSpecificationRDBMapper extends AbstractPersistenceMapper
{
protected Object getObjectFromStorage( OID oid )
{
ResultSet rs =
   RDBOperations.getInstance().getProductSpecificationData( oid );

ProductSpecification ps = new ProductSpecification();
ps.setPrice( rs.getDouble( "PRICE" ) );
ps.setOID( oid );
return ps;
}
```

The following benefits accrue from this Pure Fabrication:

- Ease of maintenance and performance tuning by an expert. SQL optimization requires a SQL aficionado, rather than an object programmer. With all the SQL embedded in this one class, it is easy for the SQL expert to find and work on it.

- Encapsulation of the access method and details. For example, hard-coded SQL could be replaced by a call to a stored procedure in the RDB in order to obtain the data. Or a more sophisticated **metadata**-based approach to generating the SQL could be inserted, in which SQL is dynamically generated from a metadata schema description read from an external source.

As an architect, the interesting aspect of this design decision is that it is influenced by developer skills. A trade-off between high cohesion and convenience for a specialist was made. Not all design decisions are motivated by "pure" software engineering concerns such as coupling and cohesion.

34.16 Transactional States and the State Pattern

Transactional support issues can get complex, but to keep things simple for the present—to focus on the GoF State pattern—assume the following:

- Persistent objects can be inserted, deleted, or modified.

- Operating on a persistent object (for example, modifying it) does not cause an immediate database update; rather, an explicit *commit* operation must be performed.

In addition, the response to an operation depends on the transactional state of the object. As an example, responses may be as shown in the statechart of Figure 34.12.

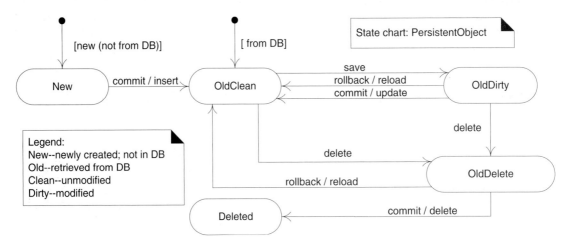

Figure 34.12 Statechart for PersistentObject.

For example, an "old dirty" object is one retrieved from the database and then modified. On a commit operation, it should be updated to the database—in contrast to one in the "old clean" state, which should do nothing (because it hasn't changed). Within the object-oriented PFW, when a delete or save operation is performed, it does not immediately cause a database delete or save; rather, the persistent object transitions to the appropriate state, awaiting a commit or rollback to really do something.

As a UML comment, this is a good example of where a statechart is helpful in succinctly communicating information that is otherwise awkward to express.

In this design, assume that we will make all persistent object classes extend a *PersistentObject* class,[6] that provides common technical services for persistence.[7] For example, see Figure 34.13.

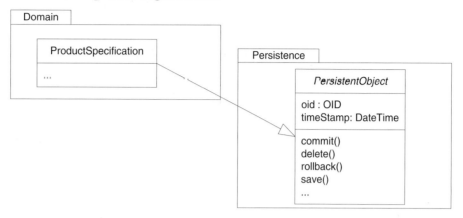

Figure 34.13 Persistent objects.

Now—and this is the issue that will be resolved with the State pattern—notice that *commit* and *rollback* methods require similar structures of case logic, based on a transactional state code. *commit* and *rollback* perform different actions in their cases, but they have similar logic structures.

```
public void commit()
{
switch ( state )
{
case OLD_DIRTY:
    // ...
    break;
case OLD_CLEAN:
    //...
    break;
...
}
```

```
public void rollback()
{
switch ( state )
{
case OLD_DIRTY:
    // ...
    break;
case OLD_CLEAN:
    //...
    break;
...
}
```

An alternative to this repeating case logic structure is the GoF State pattern.

---

6. [Ambler00b] is a good reference on a *PersistentObject* class and persistence layers, although the idea is older.

7. Some issues with extending a *PersistentObject* class are discussed later. Whenever a domain object class extends a technical services class, it should be pause for reflection, as it mixes architectural concerns (persistence and application logic).

State

Context / Problem

An object's behavior is dependent on its state, and its methods contain case logic reflecting conditional state-dependent actions. Is there an alternative to conditional logic?

Solution

Create state classes for each state, implementing a common interface. Delegate state-dependent operations from the context object to its current state object. Ensure the context object always points to a state object reflecting its current state.

Figure 34.14 illustrates its application in the persistence subsystem.

State-dependent methods in *PersistentObject* delegate their execution to an associated state object. If the context object is referencing the *OldDirtyState*, then 1) the *commit* method will cause a database update, and 2) the context object will be reassigned to reference the *OldCleanState*. On the other hand, if the context object is referencing the *OldCleanState*, the inherited do-nothing *commit* method executes and does nothing (as to be expected, since the object is clean).

Observe in Figure 34.14 that the state classes and their behavior correspond to the state chart of Figure 34.12. The State pattern is one mechanism to implement a state transition model in software.[8] It causes an object to transition to different states in response to events.

As a performance comment, these state objects are—ironically—stateless (no attributes). Thus, there does not need to be multiple instances of a class—each is a singleton. Thousands of persistent objects can reference the same *OldDirtyState* instance, for example.

34.17 Designing a Transaction with the Command Pattern

The last section took a simplified view of transactions. This section extends the discussion, but does not cover all transaction design issues. Informally, a transaction is a unit of work—a set of tasks—whose tasks must all complete successfully, or none must be completed. That is, its completion is atomic.

---

8. There are others, including hard-coded conditional logic, state machine interpreters, and code generators driven by state tables.

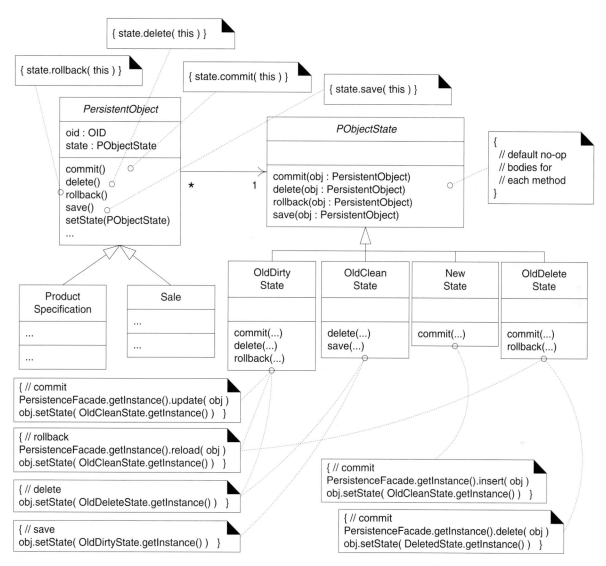

Figure 34.14 Applying the State pattern.[9]

In terms of the persistence service, the tasks of a transaction include inserting, updating, and deleting objects. One transaction could contain two inserts, one update, and three deletes, for example. To represent this, a *Transaction* class is added [Ambler00b].[10] As pointed out in [Fowler01], the order of database tasks within a transaction can influence its success (and performance).

---

9. The *Deleted* class is omitted due to space constraints in the diagram.

10. This is called a UnitOfWork in [Fowler01].

For example:

1. Suppose the database has a referential integrity constraint such that when a record is updated in TableA that contains a foreign key to a record in TableB, the database requires that the record in TableB already exists.

2. Suppose a transaction contains an INSERT task to add the TableB record, and an UPDATE task to update the TableA record. If the UPDATE executes before the INSERT, a referential integrity error is raised.

Ordering the database tasks can help. Some ordering issues are schema-specific, but a general strategy is to first do inserts, then updates, and then deletes.

Mind that the order in which tasks are added to a transaction by an application may not reflect their best execution order. The tasks need to be sorted just before their execution.

This leads to another GoF pattern: Command.

Command

Context / Problem

How to handle requests or tasks that need functions such as sorting (prioritizing), queueing, delaying, logging, or undoing?

Solution

Make each task a class that implements a common interface.

This is a simple pattern with many useful applications; actions become objects, and thus can be sorted, logged, queued, and so forth. For example, in the PFW, Figure 34.15 shows Command (or task) classes for the database operations.

There is much more to completing a transaction solution, but the key idea of this section is to represent each task or action in the transaction as an object with a polymorphic *execute* method; this opens up a world of flexibility by treating the request as an object itself.

The quintessential example of Command is for GUI actions, such as cut and paste. For example, the *CutCommand's execute* method does a cut, and its *undo* method reverses the cut. The *CutCommand* will also retain the data necessary to perform the undo. All the GUI commands can be kept in a history stack, so that they can be popped in turn, and each undone.

Another common use of Command is for server-side request handling. When a server object receives a (remote) message, it creates a Command object for that request, and hands it off to a *CommandProcesser* [BMRSS96], which can queue, log, prioritize, and execute the commands.

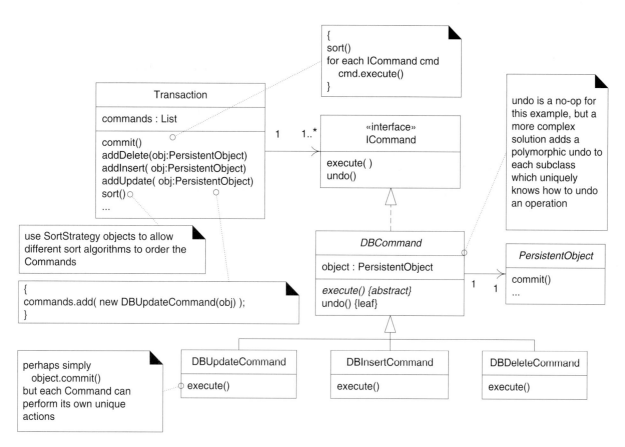

Figure 34.15 Commands for database operations.

34.18   Lazy Materialization with a Virtual Proxy

It is sometimes desirable to defer the materialization of an object until it is absolutely required, usually for performance reasons. For example, suppose that *ProductSpecification* objects reference a *Manufacturer* object, but only very rarely does it need to be materialized from the database. Only rare scenarios cause a request for manufacturer information, such as manufacturer rebate scenarios in which the company name and address are required.

The deferred materialization of "children" objects is known as **lazy materialization**. Lazy materialization can be implemented using the Virtual Proxy GoF pattern—one of many variations of Proxy.

A **Virtual Proxy** is a proxy for another object (the *real subject*) that materializes the real subject when it is first referenced; therefore, it implements lazy materialization. It is a lightweight object that stands for a "real" object that may or may not be materialized.

A concrete example of the Virtual Proxy pattern with *ProductSpecification* and *Manufacturer* is shown in Figure 34.16. This design is based on the assumption that proxies know the OID of their real subject, and when materialization is required, the OID is used to help identify and retrieve the real subject.

Note that the *ProductSpecification* has attribute visibility to an *IManufacturer* instance. The *Manufacturer* for this *ProductSpecification* may not yet be materialized in memory. When the *ProductSpecification* sends a *getAddress* message to the *ManufacturerProxy* (as though it were the materialized manufacturer object), the proxy materializes the real *Manufacturer*, using the OID of the *Manufacturer* to retrieve and materialize it.

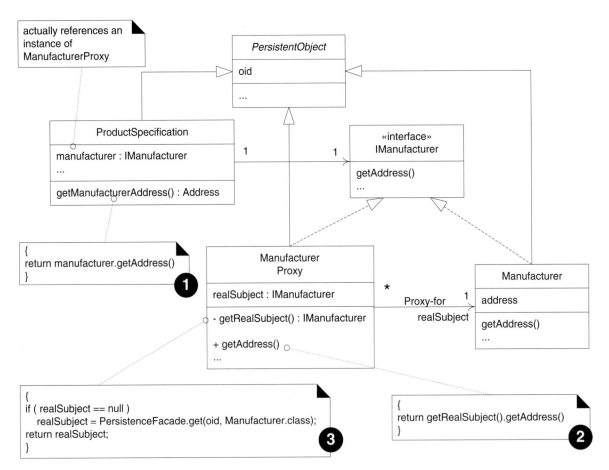

Figure 34.16 Manufacturer Virtual Proxy.

Implementation of a Virtual Proxy

The implementation of a Virtual Proxy varies by language. The details are outside the scope of this chapter, but here is a synopsis:

Language	Virtual Proxy Implementation
C++	Define a templatized smart pointer class. No *IManufacturer* interface definition is actually needed.
Java	The *ManufacturerProxy* class is implemented. The *IManufacturer* interface is defined. However, these are not normally manually coded. Rather, one creates a code generator that analyzes the subject classes (e.g., *Manufacturer*) and generates *IManufacturer* and *ProxyManufacturer*. Another Java alternative is the Dynamic Proxy API.
Smalltalk	Define a Virtual Morphing Proxy (or Ghost Proxy), which uses *#doesNotUnderstand:* and *#become:* to morph into the real subject. No *IManufacturer* definition is needed.

Who Creates the Virtual Proxy?

Observe in Figure 34.16 that the *ManufacturerProxy* collaborates with the *PersistenceFacade* in order to materialize its real subject. But who creates the *ManufacturerProxy*? Answer: The database mapper class for *ProductSpecification*. The mapper class is responsible for deciding, when it materializes an object, which of its "child" objects should also be eagerly materialized, and which should be lazily materialized with a proxy.

Consider these alternative solutions: one uses eager materialization, the other lazy materialization.

```
// EAGER MATERIALIZATION OF MANUFACTURER

class ProductSpecificationRDBMapper extends AbstractPersistenceMapper
{
protected Object getObjectFromStorage( OID oid )
{
ResultSet rs =
   RDBOperations.getInstance().getProductSpecificationData( oid );

ProductSpecification ps = new ProductSpecification();
ps.setPrice( rs.getDouble( "PRICE" ) );
```

```
    // here's the essence of it

String manufacturerForeignKey = rs.getString( "MANU_OID" );
OID manuOID = new OID( manufacturerForeignKey );
ps.setManufacturer( (IManufacturer)
    PersistenceFacade.getInstance().get(manuOID,Manufacturer.class);
...
}
```

Here is the lazy materialization solution:

```
// LAZY MATERIALIZATION OF MANUFACTURER

class ProductSpecificationRDBMapper extends AbstractPersistenceMapper
{
protected Object getObjectFromStorage( OID oid )
{
ResultSet rs =
    RDBOperations.getInstance().getProductSpecificationData( oid );

ProductSpecification ps = new ProductSpecification();
ps.setPrice( rs.getDouble( "PRICE" ) );

    // here's the essence of it

String manufacturerForeignKey = rs.getString( "MANU_OID" );
OID manuOID = new OID( manufacturerForeignKey );
ps.setManufacturer( new ManufacturerProxy( manuOID ) );
...
}
```

34.19   How to Represent Relationships in Tables

The code in the prior section relies on a MANU_OID foreign key in the PRODUCT_SPEC table to link to a record in the MANUFACTURER table. This highlights the question: How are object relationships represented in the relational model?

The answer is given in the **Representing Object Relationships as Tables** pattern {BW96], which proposes the following:

- **one-to-one** associations
  - ○ Place an OID foreign key in one or both tables representing the objects in relationship.
  - ○ Or, create an associative table that records the OIDs of each object in relationship.

- **one-to-many** associations, such as a collection
  - ○ Create an associative table that records the OIDs of each object in relationship.

- **many-to-many** associations
  - ○ Create an associative table that records the OIDs of each object in relationship.

34.20 PersistentObject Superclass and Separation of Concerns

A common partial design solution to providing persistence for objects is to create an abstract technical services superclass *PersistentObject* that all persistence objects inherit from (see Figure 34.17). Such a class usually defines attributes for persistence, such as a unique OID, and methods for saving to a database.

This is not wrong, but it suffers from the weakness of coupling the class to the *PersistentObject* class—domain classes end up extending a technical services class.

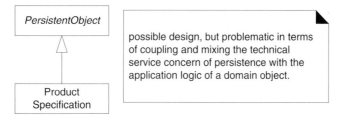

Figure 34.17 Problems with a PersistentObject superclass.

This design does not illustrate a clear separation of concerns. Rather, technical services concerns are mixed with domain layer business logic concerns by virtue of this extension.

On the other hand, "separation of concerns" is not an absolute virtue that must be followed at all costs. As discussed in the Protected Variations introduction, designers need to pick their battles at the truly likely points of expensive instability. If in a particular application making the classes extend from *Persistent-Object* leads to a neat and easy solution and does not create longer-term design or maintenance problems, why not? The answer lies in understanding the evolution of the requirements and design for the application. It is also influenced by the language: those with single inheritance (such as Java) have had their single precious superclass *consumed*.

34.21   Unresolved Issues

This has been a very brief introduction to the problems and design solutions in a persistence framework and service. Many important issues have been glossed over, including:

- dematerializing objects

  - Briefly, the mappers must define *putObjectToStorage* methods. Dematerializing composition hierarchies requires collaboration between multiple mappers and the maintenance of associative tables (if an RDB is used).

- materialization and dematerialization of collections

- queries for groups of objects

- thorough transaction handling

- error handling when a database operation fails

- multiuser access and locking strategies

- security—controlling access to the database

PART 6 SPECIAL TOPICS

ON DRAWING AND TOOLS

Bubbles don't crash.

—Bertrand Meyer

Objectives

- Learn tips for drawing UML diagrams on a project.
- Illustrate some common functions in UML CASE tools.

Introduction

On a real project, doing some analysis or design while drawing UML diagrams does not happen neatly as in the pages of a book. It happens in the context of a busy software development team working in offices or rooms, scribbling on whiteboards and perhaps using a tool, and often with a tendency to want to start programming rather than work through some details via diagramming. If the UML tool or process of drawing is bothersome or fussy, or feels less valuable than programming, it will be avoided.

This chapter offers some suggestions on striking a balance between programming and drawing, and on fostering a supportive environment to make drawing convenient and useful rather than awkward.

35.1 On Speculative Design and Visual Thinking

The designs illustrated in UML diagrams will be incomplete, and only serve as a "springboard" to the programming. Too much diagramming before programming leads to time wasted in speculative design directions, or time wasted fussing with UML tools. There's nothing like real code to tell you what works. Bertrand Meyer said it best: "Bubbles don't crash."

Nevertheless, I vigorously encourage *some* forethought through diagramming before programming, and know it can add value, especially to explore the major design strategies. The interesting question is "How much diagramming before programming?" In part, the answer is a function of the experience and cognitive style of the designers.

Some people are very spatial/visual thinkers, and expressing their software design thoughts in a visual language complements their nature; others aren't. A large percentage of the brain is dedicated to visual or iconic thinking and processing, rather than textual processing (code). Visual languages such as the UML play to a natural mental strength of most people. Those educated in the UML obviously have an easier time at it than those who are not. And in general, more experienced object designers can effectively design by drawing without straying into unrealistic speculation, because of their experience and judgment. Applied by adepts, diagrams can help a group move more quickly toward a skillful design, due to the ability to ignore details and focus on the big picture.

One exception to this "light" diagramming suggestion is systems that are naturally modeled as state machines. There are some CASE tools that can do an impressive job at full code generation based on detailed UML statecharts for all the classes. But not all domains naturally fit a strong statemodel-centric approach; as examples, machine control and telecommunications often fit well, business information systems often don't.

35.2 Suggestions for UML Drawing Within the Development Process

Level of Effort

As a guideline, consider diagramming in pairs for the following period, before serious programming in the iteration.

2-week iteration	half-day to one-day near the start of the iteration (e.g., Monday or Tuesday)
4-week iteration	one or two days near the start

In both cases, drawing does not have to stop after this early focussed effort. During the iteration, developers may head—ideally in pairs—"to the whiteboard" for short sessions to sketch out ideas before more programming. And they may do another longer half-day session partway through the iteration, as they hit a complex problem within the scope of their initial task, or finish their first task and move on to a second.

Other Suggestions

- Draw in pairs, not alone. Most importantly, the synergy leads to better designs. Secondly, the pair quickly learns design skills from each other, and thus both become better designers. It is hard to grow as a software designer when one designs in isolation. Regularly rotate with new drawing/design partners to gain broad exposure to another's knowledge.

- To clarify a point alluded to several times, in iterative processes (such as the UP), the programmers are also the designers; there is not a separate team that draws designs and hands them over to programmers. The developers put on their UML hats, and draw a little. Then they put on their programmer hats and implement, and continue to design while programming.

- If there are ten developers, suppose that there are five drawing teams working for one day at different whiteboards. If the architect spends time rotating through the five teams, he or she will come to see points of dependency, conflict, and cross-pollinating ideas. The architect can then act as a liaison to bring the designs into some harmony, and clarify the dependencies.

- Hire a technical writer for the project and educate the writer in some UML notation and basic OOA/D concepts (so he or she understand the context). Have the writer help by doing the "fussy work" with UML CASE tools, reverse-engineering diagrams from code, printing and displaying large plotter prints of diagrams, and so forth. The developers spend their (more expensive) time doing what they do best: figuring out designs and programming. A technical writer supports them by handling diagram management, in addition to true technical writing responsibilities such as working on the end-user documents. This is known as the Mercenary Analyst pattern [Coplien95a].

- Arrange the development area with many large whiteboards in close proximity.

- To generalize, maximize the work environment for convenient drawing on walls. Create a "drawing-friendly" and "hanging diagrams"-friendly environment. You can't expect a successful visual modeling culture in an environment where developers are struggling to draw on small two-foot by three-foot whiteboards, regular size computer monitors, or pieces of paper. Comfortable drawing takes very large, open drawing spaces—physical or virtual.

- As an adjunct to whiteboards, use thin plastic "static cling" white sheets (they come in packages of 20 or more) that can be placed on the walls; they are available at many stationary stores. They remain attached to the wall by static cling, and can be used like a whiteboard with an erasable marker. These can be plastered across a wall space to create massive, temporary "whiteboards." I have coached groups where we wallpapered every wall—top to bottom—of the project room with these, and found them a great communication aid.

- If using a whiteboard for UML drawings, use a device (there is at least one on the market) that captures the hand drawings and transmits them to a computer as a graphics file. One design involves a receiving part that snaps on to a corner of the whiteboard and special transmitting sleeves that marker pens insert into.

- Alternatively, if using a whiteboard for UML drawings, use a digital camera to capture the images, usually in two or three sections. This is a fairly common and effective diagramming practice.

- Another whiteboard technology is a "printing" whiteboard, which is usually a two-sided whiteboard with a scanner and attached printer. These are also useful.

- Print out the hand-drawn UML images (captured by camera or whiteboard device) and hang them visibly *very* near to the programming workstation. The point of the diagrams is to provide some inspiration for the direction of the programming, so that the programmers can glance at them while programming. If they are drawn but "buried," there was little point in drawing them.

- If drawing UML by hand, use simple notation chosen for speed and ease of drawing.

- Even if doing creative design on a whiteboard, use a UML CASE tool to generate package and class diagrams by reverse-engineering the source code (from the last iteration) at least at the beginning of each subsequent iteration. Then, use these reverse-engineered diagrams as the starting point for subsequent creative design.

- Periodically print out freshly reverse-engineered interesting/unstable/difficult package and class diagrams in an enlarged size (for viewing ease) on a plotter that can print on a continuous sheet of three- or four-foot-wide paper. Hang these on walls very close to the developers as visual aids. The technical writer, if present, can do this work. Encourage developers to draw and scribble on the plots during creative design work.

- With respect to reverse-engineering, a few UML tools support reverse-engineering of sequence diagrams—not just class diagrams—from source code. If available, use one to generate sequence diagrams for architecturally significant scenarios, print them in large size on the plotter, and hang them for easy viewing.

- If using a UML CASE tool (indeed, do this for all programming work), use a dual-monitor workstation (two regular-size flat-panel displays are cheaper than a single large flat-panel display). Modern operating systems support (at least) dual video cards and thus two displays. Organize your windows within the UML tool across the two displays. Why? One small monitor is psychologically or creatively inhibiting in terms of drawing and visual languages because the visual canvas space is too small and cramped. A developer can get into the discouraged attitude of "the design is finished because the window is full, and it looks too cluttered."

- When using a UML CASE tool and doing creative design in pairs or small groups, attach two computer projectors to the two video cards of the computer and align the projections on the wall so that the team can see and work with a large visual canvas space. A small canvas and hard-to-see diagrams are a psychological and social impediment to small-group collaborative visual design.

35.3 Tools and Sample Features

This Book Is Tool-Neutral

It would be slightly odd not to mention any UML CASE (computer-aided software engineering) tools, because the book is in part about drawing in the UML, which happens with a CASE tool, or at a whiteboard. At the same time, not all tools can be equally covered, and proper evaluations are beyond the scope of the book. To be impartial:

> This book does not endorse any UML CASE tool. The following examples are only to illustrate some typical and key features found in UML CASE tools.

Tools Have Inconsistent UML Conformance

Few tools draw all UML notation correctly, conforming to the current version of the UML specification—or indeed any version. Although this would be nice, it should not be a factor in choosing a tool, because much more important is its functionality and ease of use.

Example One

In Figure 35.1 and Figure 35.2, Together from TogetherSoft is used to illustrate and define two key functions of a UML CASE tool: **forward-engineering** and **reverse engineering**. These functions are at the heart of what distinguishes a UML CASE tool from a drawing tool.

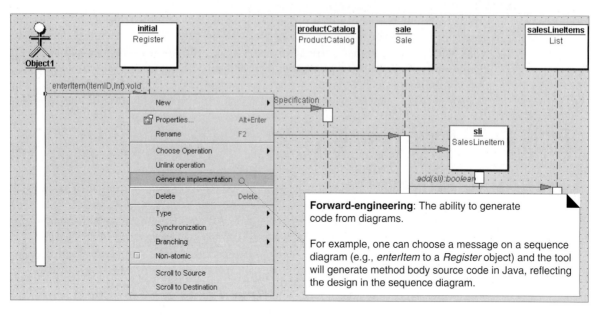

Figure 35.1 Forward-engineering.

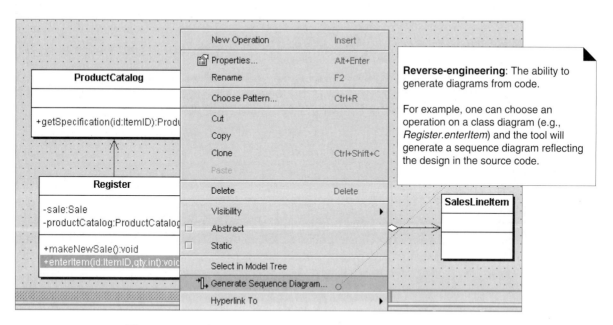

Figure 35.2 Reverse-engineering.

35.4 Example Two

In Figure 35.3 and Figure 35.4, Rational Rose is used to illustrate some other core functions in a UML CASE tool.

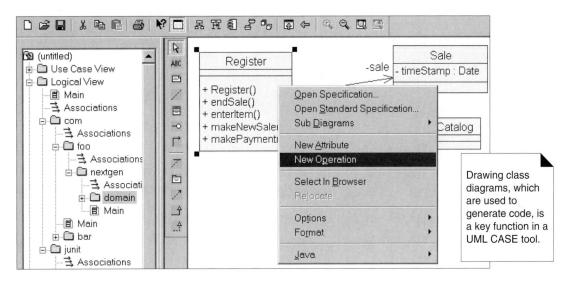

Figure 35.3 Creating class diagrams.

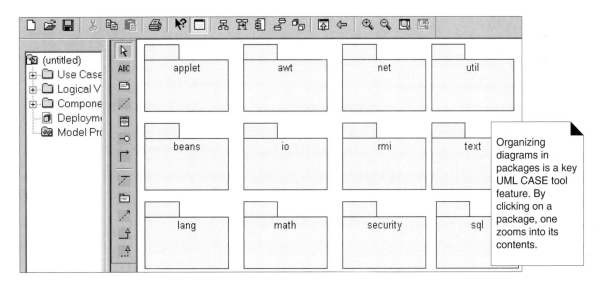

Figure 35.4 Managing packages.

UML CASE Tool Vendor Requests

I suggest consumers make four requests of UML CASE tool vendors:

1. Implement correct, current UML notation in the tool.

2. Have the CASE tool development team itself seriously draw, read, and review UML diagrams (including reverse-engineered diagrams) in the process of building the UML tool itself.

3. Use version N of the UML tool to create version N+1.

4. Provide support for reverse- and forward-engineering of sequence diagrams; most tools only support this for class diagrams.

Microsoft advocates that tool creators "eat their own dogfood." Good advice.

INTRODUCTION TO ITERATIVE PLANNING AND PROJECT ISSUES

Prediction is very difficult, especially if it's about the future.

—*anonymous*

Objectives

- Rank requirements and risks.
- Compare and contrast adaptive and predictive planning.
- Define the UP Phase Plan and Iteration Plan.
- Introduce requirements tracking tools for iterative development.
- Suggest how to organize project artifacts.

Introduction

Project planning and management issues are large topics, but a brief exploration of some key questions related to iterative development and the UP is helpful, such as:

- What to do in the next iteration?
- How to track requirements in iterative development?
- How to organize project artifacts?

36.1   Ranking Requirements

Early Iteration Drivers: Risk, Coverage, Criticality, Skills Development

What to do in the earliest iterations? Organize requirements and iterations by risk, coverage, and criticality [Kruchten00]. Requirement risk includes both technical complexity and other factors, such as uncertainty of effort, poor specification, political problems, or usability. Ranking requirement risks is to be contrasted with ranking project risks, which is covered in a later section.

Coverage implies that all major parts of the system are at least touched on in early iterations—perhaps a "wide and shallow" implementation across many components. Criticality refers to functions of high business value; that is, primary functions should have at least partial implementations for main success scenarios in the earlier iterations, even if not technically risky.

On some projects, another driver is skills development—a goal is to help the team master new skills such as adopting object technologies. On such projects, skills development is a heavily weighted prioritization factor which tends to reorganize the iterations into less risky or simpler requirements in early iterations, motivated by learning rather than risk reduction goals.

What to Rank?

The UP is use-case driven, which includes the practice of ranking use cases (and scenarios of use cases) for implementation. Also, some requirements are expressed as high-level features unrelated to a particular use case, usually because they span many use cases or are a general service, such as logging services. These non-use case functions will be recorded in the Supplementary Specification. Therefore, include both use cases and other high-level features in a ranking list.

Requirement	Type	. . .
Process Sale	UC	. . .
Logging	Feature	. . .
. . .	. . .	. . .

Group Qualitative Methods for Ranking

Based on the drivers, requirements are ranked, and high priorities are handled in early iterations. The ranking may be informal and qualitative, generated in a group meeting by members mindful of these drivers.

Suggestion

To informally prioritize requirements, tasks, or risks via a group meeting, use iterative "dot voting." List the items on a whiteboard. Everyone gets, for example, 20 sticky dots. As a group, and in silence (to reduce influence), all approach the board and apply dots to the items, reflecting the voter's priorities. A voter can assign many dots to one item. On completion, sort and discuss. Then do a second round of silent dot voting to reflect updated insight based on first round voting and discussion. This second round provides the feedback and adaptation by which decisions improve.

The requirements or risk ranking will be done before iteration 1, but then again before iteration 2, and so forth.

Quantitative Methods for Ranking

Group discussion and something like dot voting for requirements or risk ranking are probably sufficient—a fuzzy qualitative approach. For the more quantitatively minded, variations on the following have been used. The example values and weights are only suggestive; the point is that numeric values and weights can be used to reason about priorities.

Requirement	Type	AS	Risk	Criticality	W. Sum
Process Sale	UC	3	2	3	15
Logging	Feat	3	0	1	7
Handle Returns	UC	1	0	0	2
. . .	. . .	. . .	. . .	. . .	. . .
		Weight	Range		
AS: achitecturally significant		2	0-3		
Risk: tech, complex, novel,...		3	0-3		
Criticality: *early* high biz value		1	0-3		

On any project, the exact values should not be taken too seriously; on completion, the numeric scoring can be used to help group the requirements into fuzzy sets of high, medium, and low ranking. Clearly, *Process Sale* appears important to work on in early iterations.

The numbers don't tell the whole story. Even though logging is a low-risk, simple feature, it is architecturally significant because it needs to be integrated throughout the code from the start. It would be awkward and diminish architectural integrity to add it as an afterthought.

Ranking the NextGen POS Requirements

Based on some ranking method, a fuzzy grouping of requirements is possible. In terms of UP artifacts, this ranking is recorded in the UP Software Development Plan.

Rank	Requirement (use case or feature)	Comment
High	Process Sale Logging . . .	Scores high on all ranking criteria. Pervasive. Hard to add late. . . .
Medium	Maintain Users Authenticate User . . .	Affects security subdomain. Important process but not too difficult. . . .
Low	Cash Out Shut Down . . .	Easy; minimal effect on architecture. Ditto. . . .

The "Start Up" and "Shut Down" Use Cases

Virtually all systems have a *Start Up* use case, implicit if not explicit. Although it may not rank high by other criteria, it is necessary to tackle at least some simplified version of *Start Up* in the first iteration so that the initialization assumed by other cases is provided. Within each iteration, the *Start Up* use case is incrementally developed to satisfy the start up needs of the other use cases. Similarly, systems often have a *Shut Down* use case. In some systems, it is quite complex, such as shutting down an active telecommunications switch. In terms of planning, if simple, these use cases can be informally listed in the Iteration Plan, such as "implement startup and shutdown as required." Obviously, complex versions need more careful requirements and planning attention.

A Caveat: Project Planning vs. Learning Goals

The book goal is to offer a learning aid for introductory analysis and design, rather than actually run the NextGen POS project. Therefore, some license has been taken in the choice of what is tackled in the early iterations of the case study, motivated by learning rather than project goals.

36.2   Ranking Project Risks

A useful method to prioritize overall project risks is to estimate their probability and impact (in cost, time, or effort). The estimates may be quantitative (which are usually very speculative) or simply qualitative (for example, high-medium-low, based on discussion and group dot-voting). The worst risks are naturally those both probable and of high impact. For example:

Risk	Prob-ability	Impact	Mitigation Ideas
Insufficient number and quality of skilled object-oriented developers.	H	H	Read the book. Hire temporary consultants. Classroom education & mentoring. Design and programming in pairs.
Demo not ready for the upcoming POS-World convention in Hamburg.	M	H	Hire temporary consultants who are specialists in Java POS systems development. Identify "sexy" requirements that show well in a demo, and prioritize those, over others. Maximize the use of pre-built components.
. . .	. . .	. . .	. . .

In terms of UP artifacts, this is part of the Software Development Plan.

36.3   Adaptive vs. Predictive Planning

One of the big ideas of iterative development is to adapt based on feedback, rather than to attempt to predict and plan *in detail* the entire project. Consequently, in the UP, one creates an Iteration Plan for only the *next* iteration. Beyond the next iteration the detailed plan is left open, to adaptively adjust as the future unfolds (see Figure 36.1). In addition to encouraging flexible, opportunistic behavior, one simple reason for not planning the entire project in detail is that in iterative development not all the requirements, design details, and thus steps are known near the start of the project.[1] Another is the preference to trust the planning judgement of the team as they proceed. Finally, suppose there was a fine-grained detailed plan laid out at the start of the project, and the team "deviates" from it to exploit better insight in how to best run the project.

From the outside, this might be viewed as some kind of failure, when it in fact it is just the opposite.

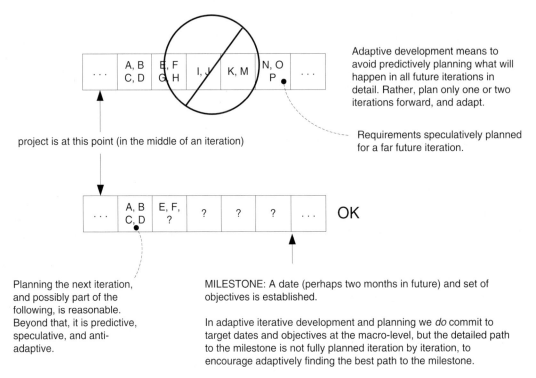

Adaptive development means to avoid predictively planning what will happen in all future iterations in detail. Rather, plan only one or two iterations forward, and adapt.

Requirements speculatively planned for a far future iteration.

project is at this point (in the middle of an iteration)

Planning the next iteration, and possibly part of the following, is reasonable. Beyond that, it is predictive, speculative, and anti-adaptive.

MILESTONE: A date (perhaps two months in future) and set of objectives is established.

In adaptive iterative development and planning we *do* commit to target dates and objectives at the macro-level, but the detailed path to the milestone is not fully planned iteration by iteration, to encourage adaptively finding the best path to the milestone.

Figure 36.1 Milestones are important, but avoid detailed predictive planning into the far future.

However, there *are* still goals and milestones; adaptive development doesn't mean the team doesn't know where they are going, or the milestone dates and objectives. In iterative development, the team still does commit to dates and objectives, but the detailed path to these is flexible. For example, the NextGen team may set a milestone that in three months, use cases *Process Sale, Handle Returns*, and *Authenticate User*, and the logging and pluggable rules features will be completed. But—and this is the key point—the fine-grained plan or path of two-week timeboxed iterations to that milestone is not defined in detail. The order of steps, or what to do in each iteration over the following three months, is not fixed. Rather, just the next two-week iteration is planned, and the team adapts step by step, working to fulfill the objectives by the milestone date. Of course, dependencies in components and resources naturally constrain some ordering of the work, but not all activities need to be planned and scheduled in fine-grained detail.

---

1. They aren't really or reliably known on a "waterfall" project either, although detailed planning for the entire project may occur as though they were.

External stakeholders see a macro-level plan (such as at the three-month level) to which the team makes some commitment. But the micro-level organization is left up to the best—and adaptive—judgment of the team, as it takes advantage of new insights (see Figure 36.1).

Finally, although adaptive fine-grained planning is preferred in the UP, it *is* increasingly possible to successfully plan forward two or three iterations (with increasingly levels of unreliability) as the requirements and architecture stabilize, the team matures, and data is collected on the speed of development.

36.4   Phase and Iteration Plans

At a macro level, it is possible to establish milestone dates and objectives, but at the micro level, the plan to the milestone is left flexible except for the near future (for example, the next four weeks). These two levels are reflected in the UP **Phase Plan** and **Iteration Plan**, both of which are part of the composite Software Development Plan. The Phase Plan lays out the macro-level milestone dates and objectives, such as the end of phases and mid-phase pilot test milestones. The Iteration Plan defines the work for the current and next iteration—not all iterations (see Figure 36.2).

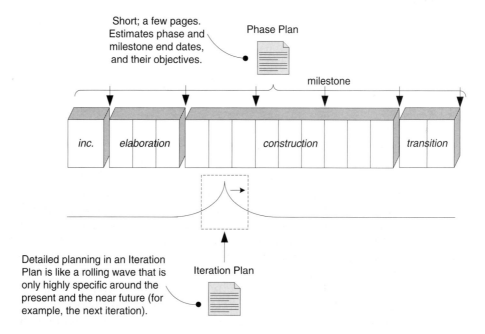

Figure 36.2 Phase and Iteration Plans.

During inception, the milestone estimates in the Phase Plan are vague "guesstimates." As elaboration progresses, the estimates improve. One goal of the elaboration phase is, at its completion, to have enough realistic information for the team to commit to major milestone dates and objectives for the end of construction and transition (that is, project delivery).

36.5   Iteration Plan: What to Do in the Next Iteration?

The UP is use-case driven, which in part implies that work is organized around use-case completion. That is to say, an iteration is assigned to implement one or more use cases, or scenarios of use cases when the complete use case is too complex to complete in one iteration. And since some requirements are not expressed as use cases, but rather as features, such as logging or pluggable business rules, these too are allocated to one or more iterations (see Figure 36.3).

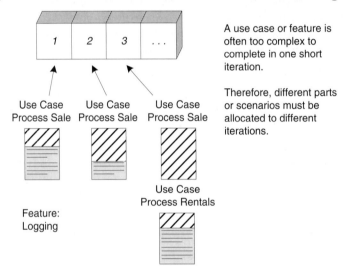

Figure 36.3 Work allocated to an iteration.

Usually, the first iteration of elaboration is consumed with myriad overhead tasks such as tool and component installation and tweaking, requirements clarification, and so forth.

The ranking of requirements guides the choice of early work. For example, the *Process Sale* use case is clearly important. Therefore, we start to tackle it in the first iteration. Yet, not all scenarios of *Process Sale* are implemented in the first iteration. Rather, some simple, happy path scenario, such as for a cash-only payment, is chosen. Although the scenario is simple, its implementation starts to develop some core elements of the design.

Different architecturally significant requirements related to this use case will be tackled during the elaboration iterations, forcing the team to touch on many aspects of the architecture: the major layers, the database, the user interface, the interfaces between major subsystems, and so forth. This leads to the early creation of a "wide and shallow" implementation across many parts of the system—a common goal in the elaboration phase.

36.6   Requirements Tracking Across Iterations

The task of creating the first Iteration Plan brings us to a noteworthy issue in iterative development, illustrated in Figure 36.3.

As indicated in the last section, not all scenarios of *Process Sale* will be implemented in the first iteration. Indeed, this complex use case may take many two-week iterations over a six-month period to complete. Each iteration will tackle new scenarios or parts of scenarios.

When fulfilling all the scenarios of a use case in one iteration is not possible, there arises a problem in requirements tracking. How does one record what parts of a use case are complete, are currently being worked on, or are not yet done? A requirements tool built for the job provides one solution.

Rational's RequisitePro offers an example, and is worth a moment's study to understand how these tools work to track partially completed use cases across iterations. This is not an endorsement of the tool, but the presentation is offered to illustrate one solution to this very important tracking problem.

An Example Requirements Management Tool

RequisitePro integrates with Microsoft Word so that one may enter and edit requirements in Word, select a phrase, and define the selected phrase as a tracked requirement in RequisitePro.

Each requirement can have a variety of attributes, such as status, risk, and so forth (see Figure 36.4 and Figure 36.5). With such a tool, the problem of tracking partial use case completion across iterations is manageable.

All statements in the main success and extension scenarios can be individually represented as tracked requirements, and each identified with various status values such as *proposed*, *approved*, and so on.

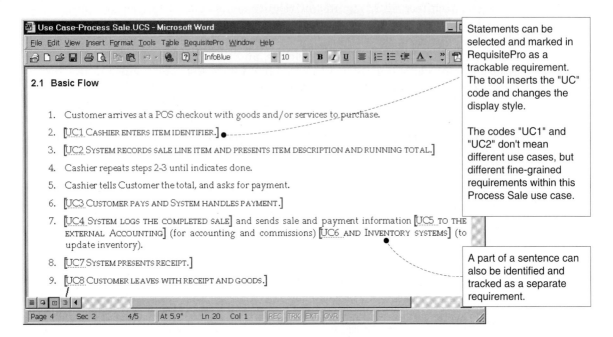

Figure 36.4 Basic tagging of use case phrases as requirements.

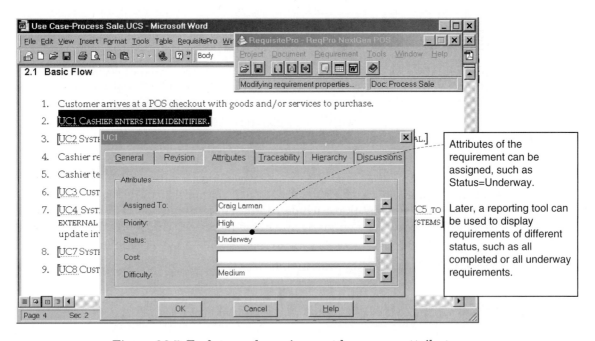

Figure 36.5 Each tagged requirement has many attributes.

36.7   The (In)Validity of Early Estimates

Garbage in, garbage out. Estimates done with unreliable and fuzzy information are unreliable and fuzzy. In the UP it is understood that estimates done during inception are not dependable (this is true of all methods, but the UP acknowledges it). Early inception estimates merely provide guidance if the project is worthy of some real investigation in elaboration, to generate a good estimate. After the first elaboration iteration there is some realistic information to produce a rough estimate. After the second iteration, the estimate starts to develop credibility (see Figure 36.6).

> Useful estimates require investment in some elaboration iterations.

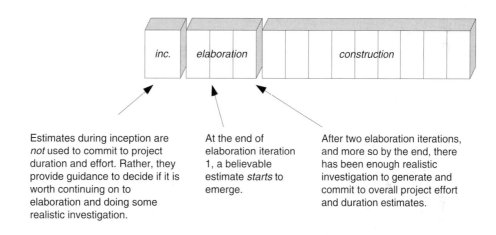

Estimates during inception are *not* used to commit to project duration and effort. Rather, they provide guidance to decide if it is worth continuing on to elaboration and doing some realistic investigation.

At the end of elaboration iteration 1, a believable estimate *starts* to emerge.

After two elaboration iterations, and more so by the end, there has been enough realistic investigation to generate and commit to overall project effort and duration estimates.

Figure 36.6 Estimation and project phases.

This is not to imply that it is impossible or worthless to attempt early, accurate estimates. If possible, very good. However, most organizations do not find this to be the case, for reasons that include continuous introduction of new technologies, novel applications, and many other complications. Thus, the UP advocates some realistic work in elaboration before generating estimates used for project planning and budgeting.

36.8   Organizing Project Artifacts

The UP organizes artifacts in terms of disciplines. The Use-Case Model and Supplementary Specifications are in the Requirements discipline. The Software

Development Plan is part of the Project Management discipline, and so forth. Therefore, organize folders in your version control and directory system to reflect the disciplines, and place the artifacts of a discipline within the related discipline folder (see Figure 36.7).

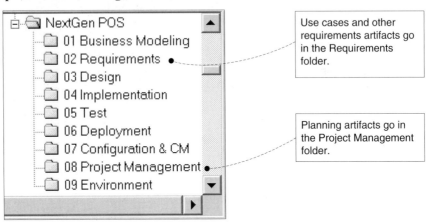

Figure 36.7 Organize UP artifacts into folders corresponding to their disciplines.

This organization works for most non-implementation elements. Some implementation artifacts, such as the actual database or executable files, are commonly found in different locations for a variety of implementation reasons.

Suggestion

After each iteration, use the version control tool to create a labeled and frozen checkpoint of all the elements in these folders (including source code). There will be an "Elaboration-1," "Elaboration-2," and so on, version of each artifact. For later estimation of team velocity (on this or other projects), these checkpoints provide raw data of how much work got done per iteration.

36.9   Some Team Iteration Scheduling Issues

Parallel Development Teams

A large project is usually broken into parallel development efforts, where multiple teams work in parallel. One way to organize the teams is along architectural lines: by layers and subsystems. Another organizational structure is by feature set, which may very well correspond to architectural organization.

For example:

- Domain layer team (or domain subsystem team)
- User interface team
- Internationalization team
- Technical service team (persistence team, and so on)

Teams on Different Iteration Lengths

Sometimes, developing a subsystem (such as the persistence service) to any meaningfully usable level requires a relatively long time, especially during its early stages. Rather than stretch the overall iteration length for all teams, an alternative is to keep the iterations short (in general, a worthy goal) for most teams, and of double length for the "slower" team (see Figure 36.8).

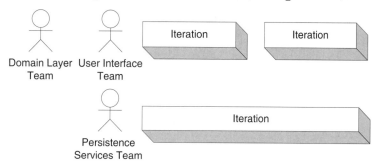

Figure 36.8 Varying iteration lengths.

Team Speed and Incremental Process Adoption

In addition to needing longer iterations for massive teams, another reason to lengthen an iteration (for example, from three weeks to four), is related to the speed and experience of the team. A team new to many of the practices or technologies will naturally go slower, and needs more time to complete an iteration. Less experienced teams benefit from *slightly* longer and fewer iterations than more experienced teams.

Note that iterative development provides a mechanism to improve estimating speed: the actual progress in early iterations informs estimates for later ones.

Related to this is the strategy of **incremental process adoption**. In early iterations, less experienced teams take on a small set of practices. As the team members digest and master these, add more—assuming they're useful! For example, in early iterations the team may do one daily system build and test. In later iterations, it may adopt continuous integration and system testing (which happens many times each day) with a continuous integration tool such as the open-source Cruise Control (cruisecontrol.sourceforge.net).

36.10 You Know You Didn't Understand Planning in the UP When...

- All the iterations are speculatively planned in detail, with the work and objectives for each iteration predicted.

- Early estimates in inception or the first iteration of elaboration are expected to be reliable, and are used to make long-term project commitments; to generalize, reliable estimates are expected with trivial or light-weight investigation.

- Easy problems or low-risk issues are tackled in early iterations.

If an organization's estimation and planning process looks something like the following, planning in the UP was not understood:

1. At the start of an annual planning phase, new systems or features are identified at a high level; for instance, "Web system for account management."

2. Technical managers are given a short period to speculatively estimate the effort and duration for large, expensive, or risky projects, often involving new technologies.

3. The plan and budget of projects are established for the year.

4. Stakeholders are concerned when actual projects do not match original estimates. Go to Step 1.

This approach lacks realistic and iteratively refined estimation based upon serious investigation as promoted by the UP.

36.11 Further Readings

Software Project Management: A Unified Framework by Royce provides an iterative and UP perspective on project planning and management.

Cockburn's *Surviving Object-Oriented Projects: A Manager's Guide* contains more useful information on iterative planning, and the transition to iterative and object technology projects.

Kruchten's *The Rational Unified Process: An Introduction* contains useful chapters specifically on planning and project management in the UP.

As a caution, there are some books that purport to discuss planning for "iterative development" or the "Unified Process" that actually belie a waterfall or predictive approach to planning.

Rapid Development [McConnell96] is an excellent overview of many practices and issues in planning and project management, and project risks.

COMMENTS ON ITERATIVE
DEVELOPMENT AND THE UP

*You should use iterative development only on
projects that you want to succeed.*

—*Martin Fowler*

Objectives

- Introduce and expand on some UP topics.

- Introduce other practices applicable to iterative development.

- Examine how the iterative lifecycle can help reduce some development problems.

37.1 Additional UP Best Practices and Concepts

The central idea to appreciate and practice in the UP is short timeboxed iterative, adaptive development. Some additional best practices and key concepts in the UP include:

- **Tackle high-risk and high-value issues in early iterations**—For example, if the new system is a server application that has to handle 2,000 concurrent clients with sub-second transaction response time, do not wait for many months (or years) to design and implement this high risk requirement. Rather, quickly focus on designing, programming, and proving the essential software components and architecture for this risky issue; leave the easier work till later iterations. The idea is to drive down the high risks in the early iterations, so that the project does not "fail late," which is a characteristic of waterfall projects that defer hard, risky concerns till later in the lifecycle. Better to "fail early" if at all, by doing the hard things first. Thus, the UP is said to be **risk driven**. Finally, notice that risk comes in many forms: lack of skills or resources, technical challenges, usability, politics, and so on. All these forms influence what is addressed in early iterations.

- **Continuously engage users**—Iterative development and the UP is about quickly taking small steps and getting feedback. It requires continuous attention and engagement by business stakeholders and subject matter experts to clarify and steer the project. At first, business may feel this is an imposition. However, the majority of failed projects are correlated with lack of user engagement [Standish94], and this approach gives business the ability to shape the software as they truly need it. On projects where the "user" is speculative, such as a new website or consumer product, focus groups may act as proxies.

- **Early attention to building a cohesive, core architecture**—That is, the UP is **architecture-centric**. This is related to tackling the high-risk concerns in early iterations, since getting the core of the architecture established is usually a risky or critical element. Early iterations typically focus on a "wide and shallow" architectural implementation, establishing the major design themes, and the subsystems with their interfaces and responsibilities. The team will "spike" into vertically deep areas for particular hard or risky requirements, such as the requirement for sub-second transactions with 2,000 concurrent clients.

- **Continuously verify quality, early and often**—Quality in this context includes correctly meeting or exceeding the requirements in a sustainable and repeatable process, with maintainable and scalable software. One motivation for an early, continuous, and intensive campaign of testing, inspection, and quality assurance is that the expense of a lingering defect increases nonlinearly through the phases of a project. Furthermore, iterative development is based on feedback and adaptation; therefore, early realistic testing and evaluation are critical activities to obtain meaningful feedback. This is in contrast to a waterfall project, where the significant quality assurance step is done near the end of a project, when response is the most difficult and expensive. In the UP, quality verification is continuously integrated from the start, so that there are not big surprises near the end of the project. Note that in the UP, quality verification also refers to process quality—each iteration, assessing how well the team is doing.

- **Apply use cases**—Informally, use cases are written stories of using a system. They are a mechanism to explore and record functional requirements, in contrast to the older style function lists or "the system shall do. . ." lists. The UP recommends applying use cases as the primary form for requirements capture, and as a driving force in planning, designing, testing, and writing end-user documentation.

- **Model software visually**—An extraordinary percentage of the human brain is involved in visual processing, which is a motivation behind the visual or graphical presentation of information [Tufte92]. It is therefore skillful to employ not only textual languages (such as prose or code), but also iconic, diagrammatic, spatially-oriented visual languages such as the UML, because this exploits the brain's natural strengths.[1] In addition, *abstraction* is a useful practice in thinking about and communicating software designs, because this allows us to focus on important aspects, while hiding or ignoring noisy details. A visual language such as the UML allows us to visualize and reason about abstract models of software, moving quickly with diagrammatic sketches of the big ideas in the design. But as will be explored later, there is a "UML sweet spot" between too little and too much diagramming.

- **Carefully manage requirements**—This does not mean employing the waterfall practice of fully defining and freezing the requirements in the first phase of a project. Rather, it implies not being sloppy—that is, being skillful in the elicitation, recording, prioritization, tracing, and lifecycle tracking of requirements, usually with tool support. This sounds obvious, but seems to be seldom well-practiced. Poor requirements management is a common factor on troubled projects [Standish94].

- **Control changes**—This practice encompasses several ideas: First, change request management. Although an iterative UP project embraces change, it does not embrace chaos. When new requirement requests emerge during the iterations, rather than a blithe "Sure, no problem!" there is a rational evaluation of their effort and impact, and if accepted, the schedule modified. It also includes the idea of tracking the lifecycle of all change requests (requested, underway, ...). Second, configuration management. Configuration and build management tools are used to support frequent (ideally, at least daily) system integration and test, parallel development, separate developer workspaces and configurations, and version control—from the start of the project. In the UP, all project assets (not just code) should be under configuration and version control.

37.2   The Construction and Transition Phases

Construction

Elaboration ends when the high risk issues have been resolved, the architectural core or skeleton is complete, and "most" requirements are understood. At the end of elaboration, it is possible to more realistically estimate the remaining effort and duration for the project.

It is followed by the **construction phase**, whose purpose is essentially to finish building the application, alpha testing, prepare for beta testing (in the transition phase), and prepare for deployment, through activities such as writing the user guides and online help. It is sometimes summarized as putting the "flesh on the skeleton" created in elaboration. Whereas elaboration can be character-

---

1. It is also a motivation for the use of color in diagramming (unless some team members have a color blindness). For example, see [CDL99].

ized as building the risky and architecturally significant core of the system, construction can be described as building the remainder. As before, development proceeds via a series of timeboxed iterations. In terms of staffing, it is recommended to use a small, cohesive team during elaboration, and then expand the team size during construction; in addition, there will probably be more parallel team development during this phase.

Transition

Construction ends when the system is deemed ready for operational deployment, and all supporting materials are complete, such as user guides, training materials, and so on. It is followed by the **transition phase**, whose purpose is to put the system into production use. This may include activities such as beta testing, reacting to beta test feedback, fine-tuning, data conversion, training, marketing roll-out, parallel operation of the old and new system, and the like.

37.3   Other Interesting Practices

This is not an exhaustive list, but some interesting practices—not explicitly documented in the UP—that have been of value on iterative projects include:

- The **SCRUM** process pattern [BDSSS00]; see also www.controlchaos.com. The most concrete is a daily "15-minute" stand-up SCRUM meeting. The project coach asks from each person: 1) items done since last meeting; 2) goals for next day; and 3) blocks for the coach to remove. I've also asked each member for noteworthy insights he or she want to share with the team. The meeting promotes adaptive, emergent team behavior, fine-grained measurement of progress, high density communication, and project socialization. Other key ideas include: The team is freed of all external distractions, has no additional work added (from outside the team) during an iteration, and management's job is to remove all blocks and distractions, so the team can focus.

- Some **Extreme Programming** (XP) [Beck00] practices, such as **test-first programming**: Write a unit test *before* the code to be tested, and write tests for virtually all classes. If working in Java, **JUnit** (www.junit.org) is a popular, free unit testing framework. Write a little test, write a little code, make it pass, repeat. Writing the test *first* is essential to experience the value of this approach.

- **Continuous integration**, another XP practice; see [Beck00] for an introduction and www.martinfowler.com for details. The UP includes the best-practice of integrating the entire system at least once every iteration. This is often shortened to the practice of a **daily build**. *Continuous* integration shortens this still further, integrating all new checked-in code (at least) every few hours. Although this can be done manually, an alternative is to use an automated, continuous integration and test environment on a fast build machine running a daemon process. It periodically wakes up (such as every two minutes) and looks for new checked-in code, which triggers running a rebuild and test script. A continuous integration system for Java projects called **Cruise Control** is freely available and open-source at SourceForge (cruisecontrol.sourceforge.net).

37.4   Motivations for Timeboxing an Iteration

There are at least four motivations for timeboxing an iteration.

First, **Parkinson's law**. Parkinson wryly observed that "Work expands so as to fill the time available for its completion" [Parkinson58]. Distant or fuzzy completion dates (for example, six months away), exacerbate this effect. Near the start of a project, it can feel like there is plenty of time to proceed leisurely. But if the end date for the next iteration is only *two weeks* away, and an executable, tested partial system must be in place on that date, the team has to focus, make decisions, and get moving.

Second, **prioritization** and **decisiveness**. Short timeboxed iterations force a development team to make decisions regarding the priority of work and risks, identify what is of highest business or technical value, and estimate some work. For example, if embarking on the first iteration, chosen to be exactly four weeks in length, there is not much latitude to be vague—concrete decisions about what will really be done within the first four weeks must be made.

Third, **team satisfaction**. Short timeboxed iterations lead to a quick and repeating sense of completion, competency, and closure. On regular two- or four-week cycles, the team has the experience of finishing something, rather than work lingering on for months without completion. These psychological factors are important for individual work satisfaction, and for building team confidence.

Fourth, **stakeholder confidence**. When a team makes a public commitment to producing something executable and stable within a short time period, on a particular date, such as two weeks in the future, and does so, business and other stakeholders develop increased confidence in the team and the project.

37.5   The Sequential "Waterfall" Lifecycle

In contrast to the iterative lifecycle of the UP, an old alternative is the sequential, linear, or "waterfall" lifecycle [Royce70], associated with heavy and predictive processes. In common usage, a waterfall lifecycle defines steps similar to the following:

1. Clarify, record, and commit to a set of final requirements.

2. Design a system based on these requirements.

3. Implement, based on the design.

4. Integrate disparate modules.

5. Evaluate and test for correctness and quality.

A development process based on the waterfall lifecycle is associated with these behaviors or attitudes:

- Carefully and fully define an artifact (for example, the requirements or design) before carrying on to the next step.

- Commit to a frozen set of detailed requirements.

- Deviation from the requirements or design during later steps indicates a failure in not having been sufficiently skillful or thorough. Next time, try harder to get it right.

A waterfall process is similar to the engineering approach by which buildings and bridges are constructed. Its adoption made software development appear more structured and similar to engineering in some other fields. For some time, a waterfall process was the approach most software developers, managers, authors, and teachers were taught when they were students (and then repeated), without critical research into its suitability for software development.

Some things should be built like buildings—such as, well...buildings—but not usually software.

A mentioned in the opening chapter on the UP, a two year study reported in the *MIT Sloan Management Review* of successful software projects identified four common factors for success; iterative development, rather than a waterfall lifecycle, was first on the list [MacCormack01].

Some Problems with the Waterfall Lifecycle

> The building metaphor has outlived its usefulness. It is time to change again. If, as I believe, the conceptual structures we construct today are too complicated to be accurately specified in advance, and too complex to be built faultlessly, then we must take a radically different approach (iterative, incremental development).
>
> *—Frederick Brooks, "No Silver Bullet," The Mythical Man-Month*

Within a certain time scale, doing some requirements before design, and some design before implementation, is inevitable and sensible. For a short two month project, a sequential lifecycle is workable. And a single iteration in iterative development is like a short waterfall project.

However, difficulties start to arise as the time scale lengthens. The complexity becomes high, speculative decisions increase and compound, there is no feedback, and in general high risk issues are not being tackled early enough. By definition, one attempts to do all or most of the requirements for the entire system before moving on, and most of the design before moving on.

Large steps are taken in which many decisions are made without the benefit of concrete feedback from realistic implementation and testing. On the scale of a two-week mini-project (that is, an iteration), a linear requirements-design-implementation sequence is workable; the degree of speculative commitment to some requirements and design is not in the danger zone. However, as the scale expands, so do the speculation and risk.

Problems with a waterfall process at the scale of the entire project include:

- delayed risk mitigation; tackling high risk or difficult problems late
- requirements and design speculation and inflexibility
- high complexity
- low adaptability

Mitigation of Some Problems with the Waterfall Lifecycle

Iterative development is not a magic bullet for the challenges of software development. Yet, it offers support to reduce some problems exacerbated by a linear waterfall lifecycle.

Problem: Delayed Risk Mitigation

Risks come in many forms: the wrong design, the wrong set of requirements, a strange political environment, lack of skills or resource, usability, and so forth.

In a waterfall lifecycle, there is *not* an active attempt to identify and mitigate the riskiest issues first. As an example, the wrong architecture for a high-load high-availability website can cause costly delays, or worse. In a waterfall process, validation of the architecture's suitability happens *long* after all requirements and all design are specified (inevitably imperfectly), during the later major step of implementation. This could be many months or even years after inception of the project (see Figure 37.1). And there is no shortage of stories where separate teams have built subsystems over a long period, and then attempted to integrate these and start overall system testing near the end of the project—with predictably painful results.

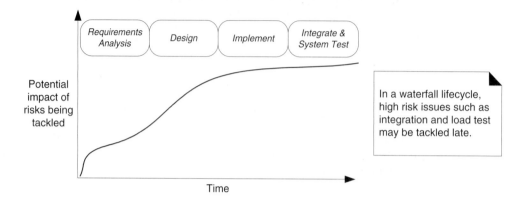

Figure 37.1 Waterfall lifecycle and risks.

Mitigation

In contrast, in iterative development the goal is to identify and mitigate the riskiest issues early. The high risks might be in the core architectural design, the usability of the interface, disengaged stakeholders. Whatever, they are tackled first. As illustrated in Figure 37.2, early iterations focus on driving down the risk. Continuing with the prior high-load website example, in an iterative approach, before much investment in other requirements or design work, the team first designs, implements, and realistically tests enough of the core architecture to prove it is on the right track with respect to load and availability. If the tests prove them wrong, they adapt the core design in the early stages of the project, rather than near the end.

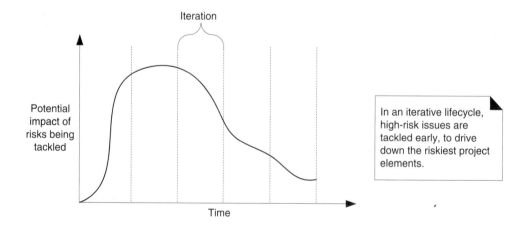

Figure 37.2 Iterative lifecycle and risks.

Problem: Requirements Speculation and Inflexibility

A fundamental assumption in a waterfall process is that requirements can be relatively fully specified and then frozen in the first phase of a project. On such projects, there is an effort to first do thorough requirements analysis, culminating in a set of requirements artifacts that are reviewed and "signed off."

It turns out this is usually a flawed assumption. The effort to get all the requirements defined and signed-off before any design and implementation work is ironically likely to increase project difficulties rather than ameliorate them. It also makes it difficult to respond late in a project to a new business opportunity via a change in the software.

Granted, there are some projects where an effort to first fully and accurately specify the requirements is necessary. This is especially true when the software is coupled with the building of physical components. Examples include aircraft and medical devices. But note that even in this case, iterative development can still be profitably applied to the design and implementation process.

The most compelling research deconstructing the myth of being able to successfully first define all requirements comes from [Jones97]. As illustrated in Figure 37.3, in this large study of 6,700 projects, creeping requirements—those not anticipated near the start—are a very significant fact of software development life, ranging from around 25% on average projects, up to 50% on larger ones; Boehm and Papaccio present similar research-based conclusions in [BP88]. Waterfall attitudes, which struggle against (or simply deny) this fact by assuming requirements and designs can be specified and frozen, are incongruous with most project realities.

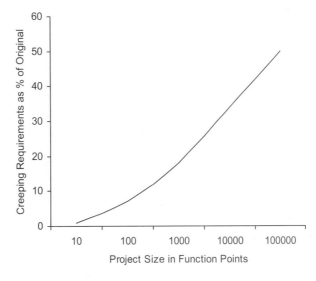

Figure 37.3 Changing requirements are an inevitable force in development.[2]

Thus, "the only constant is change," usually because:

■ the stakeholders change their minds or cannot fully envision what they want until they see a concrete system[3]

■ the market changes

■ correctly validated, detailed, and precise specification is a psychological and organizational challenge for most stakeholders [Kruchten00]

And so, there are predictable and often-seen problems that arise in waterfall projects. Since in reality significant change is inevitable, these include:

■ as described earlier, delayed discovery and mitigation of high risks

■ a negative feeling among team members of "living a fiction" or failure on the project, as the reality of changes does not correspond to the ideal

■ making a large (costly) investment in the wrong design and implementation (since it is based on incorrect requirements)

■ lack of responsiveness to changing user wishes or market opportunities

Mitigation

In iterative development, not all requirements are specified before design and implementation, and requirements are not stabilized until after at least several iterations. For example:

First, a subset of core requirements is defined, for example, within a two-day requirements workshop. Then, the team chooses a subset of those to design and implement (based usually on highest risk or business value). After a four-week iteration, stakeholders meet in a second one- or two-day requirements workshop, intensively review the partial system, and clarify and modify their requests. After a second (shorter) two-week iteration of incrementally implementing the system, stakeholders meet in a third requirements workshop, and refine again. At this point, the requirements start to stabilize and represent the true scope and clarified intentions of the stakeholders. At this point, a somewhat realistic plan and estimate of the remaining work is possible. These iterations may be characterized as part of the UP elaboration phase.

Later requirements changes are still acceptable. However, the interplay in early iteration of parallel implementation work and requirements analysis that obtains feedback from the partial implementation leads to better requirements definition in the elaboration phase.

---

2. Function points describe system complexity with a programming language-independent metric (see www.ifpug.org).

3. Barry Boehm has called this the "I'll know it when I see it" effect.

Problem: Design Speculation and Inflexibility

Another central idea in the waterfall lifecycle is that the architecture and majority of the design can and should be relatively fully specified in the second major phase of a project, once the requirements are clarified. On such projects, there is an effort to thoroughly describe the complete architecture, object designs, user interface, database schema, and so forth, before implementation begins. Some problems associated with this assumption:

1. Since requirements will change, the original design may not be reliable.

2. Immature or misunderstood tools, components, and environments make speculative design decisions risky; they may be proven wrong upon implementation because "the application server wasn't supposed to do that, ..."

3. In general, lack of feedback to prove or disprove the design, until long after the design decisions were made.

Mitigation

These problems are mitigated in iterative development by quickly building part of the system and validating the design and third-party components through testing.

37.6 Usability Engineering and User Interface Design

There is probably no skill with a greater disparity between its importance to successful software and its lack of formal attention and education than **usability engineering** and user interface (UI) design. Although outside the scope of this introduction to OOA/D and the UP, note that the UP does include recognition of this activity; usability and UI models are part of the Requirements discipline. In UP terminology, **use-case storyboards** can be used to abstractly describe the interface elements, and the navigation between them, as related to use-case scenarios.

Useful books include *Software for Use* by Constantine and Lockwood, *The Usability Engineering Lifecycle* by Mayhew, and *GUI Bloopers* by Johnson.

37.7 The UP Analysis Model

The UP contains an artifact called the **Analysis Model**; it is not necessary, and few create it. The **Analysis Model** is perhaps not ideally named, as it is actually a kind of design model. In conventional usage (for example, see [Coleman+94, MO95, Fowler96]), an analysis model suggested essentially a domain object model—an investigation and description of domain concepts. But the UP

"Analysis Model" is an early version of the UP Design Model—it describes collaborating software objects with responsibilities. To quote, "The analysis model is an abstraction, or generalization, of the design" [Kruchten00]. And, "An analysis model can be viewed as a first cut at a design model" [JBR99].

The RUP product team emphasizes that it is optional and of infrequent value, and does not encourage its regular creation—as it is yet another set of diagrams to create before implementation, and is seldom used by most methodologists and expert architects.

37.8   The RUP Product

The RUP product is a cohesive and well-crafted Web-based documentation set (HTML pages) sold by Rational Software that describes the Rational Unified Process, an updated and detailed refinement to the more general UP. It describes all artifacts, activities, and roles, provides guidelines, and includes templates for most artifacts (see Figure 37.4).

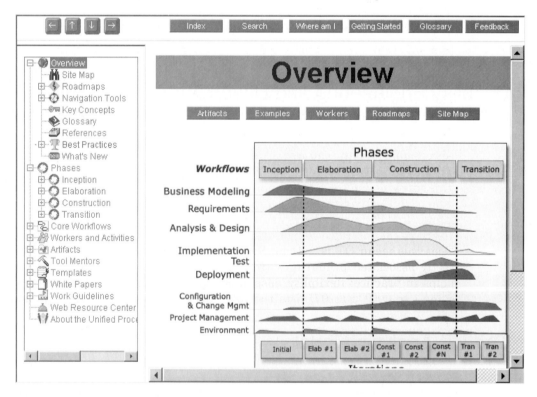

Figure 37.4 The RUP product.

The UP can be applied or adopted with the aid of process mentors and books; the basic ideas, such as iterative development, are described in this and other books.

Consequently, it is not required to own the RUP product. Nevertheless, some organizations find that placing this Web-based product (and its templates) on their intranet (licensing respected) at a visible location to be a simple, effective mechanism to gradually spread its adoption. Moving an organization to a new development process beyond a superficial level requires several modes of support. In addition to process mentoring, pilot projects, and classroom education, the Web-based documentation and templates provided by the RUP product are definitely useful aids worth evaluating.

37.9 The Challenge and Myths of Reuse

The UP is developed with object technology (OT) projects in mind, and the adoption of OT has often been promoted in order to achieve software **reuse**. Significant reuse is a laudable goal, but difficult. It is a function of much more than adopting OT and writing classes; OT is but one enabling technology in a suite of technical, organizational, and social changes that have to occur to see meaningful reuse. Certainly, libraries of classes for technical services, such as the Java technology libraries, provide a great example of reuse, but I am referring to the difficulty of reuse of code created within an organization, not core libraries.

In a survey of organizations that had adopted OT, they were asked the actual value of its adoption. Interesting, reuse was at the *bottom* of the list [Cutter97]. Among experienced OT practitioners and organizations, this is not a surprise: They know that the popular press's description of OT for reuse is to some degree a myth; most organization see little of it. This is not to imply it isn't a valuable goal, or that there is no reuse—it is worthy, and there has been some. But not the high levels of reuse some articles and books suggest. And many an experienced OT developer can tell you a war story about the misguided large-scale attempt by an organization to create the grand "reusable libraries" or services for the company, spending a year and million dollars, and ending with a failed project, or one that misses the mark. Reuse is hard, and arguably more a function of social and organizational issues than technical ones.

Does this mean OT is without value? Not at all, but its value has been incorrectly associated primarily with reuse, rather than how it most prominently helps in practice: flexibility, ease of change, and complexity management. The same survey [Cutter97] lists the top values actually experienced by adopting OT: easier application maintenance and cost savings. Object systems—if designed well—are relatively easier or faster to modify and extend, than if using non-OT technologies. This is important; many organizations find that the majority of the overall long-term cost of an application is in revision and maintenance, not original development, and thus, strategies to reduce revision costs are important. Although it is rational to want to reduce new system development costs, there is a certain irony that few stakeholders ask the follow-up question, "How can we reduce the cost to revise and maintain it?" when that is often the largest expense. It is here that OT can make a contribution, in addition to its power and elegance in tackling complex systems.

MORE UML NOTATION

38.1   General Notation

Stereotypes and Property Specifications with Tags

Stereotypes are used in the UML to classify an element (see Figure 38.1).

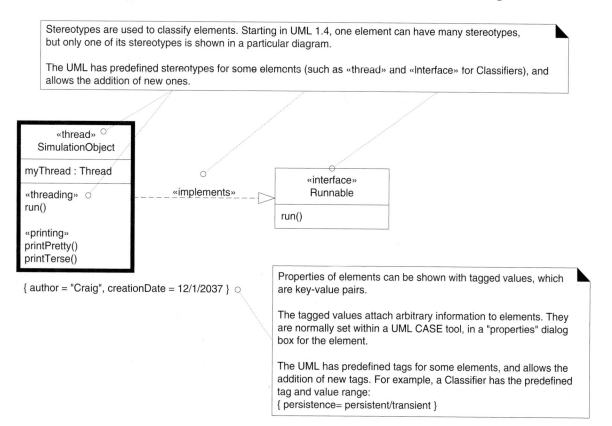

Stereotypes are used to classify elements. Starting in UML 1.4, one element can have many stereotypes, but only one of its stereotypes is shown in a particular diagram.

The UML has predefined stereotypes for some elements (such as «thread» and «Interface» for Classifiers), and allows the addition of new ones.

Properties of elements can be shown with tagged values, which are key-value pairs.

The tagged values attach arbitrary information to elements. They are normally set within a UML CASE tool, in a "properties" dialog box for the element.

The UML has predefined tags for some elements, and allows the addition of new tags. For example, a Classifier has the predefined tag and value range:
{ persistence= persistent/transient }

Figure 38.1 Stereotypes and properties.

Package Interfaces

A package can be illustrated as implementing an interface (see Figure 38.2).

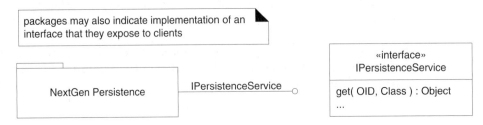

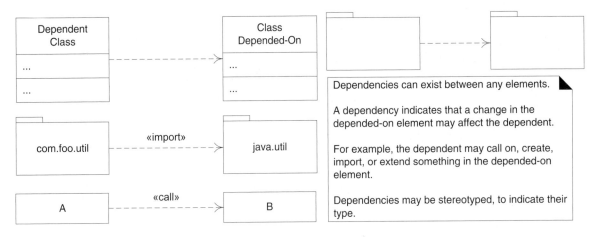

Figure 38.2 Interface of a package.

Dependency

Dependencies can exist between any elements, but they are probably most often used in UML package diagrams to illustrate package dependencies (see Figure 38.3)

Figure 38.3 Dependencies.

38.2   Implementation Diagrams

The UML defines several diagrams that can be used to illustrate implementation details. The most commonly used is a deployment diagram, to illustrate the deployment of components and processes to processing nodes.

Component Diagrams

To quote: A **component** represents a modular, deployable, and replaceable part of a system that encapsulates implementation and exposes a set of interfaces [OMG01]. It may, for example, be source code, binary, or executable. Examples include executables such as a browser or HTTP server, a database, a DLL, or a JAR file (such as for an Enterprise Java Bean). UML components are usually shown within deployment diagrams, rather than on their own. Figure 38.4 illustrates some common notation.

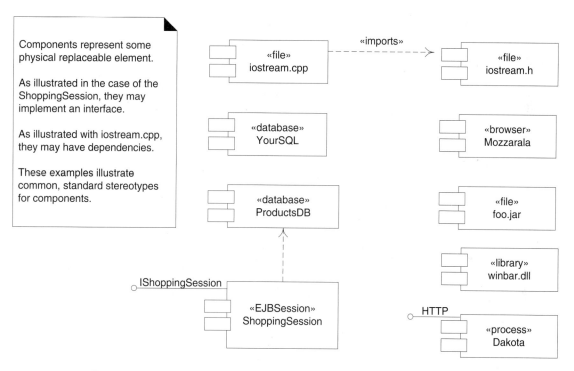

Figure 38.4 UML components.

Deployment Diagrams

A deployment diagram shows how instances of components and processes are configured for run-time execution on instances of processing **nodes** (something with memory and processing services; see Figure 38.5).

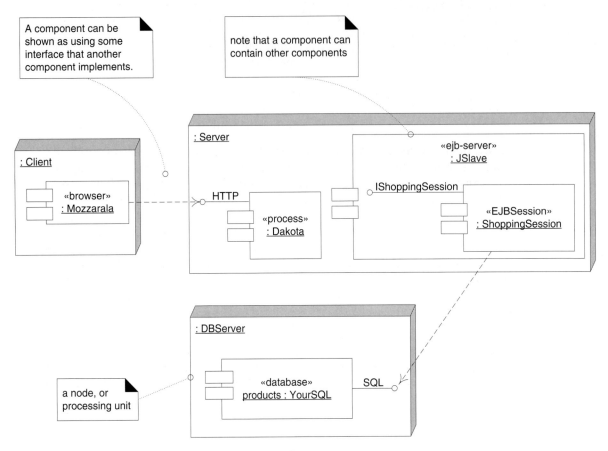

Figure 38.5 A deployment diagram.

38.3   Template (Parameterized, Generic) Class

Template classes and their instantation are shown in Figure 38.6.

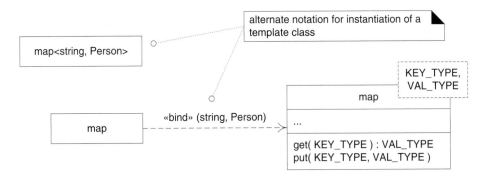

Figure 38.6 Template classes.

Some languages, such as C++, support templatized, generic, or parameterized classes. In addition, this feature will be added to the Java language. For example, in C++, *map<string, Person>* declares the instantiation of a template class with keys of type *string*, and values of type *Person*.

38.4 Activity Diagrams

A UML **activity diagram** offers rich notation to show a sequence of activities. It may be applied to any purpose (such as visualizing the steps of a computer algorithm), but is considered especially useful for visualizing business workflows and processes, or use cases. One of the UP workflows (disciplines) is **Business Modeling**; its purpose is to understand and communicate "the structure and the dynamics of the organization in which a system is to be deployed" [RUP]. A key artifact of the Business Modeling discipline is the **Business Object Model** (a superset of the UP Domain Model), which essentially visualizes how a business works, using UML class, sequence, and activity diagrams. Thus, activity diagrams are especially applicable within the Business Modeling discipline of the UP.

Some of the outstanding notation includes parallel activities, swimlanes, and action-object flow relationships, as illustrated in Figure 38.7 (adapted from [OMG01, FS00]). Formally, an activity diagram is considered a special kind of UML statechart diagram in which the states are actions, and event transition is automatically triggered by action completion.

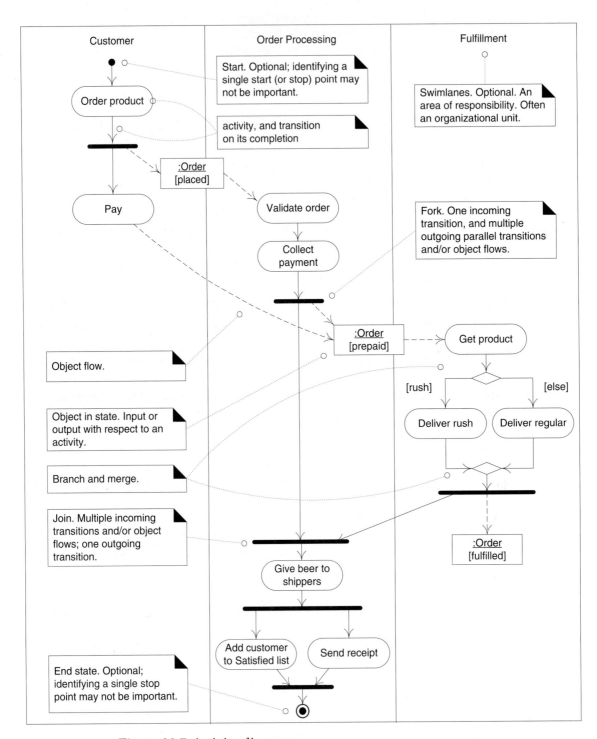

Figure 38.7 Activity diagram.

BIBLIOGRAPHY

Abbot83   Abbott, R. 1983. Program Design by Informal English Descriptions. *Communications of the ACM* vol. 26(11).

AIS77   Alexander, C., Ishikawa, S., and Silverstein, M. 1977. *A Pattern Language—Towns-Building-Construction.* Oxford University Press.

Ambler00   Ambler, S. 2000. *The Unified Process—Elaboration Phase.* Lawrence, KA.: R&D Books

Ambler00a   Ambler, S., Constantine, L. 2000. Enterprise-Ready Object IDs. *The Unified Process—Construction Phase.* Lawrence, KA.: R&D Books

Ambler00b   Ambler, S. 2000. Whitepaper: *The Design of a Robust Persistence Layer For Relational Databases.* www.ambysoft.com.

BDSSS00   Beedle, M., Devos, M., Sharon, Y., Schwaber, K., and Sutherland, J. 2000. SCRUM: A Pattern Language for Hyperproductive Software Development. *Pattern Languages of Program Design* vol. 4. Reading, MA.: Addison-Wesley

BC87   Beck, K., and Cunningham, W. 1987. *Using Pattern Languages for Object-Oriented Programs.* Tektronix Technical Report No. CR-87-43.

BC89   Beck, K., and Cunningham, W. 1989. A Laboratory for Object-oriented Thinking. *Proceedings of OOPSLA 89.* SIGPLAN Notices, Vol. 24, No. 10.

BCK98   Bass, L., Clements, P., and Kazman, R. *Software Architecture in Practice.* Reading, MA.: Addison-Wesley.

Beck94   Beck, K. 1994. Patterns and Software Development. *Dr. Dobbs Journal.* Feb 1994.

Beck00   Beck, K. 2000. *Extreme Programming Explained—Embrace Change.* Reading, MA.: Addison-Wesley.

BF00   Beck, K., Fowler, M., 2000. *Planning Extreme Programming.* Reading, MA.: Addison-Wesley.

BJ78   Bjørner, D., and Jones, C. editors. 1978. The Vienna Development Method: The Meta-Language, *Lecture Notes in Computer Science.* vol. 61. Springer-Verlag.

BJR97   Booch, G., Jacobson, I., and Rumbaugh, J. 1997. The UML specification documents. Santa Clara, CA.: Rational Software Corp. See documents at www.rational.com.

BMRSS96   Buschmann, F., Meunier, R., Rohnert, H., Sommerlad, P.,and Stal, M. 1996. *Pattern-Oriented Software Architecture: A System of Patterns.* West Sussex, England: Wiley.

Boehm88   Boehm. B. 1988. A Spiral Model of Software Development and Enhancement. *IEEE Computer.* May 1988.

Boehm00+ Boehm, B., et al. 2000. *Software Cost Estimation with COCOMO II*. Englewood Cliffs, NJ.: Prentice-Hall.

Booch94 Booch, G., 1994. *Object-Oriented Analysis and Design*. Redwood City, CA.: Benjamin/Cummings.

Booch96 Booch, G., 1996. *Object Solutions: Managing the Object-Oriented Project*. Menlo Park, CA.: Addison-Wesley.

BP88 Boehm, B., and Papaccio, P. 1988. Understanding and Controlling Software Costs. *IEEE Transactions on Software Engineering*. Oct 1988.

BRJ99 Booch, G., Rumbaugh, J, and Jacobson, I., . 1999. *The Unified Modeling Language User Guide*. Reading, MA.: Addison-Wesley.

Brooks75 Brooks, F., 1975. *The Mythical Man-Month*. Reading, MA.: Addison-Wesley.

Brown01 Brown, K., 2001. The *Convert Exception* pattern is found online at the Portland Pattern Reposity, http://c2.com.

BW95 Brown, K., and Whitenack, B. 1995. *Crossing Chasms, A Pattern Language for Object-RDBMS Integration*, White Paper, Knowledge Systems Corp.

BW96 Brown, K., and Whitenack, B. 1996. Crossing Chasms. *Pattern Languages of Program Design* vol. 2. Reading, MA.: Addison-Wesley.

CD94 Cook, S., and Daniels, J. 1994. *Designing Object Sysetms*. Englewood Cliffs, NJ.: Prentice-Hall.

CDL99 Coad, P., De Luca, J., Lefebvre, E. 1999. *Java Modeling in Color with UML*. Englewood Cliffs, NJ.: Prentice-Hall.

CL99 Constantine, L, and Lockwood, L. 1999. *Software for Use: A Practical Guide to the Models and Methods of Usage-Centered Design*. Reading, MA.: Addison-Wesley.

CMS74 Constantine, L., Myers, G., and Stevens, W. 1974. Structured Design. *IBM Systems Journal*, vol. 13 (No. 2, 1974), pp. 115-139.

Coad95 Coad, P. 1995. *Object Models: Stategies, Patterns and Applications*. Englewood Cliffs, NJ.: Prentice-Hall.

Cockburn92 Cockburn, A. 1992.. Using Natural Language as a Metaphoric Basis for Object-Oriented Modeling and Programming. *IBM Technical Report TR-36.0002*, 1992.

Cockburn97 Cockburn, A. 1997. Structuring Use Cases with Goals. *Journal of Object-Oriented Programming*, Sep-Oct, and Nov-Dec. SIGS Publications.

Cockburn01 Cockburn, A. 2001. *Writing Effective Use Cases*. Reading, MA.: Addison-Wesley.

Coleman+94 Coleman, D., *et al.* 1994. *Object-Oriented Development: The Fusion Method*. Englewood Cliffs, NJ.: Prentice-Hall.

Constantine68 Constantine. L. 1968. Segmentation and Design Strategies for Modular Programming. In Barnett and Constantine (eds.), *Modular Programming: Proceedings of a National Symposium*. Cambridge, MA.: Information & Systems Press.

Constantine94 Constantine, L. 1994. Essentially Speaking. *Software Development* May. CMP Media.

Conway58 Conway, M. 1958. Proposal for a Universal Computer-Oriented Language. *Communications of the ACM*. 5-8 Volume 1, Number 10, October.

Coplien95 Coplien, J. 1995. *The History of Patterns*. See http://c2.com/cgi/wiki?HistoryOfPatterns.

Coplien95a	Coplien, J. 1995. A Generative Development-Process Pattern Language. *Pattern Languages of Program Design* vol. 1. Reading, MA.: Addison-Wesley.
CS95	Coplien, J., and Schmidt, D. eds. 1995. *Pattern Languages of Program Design* vol. 1. Reading, MA.: Addison-Wesley.
Cunningham96	Cunningham, W. 1996. EPISODES: A Pattern Language of Competitive Development. *Pattern Languages of Program Design* vol. 2. Reading, MA.: Addison-Wesley.
Cutter97	Cutter Group. 1997. *Report: The Corporate Use of Object Technology.*
CV65	Corbato, F., and Vyssotsky, V. 1965. Introduction and overview of the Multics system. *AFIPS Conference Proceedings 27*, 185-196.
Dijkstra68	Dijkstra, E. 1968. The Structure of the THE-Multiprogramming System. *Communications of the ACM*, 11(5).
Eck95	Eck, D. 1995. *The Most Complex Machine.* A K Paters Ltd.
Fowler96	Fowler, M. 1996. *Analysis Patterns: Reusable Object Models.* Reading, MA.: Addison-Wesley.
Fowler00	Fowler, M. 2000. Put Your Process on a Diet. *Software Development.* December. CMP Media.
Fowler01	Fowler, M. 2001. Draft patterns on object-relational persistence services. www.martinfowler.com.
FS00	Fowler, M., and Scott, K. 2000. *UML Distilled.* Reading, MA.: Addison-Wesley.
Gartner95	Schulte, R., 1995. *Three-Tier Computing Architectures and Beyond.* Published Report Note R-401-134. Gartner Group.
Gemstone00	Gemstone Corp., 2000. A set of architectural patterns at www.javasuccess.com.
GHJV95	Gamma, E., Helm, R., Johnson, R., and Vlissides, J. 1995. *Design Patterns.* Reading, MA.: Addison-Wesley.
Gilb88	Gilb, T. 1988. *Principles of Software Engineering Management.* Reading, MA.: Addison-Wesley.
GK00	Guiney, E., and Kulak, D. 2000. *Use Cases: Requirements in Context.* Reading, MA.: Addison-Wesley.
GK76	Goldberg, A., and Kay, A. 1976. *Smalltalk-72 Instruction Manual.* Xerox Palo Alto Research Center.
GL00	Guthrie, R., and Larman, C. 2000. *Java 2 Performance and Idiom Guide.* Englewood Cliffs, NJ.: Prentice-Hall.
Grady92	Grady, R. 1992. *Practical Software Metrics for Project Management and Process Improvement.* Englewood Cliffs, NJ.: Prentice-Hall.
Groso00	Grosso, W., 2000. *The Name The Problem Not The Thrower* exceptions pattern is found online at the Portland Pattern Repository, http://c2.com.
GW89	Gause, D., and Weinberg, G. 1989. *Exploring Requirements.* NY, NY.: Dorset House.
Harrison98	Harrison, N., 1998. Patterns for Logging Diagnostic Messages. *Pattern Languages of Program Design* vol. 3. Reading, MA.: Addison-Wesley.
Hay96	Hay, D. 1996. *Data Model Patterns: Conventions of Thought.* NY, NY.: Dorset House.
Highsmith00	Highsmith, J. 2000. *Adaptive Software Development: A Collaborative Approach to Managing Complex Systems.* NY, NY.: Dorset House.

HNS00   Hofmeister, C., Nord, R., and Soni, D. 2000. *Applied Software Architecture*. Reading, MA.: Addison-Wesley.

Jackson95   Jackson, M. 1995. *Software Requirements and Specification*. NY, NY.: ACM Press.

Jacobson92   Jacobson, I., *et al.* 1992. *Object-Oriented Software Engineering: A Use Case Driven Approach*. Reading, MA.: Addison-Wesley.

JAH00   Jeffries, R., Anderson, A., Hendrickson, C. 2000. *Extreme Programming Installed*. Reading, MA.: Addison-Wesley.

JBR99   Jacobson, I., Booch, G., and Rumbaugh, J. 1999. *The Unified Software Development Process*. Reading, MA.: Addison-Wesley.

Jones97   Jones, C., 1997. *Applied Software Measurement*. NY, NY.: McGraw-Hill.

Jones98   Jones, C. 1998. *Estimating Software Costs*. NY, NY.: McGraw-Hill.

Kay68   Kay, A. 1968. *FLEX, a flexible extensible language*. M.Sc. thesis, Electrical Engineering, University of Utah. May. (Univ. Microfilms).

Kovitz99   Kovitz, B. 1999. *Practical Software Requirements*. Greenwich, CT.: Manning.

Kruchten00   Kruchten, P. 2000. *The Rational Unified Process—An Introduction*. 2nd edition. Reading, MA.: Addison-Wesley.

Kruchten95   Kruchten, P. 1995. The 4+1 View Model of Architecture. *IEEE Software* 12(6).

Lakos96   Lakos, J. 1996. *Large-Scale C++ Software Design*. Reading, MA.: Addison-Wesley.

Lieberherr88   Lieberherr, K., Holland, I, and Riel, A. 1988. Object-Oriented Programming: An Objective Sense of Style. *OOPSLA 88 Conference Proceedings*. NY, NY.: ACM SIGPLAN.

Liskov88   Liskov, B. 1988. Data Abstraction and Hierarchy, *SIGPLAN Notices*, 23,5 (May, 1988).

LW00   Leffingwell, D., and Widrig, D. 2000. *Managing Software Requirements: A Unified Approach*. Reading, MA.: Addison-Wesley.

MacCormack01   MacCormack, A. 2001. Product-Development Practices That Work. *MIT Sloan Management Review*. Volume 42, Number 2.

Martin95   Martin, R. 1995. *Designing Object-Oriented C++ Applications Using the Booch Method*. Englewood Cliffs, NJ.: Prentice-Hall.

McConnell96   McConnell, S. 1996. *Rapid Development*. Redmond, WA.: Microsoft Press.

MO95   Martin, J., and Odell, J. 1995. *Object-Oriented Methods: A Foundation*. Englewood Cliffs, NJ.: Prentice-Hall.

Moreno97   Moreno, A.M. Object Oriented Analysis from Textual Specifications. *Proceedings of the 9th International Conference on Software Engineering and Knowledge Engineering*, Madrid, June 17-20 (1997).

MP84   McMenamin, S., and Palmer, J. 1984. *Essential Systems Analysis*. Englewood Cliffs, NJ.: Prentice-Hall.

MW89   1989. *The Merriam-Webster Dictionary*. Springfield, MA.: Merriam-Webster.

Nixon90   Nixon, R. 1990. *Six Crisis*. NY, NY.: Touchstone Press.

OMG01   Object Management Group, 2001. *OMG Unified Modeling Language Specification*. www.omg.org.

Parkinson58   Parkinson, N. 1958. *Parkinson's Law: The Pursuit of Progress*, London, John Murray.

Parnas72   Parnas, D. 1972. On the Criteria To Be Used in Decomposing Systems Into Modules, *Communications of the ACM*, Vol. 5, No. 12, December 1972. ACM.

PM92   Putnam, L., and Myers, W. 1992. *Measures for Excellence: Reliable Software on Time, Within Budget*. Yourdon Press.

Pree95   Pree, W. 1995. *Design Patterns for Object-Oriented Software Development*. Reading, MA.: Addison-Wesley.

Renzel97   Renzel, K., 1997. *Error Handling for Business Information Systems: A Pattern Language*. Online at http://www.objectarchitects.de/arcus/cookbook/exhandling/

Rising00   Rising, L. 2000. *Pattern Almanac 2000*. Reading, MA.: Addison-Wesley.

RJB99   Rumbaugh, J., Jacobson, I., and Booch, G. 1999. *The Unified Modeling Language Reference Manual*. Reading, MA.: Addison-Wesley.

Ross97   Ross, R. 1997. *The Business Rule Book: Classifying, Defining and Modeling Rules*. Business Rule Solutions Inc.

Royce70   Royce, W. 1970. Managing the Development of Large Software Systems. *Proceedings of IEEE WESCON*. Aug 1970.

Rumbaugh91   Rumbaugh, J., *et al.* 1991. *Object-Oriented Modelling and Design*. Englewood Cliffs, NJ.: Prentice-Hall.

RUP   The Rational Unified Process Product. The browser-based online documentation for the RUP, sold by Rational Corp.

Rumbaugh97   Rumbaugh, J. 1997. Models Through the Development Process. *Journal of Object-Oriented Programming* May 1997. NY, NY: SIGS Publications.

Shaw96   Shaw, M. 1996. Some Patterns for Software Architectures. *Pattern Languages of Program Design* vol. 2. Reading, MA.: Addison-Wesley.

Standish94   Jim Johnson. 1994. *Chaos: Charting the Seas of Information Technology*. Published Report. The Standish Group

SW98   Schneider, G., and Winters, J. 1998. *Applying Use Cases: A Practical Guide*. Reading, MA.: Addison-Wesley.

TK78   Tsichiritzis, D., and Klug, A. The ANSI/X3/SPARC DBMS framework: Report of the study group on database management systems. *Information Systems*, 3 1978.

Tufte92   Tufte, E. 1992. *The Visual Display of Quantitative Information*. Graphics Press.

VCK96   Vlissides, J., et al. 1996. *Patterns Languages of Program Design* vol. 2. Reading, MA.: Addison-Wesley.

Wirfs-Brock93   Wirfs-Brock, R. 1993. Designing Scenarios: Making the Case for a Use Case Framework. *Smalltalk Report* Nov-Dec 1993. NY, NY: SIGS Publications.

WK99   Warmer, J., and Kleppe, A. 1999. *The Object Constraint Language: Precise Modeling With UML*. Reading, MA.: Addison-Wesley.

WWW90   Wirfs-Brock, R., Wilkerson, B., and Wiener, L. 1990. *Designing Object-Oriented Software*. Englewood Cliffs, NJ.: Prentice-Hall.

GLOSSARY

abstract class A class that can be used only as a superclass of some other class; no objects of an abstract class may be created except as instances of a subclass.

abstraction The act of concentrating the essential or general qualities of similar things. Also, the resulting essential characteristics of a thing.

active object An object with its own thread of control.

aggregation A property of an association representing a whole-part relationship and (usually) lifetime containment.

analysis An investigation of a domain that results in models describing its static and dynamic characteristics. It emphasizes questions of "what," rather than "how."

architecture Informally, a description of the organization, motivation, and structure of a system. Many different levels of architectures are involved in developing software systems, from physical hardware architecture to the logical architecture of an application framework.

association A description of a related set of links between objects of two classes.

attribute A named characteristic or property of a class.

class In the UML, "The descriptor of a set of objects that share the same attributes, operations, methods, relationships, and behavior" [RJB99]. May be used to represent software or conceptual elements.

class attribute A characteristic or property that is the same for all instances of a class. This information is usually stored in the class definition.

class hierarchy A description of the inheritance relations between classes.

class method A method that defines the behavior of the class itself, as opposed to the behavior of its instances.

classification Classification defines a relation between a class and its instances. The classification mapping identifies the extension of a class.

collaboration Two or more objects that participate in a client/server relationship in order to provide a service.

composition   The definition of a class in which each instance is comprised of other objects.

concept   A category of ideas or things. In this book, used to designate real-world things rather than software entities. A concept's intension is a description of its attributes, operations and semantics. A concept's extension is the set of instances or example objects that are members of the concept. Often defined as a synonym for domain class.

concrete class   A class that can have instances.

constraint   A restriction or condition on an element.

constructor   A special method called whenever an instance of a class is created in C++ or Java. The constructor often performs initialization actions.

container class   A class designed to hold and manipulate a collection of objects.

contract   Defines the responsibilities and postconditions that apply to the use of an operation or method. Also used to refer to the set of all conditions related to an interface.

coupling   A dependency between elements (such as classes, packages, subsystems), typically resulting from collaboration between the elements to provide a service.

delegation   The notion that an object can issue a message to another object in response to a message. The first object therefore delegates the responsibility to the second object.

derivation   The process of defining a new class by reference to an existing class and then adding attributes and methods The existing class is the superclass; the new class is referred to as the subclass or derived class.

design   A process that uses the products of analysis to produce a specification for implementing a system. A logical description of how a system will work.

domain   A formal boundary that defines a particular subject or area of interest.

encapsulation   A mechanism used to hide the data, internal structure, and implementation details of some element, such as an object or subsystem. All interaction with an object is through a public interface of operations.

event   A noteworthy occurrence.

extension   The set of objects to which a concept applies. The objects in the extension are the examples or instances of the concept.

framework   A set of collaborating abstract and concrete classes that may be used as a template to solve a related family of problems. It is usually extended via subclassing for application-specific behavior.

generalization   The activity of identifying commonality among concepts and defining a superclass (general concept) and subclass (specialized concept) relationships. It is a way to construct taxonomic classifications among concepts which are then illustrated in class hierarchies. Conceptual subclasses conform to conceptual superclasses in terms of intension and extension.

inheritance — A feature of object-oriented programming languages by which classes may be specialized from more general superclasses. Attributes and method definitions from superclasses are automatically acquired by the subclass.

instance — An individual member of a class. In the UML, called an object.

instance method — A method whose scope is an instance. Invoked by sending a message to an instance.

instance variable — As used in Java and Smalltalk, an attribute of an instance.

instantiation — The creation of an instance of a class.

intension — The definition of a concept.

interface — A set of signatures of public operations.

link — A connection between two objects; an instance of an association.

message — The mechanism by which objects communicate; usually a request to execute a method.

metamodel — A model that defines other models. The UML metamodel defines the element types of the UML, such as Classifier.

method — In the UML, the specific implementation or algorithm of an operation for a class. Informally, the software procedure that can be executed in response to a message.

model — A description of static and/or dynamic characteristics of a subject area, portrayed through a number of views (usually diagrammatic or textual).

multiplicity — The number of objects permitted to participate in an association.

object — In the UML, a instance of a class that encapsulates state and behavior. More informally, an example of a thing.

object identity — The feature that the existence of an object is independent of any values associated with the object.

object-oriented analysis — The investigation of a problem domain or system in terms of domain concepts, such as conceptual classes, associations, and state changes.

object-oriented design — The specification of a logical software solution in terms of software objects, such as their classes, attributes, methods, and collaborations.

object-oriented programming language — A programming language that supports the concepts of encapsulation, inheritance, and polymorphism.

OID — Object Identifier.

operation — In the UML, "a specification of a transformation or query that an object may be called to execute" [RJB99]. An operation has a signature, specified by its name and parameters, and it is invoked via a message. A method is an implementation of an operation with a specific algorithm.

pattern A pattern is a named description of a problem, solution, when to apply the solution, and how to apply the solution in new contexts.

persistence The enduring storage of the state of an object.

persistent object An object that can survive the process or thread that created it. A persistent object exists until it is explicitly deleted.

polymorphic operation The same operation implemented differently by two or more classes.

polymorphism The concept that two or more classes of objects can respond to the same message in different ways, using polymorphic operations. Also, the ability to define polymorphic operations.

postcondition A constraint that must hold true after the completion of an operation.

precondition A constraint that must hold true before an operation is requested.

private A scoping mechanism used to restrict access to class members so that other objects cannot see them. Normally applied to all attributes, and to some methods.

public A scoping mechanism used to make members accessible to other objects. Normally applied to some methods, but not to attributes, since public attributes violates encapsulation.

pure data values Data types for which unique instance identity is not meaningful, such as numbers, booleans, and strings.

qualified association An association whose membership is partitioned by the value of a qualifier.

receiver The object to which a message is sent.

recursive association An association where the source and the destination are the same object class.

responsibility A knowing or doing service or group of services provided by an element (such as a class or subsystem); a responsibility embodies one or more of the purposes or obligations of an element.

role A named end of an association to indicate its purpose.

state The condition of an object between events.

state transition A change of state for an object; something that can be signaled by an event.

subclass A specialization of another class (the superclass). A subclass inherits the attributes and methods of the superclass.

subtype A conceptual superclass. A specialization of another type (the supertype) that conforms to the intension and extension of the supertype.

superclass   A class from which another class inherits attributes and methods.

supertype   A conceptual superclass. In a generalization-specialization relation, the more general type; an object that has subtypes.

transition   A relationship between states that is traversed if the specified event occurs and the guard condition met.

visibility   The ability to see or have reference to an object.

INDEX

2

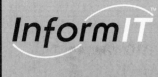

Sequence Diagram

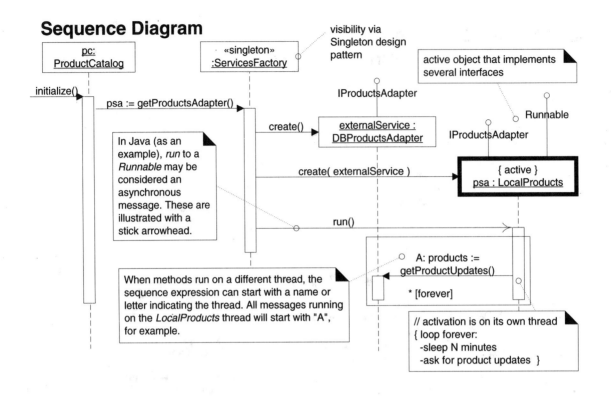

visibility via
Singleton design
pattern

active object that implements
several interfaces

pc:
ProductCatalog

«singleton»
:ServicesFactory

IProductsAdapter

IProductsAdapter

Runnable

initialize()

psa := getProductsAdapter()

create()

externalService :
DBProductsAdapter

In Java (as an
example), *run* to a
Runnable may be
considered an
asynchronous
message. These are
illustrated with a
stick arrowhead.

create(externalService)

{ active }
psa : LocalProducts

run()

A: products :=
getProductUpdates()

* [forever]

When methods run on a different thread, the
sequence expression can start with a name or
letter indicating the thread. All messages running
on the *LocalProducts* thread will start with "A",
for example.

// activation is on its own thread
{ loop forever:
 -sleep N minutes
 -ask for product updates }

Collaboration Diagram

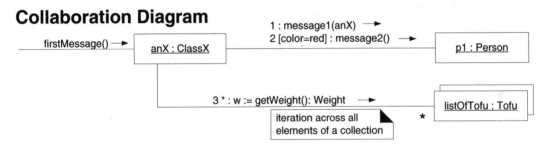

firstMessage() →

anX : ClassX

1 : message1(anX) →
2 [color=red] : message2() →

p1 : Person

3 * : w := getWeight(): Weight →

iteration across all
elements of a collection

listOfTofu : Tofu

*

More Class Diagram Notation

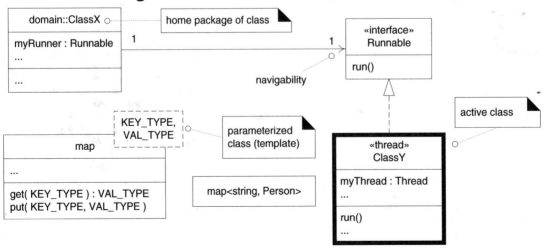

domain::ClassX

home package of class

«interface»
Runnable

myRunner : Runnable
...

1

1

run()

...

navigability

active class

KEY_TYPE,
VAL_TYPE

parameterized
class (template)

«thread»
ClassY

map

...

get(KEY_TYPE) : VAL_TYPE
put(KEY_TYPE, VAL_TYPE)

map<string, Person>

myThread : Thread
...

run()
...